Cyber Security and the Politics of Time

Tim Stevens

King's College London

CAMBRIDGE
UNIVERSITY PRESS

CAMBRIDGE
UNIVERSITY PRESS

University Printing House, Cambridge CB2 8BS, United Kingdom

Cambridge University Press is part of the University of Cambridge.

It furthers the University's mission by disseminating knowledge in the pursuit of
education, learning and research at the highest international levels of excellence.

www.cambridge.org
Information on this title: www.cambridge.org/9781107109421

© Tim Stevens 2016

First published 2016

A catalogue record for this publication is available from the British Library

Library of Congress Cataloguing in Publication data
Stevens, Tim, 1973–
Cyber security and the politics of time / Tim Stevens, King's College London.
  pages cm
ISBN 978-1-107-10942-1 (hardback)
1. Technology and international relations. 2. Internet and international
relations. 3. Computer security – Government policy. 4. Cyberspace –
Security measures – Government policy. 5. Computer networks – Security
measures – Government policy. I. Title.
JZ1254.S74 2015
327.10285′58–dc23

2015016413

ISBN 978-1-107-10942-1 Hardback

I dedicate this book to the memory of my maternal grandfather, Paul Pedrick McCord (1903–89), forester and soldier.

Cyber Security and the Politics of Time

'Cyber security' is a recent addition to the global security agenda, concerned with protecting states and citizens from the misuse of computer networks for war, terrorism, economic espionage and criminal gain. Many argue that the ubiquity of computer networks calls for robust and pervasive counter-measures, not least governments concerned at their potential effects on national and economic security. Drawing on critical literature in International Relations, security studies, political theory and social theory, this is the first book that describes how these visions of future cyber security are sustained in the communities that articulate them. Specifically, it shows that conceptions of time and temporality are foundational to the politics of cyber security. It explores how cyber security communities understand the past, present and future, thereby shaping cyber security as a political practice. Integrating a wide range of conceptual and empirical resources, this innovative book provides insight for scholars, practitioners and policymakers.

Tim Stevens is Teaching Fellow in the Department of Politics and International Relations, Royal Holloway, University of London. He is the co-author of *Cyberspace and the State* (2011) and has published widely on cyber security and related issues in journals like *International Political Sociology*, *Security Dialogue* and *Contemporary Security Policy*.

Preface

The topic of this study originated from my initial reading of Aristotle's *Nicomachean Ethics* (NE) more than thirty years ago. Perplexed by the two accounts of happiness in books I and X of Aristotle's work, I was unable to reconcile the idea that happiness consists in a mixture of intellectual and political activities with the notion that true happiness is constituted by intellectual contemplation alone. The scholarly attempts to explain the discrepancy proved unsatisfactory, since they assumed different dates of composition, interpolations of later editors or a development of the theory of happiness within the work itself. These explanations posited assumptions that were impossible to demonstrate and were often contradictory. The modern accounts of the two notions of happiness reflect the very same approaches that the medieval commentators used to explain Aristotle's concept of human goodness. Still the reader of Aristotle is left to wonder whether the Philosopher himself did not notice the different accounts of an essential moral idea that appeared in his most important work on moral philosophy.

In the course of the study of the text I came to the conclusions that Aristotle's primary moral concept was not that of happiness (*eudaimonia*) but one of practical wisdom (*phronesis*). In elevating *phronesis* to the central theme of the Ethics I was able to construct a way in which the contradictory nature of the text might be explained. I believe that while Aristotle certainly attempted to explain the meaning of human goodness, he had in fact constructed a text concerned primarily with the proper way to attain it, and that practical wisdom governs all activities of the soul that lead to moral and intellectual excellence. Despite Aristotle's clear assertion that the supreme virtue of the human soul is intellectual wisdom (*sophia*), the primary human, and hence moral, virtue is practical wisdom. In itself the uninterrupted contemplative activity of the intellect elevates human beings to a divine state in which the object and subject of the process of knowledge are united in the act of the intellect (*nous*). Human beings, however, are not purely intellectual beings like the gods, and regardless of their participation in the intellectual life they must arrange various pursuits properly in order to achieve the state that Aristotle calls happiness. Wisdom may be the supreme virtue, but practical wisdom regulates all human activity including theoretical pursuits in order that the practically wise person may recognize what is good and how best to attain it. In elevating *phronesis* to the most important virtue, Aristotle offers a human standard of conduct by which a life is measured against the practices of the best citizens, and rejects any universal moral imperatives that do not arise from human action.

In the first chapter of this work I examine various medieval and modern interpretations of some important concepts in Aristotle's moral philosophy. In Chapter 2 the meaning of happiness in Aristotle's Ethics, especially in light of its relation to the virtues of practical wisdom and theoretical wisdom, is considered. In Chapter 3 the works of William of Auxerre and Philip the Chancellor reveal a new understanding of moral principles in light of the ideas of natural law and *synderesis*, which is an innate habit by which universal moral commands are recognized. In Chapter 4 the partial commentaries on the *Nicomachean Ethics* composed before 1248 provide a second stream of interpretation of Aristotle's text, in which the main intention of the authors is to explain carefully the meaning of Aristotle's words. The subsequent two chapters consider the contributions on the topic of Albertus Magnus, whose commentaries on Aristotle were the most influential instrument in directing the medieval understanding of ancient ethics. Albert's work influenced nearly all the later medieval expositors of Aristotle, even when his most famous student, Thomas Aquinas, disagreed with some of his teacher's conclusions on the meaning of happiness. Chapter 7 examines these theories of Thomas and those of Bonaventure, which have significant differences from the doctrines of their predecessors. The discussion on Thomas is relatively short because every aspect of his moral philosophy has provoked a great number of studies in the past century. In the questions considered here Thomas' influence is not quite so great as that of his former teacher.

In all these medieval commentaries a constant theme emerges, one that insists upon the idea of the eternal existence of immutable moral laws and the ability of all human beings to recognize them. In the acceptance of natural law and *synderesis* the medieval authors transform Aristotle's Ethics from one based upon a human standard into one that depends upon a divine foundation. In so doing they change the range of practical wisdom in that it no longer determines independently moral universals, but merely deduces logically correct means that follow from predetermined ends. The development of the concepts of happiness, natural law, prudence and virtue in two late thirteenth-century commentaries on the NE forms the greater part of Chapter 8. Two sets of questions on Aristotle's text, those of an anonymous author in a manuscript in Erfurt and those of Radulphus Brito, a Parisian Arts master, show how later medieval commentators were content to explain carefully the text and to determine Aristotle's intention. They generally avoided controversy and were greatly influenced by the work of their Dominican predecessors, Albertus Magnus and Thomas Aquinas. Finally in the Conclusion I examine ideas concerning the transformation from Aristotle's morality of practical wisdom to the medieval acceptance of prudential reasoning from the eternal principles of action. Aristotle recognized the difficulty in defining practical wisdom but he did not leave us without guidance, since he advises us that the best way to understand practical wisdom is to identify those persons to whom we attribute it.

I would like to thank the Fulbright Program, the Deutscher Akademischer Austauschdienst, the National Endowment for the Humanities and Stonehill College for their support of my research. I would like to express my gratitude to the faculty and staff of the departments of Philosophy and Catholic Theology, and of the Bibliotheca Amploniana and the University of Erfurt for their gracious hospitality and assistance during my several stays in their beautiful city. I am also very grateful to Doctor Hilary Gaskin of the Cambridge University Press for her helpful and insightful comments on my work.

Preliminary considerations

I Interpretations of Aristotle's *Nicomachean Ethics*

Few works in the history of philosophy have provoked as much discussion and diverse opinions as Aristotle's *Nicomachean Ethics* (NE). Philosophers and scholars in different eras have examined a number of moral topics, such as the best life for a human being, the meaning of virtue, the ideal of natural law and the reasons for moral actions, as a result of their reading of Aristotle's text.[1] Aristotle's work, however, is not merely a historical artifact, but continues to inspire contemporary thinkers in their quest to answer significant questions concerning human ethical action. Nancy Sherman comments upon the manner in which Aristotle contributes to contemporary moral topics: "No longer do utilitarianism and Kantian ethics alone dominate the moral landscape. Now Aristotelian themes fill out that landscape with such issues as the importance of friendship and emotions in a good life, the role of moral perception in wise choice, the nature of happiness and its constitution, moral education and habituation."[2] One might add to these subjects the theory of universal basic goods, the role of fortune in a human life and the process of moral reasoning to which the philosophy of Aristotle has contributed. The flexibility and broad scope that are characteristics of Aristotle's efforts have also led to many disputes about the precise meaning of the topics listed here. This chapter will examine some of the contemporary discussions of these themes, while subsequent chapters will treat Aristotle's own doctrine and its various medieval interpretations.

---

[1] A recent discussion of the way in which the NE has been interpreted in different eras can be found in *The Reception of Aristotle's Ethics*, ed. J. Miller (Cambridge: Cambridge University Press, 2013).

[2] Introduction to *Aristotle's Ethics: Critical Essays*, ed. N. Sherman (Lanham: Rowman and Littlefield, 1999), p. vii.

a The accounts of happiness

Aristotle's two accounts of happiness that appear in books I and X of the NE
have led his expositors to different views on its nature and constitution. John
Cooper summarizes the frustration of Aristotle's readers on this topic when
he says, "Perhaps, in the end, one should admit that Aristotle works with
two distinct mutually incompatible conceptions of human happiness in
the Ethics."[3] Many modern scholars have agreed with Cooper and have
found the two descriptions of happiness in the NE to be contradictory.[4]
Cooper, however, like many others attempting to explain Aristotle's thought,
persists in his attempts to explain the true doctrine of Aristotelian happiness
despite its difficulty. He admits that he originally maintained that Aristotle's
notion of *eudaimonia* (happiness) consisted exclusively in contemplative
activity and left no room for morality as normally understood.[5] After reflection Cooper came to accept the notion that "... happiness requires the
activity of the best virtue, *along with the others*: happiness requires the
perfection of our nature as human ..."[6] Cooper describes here what has
come to be known as the 'inclusive theory' of Aristotelian happiness, which
W.F.R. Hardie distinguished from the 'dominant theory' that considers all
human actions to lead to the supreme virtue of theoretical wisdom.[7]
Anthony Kenny, like many modern readers of the NE, understands
Aristotle to have made theoretical wisdom the dominant characteristic of
happiness to which all other human pursuits are ultimately directed:
"Aristotle ... considers happiness only in the dominant sense ... Aristotle

[3] J. Cooper, "Contemplation and Happiness: A Reconstruction," *Synthese*, 72 (1987), p. 190.
[4] Foremost among them are J. Ackrill, "Aristotle on Eudaimonia," *Aristotle's Ethics: Critical Essays*, pp. 57–77; M. Nussbaum, *The Fragility of Goodness: Luck and Ethics in Greek Tragedy and Philosophy* (Cambridge: Cambridge University Press, 1986), esp. pp. 373–378; W. Hardie, "The Final Good in Aristotle's Ethics," *Philosophy*, 40 (1965), pp. 277–295; repr.in *Aristotle: A Collection of Critical Essays*, ed. J. Moravcsik (Garden City, NY: Anchor Books, 1967), pp. 297–322.
[5] J. Cooper, "Contemplation and Happiness ...," p. 190. For a discussion on the translation of *eudaimonia* as happiness, see R. Kraut, *Aristotle on the Human Good* (Princeton: Princeton University Press, 1989), p. 3.
[6] J. Cooper, "Contemplation and Happiness ...," pp. 203–204 (italics added).
[7] W.F.R. Hardie, "The Final Good in Aristotle's Ethics," and *Aristotle's Ethical Theory* (Oxford: Oxford University Press, 1968). Hardie reconsiders the adequacy of such termi-nology in "Aristotle on the Best Life for a Man," *Philosophy* 54 (1979), pp. 35–50, but modern scholars continue to use the terms 'dominant' and 'inclusive' in order to distin-guish Aristotle's descriptions of happiness. Despite much research in the past fifty years, no consensus on Aristotle's doctrine of happiness has been reached. For an extensive list of the publications on this topic see H. Curzer, *Aristotle and the Virtues* (Oxford: Oxford University Press, 2012), pp. 390–391, nn. 5–6.

seeks to show that happiness is identical with philosophic contemplation."[8] These different readings on the nature of Aristotelian happiness are also apparent in the medieval commentaries on the NE. Although the terminology differs, most medieval interpreters of Aristotle followed the lead of Albert the Great, who argued that human happiness primarily consisted in contemplation. A second type of happiness, which Albert called 'civic' and which was comprised of moral virtues, contributed to the primary form of happiness by calming desires and passions so that a person might be free to consider immutable truth.[9] In the thirteenth and early fourteenth centuries Thomas Aquinas and Boethius of Dacia, a master in the Parisian Arts Faculty in the 1270s, accepted what today would be termed the inclusive theory of happiness. They understood happiness to result from both the knowledge of truth and also the exercise of moral virtue.

b The relation of virtue to happiness

A second problem concerning Aristotle's concept of happiness involves the question that Julia Annas calls the most important and central one in ancient ethics: "In what does happiness consist?"[10] To both modern and medieval readers of the NE the more specific question becomes: What is the relation between virtuous activity and happiness? Aristotle's assertions that happiness is a final (or complete) activity and that those possessing virtue may not be able to exercise it in sleep or misfortune have produced different ideas on the role of virtue in the production of happiness.[11] Aristotle's final definition of the human good as the activity of the soul in accordance with virtue (τὸ ἀνθρώπινον ἀγαθὸν ψυχῆς ἐνέργεια γίνεται κατ᾽ ἀρετήν: NE 1098a15–16) has done little to resolve the question definitively. Richard Kraut declares categorically that "... happiness consists in just one good: this is the virtuous exercise of the theoretical part of reason that is the activity called *theoria*. Every other good (including the

---

[8] A. Kenny, "Happiness," *Proceedings of the Aristotelian Society*, New Series 66 (1965–1966), p. 99.
[9] See Chapters 5 and 6. For a modern view similar to that of Albert see S. Clark, *Aristotle's Man* (Oxford: Clarendon Press, 1975), p. 197 where he says that the practice of virtue "clears the way to the knowledge of the god."
[10] J. Annas, *The Morality of Happiness* (New York and Oxford: Oxford University Press, 1993), p. 46.
[11] NE 1097a30–31 where Aristotle claims that happiness is τὸ τούτων τελειότατον, the most final of them (goods). τελειότατον has been translated as "most complete," "most final" or "most perfect." For those possessing virtue and not able to exercise it, see NE 1095b32–33.

ethical virtues) is desirable for the sake of this one activity."[12] Annas rejects this view of Aristotelian happiness and remarks that a number of other activities and goods are needed for one to achieve human happiness. In her reading of the NE Aristotle rejects the idea that virtue is sufficient for happiness, and remarks that such a concept in Aristotle's view would be grossly counterintuitive.[13]

Aristotle's puzzling definition of *eudaimonia* led interpreters of the NE in the early thirteenth century to relegate virtue to a means whereby happiness might be achieved. They failed to see the close connection between the activity of virtue and human goodness. Later in the century more sophisticated thinkers, such as Albert the Great and Thomas Aquinas, rejected this view and stressed the importance of the activity of virtue in the production of human happiness. Still they had some difficulty in determining the exact role of virtue in the human attainment of happiness. Aristotle's doctrine of human goodness continues to lead to erroneous conclusions and frustration. Kenny claims that "Aquinas, adapting Aristotle, denied that the search for happiness involved any awareness of God."[14] It is hard to determine exactly what Kenny means by this statement since *cognitio Dei* is an absolutely essential element in Thomas's doctrines of human happiness, imperfect beatitude and perfect beatitude. Thomas rightly views the supreme object of contemplation in Aristotle's thought as divine beings.[15] Aristotle continues to thwart those seeking precise formulations in his ethical treatises. His method of avoiding absolute precision in ethics leads Annas to conclude that "What Aristotle says about virtue and happiness ... reflects commonsense Greek ethical thought, which is tempted ... in both of two conflicting directions ... If we find what he says unsatisfactory, it is because we think that ethical theory, even of Aristotle's kind, must take sides in a way that Aristotle does not."[16] Like his predecessors, Socrates and Plato, Aristotle creates the elements for a philosophical dialogue that continues even to the present day.

[12] R. Kraut, *Aristotle on the Human Good*, p. 5.
[13] J. Annas, "Aristotle on Virtue and Happiness," in *Aristotle's Ethics: Critical Essays*, p. 35 and *The Morality of Happiness*, pp. 375–377.
[14] A. Kenny, "Happiness," p. 99.
[15] Thomas Aquinas, *Sententia libri Ethicorum* (=SLE), ed. Leon., 47, 1–2, (Rome, 1969) p. 583, ll. 80–93: ... quod felicitas est optima operatio. Optima autem inter operationes humanas est speculatio veritatis ... alio modo ex parte obiecti, quod dat speciem operationi, secundum hoc etiam haec operatio est optima, quia inter omnia cognoscibilia optima sunt intelligibilia et praecipue divina. Et sic in eorum operatione consistat perfecta humana felicitas.
[16] J. Annas, "Aristotle on Virtue and Happiness," p. 50.

c Natural law

The few lines in book V of the NE on the distinction between natural and conventional justice (τοῦ δὲ πολιτικοῦ δικαίου τὸ μὲν φυσικόν ἐστι τὸ δὲ νομικόν: NE 1134b18) led medieval moralists to regard Aristotle as an advocate of the theory of natural and universal law.[17] While acknowledging Aristotle's acceptance of the notion of natural law, the medieval authors relied more heavily on Christian sources for the development of their own theory. As is clear in the subsequent chapters, the main inspiration for the content and principles of natural law are the writings of Paul and the Church Fathers, especially Augustine.[18] While there is very little dispute about the presence of a natural law theory in the NE among medieval authors, such is not the case in contemporary thought. Aristotle's text is again the cause of diametrically opposed interpretations, since he asserts the existence of natural justice and then shortly thereafter says "for us [human beings] although there is something like natural justice, it is still changeable" (κινητὸν: NE 1134b28–29). Modern political, religious and legal philosophers, who have developed a new theory of natural law, trace its origins to the work of Aristotle. Foremost among them is John Finnis, who cites another passage in the NE as support for the idea of moral absolutes: "Not every action . . . admits of a mean . . . It is not possible then ever to be right with regard to them; one must always be wrong" (NE 1107a9–13).[19] Hardie disputes this interpretation and argues that Aristotle is here making a purely logical point that arises from the way in which certain words are used to describe actions.[20]

---

[17] For Thomas Aquinas's explanation of Aristotle's text see SLE, pp. 304–306, ll. 1–168.
[18] For a survey of theories of natural law in the Middle Ages, see J. Porter, "Contested Categories: Reason, Nature and Natural Order in Medieval Accounts of the Natural Law," *The Journal of Religious Ethics*, 24 (1996), pp. 207–232.
[19] J. Finnis, *Moral Absolutes: Tradition, Revision and Truth* (Washington, DC: Catholic University of America Press, 1991), p. 31; also J. Finnis, *Natural Law and Natural Rights* (New York and Oxford: Oxford University Press, 2011); J. Finnis, "Natural Law: The Classical Tradition," The Oxford Handbook of Jurisprudence and Philosophy of Law, ed. J. Coleman and S. Shapiro (New York and Oxford: Oxford University Press, 2002), pp. 1–60. Finnis and other 'neo-natural law' theorists acknowledge a greater debt to Thomas Aquinas, but still attribute the theory to Aristotle as well. G. Grisez, *Way of the Lord Jesus, v. 1: Christian Moral Principles* (Chicago: Franciscan Herald Press, 1983), c. 7; G. Grisez, J. Boyle, and J. Finnis, "Practical Principles, Moral Truth and Ultimate Ends," *American Journal of Jurisprudence*, 58 (1987), pp. 99–151. See also R. Hittinger, *A Critique of the New Natural Law Theory* (Notre Dame: Notre Dame University Press, 1987).
[20] W.F.R. Hardie, *Aristotle's Ethical Theory*, p. 137.

Again Aristotle's desire to sketch possible answers to moral questions leads to vastly different explanations of his text.[21]

A feature of the new natural law theory is the idea of basic human goods: "There is no reason to doubt that each of the basic aspects of human well-being is worth seeking to realize. But there are many such basic forms of human good; I identified seven. And each of them can be participated in and promoted . . ."[22] Moral choices are ultimately justified by "what is intelligent to take an interest in," and intelligence indicates always the pursuit of basic goods.[23] Among such basic goods are life, knowledge, play, creativity, friendship, religious observance and loyalty. These activities are necessary for the attainment of the good life. The adherents of this theory believe that the concept of basic goods specifies the constituent elements to the Aristotelian doctrine of human happiness.[24] The proponents of the theory of natural law recognize the importance of the use of practical reason in order to determine the best application of legal and moral principles. Reason, however, has limitations since it cannot arrange hierarchically the incommensurable goods when they make conflicting demands on the moral agent. Since no basic good may be reduced, or subordinated, to another, any of them may be reasonably chosen at the expense of the other.[25] Although influenced by Aristotle and Thomas Aquinas, the proponents of natural basic goods have departed from the philosophy that inspired them. There is no doctrine of basic goods in either Aristotle or Thomas, and certainly Thomas arranges the principles of natural law in an ascending order, as is clear from the subsequent discussions.

The theory of basic goods rests upon a misunderstanding of a concomitant aspect of Aristotle's description of human goodness, which considers the self-sufficiency of an activity done for its own sake alone. Self-containment does not necessarily convey goodness to all activities done *propter se*. The idea that the nature of happiness allows for the generalization that all actions done for their own sake are always choice worthy is a

---

[21] In his review of the various readings of Aristotle, J. Vega rejects the presence of any invariable principles of law in the work of Aristotle. "Aristotle's Concept of Law: Beyond Positivism and Natural Law," *Journal of Ancient Philosophy*, 4 (2010), pp. 1–31.

[22] J. Finnis, *Natural Law and Natural Rights*, p. 100.

[23] J. Finnis, *Fundamentals of Ethics* (Washington, DC: Georgetown University Press, 1983), p. 63.

[24] J. Finnis, *Fundamentals of Ethics*, p. 68.

[25] J. Finnis, "Practical Reasoning, Human Goods and the End of Man," *Proceedings of the American Catholic Philosophical Association*, 58 (1984), p. 26.

serious misunderstanding of Aristotle's argument in the NE.[26] Aristotle certainly prefers a life with an activity done for its own sake as a better alternative to one devoted solely to production. But in so doing, he does not dismiss productive actions as universally inferior to operations desired for themselves alone. Production is necessary in order to attain certain human goods that contribute to the good life. The products of these actions are superior to the acts themselves (NE 1094a5–8 and 1101a14–17). Aristotle limits his praise of self-contained acts to a few activities, and especially to contemplation, which perfects human nature more than any other endeavor. For both Aristotle and Thomas Aquinas the goodness of contemplation does not arise from the action's self-sufficiency, but rather from the intellect's ability to perfect the intellectual potentiality of human beings. Self-sufficiency is merely a concomitant feature of theoretical wisdom. Aristotle and Thomas realize that there is nothing intrinsically meritorious in self-contained acts, since they stress the type of action and its contribution to the perfection of the moral agent. All actions are ultimately measured according to their ability to lead one to the state of happiness. Once again one can see how the work of Aristotle leads to various interpretations of his moral doctrine.

d Moral action theory

The medieval theory of moral actions has its origins in Aristotle's concept of right reason and Augustine's notion of free choice (*liberum arbitrium*). For Aristotle practical choices mimic the deductive process of theoretical reason in which a particular option may be deduced from a universal proposition.[27] The logically deduced conclusion combines an awareness of a universal moral principle with the recognition of a relevant particular instance. Aristotle himself refrains from providing specific examples of universal ethical imperatives, most likely because he bases his moral philosophy on human practice. His examples, however, do illustrate the

---

[26] R. Sokolowski, *Moral Action: A Phenomenological Study* (Bloomington: Indiana University Press, 1985), p. 102; J. Finnis, "Practical Reasoning, Human Goods and the End of Man," pp. 24–26. For a fuller critique of this reading of Aristotle, see A. Celano, "Play and the Theory of Basic Human Goods," *American Philosophical Quarterly*, 28 (1991), pp. 137–146.

[27] Aristotle's theory of moral action is not so controversial as the other doctrines discussed here. For a summary of his position and his influence on modern moral theorists see M. Homiak, "Moral Character," *The Stanford Encyclopedia of* Philosophy, ed. E. N. Zalta (Spring 2011 Edition) http://plato.stanford.edu/archives/spr2011/entries/moral-character/.

nature of practical moral reasoning, as in the rules that stagnant water is to be avoided as unhealthy, and that light meat is beneficial. In the discovery of both the universal and particular premises, experience is a fundamental requirement, since there is no a *priori* knowledge of either proposition. Only after repeated experience, reflection and teaching can one accept the truth of the statements that stagnant water is unhealthy and that this body of water is indeed stagnant. The awareness of both premises provides the basis for the judgment that one should not drink this water. The most basic formulation of universal moral principles would be that human actions should seek to produce happiness, and these actions are conducive to that end. Again experience is required to recognize those actions that produce happiness, and if the required background is operative, then the agent would always choose correctly.

Aristotle recognizes that human beings do not always follow the dictates of right reason, and he explains moral weakness as an error in the process of practical reasoning. In book VII of the NE he indicates that a weak person primarily errs with respect to the minor premise. Although Aristotle does recognize the possibility of absolute moral reprobation in intemperate persons, who believe that their evil choices are justified, he considers the problem of moral weakness (*akrasia* or *incontinentia*) to be far more common. Morally weak persons do not think that what they do is right (NE 1146b22–24), but overcome by unrestrained desires or passions, they choose to ignore the dictates of a rational moral principle (NE 1147b6–12). Unlike Socrates, who determines such a choice to be the result of faulty intellectual reasoning, Aristotle understands that a particular choice (*prohairesis*) may be made in spite of the intellectual awareness of moral principles. One may accept intellectually that drinking to excess is to be avoided, but a desire to enjoy a night out with friends may obscure the acceptance of the final term of the practical syllogism, which would command a cessation of drinking at a reasonable point.

Christian moral theory accepts the basic idea of Greek philosophy that all humans seek a single end. In Christian moral thought the single goal is perfect beatitude, which consists ultimately in the soul's union with God. Christian moralists, however, attempt to explain the decision-making process with the concept of the will, since they were convinced that the exalted faculty of reason could not be led astray by the far inferior powers of emotion and desire. Augustine, whose writings are more influential in the Middle Ages than any source other than the scriptures, was particularly important for the development a new Christian theory of moral action. Mary Clark describes his contribution as follows:

The moral theory of Augustine was both like and unlike that of the Greek philosophers. It was like Greek moral theory in placing happiness as the end of all human striving, and it was like the Neoplatonic philosophers in relating human goodness to a choice of greater over lesser goods, with God as the true source of happiness. Unlike the Greeks, who emphasized knowledge and self-sufficiency, Augustine taught that the human person reaches union with God with God's help by loving him in response to his love ... He emphasized right will in addition to true knowledge as the way to happiness of being united to God ...[28]

Augustine, certainly aware of the conflicting desires that marked his early life, was particularly interested in an explanation for the human dilemma of willing what is not good as presented by Paul in *Romans* 7:19–25: "For the good which I will, I do not, but the evil which I will not, that I do ... But I see another law in my members, fighting against the law of my mind ..."

Augustine determines the final element in action to be the will that provides human beings with autonomy, self-determination and the ability to choose between right and wrong. Although he accepts the Stoic idea of a natural cognition of universal principles of eternal law, Augustine also recognizes the will's ability to accept or reject its dictates. Rather than attribute moral error to an intellectual failure, he explains it in terms of the will's free decision to choose between alternatives. J. Müller notes that Augustine recognizes the ancient concept of the rational striving toward a recognized good, but after the fall of Adam, reason is not strong enough to determine right action without the assistance of divine grace. Augustine introduces a new idea of decisive wanting, which ultimately directs the conflicted will toward a particular action. The human will is the crucial factor in Augustine's moral theory, providing the basis for freedom and individual responsibility.[29] The good will is the cause of "turning and adhering to" the perfect being rather than to a less than perfect one, and the evil will is a desertion or rejection of God.[30] The concept of will allows Augustine to explain how any person may freely disobey the moral law, even though one may recognize intellectually its obligatory nature.

The Latin translations of Aristotle's NE and the Greek commentaries that appeared in the late twelfth and thirteenth centuries provided an impetus for a renewed interest in, and more extensive treatment of, ethical questions. The moral theorists of this era combined the deductive process

---

[28]　M. Clark, *Augustine* (London, New York: Continuum Press, 1994), p. 42.
[29]　J. Müller, *Willenschwäche in Antike und Mittelalter. Eine Problemgeschichte von Sokrates bis zum Johannes Duns Scotus* (Leuven: Leuven University Press, 2009), p. 362.
[30]　Augustine, *De civitate Dei*, XII, 9, ed. B. Dombart and A Kalb, *Corpus christianorum series latina*, 47–48 (Turnhout: Brepols, 1955).

of the rational syllogism with the eternal dictates of natural law. Early in the thirteenth century, authors such as William of Auxerre and Philip the Chancellor located the universal principles of moral reason that are identical with the eternal law in the human innate power, or habit, of *synderesis*. Every single person has an innate ability after certain experiences to recognize the infallibility and immutability of certain moral principles. The dictates of *synderesis* form the major premises of the practical syllogism in the theories on moral choice of Albert the Great and Thomas Aquinas later in the century.[31]

Thomas Aquinas develops the ideas of his former teacher, Albert the Great, when he argues that moral choice follows a judgment that functions as a conclusion in the practical syllogism. The end in all practical decisions functions as a first principle and not as a conclusion. The end insofar as it is an end does not fall within the elective process (*electio*). Just as nothing prevents a speculative principle of one science from being a conclusion in another, no end in one decision is prohibited from being ordered to a further goal. In medicine, for example, health is the end about which no doctor deliberates. The physician intuits the goal of restoring or maintaining health and selects the proper means. Bodily health, however, may be ordered to the good of the soul, and one entrusted with care of the soul may at times have to sacrifice corporeal health for a superior end.[32] No one can choose what lies beyond one's abilities or power to accomplish. The will is the bridge between the intellect and the external operation, since the intellect proposes its object to the will, which in turn is the motivating force to action. The intellect that comprehends something as good in the universal sense drives the will to action. The perfection of the voluntary action develops according to the order leading to the operation by which one strives to attain the object of desire. The voluntary act's perfection results from the performance of some good that lies within the agent's power.[33]

Both Albert and Thomas attempt to explain how reason may fail to function in a rational manner and thus produce incorrect moral action. For Albert the failure is one of reason because the agent may perceive the minor premise but does not really know its relevance due to influence of passion. The morally weak person does not intend to do wrong, and his act is not

---

[31] A. Celano, "*Phronesis*, Prudence and Moral Goodness in the Thirteenth Century Commentaries on the *Nicomachean Ethics*," *Mediaevalia Philosophica Polonorum*, 36 (2007), pp. 5–27.

[32] Summa theologiae (=S. th.) I–II, 13, 3.   [33] S. th. I–II, 13, 5 ad 1.

the result of will but rather unwanted ignorance.[34] Thomas generally agrees with Albert's understanding of moral weakness wherein the general moral principle is obscured in a specific instance because of the effect of passion.[35] Thomas, however, grants a larger role to the will in such decisions, since choice consists in the will's selection according to pleasure. Reason itself can never be the efficient cause of human choice, which depends upon the will, but is rather the final cause of action in its function as that which proposes and judges a goal as good.[36]

Aristotle's explanation of moral action that depends upon the human standard of the rational person was altered by medieval authors, who sought a more secure foundation for the principles of moral reasoning. The dictates of eternal law provide the content for the universal premises that govern ethical deliberation. Aristotle's practical wisdom, which governs the entire range of choices within a lifetime, becomes limited to the deductive process by which moral virtues alone are exercised. The medieval interpretation of practical wisdom allows more easily for Kant's critique of practical wisdom, since *prudentia* commands acts insofar as they are means to an individual end.[37] While prudence in medieval moral theory must recognize a proper moral end, it does not set the ends themselves, which arise from an innate awareness of eternal laws. Aristotle's cryptic style and his adherence to his own dictum to refrain from scientific certainty in practical philosophy have led to disputes about the exact meaning of a number of his moral doctrines. His explanations of the meaning of happiness, the relation of virtue to happiness and the possibility of universal justice have led both medieval and modern readers to extremely different conclusions. While his theory of moral action is less controversial, medieval interpreters attempted to shift the standard of action from the best practices of human beings to that of eternal law. In the subsequent chapters these topics are considered both in Aristotle's works and the writings of medieval authors.

---

[34] J. Müller, *Willenschwäche in Antike und Mittelalter*, p. 507 and M. Tracey, M., "Albert on Incontinence, Continence and Divine Virtue," *Das Problem der Willenschwäche in der Mittelalterlichen Philosophie, Rechérches de Théologie et Philosophie médiévales: Bibliotheca*, 8, ed. T. Hoffmann, J. Müller and M. Perkhams (Louvain: Peeters, 2006), pp. 212–213.

[35] S. th. I–II, 77, 2.   [36] J. Müller, *Willenschwäche in Antike und Mittelalter*, p. 514.

[37] I. Kant, *Grundlegung zur Metaphysik der Sitten*, Akademie Textausgabe (Berlin: Walter de Gruyter, 1903/1911), IV, p. 416.

2

Practical wisdom in the moral theory of Aristotle

Aristotle identifies the purpose of moral philosophy as neither speculation about the nature of goodness, nor analysis of the language of obligation, but rather the practical task of making people good. Aristotle introduces the method of attaining moral knowledge in a passage that alerts the reader to his approach: "Now fine and just actions, which political science investigates, admit of much variety and fluctuation of opinion, so that they may be thought to exist only by convention and not by nature."[1] While Aristotle rejects the idea that politics exists solely by convention, he does allow for great differences within individual moral agents and within different societies. The aim of the moral philosopher is not to create an abstract science, but rather to make himself and others good. Aristotle's method leads to a concrete discussion concerning the conditions and causes of human goodness within his own particular circumstances. He is not so much interested in an abstract discussion of a universally applicable definition of goodness than he is in a description of a good person within his own society. This particular concern does not, however, limit Aristotle's moral theory to a privileged few within ancient Athens. His method directs his readers to seek out those conditions within a particular time and place that contribute to the moral and intellectual excellence of its inhabitants. In the *Politics,* which Aristotle considered the culmination of the study of ethics, his extensive discussion of educational practices pertain to his own community, but many of his ideas retain their relevance for all societies. Aristotle would have hardly argued that years of musical study would have been appropriate to

---

[1] *Nicomachean Ethics* (=NE), *Aristotelis Ethica Nicomachea*, ed. I. Bywater (Oxford: Clarendon Press, 1894), 1094b15–17. I have used the translation of W. D. Ross (Oxford, 1908), with minor changes.

Spartan or barbarian societies.[2] Education serves its environment best when it teaches students how to flourish within a particular community. Aristotle in the *Politics* mocks philosophers who think that they can introduce a radically novel educational system in order to make a city good. A city cannot be well regulated by an imposition of a new moral system, but rather by its traditional manners, customs and laws. Aristotle thinks the state should be made cohesive and unified by means of education. He considers it strange for philosophers to introduce a system of education and think that such an imposition of new ways could make a city morally good. Aristotle clearly prefers to use existing manners, culture and laws.[3] A good society does not arise from theoretical musings about ideal practices, but from traditional ways that instill appropriate skills within the young. Every society adjusts its schools to its needs, but does so gradually since the practical requirements demand long and constant evaluation of societal needs. All could reasonably argue that the general goals for schools would be to produce productive and informed citizens, but disagree about specific methods to produce such ends. The same claim could be made about moral teaching because methods and arguments may differ, although all would agree that the end of ethics is to produce good people. Methods of education change to meet new conditions, as home economics and nuclear radiation drills in American schools have been replaced by computer training and gun safety awareness. The type of practical wisdom envisioned by Aristotle demands constant attention toward the fluctuating conditions within institutions, as well as toward the diverse talents within the communities. Aristotle's introduction to his method of investigating ethical behavior does not merely note the flexibility needed to investigate various behaviors, but also how such variety influences opinions about what is truly good: "Now fine and just actions, which political science investigates, admit of much variety and fluctuation of opinion, so that they may be thought to exist only by convention, and not by nature" (NE 1094b15–17). While Aristotle does not completely accept the idea that human goodness exists solely by convention, he does allow a great measure of latitude to wise individuals, who ultimately determine which actions make them morally good.

[2] For the importance of education in the development of citizens in the ancient world, see W. Jaeger's three-volume study, *Paideia: The Ideals of Greek Culture*, tr. G. Highet (Oxford: Oxford University Press, 1986) and H. I. Marrou, A *History of Education in Antiquity*, tr. G. Lamb (New York: Sheed and Ward, 1956).
[3] *Politics*, ed. W. D. Ross, *Aristotle's Politica* (Oxford: Clarendon Press, 1957), 1263b36–1264a5.

When Aristotle speaks of nature in his writings on ethics, he does not regard the term in the same way as Hume, who sees in nature a cause of great differences in all human beings, or as Locke and Kant, who regard nature as a foundation for the postulation of universal rights and obligations within a political or moral system. For Aristotle nature provides both guidelines for human goodness and limitations on human achievement. Human nature is understood best by examining the composite physical being comprised of body and soul. Because the soul (ψυχή = *psyche*) is the principle of action and thought, Aristotle analyzes it in far greater detail than he does the body, although he does not neglect the effects of corporeal factors within the moral life. The good person must recognize the effects of emotions and desires that arise within the composite of body and soul. One must acknowledge the power of emotions and the ability of the rational mind to overcome their power. H.H. Joachim describes the good man as one "whose conduct must embody the mean or right amount of feeling (as its material). This amount (μέσον) fluctuates within certain limits. It is definite in the sense that it is determined by a proportion or rule."[4] The problem for one trying to grasp Aristotle's meaning arises from his reluctance to state any concrete rule concerning the proper control of an emotional reaction. He merely claims that only a good person can rightly determine the rule. There is no universal natural principle by which moral actions may be measured. Aristotle's repeated use of the good person as the moral standard can be particularly frustrating to those seeking a uniform code of conduct. Throughout the NE, Aristotle assumes that well-intentioned observers of practical endeavors have the ability to recognize those traits and characteristics that render actions and people good.

a The meaning of happiness

Aristotle starts his ethical deliberations with a discussion on the meaning of happiness (εὐδαιμονία = *eudaimonia*). All human actions are directed toward its attainment, and it can therefore be considered as the directive principle of human goodness.[5] Aristotle refers to happiness as the first principle (ἀρχή) of ethical deliberation, not as a proposition of reason, but rather as a unifying element in moral theory. That happiness is the universal good is obvious to all, but such a statement tells little about the

---

[4] H. H. Joachim, *Aristotle the Nicomachea Ethics*, ed. D. A. Rees (Oxford: Clarendon Press, 1955), p. 163, ad 1138b18–25.
[5] NE 1102a1–4.

actions that cause it. An important theme in all Aristotle's works on practical philosophy is the description of the ways in which human beings attain happiness.

Since happiness is a certain activity of the rational soul according to complete virtue, it is essentially a human achievement. Animals cannot be happy because they cannot live according to rational principles. Despite some imprecision in language, Aristotle precludes divine beings from the attainment of happiness and calls them 'blessed', since their entire existence is marked by continuous contemplation. They need not be concerned with the rational activities that comprise human moral virtues, since they are never subject to the changes that occur within human existence. Aristotle examines the meaning of happiness primarily in the context of human nature and its virtues. While he does not ignore the effects of the body on human nature, he insists that human goodness must primarily be an activity of the soul.[6]

What is specifically human does not involve purely biological functions, since they are common to all living things. Although human beings must provide for their material needs, these necessities are not a primary concern of moral theory. Human goodness and virtue principally result from actions of the soul, and the moral philosopher must have some awareness of its nature and abilities (NE 1102a16–19). Aristotle initially divides the soul into that which is rational (λόγον ἔχον) and that which is irrational (ἄλογον). Aristotle dismisses the question whether this division denotes two distinct parts (μόρια) or merely distinguishes them in thought as unimportant (NE 1102a28–33). The irrational element of the soul can be further subdivided into that which is common to all living beings and that which, though irrational, can be ruled by reason. The irrational part controls biological functions and operates without rational planning. Aristotle deems it reasonable to disregard it in an analysis of human moral achievement (NE 1102a32). The second component of the irrational soul may not be able to regulate action, but it can obey the imperatives of reason. This faculty is the appetitive or, more generally, the desiring element (τὸ δ' ἐπιθυμητικὸν καὶ ὅλως ὀρεκτικὸν).[7] Aristotle notes that this element within the soul is the source of moral weakness and conflict. A person with self-control merits praise for restraining desires, just as one is lauded for heeding good advice. A morally weak person, however,

---

[6] NE 1102a16–18: ἀρετὴν δὲ λέγομεν ἀνθρωπίνην οὐ τὴν τοῦ σώματος ἀλλὰ τὴν τῆς ψυχῆς· καὶ τὴν εὐδαιμονίαν δὲ ψυχῆς ἐνέργειαν λέγομεν.

[7] NE 1102b30. See Joachim, p. 62, ad 1102b13–1103a10.

provokes criticism for yielding to unrestrained desires (NE 1102a29–1103a1). Aristotle stresses again the importance of the society in which virtues develop. Without the proper direction of morally wise friends and teachers, one would find little direction concerning the formation of morally good habits, and could not distinguish between appropriate and inappropriate desires.

   The purely rational principle of the soul is the final element in Aristotle's short account of his psychology in the NE. The subdivision within this component of the soul gives rise to a number of questions, which unto this day remain the subject of debate. The primary question concerns the relationship between the intellectual and the moral life, and the corresponding virtues that arise from the respective faculties of the soul. The salient issue is whether the moral virtues that arise from habitual actions comprise merely a preparatory requirement for the fuller life of intellectual excellence. Such is the opinion of Joachim who writes:

> The moral virtues . . . would then appear to be good states of character, so far as the agent in question has not passed beyond a certain immaturity of development. Many people, presumably, would always remain incapable of rising above this level of goodness, for they would never be able to think out their ideals for themselves. And all people, presumably, would have to pass through this lower level of goodness on their way to intelligent or perfect goodness.[8]

While Joachim most likely restricts his analysis here to the development of moral virtue, which proceeds from mere imitative action to reflective awareness of reasons for such acts, he does address an important issue in interpreting Aristotle's theory of happiness. Do human beings pass from a practical stage of correct actions to a fuller, more complete life dominated by theoretical speculation, or do the moral habits complement intellectual accomplishments in the performance of a good life? Aristotle's distinctions within the soul provide the foundation for subsequent conclusions concerning happiness, virtue and human purpose. The way in which the demands of the political life may conflict with the isolated pursuit of theoretical knowledge has led both medieval and modern commentators to different opinions on the exact nature of happiness. Some argue that Aristotle's concept of happiness includes both action and theory (πρᾶξις = *praxis* and θεωρία = *theoria*), while others argue that the contemplative life is the dominant factor within the attainment of *eudaimonia*. The text of Aristotle provides support for both theories and the attempts to reconcile the conflicting accounts have been largely unsuccessful. A resolution may perhaps be found not in the

[8] Joachim, p. 70, ad 1103a3–10.

notion of happiness itself, but rather in an analysis of Aristotle's theory of practical wisdom (φρόνησις = *phronesis*). When Aristotle does consider the intellectual virtues in book VI of the NE, he regards the virtues of wisdom (σοφία = *sophia*) and practical wisdom (*phronesis*) as complementary elements to the good life. *Phronesis* seems here to be the guiding accomplishment that produces goodness in all spheres of human endeavor. Whether Aristotle limits the domain of *phronesis* to practical moral decisions alone or extends its effects to all human actions can be answered only by an examination of his understanding of the human end or general purpose (τέλος). Aristotle argues that it would be unreasonable to think that a human being has no specific function while every natural object and even every bodily part does.[9] This end or goal for all persons can only be happiness.

In determining the nature of *eudaimonia* Aristotle employs his usual method of examining first the undemonstrated opinions of experienced or wise persons (NE 1143b10–12). Such opinions provide the raw data that Aristotle may refine into a more sophisticated theory of moral goodness. This science, which is based on a variety of experiences and suited to individual differences, can never be marked by the type of exactitude found in mathematics or physics. The variety of opinions may lead one to conclude that ethics may be thought of as existing only by convention, but Aristotle tries to find some universal characteristics to human excellence. In the opening chapters of the NE he provides a broad outline of a true, more general, theory, and considers its veracity in light of subsequent conclusions (NE 1094b13–25).

Aristotle combines seemingly disparate elements into his moral theory. The union of subjective and objective premises, the appeal to nature and the consideration of individual differences, and the seemingly contradictory explanations of central themes have long produced great difficulties in interpretation. Concerning human goodness, Aristotle admits that there may be general agreement on its designation, but there is a wide divergence of views on its formation. All would agree that happiness is the human good, which is best defined as living and acting well (τὸ δ' εὖ ζῆν καὶ τὸ εὖ πράττειν). Despite such verbal agreement, many people (οἱ πολλοὶ) have a different understanding concerning happiness than the wise (οἱ σοφόι). The former often consider happiness to be an obvious good, such as wealth, honor or pleasure and they often change their opinion depending upon

---

[9] See F. Sparshot, *Taking Life Seriously – A Study of the Argument for the Nicomachean Ethics* (Toronto: University of Toronto Press, 1996), pp. 15–27.

shifting fortunes. When sick, they seek to become healthy, when poor, wealthy (NE 1095a17–25). Aristotle does not dismiss completely these popular notions, but incorporates them into his own discussion of human goodness. It would be just as foolish for a moral philosopher to ignore common opinions, as it would be for a builder to overlook mathematical formulas in his craft.

Aristotle, in seeking to refine the meaning of happiness, first provides a description of its essential characteristics. In a general way the good may be thought to be that at which all things aim (NE 1094a1–3). Aristotle provides many examples in order to illustrate how the good in any area of human enterprise is the goal and directive force for any subsequent particular action. In military science, the goal is victory; in construction, the building; in medicine, the health of the patient. While there may be a long and arduous deliberative process about the best means to any end, the goal remains ever in the mind of the agent. Every action or choice is judged in relation to the realization of the desired objective. When Aristotle considers the supreme human good, he describes it as that which we desire for its own sake, and never for the sake of anything else. This principal good (τἀγαθὸν καὶ τὸ ἄριστον) is placed within a practical context. Aristotle has little interest in discussing a separate perfect ideal of good-ness, for were such a good to exist, it would contribute nothing to our understanding of moral purpose (NE 1096b30–35). Aristotle's inclusion of the phrase, "of the things we do" (τῶν πρακτῶν, NE 1094a19) concerning ultimate human goodness, emphasizes the main topic of his work: to discover what conditions lie in the human power that allow for the perfection of the potential within the human soul. Aristotle limits the scope of his search by asserting the finite process by which human beings attain moral goodness. If there were an infinite hierarchy of human pur-suits, he would search in vain for a unifying moral element to moral behavior.[10] The final human good, as a certain goal (τί τό τέλος), completes or fulfills human existence, and perfection results only in the attainment of the end. The teleological view of nature that is an important feature of Aristotle's natural philosophy appears just as prominently in the discus-sions on *eudaimonia*.

In his treatment of the general traits characterizing goodness, Aristotle seeks to discover that good which is achieved through human practice.[11]

---

[10] R.-A. Gauthier and Y. Jolif, *L'Éthique à Nicomaque, trans. et comm.* (Louvain: Publications Universitaires, 1970), ad 1096b30–35.
[11] NE 1095a15–17.

As he repeatedly indicates, the goal of ethics is not simply to expound a theory of moral principles, but to specify individual operations that make a person good.[12] The insistence upon a practical end of human endeavors does not lead Aristotle to exclude all theoretical activity from the definition of happiness. 'Praxis' includes all operations that actualize human potentialities within the soul, and contemplation itself is an action that perfects the noetic ability of all human beings.

Another feature of *eudaimonia* is the necessity of self-sufficiency (αὐτάρκεια), as was indicated briefly above. Happiness, therefore, is desired for its own sake, and never because it leads to any further activity.[13] By 'self-sufficiency' Aristotle does not mean that the moral person should live a solitary life without common social and political interaction, but rather that the supreme human good cannot be made more desirable by the addition of any further good. 'Self-sufficient' qualifies not the happy person, but rather refers to the state of happiness, which, viewed analytically, makes a life desirable and lacking nothing (NE 1097b15–18). Aristotle adds one final qualification to his general description of *eudaimonia* when he claims that it should never be numbered as one good among many others. If it were to be so considered, it could be made more desirable by the addition of the smallest of goods (NE 1097b17–20). Aristotle seems to regard happiness in absolute terms: one is either happy or is not. He would probably reject the claim that some people are happier than others. Some may be more blessed by fortune, but happiness is a state determined by excellence in human action.

The broad account of happiness as a final, self-sufficient activity, and the end to which all operations are directed tells one little about its specific nature, as Aristotle readily admits (NE 1097a22–23). The general characteristics of goodness pertain to any object or inquiry in Aristotle's view, but in order to determine human goodness he deems it necessary to examine the specific function of human beings. Their endeavors are judged according to how well they contribute to the performance of their particular purpose. Inspired by Socrates's example of good craftsmen, Aristotle asks whether we would not assume that the shoemaker and carpenter have definite purposes and functions but that a human being would be naturally functionless (ἀργὸν πέφυκεν).[14] Just as the particular artisans are judged

[12] NE 1095a6–7.

[13] Aristotle says that the supreme good appears to be something final or complete: NE 1097a28: τὸ δ' ἄριστον τέλειόν τι φαίνεται.

[14] R. Parry, "Episteme and Techne," *Stanford Encyclopedia of Philosophy*, ed. E. Zalta (Fall 2007), http://plato.stanford.edu/entries/episteme-techne/#Bib.

by how well they perform their specific tasks, so too will a person be assessed according to actions that contribute to actualizing the human function (NE 1097b29–34). The element of judging other people is an integral part to Aristotle's ethics, since it allows citizens to discern which characteristics are to be emulated, and which persons should be deemed to have acted wisely. These judgments not only allow for the transmission of the moral tradition to future generation, but also provide a foundation for adopting novel elements into the culture. The ability to recognize better and innovative methods in the pursuit of goodness promotes moral progress within a particular society.

As has been noted, Aristotle thinks it strange to regard every part of the human body to have a particular function (ἔργον) and not the human being as a whole. Human goodness then must be discovered in those actions that perfect the human being as such. The human function differentiates the species from all other things, and its fulfillment actualizes the various elements of human nature. Aristotle's general principle of nature is "that the good or well being of anything which has a work (or function), depends upon its doing that work well" (NE 1097b26–27).[15] The soul (*psyche*) is the most important part of the human nature. Life and perception are not specifically human since they are common to all animals. What remains as fitting to humans is the active life of that which has reason (λείπεται δὴ πρακτική τις τοῦ λόγον ἔχοντος: NE 1098a3–4). In addition to the obvious identification of the human *ergon* with the ability to arrange actions according to reason, Aristotle again emphasizes the importance of *praxis*. By so doing he does not limit moral goodness to the politically active life. As many commentators have noted, the phrase 'πρακτική τις' here does not exclude the exercise of contemplation from the human function, but rather incorporates it into the concept of human perfection, which is part of the achievement of human efforts (τό πρακτικὸν ἀγαθόν; τέλος τῶν πρακτῶν).[16]

In order to specify the excellence of the function, Aristotle insists that the activity must be done skillfully and well, just as a good person would perform these acts. Aristotle concludes this section by summarizing the requisite conditions that characterize the human *ergon*: it is a certain kind of life, which is an activity or actions of the soul according to reason; the performance of these actions must harmonize with what a good person

---

[15] Joachim, p. 49, ad 1097b26–27.

[16] J. Stewart, *Notes on the Nicomachean Ethics* (Oxford: Clarendon Press, 1892); J. Burnet, *The Ethics of Aristotle* (London: Methuen, 1900) and Gauthier-Jolif, ad 1105a17–18.

does, and every human virtue must be well accomplished in accordance with its own particular excellence.[17] After the enumeration of these requirements, Aristotle is prepared to offer his definition of human goodness as the "the activity of the soul in accordance with virtue (κατ' ἀρετὴν), and if there are more than one virtue, in accordance with the best and most complete" (NE 1098a17–18).[18] Aristotle offers here the possibility of either a single action that constitutes human excellence (δὲ ψυχῆς ἐνέργειαν) or multiple activities (πράξεις μετὰ λόγου). In his determination of goodness, his conditional statement concerning one or more virtues is even more puzzling (εἰ δὲ πλείους αἱ ἀρεταί, κατὰ τὴν ἀρίστην καὶ τελειοτάτην). Aristotle's theory certainly includes consideration of many virtues of the soul, as the discussions in the subsequent books of the NE indicate. One may well ask whether the use of the singular adjectival form referring to the best and the final virtue in the last line of the quotation is a clear indication of his acceptance of one particular supreme virtue as the only activity worthy of perfecting the human soul, and thereby meriting the designation of happiness. If this were the case then all other activities, no matter how noble or praiseworthy in themselves, must be considered subordinate to a single best virtue. Aristotle's subsequent discussions, however, seem to indicate that he has a more complex understanding of the notion of happiness. The two interpretations concerning the number of virtues required for happiness, as well as the subsequent discussions in book X of the NE and in the *Eudemian Ethics* (EE) concerning *eudaimonia* provide no definitive answer to the problem. Rather than attempting to resolve the dilemma by examining the conflicting accounts of meaning of happiness, perhaps a better and more satisfactory path will be provided by an analysis of the virtue of practical wisdom (*phronesis*). The traditional view of Aristotle's ethics as predominantly eudaimonistic may be wrong, since he seems to indicate that even the operations of *eudaimonia* may be subject to the judgments of the man of practical wisdom (φρόνιμος = *phronimos*). In examining the significance of the virtue of practical wisdom for the attainment of moral goodness, we may be able better to resolve the seemingly incompatible views concerning the relation of virtue to happiness.

---

[17] NE 1098a13–16.

[18] A slightly different definition of best life for a human being is given in the *Politics* (1323b40–1324a2): "For the present let us take it as established that the best life whether separately for an individual or collectivity for states, is the life conjoined with virtue furnished with sufficient means for taking part in virtuous actions.

Aristotle believes that he has provided an adequate outline of the meaning of goodness that is acceptable to all (NE 1098a19–b8). His discussion of
the principles of moral reasoning indicates his conviction that he has
established the facts or the what (τὸ ὅτι) of moral goodness. The meaning
of goodness is not only sufficiently determined from his own philosophical
reasoning, but also harmonizes with common opinions. All known opinions, both philosophical and popular, agree with his own account that
asserts that the happy person lives and acts well.[19] While the moral philosopher cannot provide the same level of certainty for first principles that
scientific demonstrations demand, he may give an account of them that is
appropriate to the practical science of ethics. With his descriptions of human
function and goodness completed, Aristotle substitutes easily the term
'happiness' for 'goodness,' since he considers them almost identical with
respect to human achievement (NE 1099b23–24). Once named, happiness as
the human end has been variously thought to consist in virtue (ἀρετή =
arete), practical wisdom (*phronesis*), a certain type of wisdom (σοφία τις), or
all or some of these elements, accompanied by pleasure and external prosperity (NE 1098b23–27). As is usual in Aristotle's passages introducing a
new topic, all the possible solutions mentioned are to be taken seriously.
Aristotle has little interest in providing weak arguments that he may easily
attack, since he prefers to examine plausible ideas and to incorporate them
into his own resolution of the problem, if they are worthwhile.

Since human goodness depends upon the performance of those actions
that are proper to human beings and perfect their function, Aristotle
concentrates upon the activities of the soul. The actions of the soul that
are in accord with virtue are of two types: the excellence of that component of the soul which is regulated by reason; and the virtue of the part
that is actualized into intellectual accomplishment. The concomitant
attributes of pleasure and prosperity do not qualify as constituents of
happiness. The relation between the former qualities, which are the moral
virtues, and the latter, which constitute intellectual excellence, is an
important and difficult question for interpreting Aristotle's doctrine of
human goodness. What is immediately clear from the discussion is the
dismissal of the concomitant attributes of prosperity and pleasure as
essential components to *eudaimonia*.

---

[19] NE 1098b20–21: καὶ τὸ εὖ ζῆν καὶ τὸ εὖ πράττειν τὸν εὐδαίμονα: See Burnet, p. 15, ad
1095a19: "In the *Politics* Aristotle more and more tends to substitute this phrase (τὸ δ' εὖ
ζῆν) for the name εὐδαιμονία which he had borrowed from the Academy. It emphasizes
the view that a good life is an *ἐνέργεια*."

b Reconciling Aristotle's two accounts of happiness

Aristotle's two accounts of the nature of happiness in books I and X of the NE have caused much disagreement concerning the precise constitution of human goodness. While all may agree that happiness according to Aristotle is an activity of the soul, the question remains concerning the exact relation between the moral and intellectual virtues, or the practical and theoretical life. H.G. Gadamer notes the tension in the two accounts by Aristotle, when he considers the meaning of practical wisdom:

> It can be determined that practical wisdom (*phronesis*) and not only theoretical reason is the supreme virtue of an intellectual being. So the question remains how do both these perfections and types of knowledge relate to one another. We therefore return again to the ancient problem of the primacy of *theoria* over human *praxis*.[20]

Even as astute a reader of Aristotle as Gadamer has some difficulty in determining the relative importance of some human accomplishments in relation to others. The assertions that both practical wisdom (*phronesis*) and intellectual wisdom (σοφία = *sophia*) comprise the supreme good and that both must be considered as the highest virtue need careful consideration. The uncertainty concerning the relation between the practical and the theoretical lives arises from Aristotle's text, and Gadamer's approach seems close to what Aristotle may have intended. Any interpretation of the notion of *eudaimonia* must examine carefully the passages in book X of the NE where Aristotle seems to indicate that only contemplation can actualize human potentiality sufficiently and merit the designation of happiness. Despite the praise of the contemplative life, Aristotle also indicates the importance of the life within the *polis* and the civic and social responsibilities that comprise a good human life.

In the last chapters of the NE Aristotle praises the perfection of the intellect, the purely rational part of the soul, as the highest human activity. If happiness is truly an activity according to virtue, it is reasonable to conclude that the highest human good must consist in the virtuous action of the best element within human nature. Aristotle's discussion of this topic begins with his usual method of posing questions and considering a number of opinions. It may be that the intellect (νοῦς = *nous*) reigns supreme or that something else guides and rules human operations. It may also be that *nous* is divine or only what is most divine in us. Whatever this human power may

---

[20] H. G. Gadamer, *Nikomachische Ethik VI/Aristoteles* (Frankfurt am Main: Klostermann, 1998), p. 16.

be, Aristotle does say that an existence according to its actualization will be complete happiness. However Aristotle may answer these questions, he does incorporate many of these ideas into his conclusion that the activity of complete happiness is a contemplative or theoretical pursuit (ἡ δὲ τελεία εὐδαιμονία ὅτιθεωρητική τις ἐστιν ἐνέργεια: NE 1178b8–9). This passage is the clearest expression of the supremacy of the theoretical life, and its dominant role in the production of happiness. If these were the final words on the subject then all other actions and pursuits must be directed toward the intellectual life of contemplation. Only contemplative activity would merit the designation, 'supremely good', since it not only perfects the best part of human beings, but its objects are also supremely knowable in themselves (1177a19–22). Contemplation is the most continuous, independent and self-sufficient of human accomplishments, since it demands nothing outside the intellectual fervor and excellence of the contemplative. Aristotle can think of nothing more desirable than the pleasure of contemplating truth (NE 1177a23).

In comparing contemplation (*theoria*) with practice (*praxis*), Aristotle notes how the former is loved for its own sake, but the latter produces virtues within political and military realms that aim at external ends (NE 1177b3–15). Aristotle's most commonly cited passage on the relationship between the two types of lives seems to relegate the practical life to a secondary status: "The life according to the other kind of virtue is happy only in a secondary degree. For the activities according to it are human."[21] Aristotle has again drawn attention to the interplay between what he calls the divine and human spheres of existence. His eloquent plea "not to follow those who advise us, being human, to think of human things, and being mortal, of mortal things, but must, so far as we can, make ourselves immortal, and strain with every nerve to live in accordance with the best things in us" (NE 1177b32–1178a1) is balanced by his admonition that "such a life would be too high for a human; it is not in so far as one is human that one will live so, but in so far as something divine is present . . ." (NE 1177b27–32). The juxtaposition of these two passages suggests a fundamental dilemma in Aristotle's doctrine concerning human purpose and goodness. A person may well ask whether one should seek to overcome one's natural corporeal limitations and seek the divinely blissful contemplative life, or should one align the joy of contemplative thought with the civic and familial demands presented to all. Aristotle's treatment of the

---

[21] NE 1178a9–10.: δευτέρως δ' ὁ κατὰ τὴν ἄλλην ἀρετήν: αἱ γὰρ κατὰ ταύτην ἐνέργειαι ἀνθρωπικαί. The phrase, κατὰ τὴν ἄλλην ἀρετήν, refers clearly to practical virtue.

question remains unclear, since at times he indicates that happiness consists in a full life of many virtues, and at others his enthusiastic praise of the life devoted to theoretical wisdom seems to make all other pursuits, however noble, subordinate to the life of the intellect.

Aristotle, if pressed, would probably have had to admit that the demands of the theoretical life could at times conflict with those of practical affairs. But he never seems to have considered the problem as a serious objection to his moral thought. He does not indicate any conflict within the activities of the morally good person. Certainly one could argue that a contemplative individual would have little use for political strife within a certain society, since governmental policies are not marked by the intellectual constancy of speculative sciences. On the other hand, the adept politician would care little for questions concerning the ground of existence because an awareness of questions on the source of being would contribute little to fiscal and civic policy. Aristotle says of the search for the meaning of the separate good that "even if there is some one good which is universally predicable of goods or is capable of separate and independent existence, clearly it cannot be achieved by human beings, and we are now seeking something attainable" (NE 1096b31–35). The dismissal here of a metaphysical topic may seem to minimize the importance of theoretical activity, but Aristotle is merely noting here that an intelligent person knows the limits of ethical science. Aristotle continues to examine the place of speculation within the practical life when he maintains: "It is hard to see how a weaver or carpenter will be aided in his craft by knowing the good itself, or how one could become a better doctor or general by having viewed the idea itself" (NE 1097a8–11). It is important to note that Aristotle does not include here the term 'a better human being', because investigating the good theoretically may indeed contribute to the fulfillment of the intellectual potential of the soul, and thereby produce a better person.

Aristotle's ethics includes treatments of many virtues that are essentially practical and his use of medical analogies to explain the meaning of important moral doctrines appears throughout his works. One might gain the impression that by noting the fruitlessness of speculative pursuits to the practitioners of various human arts, Aristotle rejects the importance of any theory to the practically wise. One might also conclude that Aristotle has restricted the life of happiness to a few persons who have mastered theoretical principles and science. Neither interpretation seems to reflect the true opinion of Aristotle, who clearly considers contemplation to be perfect happiness: "The act of this [divine element] in accordance with its proper virtue will be perfect happiness. That this activity is contemplative

has already been stated."[22] Aristotle is quick to remind us that human
beings cannot be divine contemplatives:

But such a life would be too high for a human being, for it is not in so far as he is
man that he will live in such a way, but in so far as something divine is present in
him; and by so much as this is superior to our composite nature it is activity
superior to that which is the exercise of the other kind of virtue. If reason is divine
then in comparison with a human being, the life according to it is divine in
comparison with human life. (NE 1177b27–32)

Aristotle insists that despite the human desire for an immutable blessed
existence, there can only be a type of beatitude that is characterized by the
phrase "blessed as men" (μακαρίους δ'ἀνθρώπους).[23]

When Aristotle concludes the two discussions on happiness, he refers
to Solon who warned that no living person could be called happy because
a secure judgment about the state of a life can be made only after it has
ended. In book I Aristotle asks whether "should we not say that one is
happy who is active in accordance with complete virtue and is sufficiently
equipped with external goods, not for some chance period but throughout a complete lifetime." If such conditions are met, Aristotle describes
those persons as "blessed among living men in whom these conditions
are, and are to be, fulfilled – but blessed as men" (NE 1101a14–22). There
are two very significant ideas in this passage. The emphasis on the happy
person acting in accordance with complete virtue (εὐδαίμονα τὸν κατ'
ἀρετὴν τελείαν ἐνεργοῦντα) signals Aristotle's intention to include both
contemplative and habitual virtues with the notion of happiness. The
provision "sufficiently equipped with external goods," refers to the question
of the effects of chance upon happiness. Taken together, these two provisions
in Aristotle's statement lead to the conclusion that happiness is to be understood as the actualization of human potentials. Contemplation, as the
actuality of *nous*, perfects the intellective element of the soul; moral virtue
perfects the part that heeds the dictates of reason; the external goods ensure
that a person has what is necessary to maintain biological existence. In short,
happiness turns out to be the enjoyment of life, and the exercise of moral and
intellectual virtues.

In book X of the NE, Aristotle again concludes his discussion on happiness with a reference to Solon:

---

[22] NE 1177a16–18.

[23] NE 1101a21–22: In the *Politics* Aristotle argues that divine beings have no need for
external goods since they are blessed by their very nature, *Politics*, 1323b27–30. See also
A. Celano, "Aristotle on Beatitude," *Ancient Philosophy*, 5 (1985), pp. 205–214.

Solon too was perhaps sketching well the happy person when he described him as moderately furnished with externals but as having done (as Solon thought) the noblest acts and lived temperately; for one can with but moderate possession do what one ought. (NE 1179a9–13)

Despite the importance in book X of the supremacy of the life of contemplation, Aristotle's addition of the condition of moral virtue (βεβιωκότας σωφρόνως) and good fortune (ἐκτὸς κεχορηγημένους) to the supreme human activity (πεπραγότας δὲ τὰ κάλλισθ᾽) restates the notion of happiness found in the first book of the NE. Again the moral and intellectual life supplemented with external goods constitutes happiness. Aristotle's most enthusiastic praise for the life of the mind follows his analysis of Solon's opinion of happiness, but Aristotle assumes one has recognized that his prior discussion of *phronesis* provides the solution for the exact determination of what activities the good person should pursue. In itself *theoria* must be the supreme virtue and is clearly superior to the political life, which produces happiness only in a secondary way. A human life, however, is never characterized by continuous contemplation, but must also include other virtues: "For the moral activities are truly human."[24] Aristotle constantly describes contemplation as a divine activity, but the inclusion of a divine spark within the human soul does not lead to the conclusion that all endeavors should be directed toward the solitary life of theoretical wisdom. Such a life is fitting only to the gods, just as a solitary irrational existence suits only animals. Human lives lie between the two extremes, and they become fulfilled through a number of different rational acts. Aristotle repeats in the *Politics* his idea that the best life is one that incorporates a variety of rational activities:

For as regards at all events one classification of things good, putting them in three groups, external goods, goods of the soul, and goods of the body, assuredly nobody would deny that the ideally happy are bound to possess all three.[25]

For Aristotle a life without involvement within the practical affairs of the city would neglect an integral potentiality for human goodness – the contribution to a just and good society. He makes this conviction clear in the *Politics* when he says that the activities of the superior part of the soul must be preferable for those persons who are capable of attaining either all the soul's activities or two of the three.[26] Then he says justice and temperance are needed by those who are deemed very prosperous and who enjoy

---

[24] NE 1178a9–10: αἱ γὰρ κατὰ ταύτην ἐνέργειαι ἀνθρωπικαί. ταύτην here refers to moral virtue.
[25] *Politics*, 1323a23–27.   [26] *Politics*, 1333a27–30.

all blessings, like the persons, if such exist, as the poets say, that are in the islands of the blest.[27] The insistence upon the need for moral virtue even for those who dwell as eternally blessed emphasizes the importance of political and moral virtues for all who are said to be happy.

Within the practical domain, justice, courage and similar virtues are needed to produce a good human society. Virtuous practices comprise the civic duties that are typical of all good communities (NE 1178a13–14). The primary virtues among human habits is *phronesis*, but Aristotle seems unclear in the formulation of its function: "Practical wisdom, too, is linked to virtue of character, and this to practical wisdom, since the principles of practical wisdom are in accordance with the moral virtues and rightness in morals is in accordance with practical wisdom."[28] Aristotle's argument here is consistent with his account of *phronesis* throughout the NE, but he seems to construct a circular argument: practical wisdom is connected with moral virtue that is itself linked to practical wisdom. The relation between virtue and practical wisdom depends upon the agent's ability to recognize the principles (ἀρχαὶ) of *phronesis* that are determined in accordance with the moral virtues, whose standard for correct action is established by practical wisdom. The indeterminate character of such a formulation concerning the principles of moral action led later commentators on the NE, such as Albert the Great and Thomas Aquinas, to anchor the imperatives of action in the natural law. Aristotle's own notion provides few, if any, objective criteria, for recognizing a determined path of moral action.

Despite the lack of clarity concerning the origins of moral principles, Aristotle specifies the domain of practical wisdom when he claims that the moral virtues, because of their connection to the passions (τοῖς πάθεσι), concern the composite nature of human beings. These moral virtues of the composite being are specifically human, as are the life and happiness that result from their exercise.[29] The happiness that produces intellectual excellence may in itself be superior to specifically human happiness, but it is a thing apart from the composite, and, as such, is truly reserved for a higher type of existence. While human beings have a temporary glimpse of the blessed life of eternal contemplation, their lives are judged ultimately by how the capacities of their composite nature are realized through acts of justice, liberality and temperance that are precluded from the actions of divine beings.

A similar account of human happiness appears in the EE, where Aristotle identifies *eudaimonia* with the greatest and best of human goods (τῶν

---

[27] *Politics*, 1334a27–30.   [28] NE 1178a16–19.   [29] NE 1178a19–23.

ἀγαθῶν τῶν ἀνθρωπίνων). He clarifies the meaning of the term 'human', in a manner similar to that in the NE: "we say 'human' because there might very well be happiness for a higher being, such as a god."[30] This human good is realized best through the decisions of politics, economics and practical wisdom.[31] The inclusion of practical wisdom among the practical pursuits of politics and economics indicates a notion of happiness similar to that of the NE, and differs significantly from the Platonic understanding of wisdom. The concept of *phronesis* apparent in the EE makes Aristotle's description of the philosophical life particularly noteworthy. In the discussion concerning the definition of happiness, Aristotle offers three possible types of life that may constitute happiness: political, pleasurable or the philosophical. When he considers the philosophical life, he notes that it concerns practical wisdom (περὶ φρόνησιν): "Of these [three lives] the philosophical strives to be about practical wisdom and also with the contemplation of truth."[32] The passage cited here gives equal place to both practical and theoretical wisdom in the formation of human happiness. The interpretation of *phronesis* as theoretical wisdom in this work by some modern commentators arises from its appearance in the preliminary discussion of happiness, where Aristotle lists certain opinions on the meaning of *eudaimonia*: "To be happy and to live a life blessedly and well may consist primarily in three things thought to be most desirable; for some say the greatest good is

---

[30] EE1217a22–24: μέγιστον εἶναι καὶ ἄριστον τοῦτο τῶν ἀγαθῶν τῶν ἀνθρωπίνων. ἀνθρώπινον δὲ λέγομεν, ὅτι τάχ' ἂν εἴη καὶ βελτίονός τινος ἄλλου τῶν ὄντων εὐδαιμονία, οἷον θεοῦ.

[31] EE 1218b10–14: τὸ δ' οὗ ἕνεκα ὡς τέλος ἄριστον καὶ αἴτιον τῶν ὑφ' αὐτὸ καὶ πρῶτον πάντων.ὥστε τοῦτ' ἂν εἴη αὐτὸ τὸ ἀγαθὸν τὸ τέλος τῶν ἀνθρώπῳ πρακτῶν. τοῦτο δ' ἐστὶ τὸ ὑπὸ τὴν κυρίαν πασῶν. αὕτη δ' ἐστὶ πολιτικὴ καὶ οἰκονομικὴ καὶ φρόνησις. "For the object aimed at is the chief good, and is the cause of the subordinate goods and first of all; so that the Absolute Good would be this – the End of the good practicable for man. And this is the good that comes under the supreme of all practical sciences, which is Politics and Economics and [Practical] Wisdom.

[32] EE 1215b1–2: τούτων γὰρ ὁ μὲν φιλόσοφος βούλεται περὶ φρόνησιν εἶναι καὶ τὴν θεωρίαν τὴν περὶ τὴν ἀλήθειαν The English translation of H. Rackham, *Athenian Constitution, Eudemian Ethics and Virtues and Vices* (Cambridge: Harvard University Press, 1981) ignores completely the phrase περὶ φρόνησιν: "Of these the philosophic life denotes being concerned with the contemplation of truth . . ." Dirlmeier's German translation takes περὶ φρόνησιν as a reference to theoretical knowledge: "Von diesen Grundformen nämlich hat die philosophische als ihr Ziel theoretisches Wissen, das heisst die Betrachtung des wahren Seienden." F. Dirlmeier, *Eudemische Ethik Übers.und kommentiert von Franz Dirlmeier* (Berlin: Akademie Verlag, 1984), p. 504. Also C. J. Rowe, "The Meaning of *Phronesis* in the *Eudemian Ethics*," *Untersuchungen zur Eudemischen Ethik*, ed. P. Moraux et al. (Berlin: De Gruyter, 1971), pp. 73–92.

wisdom (*phronesis*), others say virtue (*arete*) and still others pleasure (ἡδονή)."[33] The use of *phronesis* here must be understood as a reference to intellectual wisdom, since it signifies a type of life that differs from those of moral virtue and pleasure. If Aristotle had meant it here to refer to practical wisdom, he would have had no need to include the life of virtue (*arete*) as a different form of life. But this concept of *phronesis is* not Aristotle's own since he seems to be referring to the Platonic understanding of *phronesis* as theoretical knowledge. The phrase that introduces the clause, 'some say' (οἵ μὲν φασιν), indicates that Aristotle is using the ideas of others to begin the discussion concerning the nature of happiness.

Aristotle examines specifically the Socratic position on wisdom in the EE when he argues that *phronesis* is a type of knowledge (ἐπιστήμη=episteme) and truth (ἀληθές τι), but the *phronimos* may miss the mark, just as an ignorant person may. For Aristotle the possession of knowledge does not immediately translate into the infallible exercise of it (EE 1246b4–8). While the practically wise are clearly good, wisdom and goodness are not coextensive terms. Socrates was correct when he said nothing is more fitting than wisdom (*phronesis*), but was wrong in calling practical wisdom knowledge (*episteme*). Phronesis is a virtue (*arete*) and a form of knowing that is different from *episteme*.[34] By distinguishing between *phronesis* and *episteme*, Aristotle has distanced his own theory of morality from that of Socrates and Plato, who based their theory on the principle that virtue is knowledge. Aristotle has also begun to formulate his idea that the good person must indeed be the same as the practically wise person. The terms 'practically wise' and 'good', are not identical, because for true human goodness human beings must also be in some way *sophoi*. Aristotle argues that all people by nature have a ruling and subservient element within them. They live properly according to a ruling principle that is two-fold: just as medicine and health are the directive principles of the practical art of healing, so too are practical wisdom and knowledge the requirements for happiness. The example of medicine as the means to establishing health is particularly relevant to Aristotle's understanding of the role of

---

[33] EE 1214a31–35: τὸ δ' εὐδαιμονεῖν καὶ τὸ ζῆν μακαρίως καὶ καλῶς εἴη ἂν ἐν τρισὶ μάλιστα, τοῖς εἶναι δοκοῦσιν αἱρετωτάτοις. οἳ μὲν γὰρ τὴν φρόνησιν μέγιστον εἶναί φασιν ἀγαθόν, οἳ δὲ τὴν ἀρετήν, οἳ δὲ τὴν ἡδονήν.

[34] EE 1246b33–36. See also *Politics*, 1260a26–30, where Aristotle agrees with Gorgias' method of considering each virtue separately, and not as different facets of knowledge. Aristotle claims to prefer Gorgias' separate enumeration of virtues to those (e.g. Socrates) who define virtue in a universal way.

contemplation in the genesis of *eudaimonia*. The guiding force of the contemplative element in the human soul is the divine being, which does not issue commands, but is the final end sought by all contemplatives. That element that directs human beings to recognize the importance of contemplation within a life is practical wisdom. Aristotle again emphasizes the importance of practical wisdom even as it directs one toward theoretical speculation. While the superior part of the soul (*nous*) is contemplative or intellectual, the rational virtue of *phronesis* issues the commands that lead to the attainment of all desired ends. Practical wisdom is like the art of medicine without which there can be no sustained health:

It is proper, therefore, here as in other matters to live with reference to the ruling factor . . . And since man consists by nature of a ruling part and a subject part, and each would properly live with reference to the ruling principle within him (and this is two-fold, for medical science is a ruling principle in one way and health is in another, and the former is a means to the latter), this is therefore the case in regard to the faculty of contemplation. For God is not a ruler in the sense of issuing commands, but is the End as a means *to which wisdom (phronesis) gives commands* . . . Therefore whatever mode of choosing and of acquiring things by nature . . . will best promote the contemplation of God, that is the best mode, and that standard is the finest.[35]

Although Aristotle compares *phronesis* to the practice of medicine, which is a means to health, he does not hesitate to claim that practical wisdom commands the methods by which contemplation is best attained.[36]

In the *Politics* Aristotle describes happiness as that which consists in a combination of activities that are governed by virtue and practical wisdom. He does not mention theoretical wisdom, but the reader may infer that its exercise falls within the judgments of the practically wise: ". . . that to each man there falls just so large a measure of happiness as he achieves of virtue

---

[35] EE1249b7–19: δεῖ δὴ ὥσπερ καὶ ἐν τοῖς ἄλλοις πρὸς τὸ ἄρχον ζῆν, καὶ πρὸς τὴν ἕξιν κατὰ τὴν ἐνέργειαν τὴν τοῦ ἄρχοντος, οἷον δοῦλον πρὸς δεσπότου καὶ ἕκαστον πρὸς τὴν ἑκάστου καθήκουσαν ἀρχήν. ἐπεὶ δὲ καὶ ἄνθρωπος φύσει συνέστηκεν ἐξ ἄρχοντος καὶ ἀρχομένου, καὶ ἕκαστον ἂν δέοι πρὸς τὴν ἑαυτῶν ἀρχὴν ζῆν (αὕτη δὲ διττή· ἄλλως γὰρ ἡ ἰατρικὴ ἀρχὴ καὶ ἄλλως ἡ ὑγίεια· ταύτης δὲ ἕνεκα ἐκείνη)· οὕτω δ᾽ ἔχει κατὰ τὸ θεωρητικόν. οὐ γὰρ ἐπιτακτικῶς ἄρχων ὁ θεός, ἀλλ᾽ οὗ ἕνεκα ἡ φρόνησις ἐπιτάττει (διττὸν δὲ τὸ οὗ ἕνεκα· διώρισται δ᾽ ἐν ἄλλοις), ἐπεὶ κεῖνός γε οὐθενὸς δεῖται. ἥτις οὖν αἵρεσις καὶ κτῆσις τῶν φύσει ἀγαθῶν ποιήσει μάλιστα τὴν τοῦ θεοῦ θεωρίαν, ἢ σώματος ἢ χρημάτων ἢ φίλων ἢ τῶν ἄλλων ἀγαθῶν, αὕτη ἀρίστη, καὶ οὗτος ὁ ὅρος κάλλιστος.

[36] J. Burnet, p. 286, ad 1144b27: "It is true that the ὀρθὸς λόγος is not an ἀρετή nor identical with φρόνησις, but yet this way of speaking is quite Aristotelian. The ὀρθὸς λόγος of health is ἰατρική, and so the ὀρθὸς λόγος of action may be regarded as the form of goodness existing in the soul of the φρόνιμος, and identical with the φρόνησις of the man who has the 'λόγος'."

and of practical wisdom, and of virtuous and wise action."[37] Later in the same work Aristotle again argues that the function for the good person or the good state needs virtue and *phronesis*, but omits a discussion of the contemplative life as irrelevant to politics. He does, however, expand the meaning of *praxis* to include theoretical actions:

But the active life is not necessarily active in relation to others, as some think, nor are only those processes of thought active that are pursued for the sake of the objects that result from action, but far more those speculations and thoughts that have their end in themselves are pursued for their own sake; for the end is to do well and is therefore a certain kind of action.[38]

Aristotle concludes this discussion by saying that those who say the political life is undesirable are partly correct, but also partly wrong. They are right in their assertion because leisure provides the opportunity for human beings to fulfill their desire for the highest enjoyment of contemplation (*Pol.* 1329a1–3); they are wrong because happiness is essentially an active pursuit (τὴν δ᾽ εὐπραγίαν καὶ τὴν εὐδαιμονίαν εἶναι ταὐτόν. *Pol.* 1325a23–24). To praise inactivity more highly than activity is ill-advised, since happiness itself is *praxis*, and just and temperate acts lead in great part to the realization of human goodness.[39]

All the activities of the composite human beings are ruled by *phronesis*, which allows the wise person to make proper judgments, not only in dealing with others, but also in organizing one's own pursuits. Joseph Owens writes:

The incessant variability makes the *kalon* [good] a moving target for practical philosophy ... practical truth is not measured by an already existent design. Its measure is correct desire, a norm that requires correct upbringing in the virtues ... Correct habituation in the virtues, an habituation arising from freely performed acts, renders the *phronimos* the measure and judge of moral goodness.[40]

Moral goodness is not limited merely to the exercise of habitual virtues regulating human passions, but is realized most fully in a completely integrated life of excellence. In the *Rhetoric*, Aristotle describes *phronesis* as that virtue by which all come to make wise decisions about good and evil. He does not limit its domain to the political or ethical decisions, but

---

[37] *Politics*, 1323b21–23: ὅτι μὲν οὖν ἑκάστῳ τῆς εὐδαιμονίας ἐπιβάλλει τοσοῦτον ὅσον περ ἀρετῆς καὶ φρονήσεως καὶ τοῦ πράττειν κατὰ ταύτας. Wise action here reflects the phrase περ ... φρονήσεως.
[38] *Politics*, 1325b17–22. [39] *Politics*, 1325a31–34.
[40] J. Owens, "Value and Practical Knowledge in Aristotle," *Essays in Ancient Greek Philosophy IV: Aristotle's Ethics*, ed. J. Anton and A. Preuss (Albany: SUNY Press, 1991), pp. 148–149. Owens is commenting upon NE 1139a29–31.

indicates that it chooses rightly about what is good for all human beings in their pursuit of happiness: "*Phronesis* is that virtue of the understanding which enables wise choices concerning good and evil already mentioned in relation to happiness."[41] The good and evil already mentioned are mostly the moral virtues, but Aristotle also includes *sophia,* theoretical wisdom, among the virtues subject to the choices of *phronesis* (*Rhetoric,* 1366b2). He clearly indicates here that the pursuit of theoretical knowledge falls under the guidance of practical wisdom.

In the discussions on virtue Aristotle acknowledges that a vague awareness of general principles is insufficient to bring about good habits. There must also be a correct interpretation, and an appropriate application, of rules. To say, however, that one must act as right rule (ὀρθὸς λόγος = *orthos logos*) dictates is no more helpful than to tell a sick person to do whatever medical science advises. The philosopher's task is to discover both the right rule and the standard (ὅρος) of action by which right rule actualizes the states of the soul (NE 1138b29–34). In order to analyze the proper states of the human being that contribute to moral goodness, Aristotle provides a refinement in his earlier division of the soul. Rationality may be considered as that power by which one contemplates objects whose causes are immutable and invariable, but it may also be viewed as the ability to analyze mutable objects. The former capacity he names the scientific facility (ἐπιστημονικόν), while the latter he specifies as the calculative or deliberative capability (λογιστικόν: NE 1139a12–14).

Although Aristotle speaks of parts (μέρη) of the soul he views the soul primarily as the unifying actuality of the human composite. While the virtues of the rational soul are divided into moral and intellectual ones, Aristotle sees them integrated within the life of goodness in order for one to attain happiness. Aristotle repeats often that the practically wise develop all virtues: "Thus it is clear that it is impossible to be practically wise without being good."[42] The term 'good' refers here to moral excellence, and so this passage demonstrates Aristotle's conviction of the close connection between the virtues of practical wisdom and goodness in general. More explicit is his statement that it is not possible simply to be good without practical wisdom. For Aristotle, one who is good without qualification and thereby happy cannot lack any virtue. He who has practical wisdom will also have all other virtues as well:

---

[41] *Rhetoric,* 1366b20–22: φρόνησις δ' ἐστὶν ἀρετὴ διανοίας καθ' ἣν εὖ βουλεύεσθαι δύνανται περὶ ἀγαθῶν καὶ κακῶν τῶν εἰρημένων εἰς εὐδαιμονίαν.

[42] NE 1144a36: ὥστε φανερὸν ὅτι ἀδύνατον φρόνιμον εἶναι μὴ ὄντα ἀγαθόν.

This is possible in respect of the natural virtues, but not in respect of those in respect of which a man is called without qualification good; *for with the presence of the one quality, practical wisdom, will be given all the virtues.* And it is plain that, even if it were of no practical value, we should have needed it because it is the virtue of the part of us in question; plain too that the choice will not be right without practical wisdom any more than without virtue . . .[43]

Some modern commentators on Aristotle's ethics read this passage as reference only to the person who possesses only moral virtue,[44] but Aristotle does not limit the virtues of the *phronimos* to rational ones alone. The close identification here of *phronesis* with goodness (ἀγαθόν) indicates that Aristotle intends to include the intellectual virtues among those exercised by the person of practical wisdom.

c The importance of practical wisdom

The virtue of *phronesis* serves as a single unifying factor in Aristotle's doctrine of human goodness. Moral decisions arise not from an immediate voluntary act, but rather after a deductive reasoning process. *Phronesis*, a virtue that allows for correct deliberation about the best manner to attain happiness, directs the process of moral syllogistic reasoning toward a successful exercise of actions needed for *eudaimonia*:

"Now it is thought to the mark of a man of practical wisdom to be able to deliberate well about what is good and expedient for himself, not in some particular respect . . . but about what sorts of things conduce to living well in general."[45] The inclusion of the phrase, to live well (τὸ εὖ ζῆν) is a clear reference to the close connection between *eudaimonia* and *phronesis*, since Aristotle in book I of the NE makes 'living well' an integral part of the definition of happiness (NE 1098b20–21). Here in book VI Aristotle

---

[43] NE 1144b35–1145a2: ἔσται· τοῦτο γὰρ κατὰ μὲν τὰς φυσικὰς ἀρετὰς ἐνδέχεται, καθ' ἃς δὲ ἁπλῶς λέγεται ἀγαθός, οὐκ ἐνδέχεται· ἅμα γὰρ τῇ φρονήσει μιᾷ ὑπαρχούσῃ πᾶσαι ὑπάρξουσιν. In *Rhetoric* II, 12 Aristotle describes the young who have many laudable characteristics but lack the practical wisdom to make the best moral decisions. See also R. Sorabji, "Aristotle on the Role of Intellect in Virtue," *Aristotle's Ethics*, ed. A. O. Rorty (Berkeley: University of California Press, 1980), p. 214: "Aristotle agrees that virtue may exist without practical wisdom, for it speaks as if people who are still young may have virtue even though they have been trained by convention." While one may have single virtues, such as courage, no one can be completely virtuous without practical wisdom.
[44] See the translations of Rackham, Dirlemeier (Es ist also offenkundig unmöglich ethische Einsicht zu haben, wenn man nicht ein ethisch hochstehender Mensch ist) and O. Gigon, *Die Nikomachische Ethik, eingeleitet und übertragen von Olof Gigon* (Zurich: Akademie Verlag, 1951): Also ist klar, dass man nicht klug sein kann, wenn man nicht tugendhaft ist.
[45] NE 1140a25–28.

emphasizes his conviction that the *phronimos* must be able to deliberate well about all matters pertaining to the good life. Since contemplation is a necessary feature of living well, it must also fall under the deliberative process of practical wisdom.

The capacity of *phronesis* for governing actions that lead to happiness makes the discussion concerning its nature an extremely important element in Aristotle's moral philosophy. Aristotle defines *phronesis* not by his usual philosophical method of analyzing moral virtues as a mean between extremes, but rather by observing those admirable people within his society who are thought to possess wisdom: "Regarding practical wisdom we shall get at the truth by considering those who are the persons we credit with it."[46] The rather imprecise description of an essential intellectual virtue permits Aristotle to characterize the ethical person as one who allows for variety and exceptions within moral practice.[47] The morally, or practically, wise person makes a decision based on conclusions derived from principles that have arisen from the context of his specific situation and circumstances. The indispensable ability to decide which course of action best contributes to individual flourishing is always intertwined with past practices and current demands. G. Verbeke characterizes the moral act in its context as follows:

The moral act is a truly personal event, for it is the result of deliberation, which is situated in the present, but which also takes account of the past and future. If the human horizon were limited to the present instant, one could not be capable of deliberating: in fact, the temporal perspective embraces life in its entirety.[48]

The *phronimos* finds his inspiration not only in reasoned arguments, but also through recognition of the best practices of the best citizens within the state. Aristotle does not limit his understanding of the good to purely philosophical determinations, but incorporates what is commonly said and done into his final resolution of the topic (NE 1098b8–12). The

[46] NE 1140a24–25: περὶ δὲ φρονήσεως οὕτως ἂν λάβοιμεν, θεωρήσαντες τίνας λέγομεν τοὺς φρονίμους.
[47] M. F. Burnyeat, "Aristotle on Learning to Be Good," *Aristotle's Ethics* (n. 39), p. 80: ". . . a mature morality must in large part continue to be what it originally was, a matter of responses deriving from sources other than reflective reason."
[48] G. Verbeke, "L'éducation morale et les arts chez Aristote et Thomas d'Aquin," *Miscellanea Mediaevalia, 22, Scientia und ars in Hoch-und Spätmittelalter*, ed. I. Craemer-Ruegenberg and A. Speer (Berlin: De Gruyter, 1994), p. 462. Thomas and his medieval contemporaries recognized the temporal continuity of the deliberative process, but they were not satisfied with situating the principles of action in the limited civic tradition. They sought to anchor the first principles of morality in the eternal laws that transcend the borders of human society, as is discussed in Chapters 2–7.

morally wise opinion may be just as an appropriate starting point for acting as general rules or deduced conclusions.

In his specific analysis of the virtue of *phronesis*, Aristotle describes it as the ability to deliberate correctly both about the best manner to attain goodness and also the best process of constructing moral syllogisms that lead to good decisions (NE 1104a24–27). Rather than analyze such premises and conclusions, Aristotle concentrates his attention upon those who best incorporate the characteristics of practical wisdom. He chooses as the primary example of the virtue not a philosopher, but rather a politician, Pericles, because he had the ability to recognize what was good (ἀγαθόν) for himself and others, and how to attain it.[49] Because he could recognize goodness and could secure it for himself, Pericles must also be described as *eudaimon*. The representatives of the theoretical life of speculative philosophy are the ancient thinkers, Thales and Anaxagoras. Aristotle dismisses them from the ranks of the *phronimoi* because they did not employ the means necessary to achieve their own goodness despite their wisdom. They, as wise men (*sophoi*), possessed important, impressive and admirable knowledge, but their theoretical understanding brought no practical rewards. In short, they were absorbed in the contemplation of eternal truth, but were neither *phronimoi* nor *eudaimones*, since they did not engage in actions that comprise human goodness.[50]

In his treatment of *phronesis*, Aristotle implies that the life of contemplation alone cannot produce happiness. When he claims that the wise men, Thales and Anaxagoras, did not attain human goodness, Aristotle makes clear his view that contemplative wisdom without practical judgment produces figures of derision, who may know the position of the stars, but cannot avoid falling in a well. Theoretical science cannot account for the variety of human experiences that contribute to the actualization of the human being. *Phronesis*, however, is directly concerned with the multifaceted decisions that lead to human fulfillment:

---

[49] See A. MacIntyre, *Whose Justice? Which Rationality?* (Notre Dame: University of Notre Dame Press, 1988), p. 99: "Aristotle, like most Greeks, recognized the existence of exceptional persons ... [who] were able to play the role of a lawgiver, providing their *polis* with a new constitution and by so doing to establish or reestablish possibilities of virtue in a *polis* that (which is in text cited) it had previously lacked. Such had been Solon at Athens and Lycurgus at Sparta. And Socrates may be regarded analogously as the founder in some sense of a philosophical community whose structure Plato institutionalized at the Academy." While MacIntyre may include Socrates among the wise men, Aristotle certainly prefers to number Pericles among them.

[50] NE 1141b3–8. For a different evaluation of the life of Thales and his practical knowledge, see *Politics*, 1259a6–23.

For philosophic wisdom (*sophia*) will consider none of those things that will make a person happy (for it is not concerned with any coming into being), and though practical wisdom does do this, for what purpose do we need it? Practical wisdom is the quality of mind concerned with things just and noble and good for man ... (NE 1143b19–25)

The phrase "for it is not concerned with any coming to being," is taken as a parenthetical insertion by modern translators such as Ross and Rackham, but it serves an important function in Aristotle's description of knowledge and its relation to human happiness. *Eudaimonia,* as the supreme good, is a type of genesis, since it occurs as the transformation of psychic potentialities into actual states. Theoretical knowledge is itself the product of generation, since one learns the immutable principles of metaphysical and mathematical sciences. But theory cannot account completely for all actions needed to make a human being happy. Theoretical knowledge, once learned, no longer is a coming to be, since the truly wise person does not gain further knowledge but takes pleasure in knowing what has already been learned. The process of generation of which Aristotle speaks falls under the regulatory power of *phronesis* that considers "everything that makes a person happy."[51]

Throughout the NE Aristotle emphasizes the importance of contemplative activity for the fullest realization of happiness, but implies that it alone cannot produce moral goodness. Only the *phronimos* can recognize the proper goals of life and the means to attain them, especially when conflict arises in the various spheres of human endeavor.[52] When different demands of human pursuits conflict, the *phronimos* determines which worthwhile actions have priority. Happiness may be the overriding goal of life, but *phronesis* unifies all moral decisions into a coherent whole. It determines when and why one should engage in contemplative, civic or even recreational pursuits. Although Aristotle claims that the life of moral virtue by itself can only constitute a secondary type of happiness, the intellectual virtue of *phronesis* arranges every decision and practice into a life of excellence. No one, says Aristotle, can be practically wise without being good (NE 1144a36–37). When Aristotle says that with *phronesis* all virtues are present, he does not limit them to the moral habits. All virtues

---

[51] NE 1143b19–20: θεωρήσει ἐξ ὧν ἔσται εὐδαίμων ἄνθρωπος.

[52] A. O. Rorty, "Virtues and Their Vicissitudes," *Midwest Studies in Philosophy,* 13 (*Ethical Theory: Character and Virtue*), ed. P. French *et al.* (Notre Dame: University of Notre Dame Press, 1988), p. 140: "It was because he thought that the proper exercise of presumptively virtuous traits requires both cognitive and character dispositions – well formed discriminating habits directed to good ends appropriately understood – that Aristotle located the master virtue in *phronesis* ... But *phronesis* is an umbrella term for a wide range of independent traits that enable a person to set, and to actualize, the goods ..."

are present within the *phronimos*, because the person with practical wisdom leads a life that will make him *eudaimon*.[53]

The conceptual unity of the NE is found not in the notion of *eudaimonia*, but rather in the specifically human virtue of *phronesis*. Despite the admonition against placing practical wisdom on a higher plane than philosophical knowledge, *phronesis* ultimately reigns over all human choices. In itself, theoretical wisdom is an activity superior to the life of practice, but human beings are not purely intellectual. If they were, then there would be no need for the practical judgments that regulate life and its conflicting demands. N. White comments upon the tension in Aristotle's ethics as follows:

Aristotle is unquestionably aware of competition among the good activities which he takes happiness to involve ... the evidence seems to me to indicate that in his opinion, conflict among them is inevitable and we have to respond to it not by showing that they are really completely consistent with each other but by finding grounds for choosing some of them, at least to some extent, over others, Happiness may include various goods, but that does not mean they are fully in harmony with each other.[54]

The supreme goal of human existence should never be restricted to a narrow pursuit of theory, but, as Gadamer points out, must include both practical and theoretical accomplishments. In the union of theory and practice *phronesis* emerges as the ideal of the most acute insight, a true virtue. It is the highest form of the unity of human practice.[55]

Aristotle's praise of *phronesis* and his advice to regard the actions of the practically wise in order to understand better the good life provide little

[53] R. Sorabji, "Aristotle on the Role of Intellect in Virtue," p. 206: "Whatever other roles practical wisdom may or may not play, I suggest that one role is this. It enables a man in light of his conception of the good life in general to perceive what ... virtue and *kalon* require of him, in the particular case, and instructs him to act accordingly."
[54] N. White, "Conflicting Parts of Happiness in Aristotle's Ethics," *Ethics*, 105 (1995), p. 269.
[55] Gadamer, *op. cit.*, p. 66. Gauthier and Jolif, however, do not view *praxis* and *theoria* as complementary aspects of a happy life. They claim ad 1138b24 that right rule is that which *phronesis* formulates, but the supreme norm to which this right rule refers is contemplation. Later ad 114031–32 they argue that the end, contemplation of God, includes without doubt a transcendent element. The recognition of this element and of its transcendence pertains to *sophia*. *Phronesis* is only indirectly concerned and only with respect to its subordination to *sophia*. *Phronesis* refers actions to the norm of contemplation. A similar interpretation is found in B. Souchard, "La singulière primauté aristotélicienne de la raison théorique sur la raison pratique," *Vers la contemplation: Études sur la syndérèse et les modalités de la contemplation de l'antiquité à la renaissance*, ed. C. Trottmann (Paris: Honoré Champion, 2007), pp. 27–45. Such an interpretation was common in the medieval commentators of the NE, foremost among them is Albertus Magnus. See A. Celano, "The 'Finis Hominis' in the Thirteenth-Century Commentaries on the *Nicomachean Ethics*," *Archives d'histoire doctrinale et littéraire du moyen âge*, 53 (1986), pp. 23–53.

insight into the exact nature of the virtue. His analysis of practical wisdom is
sometimes obscured by its function as a moral virtue and its designation as an
intellectual one. Its location at the junction of the soul's moral and intellectual
capacities led some medieval commentators to classify it as both a moral and
intellectual virtue. Aristotle himself is clear on this question, since he always
regards *phronesis* as an intellectual process despite its governance of moral
acts. Aristotle found it difficult to provide an exact definition of practical
wisdom despite its central role in his moral theory. He realizes that the
identification of wise persons is an appropriate beginning from which one
can proceed to analyze the characteristics of the virtue. In observation we can
come to understand that the *phronimoi* possess qualities that distinguish
them from ordinary citizens (NE 1140a24–25). Aristotle builds a definition in
the manner similar to that of a doctor who regards patients individually in
order to come to a more general understanding of health and healing.

d   The process of practically wise decisions

Phronesis begins with the ability to recognize wisdom in others, which is
essential to the development of moral character. Because it permits flexibility
in action, practical wisdom cannot be defined by prescribing universal rules
that would govern particular and variable circumstances. In resolving conflicting moral demands like those faced by pacifists confronted by cruel and
evil invaders, Aristotle would not advocate moral despair or ethical relativ-
ism. He would argue that the *phronimos* would choose correctly, whatever
course of action is taken, since his character has been formed by a series of
past decisions, generated initially by imitation, reinforced by repetition and
finally informed by reflective reason. Aristotle would argue further that not
all *phronimoi* choose the same option because the wise decision would
account for a variety of abilities and circumstances. A moral choice reflects
the content of an individual life, whose needs are balanced by the demands of
others and civic duty. All members of a society must recognize their own
needs in light of a moral tradition that provides a measure for judging each
individual choice. The morally wise person aligns individual choices with
what is needed to bring about what is good for the agent and others. The
ultimate model for ethical choice is a human one, that is the *phronimos* who
can recognize the benefits of a range of actions and makes choices that best
serve oneself and the community (NE 1179a9–17).[56]

---

[56] J. Stewart, ad 1144b26: "The κύριος ἀγαθός performs his virtuous acts *proprie motu*,
according to a standard which he has assimilated – with which he identifies himself." See

The complex nature of practical wisdom has provoked questions from commentators for many years, as W.F.R. Hardie notes: "[commentators] try to explain away the fact that Aristotle describes *phronesis* both as discerning means to an end determined by moral virtue (1145a5–6) and as involving a true understanding of the end (1142b31–33)."[57] Hardie is correct in his assessment and the means/ends relation is a central aspect of Aristotle's virtue of practical wisdom. In the opening line of book VI of the NE, Aristotle repeats his general definition of virtue. A good person must avoid excess and defect, and should choose the mean that is determined as right rule dictates (ὡς ὁ λόγος ὁ ὀρθὸς λέγει: NE 1138b20–21). The mean is not rigidly determined, but may fluctuate within certain limits recognized by right rule or reason. Joachim recognizes the relation between the mean and the practical wisdom in the following passage:

"Every moral virtue is a μεσότης ὡρισμένη λόγῳ (a mean determined by a rule). But what is the λόγος and how is it determined?: In Book II Aristotle had simply said: 'It is the λόγος employed by the φρόνιμος ... to determine the feeling embodied in his own action.' – i.e. it is the right λόγος, the λόγος used by the ideally good man."[58]

While one may object to the term 'feeling' reflected in action, one recognizes the accuracy in Joachim's description of how right rule is determined by the good person.

Not only is the recognition of the proper rule difficult, but its application in particular circumstances also is complicated, as M. Nussbaum observes:

The Aristotelian virtues involve a delicate balancing between general rules and the keen awareness of particulars, in which process, as Aristotle stresses, the perception of the particular takes priority. It takes priority in the sense that a good rule is a summary of wise particular choices and not a court of last resort. Like rules in medicine and in navigation, ethical rules should be held open to modification in light of new circumstances ...[59]

---

also T. Irwin, "Prudence and Morality in Greek Ethics," *Ethics* 105 (1995), p. 295: "To decide whether some good or other is really part of my happiness, I must form some conception of what is good for me, and I must decide whether that good really satisfies my conception of what is good for me. Any putative part of my happiness has to be shown to meet appropriate conditions for prudential value."

[57] W. F. R. Hardie, *Aristotle's Ethical Theory* (Oxford: Clarendon Press, 1968), p. 213.

[58] Joachim, *op. cit.*, p. 163, ad 1138b18–25.

[59] M. Nussbaum, "The Discernment of Perception: An Aristotelian Conception of Private and Public Rationality," *Proceedings of the Boston Area Colloquium of Ancient Philosophy*, 1 (1985), p. 154.

Nussbaum's analysis underscores the difficulty in identifying moral norms in the ethics of Aristotle. Particular choices generate the general rule, which in turn governs individual choices. General rules may themselves be subject to modification in changing circumstances. If a rule must be adjusted, one may ask with justification whether such a rule may be considered a true ethical principle.

Practical wisdom arises from a combination of intuition and deliberation. For Aristotle proper deliberation produces a type of truth in accordance with right desire (NE 1139b29–32). He regards the deliberative process of choice leading to correct action in a manner similar to the way in which a theoretician grasps truth. The process of deduction is similar, but the methods of recognizing principles differ. In describing the process, Aristotle reminds the reader that deliberation is limited to certain areas of human endeavor. No one deliberates about immutable events or actions that are impossible to perform. Deliberation considers only what a person may do to bring about a desired end (NE 1140a32–36; 1141b8–12). Deliberation does not consider the ends of action but only the means to attain them (NE 1112b12–20). We wish for a certain end and deliberate how best to satisfy our desire (NE 1113b3–4). One might object that human beings often deliberate about their goals and ends, for example when they ask themselves whether they should study at a university, or enter military service, or whether they should play tennis or paint the living room. But Aristotle views such questions subsumed under the more general goal of those actions which lead to happiness. Within a specific area of acting, the end is immediately grasped without deliberative reflection. A doctor never asks whether the patient should be healed, but rather what medicine or procedures best lead to the recovery of health. A general does not debate the merits of victory, but rather how best to employ troops and weapons in order to attain it. Every athlete accepts the idea that the goal of the contest is winning. Athletes may deliberate about what methods are most conducive to victory, but none would claim that losing should be considered as an end of the sport. If one were to argue that one plays merely for the enjoyment of the game, then such a person would be acting in a manner that differs from that required for athletic competition. As a human being, one might question the wisdom of winning at any cost, but no true competitor questions the desire for victory.

The practically wise person needs to know not only the universal principles of action, but also their application in particular circumstances. Unlike a theoretician, whose knowledge consists securely in eternal universal truths, the practitioner must be able to apply his knowledge to individual needs and goals. While deliberation is an element essential to practical wisdom, it is not identical to it. Deliberation concerns only the means to an end, but *phronesis* must align individual actions with the dictates of moral principles. Aristotle draws a parallel to theoretical wisdom in his analysis of practical wisdom but emphasizes different aspects of the process. Although theoretical and practical reasoning comprehend both universal principles and particular relevant instances, the theoretician concentrates primarily upon noetic principles, while the practitioner considers most of all the ultimate particular, which is not known through theory, but by perception (NE 1142a24–28). J. Stewart explains the process of practical reasoning as similar to that of a geometer:

but the ἔσχατα of φρόνησις are not like the ἴδια αἰσθητά (perceived forms) perceived by the special senses ... but they are like the perceptions of the geometer ... As the geometer solves his problem by processing shapes in the data of the eye (or touch), and recognizing this constitution ... so the φρόνιμος solves the problem of τὸ εὖ ζῆν by apprehending τὰ ἐν ταῖς πράξεσι (those things in practice) not as this pleasant or painful to sense here and now, but as things which are good or bad – i.e. fitted, or not fitted, to have a permanent place in the general plan of life.[60]

For Aristotle intuition (*nous*) is the capacity within the soul that apprehends not only the particular actions to be performed but also the universal rule:

And *nous* is concerned with the ultimate in both directions; for both the first and last term are objects of intuition and not of argument, and the intuition which is presupposed by demonstrations comprehends the unchangeable and first terms, while intuition involved in practical reasoning grasps the last and variable facts ... For the variable facts are the starting points for the apprehension of the end, since the universals are reached from the particulars; of these therefore we must have perception and this perception is intuition. (NE 1143a32–b6)

In speculative knowledge, one exercises *nous* insofar as one apprehends intuitively or immediately general truths, those indemonstrable principles that are the first premises of demonstration.[61] There is a decisive moment when individual sense experiences coalesce into a general understanding of similar objects, as when a young child after repeated attempts to eat chalk understands it to be a writing instrument. From that moment on the child recognizes the object to belong to a particular category, and comprehends it, whether it is actually present or not. At this moment language informed by *nous* signals the understanding of the essential nature of the object.

[60] Stewart, *op. cit.*, ad 1142a8.   [61] See Joachim, *op. cit.*, p. 213, ad 1143a35–b6.

Aristotle claims that in practical reasoning when one apprehends the relevance of a particular action to attain a good end, one is said to employ *nous* and to perceive rightly. Aristotle says that these perceptions are the reason why some believe that good persons naturally have good judgment, understanding and intuition, even though no one is thought to have theoretical wisdom naturally (NE 1143b6–9).

When Aristotle states that individual perception may be an instance of intuition, since it may be a mere sense impression, he means that in practical reasoning individual actions are perceived and performed in relation to a desired end. J. Stewart explains the process as follows:

There is no inconsistency in saying at once that νοῦς gives ἀρχαὶ and that ἐπαγωγή gives ἀρχαὶ, because nous, as distinguished from αἴσθησις, is the faculty which man, as rational being, possesses of taking notice of that which is common in a number of particulars presented.[62]

One of Aristotle's most famous examples to illustrate the process of practical reasoning begins with the universal statement that dry food is good for all human beings. *Nous* must recognize not only the truth of such a general assertion but also that one is a human being and that this particular food can be classified as dry (NE 1147a4–8). Another example of such reasoning asserts that light meat is healthy. This principle results only from a number of past experiences that lead to such a general formulation. *Nous* organizes the common feature of healthy meat and recognizes whether a particular dish contains light meat. If a child were to mimic his elders and claim that light meat is healthy, he may not be able to recognize which particular meats are light. In this case knowledge of the general rule does not bring practical wisdom.

Aristotle's theory is more complicated than his examples indicate. Even in theoretical knowledge the starting point for human knowledge begins in the perception of individual objects. After sufficient reflection the essential nature of common objects is discovered and *nous* comprehends the true principles governing such objects. Once the principle is apprehended then the process of scientific deduction may proceed with clarity and certainty. In practical sciences the process differs in the formulation of the universal.

[62] Stewart, ad 1147a7. Stewart has some difficulty in identifying the noetic process in practical reasoning. He argues that practical νοῦς cannot command with desire (ἐπιθυμία) ad 1139a17; that νοῦς is equivalent to διάνοια at 1139a33. He argues that νοῦς is the authoritative principle or the ἀρχή, and that διάνοια merely indicates what particular things are pursued or shunned: "Here to distinguish we may say νοῦς grasps the end immediately and διάνοια reviews the means." But Aristotle makes no such distinction.

A comprehension of both universal and particular moral elements are needed to produce practical wisdom:

Nous therefore is both beginning and end; for demonstrations are from these and about these. Therefore we ought to heed the undemonstrated sayings and opinions of experienced and older people or of the practically wise not less than to demonstration; for experience has given them the ability to judge correctly. (1143b9–13)

The formulation of general principles of conduct and their relevance for particular actions may be integral features of *phronesis*, but a vexing problem remains concerning the moral rectitude of the first premises. If the starting points of actions are wrong, then the subsequent actions must also necessarily be wrong. Aristotle does not seem to provide any secure foundation for the discovery of principles of action. He is notoriously vague on the topic, and Hardie has pointed out such a lack remains an important issue in Aristotle's conception of *phronesis*. Another modern commentator attempts to resolve the dilemma of the two-fold function of the virtue of practical wisdom by distinguishing the intuitive function that concerns the ends of actions from the discursive function that deliberates concerning the means to the end.[63] Such a division, unstated in Aristotle's work, represents an attempt to comprehend the source of moral principles and their relation to action. Aristotle himself proposes a number of mental faculties that provide the starting points of practical reasoning. At various places interpreters of Aristotle's ethics have made desire (ὄρεξις),[64] character (ἦθος),[65] desire (ἐπιθυμία),[66] intuition (νοῦς)[67] and habituation (ἐθισμός) the source of moral principles.[68] Gauthier and Jolif claim that knowledge of principles may be attributed indifferently to induction achieved by intuition, or by intuition prepared by induction.[69]

Aristotle sometimes indicates that virtue permits us to recognize and attain the ends,[70] but most often he employs the measure of right rule to ensure the goodness of the end. These various elements that try to explain

---

[63] P. Schollmeier, "Aristotle on Practical Wisdom," *Zeitschrift für philosophische Forschung*, 43 (1989), p. 124.

[64] Burnet, ad 1141b15, Stewart, ad 1139a24 and 1139a31.

[65] J. Roberts, "Aristotle on Responsibility for Action and Character," *Ancient Philosophy*, 9 (1989), p. 35.

[66] Joachim, p. 218, Stewart, ad 1139a17.   [67] Stewart, ad 1143a35.

[68] Stewart, ad 1143b5.

[69] Gauthier and Jolif, ad 1141a7–8. See ad 1143a10 where they argue that the imperative of practical wisdom requires something more, i.e. the intervention of desire rectified by moral virtues.

[70] NE 1106a22–24, 1139a 17; EE 1219a26–28; *Rhetoric* 1366a36–38.

the genesis of moral principles have contributed to the dissatisfaction with, or hostility toward, Aristotle's account of moral action.[71] Whatever presents the end to the moral agent, the goal must always be in accordance with right rule (*orthos logos*). The norm of right rule ensures the rectitude of the moral principles, but such a rule has no foundation independent of the practice of individual human beings.[72] Desire is correct when it seeks what reason (*logos*) affirms to be good, that is when desire is in harmony with reason.[73] The standard of right rule is not an external measure but rather an internal disposition toward action that the good person recognizes within himself.[74] Joachim summarizes the Aristotelian notion of right as follows:

Now the rightness of the λόγος, which the φρόνιμος possesses . . . depends in the end upon the ultimate standard of value in human life, which the φρόνιμος truly conceives . . . because he knows the true mark to aim at . . . that the λόγοι which he formulates to limit or determine the various μεσότητες (means) . . . are ὀρθοί (sound, correct).[75]

The ultimate standard of ethical value is determined by the good person who 'knows' the true end of action. Right rule is that which *phronesis* determines and *phronesis* itself is regulated by right rule.

Aristotle blithely assumes that the wise persons will recognize the truth of ethical principles if they have been educated properly in a good society. One could argue that Aristotle is content with a theory that accepts the idea that any society that is not utterly corrupt would adopt just moral actions and ideals, and abandon those which are unjust.[76] One may also question whether Aristotle's confidence in the human ability to identify the practically wise is misplaced. Certainly one can conceive of two persons, both excellent in two different areas, who advocate conflicting courses of action.

---

[71] J. Roberts, art. cit., p. 28.
[72] NE 1144b27. D. DeMoss, "Acquiring Ethical Ends," *Ancient Philosophy*, 10 (1999), p. 63: ". . . the operation of practical wisdom must assume the end for which it determines the appropriate means. This passage (1142b31–33) does not explain how the ethical end is acquired, it says only that the person of practical wisdom must have a true belief about what is the end."
[73] NE 1139a 24 and J. Stewart, ad loc. [74] NE 1144b26–28.
[75] Joachim, p. 164, ad 1138b18–25. See Stewart, ad 1139a24: "ὄρεξις is ὀρθή when it seeks (δίωξις) what λόγος or διάνοια affirms to be good . . . when to use the expression of EN I, 13, it is ὁμοφωνεῖ τῷ λόγῳ.[in harmony with reason] . . . The motive power is used rightly only when it is used to further the welfare of the whole life which reason comprehends (see *De an.* III, 10, 433b5) . . . By λόγος in EN VI, 2 we are to understand the συλλογισμός or chain of deliberative reasoning leading up to the act of προαίρεσις."
[76] For a summary of modern criticisms of Aristotle's depiction of moral development, see J. Roberts, art. cit., p. 35, n. 15.

A wealthy businessman may encourage behavior that would certainly differ from the choices of Mother Teresa. Both might argue for principles and actions that are in accordance with right reason. How then is one to decide which person should be considered the model for behavior? Aristotle does address the question, at least indirectly, when he identifies the primary characteristic of the practically wise to be the ability to deliberate well and correctly with regard to what leads to the end for which *phronesis* is the true apprehension.[77] Two conditions ensure that the person seeking guidance is not left without direction. *Phronesis* leads to a successful conclusion of any pursuit since it recognizes and selects the appropriate actions that bring about a desired end. The second factor lies in Aristotle's claim that *phronesis* must always include a true apprehension (ἀληθὴς ὑπόληψίς) of the end. Aristotle emphasizes here the ability of the *phronimos* to comprehend both the end and the means to it, but he adds the qualification, 'true'. The wise person comes to know a true end not merely by observing others, but also by being aware of how the action affects his own happiness. Aristotle attributes to human beings an "ability to internalize from a scattered range of particular cases a general evaluative attitude, which is not reducible to rules or precepts."[78] Aristotle's reluctance to introduce objective, independently grounded rules into ethical speculation does not lead him to conclude that there can be no universal goal or end for human beings. Any medical practitioner with experience understands health to be the true end of the profession without formulating universal principles from independent sources.[79]

e Happiness and practical wisdom

Aristotle argues in a general way that every action must be directed toward the achievement of happiness, and goodness is measured by its contribution

[77] NE 1142b29.   [78] M. F. Burnyeat, art. cit., p. 72.
[79] Joachim, pp. 75–76 ad 1104a7–8: "However complex and detailed a set of rules or moral principles may be, they are not in themselves adequate to guide and determine conduct ... the agent has to apply the rules which he knows, and the application is a matter of selection involving moral insight. It cannot be determined by the rules themselves ... Aristotle is not saying that action or medical treatment are decided at haphazard, on no principle ... When he insists, for example, that the decision must ultimately rest upon perception (1109b20–3), the perception in question is the trained insight of the man of practical wisdom, the φρόνιμος – the perception informed by an intelligent understanding of life. In the end the doctor has to *see* what the patient's illness is – no rules can do more than limit the field within which his medical perception will have to decide: but it is a medical perception or intuition – one formed and trained by systematic study."

to this moral goal. When choices conflict, however, how can a moral agent determine which course of action best contributes to the goal of happiness? One might ask whether one should always prefer intellectual pursuits over civic and familial duties. Aristotle certainly never makes such a claim and seems content with the assumption that the good person would choose correctly. Aristotle takes up this question in the *Politics* and says that the best life either for the individual or for the state is that life joined with virtue,[80] as was noted above. Aristotle is aware of the possibility of doubt concerning the primacy of the contemplative life over one of action. He says that the advocates of either life are both partially right and partially wrong. Some say the political life is undesirable while others say it is the best life, because the one who does nothing cannot do well. Since doing well and happiness are the same thing, they imply that a life without political involvement cannot be happy.[81] Aristotle seems finally to have made his position on happiness clear: that a life without the civic commitment of the just and practically wise cannot truly be happy. But he quickly retreats from such a clear view and says:

> But if these things are well said, and if happiness is to be defined as doing well, the active life is the best life both for the whole state collectively and for each man individually. But the active life is not necessarily active in relation to other men, as some think, nor are only the processes of thought active that are pursued for the sake of the objects that result from action, but far more those speculations and thoughts that have an end in themselves . . . for the end is to do well, and therefore is a certain form of action. (Politics 1325b14–22)

Again Aristotle leaves his reader wondering whether he considers happiness to consist in practical activity or theoretical contemplation.

When the right course of action is not immediately apparent, as in the dilemma of choosing the active or contemplative life, Aristotle would advise that one must decide as would the *phronimos*. Such a method of attaining moral rectitude may appear frustrating and unsatisfactory, but Aristotle describes virtue consistently throughout his works. He does not define virtue merely by isolating certain universal conditions and standards. To be just or brave one must do more than perform just or courageous action; one must also act in the way a just or brave person does.[82] Aristotle knows that a person could display the outward characteristics of courage because of fear of ridicule or because of manic hatred for an enemy, and not be truly brave. One could mimic the decisions of a just person in order to receive civic

---

[80] *Politics*, 1232b40–1324a2.   [81] *Politics*, 1325a24–30.   [82] NE 1105b5–12.

honors or acclaim, but not act from a true sense of what is owed to another. Such people manifest the same characteristics as the truly virtuous, but have not really developed an authentic virtuous habit.

The beginning of virtue lies in the human ability to imitate the practices of others. Aristotle makes clear his admiration for human mimetic abilities as a source of learning:

Imitation is natural to man from childhood, one of his advantages over lower animals being this, that he is the most imitative creature in the world, and learns first by imitation. And it is natural to delight in works of imitation.[83]

Two elements are to be noted in this passage: imitation is the origin of learning and that human being delight in imitation. Such imitative abilities are essential for the development of ethical virtues. No one naturally can be just or courageous without first observing such actions in others. The medieval commentators on Aristotle used the acquisition of proper grammatical speech to illustrate the theory concerning the development of practical knowledge. We begin to learn to talk by imitating patterns of speech and repeating the words of others. Soon the development of an awareness of the terms' significance leads to their proper syntactical functions within sentences. As awareness deepens a knowledge of more complicated rules concerning grammar and syntax develop. True knowledge of grammar and speech results only with the understanding of why certain constructions, such as subjunctives and conditionals, are used in particular sentences and what shades of meaning they convey. For moral knowledge one must know why one acts courageously or temperately if one is to be regarded as morally wise. Gauthier and Jolif explain the process as follows: "*Hexeis* [habits] result from corresponding activities ... the acts which produce virtue should be similar to those which virtue will produce, once acquired."[84] They further describe virtue as a certain manner of acting and one is virtuous because one acts in a virtuous manner. For Gauthier and Jolif the manner that the subject impresses upon his actions differentiates Aristotelian moral theory from that of Socrates.[85] When Aristotle claims that to be virtuous actions must be performed in the manner of virtuous persons, he does not slip completely into a circular argument.[86]

---

[83] *Politics*, 1144b4–9.   [84] Gauthier and Jolif, ad 1103b23–24.
[85] Gauthier and Jolif, ad 1105b8.
[86] Such is the criticism of J. Wallace, "Ethics and the Craft Analogy," *Midwest Studies in Philosophy* (note 54), p. 224: "In Aristotle's ethics, moral virtue is defined by reference to the determinations a practically wise man, a *phronimos*, would make. When the account of practical wisdom, *phronesis*, as (roughly) wanting the things a man

Virtuous persons perform good actions as the virtuous do, but Aristotle assumes that the performance of such actions that begin in imitation lead ultimately to an awareness of the underlying reasons why human beings should act well. Like the few who attain a true mastery of speech and grammar, the truly virtuous know what to do and why to do it. When confronted with conflicting demands from different areas of activity, they choose the appropriate course of action. They ultimately align all their choices with the pursuit of human goodness or happiness.[87]

Aristotle does not offer a progressive hierarchy of human accomplishments leading to *eudaimonia*. He understands life to be filled with possibilities for its achievement. While the solitary enjoyment of contemplative knowledge may in itself be the supreme achievement of the human being, a life devoted primarily to theoretical pursuits may not be suitable to all. Aristotle rarely appeals to any standard other than human practice, but he does indicate in the *Rhetoric* that "human beings have a sufficient natural instinct for what is true and usually arrive at the truth."[88] He does not claim to have discovered a standard independent of action, and the natural ability to recognize truth is most likely the intuitive power of *nous* that understands the general patterns within the conduct of good persons: "We believe good human beings more fully and more readily than others; this

---

possessing the virtues would want knowing how to get such things, is placed beside the account of moral virtue as (roughly) the disposition to choose in certain circumstances a *phronimos* would think one should, it is apparent that the two accounts are circular ... one is no wiser about *how* the *phronimos* properly determines what choice should be made ... Aristotle was aware of this problem (1138b30–32)." Aristotle would of course look to the standard of right reason to overcome the problem of circularity. A. MacIntyre considers the problem of circularity in *Whose Justice? Which Rationality?*, p. 118: "We cannot judge and act rightly unless we aim at what is in fact good; we cannot aim at what is good except on the basis of experience of right judgment and action. But the appearance of paradox and circularity are deceptive. In developing both our conception of the good and the habit of right judgment and action – and neither can be adequately developed without the other – we gradually learn to correct each in light of the other, moving dialectically between them." I am not convinced that Aristotle would term such a process dialectical, since he bases the beginning of moral development in *mimesis*. Still, while a person strives toward practical wisdom, there is a process similar to that which MacIntyre describes.

[87] M. F. Burnyeat, art. cit., p. 84: "He [Aristotle] will encourage us to think about our life as whole, to arrive at a reasoned view of the good for man; but to begin with, until our understanding of 'the because' has had a chance to become second nature with us, this will be superimposed upon well-established habitual patterns of motivation and response, which it will take time and practice to integrate with the wider and more adult perspective that Aristotle will help us to achieve."

[88] *Rhetoric* 1355a15–16.

is true generally whatever the question is, and absolutely true where exact certainty is impossible and opinions are divided."[89] Certainty is impossible in the study of ethics, politics and rhetoric, and the best practitioners provide the foundation for moral action and general rules may be distilled from observation, emulation and intuition:

> Consequently whenever you want to praise anyone, think what you would urge people to do: and when you want to urge the doing of anything, think what you would praise a person having done . . . Since all good things that are highly honored are objects of emulation, moral goodness in its various forms must be such an object . . .[90]

Only once does Aristotle describe a moral foundation that transcends the practices of individuals. When discussing *Antigone*, he asserts that "there really is, as every one to some extent divines, a natural justice . . . binding on all men. It is this that Sophocles' Antigone clearly means when she says that the burial of Polyneices was a just act in spite of the prohibition: she means it was just by nature."[91] We must ask ourselves whether Aristotle is merely explicating the text of Sophocles (not of today or yesterday is it, but lives eternal, none can date its birth: *Antigone* 456,7) and relating this passage to the idea of Empedocles ("Nay but an all embracing law, through the realm of the sky unbroken it stretcheth, and over the earth's immensity"[92]), or is he truly asserting the existence of a universal principle of justice. Aristotle understands Empedocles to assert a universal code of conduct that never changes according to circumstance or person, but he makes no further comment on the text. Aside from this one instance that may merely be Aristotle's interpretation of another's text, Aristotle never appeals to a law higher than that of the human practice of good. For Aristotle's ethics man remains always the measure: "For each state of character has its own idea of the noble and the pleasant, and

---

[89] *Rhetoric* 1356a6–8. See D. Wiggins, "Deliberation and Practical Wisdom," *Aristotle's Ethics*, p. 237: "I entertain the unfriendly suspicion that those who feel they *must* seek more than all this provides want a scientific theory of rationality not so much from a passion for science . . . but because they hope and desire . . . to turn such a theory into a system of rules by which to spare themselves some of the agony of thinking, and all the torments of feeling and understanding that is actually involved in reasoned deliberation."

[90] *Rhetoric* 1368a7–9 and 1388b9–11.

[91] *Rhetoric* 1375b5–10. In book V of the NE (1134b18–25): Aristotle speaks of natural justice but does not indicate any laws that transcend human practice.

[92] Empedocles, 380, in *Die Fragmente der Vorsokratiker*, ed. H. Diels and W. Kranz (Berlin: Weidmannsche Verl., 1960), p. 275.

perhaps the good man differs from others most by seeing the truth in each class of things, being as it were the norm and measure of them."[93] Not any human being is the true measure of the good life, it is the person with practical wisdom who unifies all acts into a life of virtue and wisdom.

---

[93] NE 1113a29–33. See Gauthier and Jolif, ad 1113a33 who refine the adage in noting that the measure is not simply man, it is the virtuous man. Each virtue is in effect a desire (*penchant*) that rectifies the intention and inclines one to the proper object, i.e. the good. The virtuous person who possesses all the virtues is involved in all domains concerning goodness, and this inclination assures the rectitude of moral judgment.

3

The moral theories of William of Auxerre
and Philip the Chancellor

a William of Auxerre on the principles of moral decisions

In the thirteenth century the science of ethics, infused with the recently translated texts of Aristotle and stimulated by the deliberations of canonists, considered moral questions on virtue, law and human purpose in a manner open to solutions that went beyond traditional religious answers. While the authors of the early thirteenth century did not challenge Christian authorities, they were able to see a variety of new approaches to moral problems. William of Auxerre, who was one of the ecclesiastical authorities chosen by Pope Gregory IX in 1231 to examine the works of Aristotle,[1] remained primarily influenced by Scripture and the works of Augustine, but is willing to use the conclusions of Aristotle when they are helpful in moral matters. William's *Summa aurea* contains extensive treatments of theological ideas discussed at Paris in the first half of the thirteenth century. Based primarily on Peter Lombard's *Sentences*, his discussions include topics in moral theology, such as natural law, beatitude and the cardinal virtues. In this work William makes use of the translation of Aristotle's NE that had appeared in the twelfth century.[2] The *Summa's* short section on natural

---

[1] William of Auxerre, *Summa aurea magistri Guillelmi Altissiodorensi* (=SA), ed. J. Ribaillier (Paris: Spicelegium Bonaveturianum, 18, 1980–1987), Introduction, pp. 4–5. For a short summary of the these doctrines of William and Philip the Chancellor, see D. Farrell, *The Ends of Moral Virtues and the First Principles of Practical Reason in Thomas Aquinas* (Rome: Gregorian and Biblical Press, 2012), pp. 37–47.

[2] R.-A. Gauthier, ed., *Ethica Nicomachea, Praefatio in Aristoteles Latinus* (Leiden-Brussels: Brill, Desclée de Brower, 1974), XXVI, fasc. 1, pp. xv–xvi. F. Bossier, "L'élaboration du vocabulaire philosophique chez Burgundio de Pise," *Aux origines du lexique philosophique européen. L'influence de la latinitas. Actes du Colloque international organisé à Rome (Academia Belgica, 23–25 mai 1996)*, ed. J. Hamesse, (Louvain-la-Neuve, 1997), pp. 81–116; F. Bossier, "Les ennuis d'un traducteur. Quatre annotations sur la première traduction

law, which O. Lottin calls the first theological treatment of the question,[3] follows immediately after the treatment of the cardinal virtues and contains William's assertion that "natural law is the origin and principle of all virtues and their motions."[4] Like his contemporaries, William begins with Augustine's basic premise that "the eternal law is prior to every principle of order, the work of ordaining reason."[5] The canonists had also provided a distinction within the idea of natural law that William finds useful: natural law may be understood broadly or strictly. Taken in the first way, natural law teaches all living beings certain practices, such as the union of male and female. In this understanding of natural law there is no consideration of vice or virtue. Taken strictly, natural law denotes how natural reason dictates without any, or without great deliberation, what should be done, such as God is to be loved.[6] In the strict sense of natural law William can find a basis for moral judgments about right and wrong.

Like other later medieval authors who view a passage in book V of the NE as evidence for an Aristotelian doctrine of natural law, William also finds this concept in Aristotle's philosophy. Because he was not familiar with the fifth book of the *Ethics*, William identifies the source for Aristotle's concept of natural law to be *Topics* (119a16–17). William understands the argument that what has a quality naturally must have it to a greater degree than what does not have it naturally, as an indication that what is just according to natural law must be more just than what is merely asserted by positive law. That which is generally just is so because of natural law.[7] William does not make further use of this passage from Aristotle, and bases most of his conclusions on the subject from Christian sources. He credits Prepostinus for identifying different categories within the general concept

latine de l'*Ethique à Nicomaque* par Burgundio de Pise," *Bijdragen. Tijdschrift voor filosofie en theologie*, 59 (1998), pp. 406–427.

[3] O. Lottin, "Le rôle de la raison dans la morale Albertino-Thomiste," *Psychologie et morale aux XIIᵉ et XIIIᵉ siècles* (Louvain, Gembloux: Abbaye du Mont César, Duclot, 1942–1949), III, p. 554.

[4] SA, III, tr. 18, prol. pp. 368–369: ... quoniam autem ius naturale origo et principium est omnium virtutum et motuum ipsarum.

[5] ... selon saint Augustin, la loi éternelle est avant tout principe d'ordre, oeuvre de raison ordinnatrice. O. Lottin, "La loi en general, la definition thomiste et ses antécédentes," *Psychologie et morale*, II, p. 15.

[6] SA, III, tr. 18, prol. p. 369: Sciendum ergo quod ius naturale quandoque large, quandoque stricte dicitur. Large, secundum quod ius naturale dicitur quod natura docuit omnia animalia, ut est coniunctio maris et femine; et secundum hoc ius non est virtus vel vicium ... Stricte sumitur ius naturale secundum quod ius naturale dicitur naturalis ratio sine omni deliberatione aut sine magna dictat esse faciendum, ut Deum esse diligendum et similia.

[7] SA, III, tr. 18, c. 1, p. 370.

of natural law, such as precepts, prohibitions and demonstrations. The only specific precept mentioned is the golden rule, and the primary prohibition expresses this very same rule negatively. The decalog also contains examples of prohibitions that reflect the force of natural law. Demonstrations merely identify external conditions, such as the command to the Apostles to refrain from answering force with force.[8]

In the section on natural law William does not refer explicitly to the idea of *synderesis*, but implies a connection between the two concepts when he asks how natural law may be written in the human heart. William is not the first to make the connection between natural law and the principles of *synderesis*, since a decretist, Simon de Bisiniano, had done so in the twelfth century.[9] In his solution William ignores the connection of natural law to prudence, and merely indicates that the human soul naturally has a vision of "first goodness" (*primam bonitatem*).[10] Later in this *Summa* he connects the precepts of natural law to those of *synderesis*. William understands the admonition in *Isaiah* to liars to return to the heart, in which the law is written, as an implicit reference to *synderesis*. In the heart, he says, is *synderesis* that commands what is to be done and what is to be avoided. This ability is a norm of reason, or the conformity to divine will, which informs the commands of prudence.[11] William refers again to the same passage when he considers the state of sinners' souls. There he argues that these souls are only partially weakened. One part that is *synderesis*, as the superior part of reason, remains healthy since it cannot sin. It can never judge evil to be good and always rejects evil. The lower part of reason may judge good to be evil, but *synderesis* with its infallible understanding remains untouched by error.[12]

Unlike authors later in the thirteenth century, William makes no effort to determine the nature of *synderesis* as a potency or habit. He is content to identify it merely as the superior part of reason, whose primary function is to command a human being through free choice to seek true delight or beatitude. In this way he indicates that *synderesis* functions as a power of will. As a voluntary power it does more than merely display

---

[8] SA, III, tr. 18, c. 1, pp. 370–371.
[9] O. Lottin, "La loi naturelle depuis le début du XIIe siècle jusqu'a saint Thomas d'Aquin," *Psychologie et morale aux XIIe et XIIIe siècles*, II, p. 74. For the early sources on, and the development of, the idea of *synderesis*, see A. Le Boulluec, "Recherches sur les origines du thème de la syndérèse dans la tradition patristique," *Vers la contemplation . . .* ed. C. Trottmann (Paris: Champion, 2007), pp. 61–77.
[10] SA, III, tr. 18, c. 5, p. 381.   [11] SA, III, tr. 20, c. 2, p. 394.
[12] SA, III, tr. 47, c. 1, p. 900.

what is right through reason.[13] Here William displays his obvious difficulty in determining the precise function of *synderesis*, and also in
deciding whether it is part of the will or reason. He, like his contemporaries, demonstrates further confusion concerning the exact nature of the
virtue of prudence. He begins his discussion of the cardinal virtues by
asserting their function to enable human beings to attain the theological
virtues by exterior acts that make them similar to God.[14] In passages
specifically devoted to the virtue of prudence, William asks whether it
may be identified with the moral science that is found in the book of
Solomon and in the *Ethics* of Aristotle. These works claim that its primary
function is to guide one in the choice of good over evil.[15] William
continues by dividing the judgments of reason into one of discretion,
which knows what to do, and one that is definitive and commands what is
to be done. He says here that prudence differs from moral science because
the latter merely indicates what to do, but prudence orders the proper
action. He has very briefly answered the question whether prudence is
merely science or knowledge.[16]

b Prudence and beatitude

The moral theologians of the early thirteenth century accept the intellectual nature of prudence as an important aspect of human morality, since it
must recognize the proper principles of action before it can exercise its
moral imperative function. William calls prudence a specifically unique
virtue, and not merely science, because it must decree actions according to
the dictates of reason. According to William, the ability to align all actions
to the norm of reason harmonizes prudence with the divine will.[17] Another
type of prudence that of the spirit, is a kind of knowledge that supposes all
that is knowable and useful for salvation. This 'gift' of prudence allows its
possessor to act frequently in accord with its decrees.[18] Like many medieval
authors, William notes the dual nature of the virtue of prudence and

---

[13] SA, III, tr. 47, c. 3, p. 906.   [14] SA, III, tr. 19, prol., p. 385.
[15] SA, III, tr. 20, c. 1, p. 388.
[16] SA, III, tr. 20, c. 1, p. 389. See P. Payer, "Prudence and the Principles of Natural Law: A
Medieval Development," *Speculum*, 54 (1979), pp. 55–70, esp. pp. 56–57.
[17] SA, III, tr. 20, c. 2, p. 394.
[18] SA, III, tr. 41, c. 1, p. 779. See M. Tracey, "Prudentia in the Parisian Summae of William of
Auxerre, Philip the Chancellor, and Albert the Great," *Subsidia Albertina II: Via Alberti
Texte-Quellen – Interpretationen*, ed. L. Honnefelder, H. Möhle, and S. Bullido del Barrio
(Münster: Aschendorff, 2009), pp. 272–274.

recognizes both its intellectual character as a type of knowledge as well as its moral function in the ability to command proper actions.

The goal of all human moral action is beatitude, which may be viewed as either perfect or imperfect. William does not cast this distinction in terms of theological and philosophical considerations. Rather he views imperfect beatitude in its relation to ultimate perfection and notes that the saints will have in the future what they possess presently only imperfectly. Perfect beatitude conveys the satisfaction of every desire with respect to both the present and the future. The saints who attain imperfect beatitude do not actually possess the glory and satisfaction of every desire that they will eventually enjoy.[19] William makes no effort to define the philosophical concept of happiness or the rational attainment of imperfect beatitude through moral and intellectual virtues. He also ignores the more difficult question of the relation of imperfect to perfect beatitude that many of his successors later in the century will examine at great length.

c Philip the Chancellor's *Summa de bono*

Philip the Chancellor's *Summa de bono*, written c. 1225–1228, is the first comprehensive treatment of moral topics in the thirteenth century. Although Philip states his primary intention is to investigate goodness theologically, he examines at length philosophical ideas such as the mean- ing of prudence and *synderesis*, and the composition of moral choice.[20] He interprets the opening lines of the *Nicomachean Ethics*, which assert that all things seek the good, as Aristotle's attempt to determine goodness accord- ing to the capacity of the seeker. Since the soul is created capable of attaining beatitude through the fulfillment of the intellect, Philip says it is able to *participate* in beatitude. Such participation cannot occur without the perpetuity of the soul's existence. The soul must therefore be incorrup- tible and immortal. The intellect, which makes the human being similar to God, is a greater gift than immortality in that the former element guaran- tees the latter state.[21] Philip defines goodness primarily and principally as the indivisibility of an act with its corresponding potency. The paradigm of goodness is the divine essence wherein any potency must be identical with

---

[19] SA, III, tr. 47, c. 2, p. 904.

[20] De bono autem intendimus principaliter quod ad theologiam pertinet. *Philippi Cancellarii Parisiensis Summa de Bono* (=SDB) ed. N. Wicki (*Corpus Philosophorum Medii Aevi: Opera philosophica mediae aetatis selecta, II*: Bern: Francke, 1985), v. I, p. 4, ll. 41–42.

[21] SDB I, 275, 349–356.

its act. No division whatsoever can exist within the divine being.[22] When Philip examines the problem of human goodness he discusses at length the meaning of the virtue of prudence and the habit of *synderesis*. He begins his treatment of these questions by considering the various definitions of the soul. He accepts Seneca's designation of the soul as an intellectual spirit directed in itself and in the body toward beatitude. Philip claims that Augustine also accepted this definition in the *De spiritu et anima*.[23] Throughout his *Summa* Philip displays a willingness to consider non-Christian sources when fitting, but his most important non-scriptural source remains the works of Augustine. Even if he considers moral ideas that may be viewed as primarily philosophical, his ultimate aim is always theological, since his intent is to identify those acts that ultimately lead one to God.[24]

Philip accepts the account of the soul's powers found in John Damascene's *De fide orthodoxa*: "The soul naturally has two powers: the cognitive and the 'zotica'." The latter Philip calls the moving (*motivas*) powers. He understands Damascene as having provided examples of the different psychic powers, but not actually dividing them. The cognitive faculties are understanding, mind, opinion, imagination and sensing; the moving powers are deliberation and choice.[25] Deliberative skill was reduced by Aristotle to the efficient causes, and Philip understands everything that may be related to action to involve the moving powers. He argues that Damascene orders the cognitive powers of the inferior part of the soul: imagination arises from sensation, and opinion from imagination. Damascene is said to have elaborated the mental powers by identifying the first psychic movement as understanding. If this understanding concerns some object, it is called intention; what remains and shapes the soul according to the object of understanding is termed the concept or image (*excogitatio*). This concept endures and when it is self-reflective, Philip calls it *phronesis*. *Phronesis* understood broadly orders the internal mental designation, which later becomes the spoken word.[26] Understanding considers the truth indeterminately, but with the following qualification from Damascene: "which concerns something (*que est circa aliquid*)." Understanding then signifies intention, not as the will directed toward an end, but rather as deliberative understanding. When Damascene says that

[22] SDB I, 7, 34–42.   [23] SDB I, 156, 28–30.
[24] N. Wicki, *Die Philosophie Philipps des Kanzlers: ein philosophierender Theologe des frühen 13. Jahrhunderts* (Dokimion, 29. Fribourg: Academic Press, 2005), p. 162.
[25] Ibid., p. 85.   [26] SDB I, 159, 2–16.

this understanding endures and shapes the soul, he refers to a process applied to a particular truth. The resulting mental image (*excogitatio*) endures and is self-reflective. The product of such a mental process and the manifestation of the particular truth is a perfection of the soul's interior motion through examination. Philip admits, however, that he understands *phronesis* here differently from Aristotle's concept of practical wisdom, which is an intellectual virtue.[27] Philip's notion of *phronesis* reflects the teaching of his contemporaries, who viewed this virtue as a means whereby a human being is united to God. Nothing in the soul remains imperfect because one is led to union by means of a similarity to divine virtue.[28]

d Reason, will and human freedom

The discussion of the relation of sensation to the desiderative and irascible elements within the soul begins with the observation that the philosophers added a third component in their theories, since they placed the rational power over the moving powers, whereas Scripture designates only sensation and reason. Philip categorizes free choice, the will and desire with *synderesis* as the individual moving powers of the soul. Philip will investigate the relation of these elements as well as the irrational and those faculties participative in reason. The first constituent of the moral act is the appearance of the good. One may pursue what is simply good or what is good in a particular sense. Then one wants, or desires, the perceived object, but reason commands the pursuit or avoidance of the object of desire. The appearance of what is simply good falls under the moving force of the practical intellect, while the perception of a particular good is subject to the imagination (*phantasia*). The intellect never errs, but imagination may mislead when presenting a particular object as good. When reason identifies goodness it is ordered to understanding, but when the senses pursue an object as good they are ordered to imagination.[29]

The will is characterized partly by reason and partly by desire, the latter of which is moved intemperately. To seek goodness and evil according to reason is a consequence of willing, while to do so according to sensation

---

[27] SDB I, 159–160, 17–28. See also N. Wicki, *Die Philosophie Philipps . . .*, p. 86.

[28] R.-A. Gauthier, "Arnoul de Provence et la doctrine de la 'fronesis', vertu mystique suprême," *Revue du Moyen Âge Latin*, 19 (1963), p. 146. As Gauthier notes this position is certainly not that of Aristotle. See also A. Celano, "The Understanding of Beatitude, the Perfection of the Soul, in the Early Latin Commentaries on Aristotle's *Nicomachean Ethics*," *Documenti e Studi sulla Tradizione Filosofica Medievale*, 17 (2006), pp. 1–22.

[29] SDB I, pp. 160–161, ll. 43–70.

follows from desire.[30] In order to understand fully the genesis of moral action, Philip considers the notions of natural will (*thelisis*), *synderesis*, free choice and willing (*bulesis*). Free choice differs from *synderesis*, which is a determination from the superior part of the soul with respect to judgment, in that it is flexible with respect to good and evil. Free choice according to Philip originates in the lower part of the soul. Natural will differs from deliberative will, which, taken commonly, consists in an antecedent deliberative judgment involving *synderesis* and choice (*proheresis*). Free choice encompasses every act of the rational powers enumerated by John Damascene: deliberation, enquiry, judgment, love and desire. These divisions within the intellect's moving powers seem sufficient for theological speculation.[31]

Damascene again provides Philip with a definition for understanding when he declares the comprehension of truth to be cognitive, but when understanding and truth are directed toward goodness, then the understanding governs deliberative reason.[32] Philip examines understanding's function in moral decisions more closely when he identifies the source of moral error to be the understanding's apprehension of particular mutable goods. While temporal goodness may be the proper domain of the imagination and sensation, it is the task of understanding to convert such a limited comprehension to the grasp of what is eternally good. In this transformative process, the union of the soul and body allows the corporeal nature to act like a weight dragging the soul downward.[33] Although temptation arises in sense perception, perception itself cannot provide motivation for action. The imagination when opposed to the understanding provides the impetus for irrational action.[34] In summarizing the section on the soul's powers, Philip distinguishes *synderesis* from free choice, although both are psychic potencies, and *synderesis* from *proheresis*, since the former is a habit. He will explain later how *synderesis* is both habit and potency. *Synderesis* is termed here a natural moving force toward the good, while free choice moves one either to good or evil. *Synderesis* finally is called a natural judgment concerning goodness, while *proheresis* involves deliberative judgment.[35]

Human freedom arises not only from volitional acts, but also from rational ones. The primary element of freedom originates in the will, but does not arise from the nature of any choice, but only from one that has a material principle of merit anchored in reason. The freedom of the will

---

[30] SDB I, p.161, ll. 72–78.   [31] SDB I, 162, 91–107.   [32] SDB I, 163, 133–135.
[33] SDB I, 163–164, 133–142.   [34] SDB I, 164, 158–161.   [35] SDB I, 164, 162–167.

consists principally in the act of willing in which there is a complement to merit.[36] Such a distinction explains why Augustine chose the term 'free choice' (*liberum arbitrium*), and not 'discretionary will' (*voluntas arbitraria*), in order to explain the nature of human moral freedom. Choice is the material principle of merit, and the will functions as its formal and complementary principle.[37] In his explanation of Augustine's terminology, Philip locates freedom in the will, not because there is no judgment before willing, but because the greatest freedom lies in the act of willing; choice, however, refers to reason. According to moral theory, the acts of knowing and willing belong respectively to the nature of acting well. Knowing reflects choice, but freedom remains rooted primarily in willing. Knowing is directed toward goodness according to the nature of truth; willing according to the nature of goodness. As a result the soul in its entirety may be perfected through merit and reward.[38]

Philip understands Aristotle's *Ethics* to contain a concept of the will. He argues that what comprehends truth and goodness must undoubtedly be the same. Speculative understanding becomes practical by extension, according to Philip's reading of Aristotle, and this idea provides a basis for Philip's understanding of the unity of reason and the will.[39] Although Philip considers understanding to pertain to cognition, which is rational, he says that practical understanding pertains to the moving force of the will. The designations 'practical' and 'speculative', arise from the agent's intention, and so the will may be thought of as a type of reason. Purely speculative understanding differs from purely motivating understanding not by substance, but by definition (*secundum rationem*).[40]

e Synderesis and the principles of moral actions

The question on the human powers that allow for free choice distinguishes sharply the powers of motivation within the soul, i.e. will and desire, from

---

[36] SDB I, 176, 349–355.   [37] SDB I, 177, 356–358.

[38] SDB I, 177, 401–409. N. Wicki notes how Philip distinguishes his understanding of the moral act from the prevailing opinion of his time that made the ability to choose freely an act of understanding. For Philip *liberum arbitrium* must be defined by the will. N. Wicki, *Die Philosophie Philipps* . . ., p. 164. For Philip's sources on this doctrine, see O. Lottin, "Libre arbitré et liberté jusqu'a la fin du XIIIe siècle," *Psychologie et morale*, v. I, pp. 50–52.

[39] G. Queneau, "Origine de la sentence 'Intellectus speculativus extensione fit practicus' et date du Commentaire du *De Anima* de S. Albert le Grand," *Recherches de théologie ancienne et medievale*, 21 (1954), pp. 307–312. Also N. Wicki, *Die Philosophie Philipps* . . ., p. 100.

[40] SDB I, 181, 67–72.

synderesis. Synderesis, which is a component of the superior part of the soul, directs human judgments toward goodness and away from evil. Free choice, which draws upon the powers within the lower part of the soul, is flexible with regard to both good and evil. Philip considers free choice to be in a certain manner 'concupiscibility' in the young and concupiscence, or the stimulus to sin, in adults. He distinguishes free choice, which seems to be inclined to moral error, from the natural will. Natural will encompasses deliberative will, which is described as a certain *synderesis* and choice that proceeds from a prior judgment.[41] Unlike many of his contemporaries in the thirteenth century, Philip identifies the will (*voluntas naturalis*) and *synderesis*, which, as Lottin notes, will lead to Bonaventure's concept of the *synderesis* as the will's natural inclination (*naturale pondus voluntatis*).[42] Free choice is a potency, as is *synderesis* when it functions in relation to free choice. When a specific choice (*proheresis*) is made, *synderesis* is better understood as a habit. Philip regards free choice (*liberum arbitrium*) and *synderesis* as general components to moral decisions, but he limits *proheresis* to an immediate decision. Regulated by a developed sense of right and wrong, *synderesis* is distinguished from free choice in that it naturally is moved to goodness, while choice may be attracted to evil. *Synderesis* differs from immediate choice (*proheresis*) in that it is a natural judgment concerning good, while *proheresis* is a deliberative judgment.[43]

Philip considers specifically the notion of *synderesis* in the question concerning its presence in the souls of angels. There Philip describes *synderesis* as an integral component to every moral choice. He cites Jerome's definition of *synderesis* as the spark of conscience never extinguished, but does not accept completely the identification of *synderesis* with a spark within the soul. He argues that this spark may be understood either with respect to the intellect or to desire. The spark may be considered in both ways, not only in free choice, but also in the function of *synderesis*. Philip asks whether this power could ever be extinguished even in the devil. After the fall, the devil still would wish to exist without

---

[41] SDB I, 162, 93–100.

[42] O. Lottin, "Le rôle de la raison dans la morale Albertino-Thomiste," *Psychologie et morale*, v. III, pp. 554–555.

[43] SDB I, 162–167: Respondeo quod liberum arbitrium dividitur contra synderesim ut potentia contra potentiam; proheresis autem dividitur contra synderesim, prout synderesis est habitus ... Item synderesis dividitur contra liberum arbitrium prout est motivum naturale in bonum, liberum arbitrium in bonum et malum. Item synderesis dividitur contra proheresim, prout synderesis est iudicium naturale de bono, proheresis deliberativum.

pain and would naturally desire supreme beatitude, and this natural desire would always endure.[44]

In the question devoted to the nature of *synderesis*, Philip asks whether it should be considered as a potency within the soul or a habit existing naturally within the soul. Although the form of its name seems to indicate that *synderesis* is a habit rather than a potency, Philip prefers the designation of habitual potency. This power should be considered innate, and not one attained through activity. By its nature as potency, it differs from the usually developed habits, and by nature of habit it differs from the normally undeveloped potency. According to N. Wicki, this designation of *synderesis* as a habitual potency allows Philip to move away from the usual classification of *synderesis* as understanding and closer to that of will.[45]

Like many of his contemporaries, Phillip seems to have difficulty with the concept of an innate habit. Habits normally require the exercise of activities that develop into a habitual state. *Synderesis*, while inhering naturally within every human soul, does not regulate actions until a number of moral decisions have been made. By reason of its potency, *synderesis* differs from free choice and sensuality; by its nature as habit it can be distinguished from choosing and desire.[46] Philip indicates that his position is a compromise concerning the nature of *synderesis*, which is very similar to natural will. He seems to regard *synderesis* as an element of the natural will, which extends to rational, natural and subsistent goods, but *synderesis* is limited to considering rational goods only.[47]

One may well ask whether *synderesis* should be considered the same power as free choice or reason. In his arguments against the identification of *synderesis* with choice and reason, Philip mistakenly cites Gregory as support for his denial of such an identification. In reality he uses Jerome's commentary on *Ezechiel* 1, 1 to argue for the separate existence of a fourth power within the soul that corrects errors; this power is *synderesis*.[48] In his resolution to the question, Philip claims that reason can be understood broadly so that it may encompass every moving power of the rational soul, but differs from the soul itself, which is the principle of life. When reason is

---

[44] SDB I, 102–103, 28–47: Est scinctilla quantum ad intellectum et quantum ad affectum et hec est duplex: quantum ad intellectum et affectum in libero arbitrio et quantum ad intellectum et affectum in synderesi . . . Tamen sciendum quod in ipso est scintilla que est in synderesi non est extincta in ipso [diabolo]. Vellet enim diabolus se esse sine miseria pene et vult naturaliter summam beatitudinem, et hec voluntas naturalis remanet ei etiam post corruptionem peccati.

[45] SDB I, 194, 65–69. N. Wicki, *Die Philosophie Philipps* . . ., p. 164 and p. 107.

[46] SDB I, 195, 69–73.   [47] SDB I, 195, 73–81.   [48] SDB I, 195, 5–7.

understood most generally *synderesis* may be considered as one of its parts.[49] If reason is taken generally, it will also include the desirous and irascible elements within the human being. *Synderesis* would also fall under the general abilities of reason as an element capable of intellectual comprehension. If, however, reason is considered distinct from desirous and irascible elements, then *synderesis* will be viewed as part of the unerring powers that Adam possessed in a state of innocence. It remains as a modest light leading to God in order to prevent human reason from being wholly inclined or twisted to the pursuit of temporal goods. While the rectitude of grace was wholly lost through sin, Adam retained a natural righteousness concerning judgment, will and anger. This rectitude was never completely lost by human beings, and what remains as innate correctness may be called *synderesis*.[50]

Philip gives to *synderesis* more extensive powers than do theologians later in the thirteenth century. In addition to directing one to pursue good and avoid evil, it promotes the proper contemplation of, and the desire for, the good simply. *Synderesis* functions also as the critical examining faculty (*inspectrix*) of all things in relation to the supreme good, to which it is principally related. In this way *synderesis* is not a potency apart from the other moving powers of the soul that consider good and evil, but remains steadfastly joined to them in the pursuit of goodness.[51] In extending the domain of *synderesis* to include the arrangement of good with respect to the supreme good, Philip elevates it to a supreme moral power. Not only does it allow one to attain moral virtue, but it also directs all one's activity to God. Philip thereby makes it an essential element in the acquisition of imperfect or perfect beatitude. He asserts that it is nobler than all the other powers of the soul because of its inflexible adherence to the desire for good and its aversion to evil. Philip would place *synderesis* above reason and in the understanding, if understanding signifies that which leads to supreme goodness without considering particular goods in actions. Reason may be judged as correct or incorrect with respect to specific acts of good and evil, and at times may be subject to the imagination that arises from goods comprehended through sense experience. If reason is thought to be affected by imagination, then *synderesis* is more properly thought to exist beyond reason.[52] In elevating *synderesis* above reason, Philip can preserve the infallibility of its dictates, while simultaneously accepting the

[49] SDB I, 197, 50–54.
[50] SDB I, 197–198, 57–71. See also N. Wicki, *Die Philosophie Philipps ...*, p. 108.
[51] SDB I, 198, 71–80.   [52] SDB I, 198, 81–90.

possibility of moral error. Philip is untroubled by the lack of a concept of *synderesis* in the moral writings of Aristotle.

In resolving the question concerning the manner by which *synderesis* leads one to reject evil, Philip concludes that it moves free choice by prescribing good and preventing evil. It also moves the choice toward a common good that is found in all particular good choices, but does not move one to choose common goodness in itself.[53] *Synderesis* is not characterized by a deliberative judgment, but rather by one that leads to action. Both natural will and *synderesis* are directed to natural goods, but in different manners. Natural will is like a potency, but not a habitual one like *synderesis*. The will may be directed toward other goods, whereas *synderesis* leads only to those objects good by nature. Both cognition and desire move the natural will, while an intellectual process of cognition alone governs *synderesis*.[54] Philip designates *synderesis* a habitual potency not because it may be frustrated in itself, but because it may be impeded by disobedience to reason. An act of judgment under difficult circumstances may prevent the full exercise of reason.[55]

Synderesis has a close connection to the natural will, since they are the same in subject, but they differ in that natural will is only a simple potency. Natural will, therefore, may err in judgment, but *synderesis*, as a natural potency cannot do wrong through its own power.[56] Philip's second argument declares that the soul in itself is eternally punished for sin, which is the product of the moving powers. He notes that conscience, which Gregory identified with *synderesis*, may produce error, and may not be an infallible guide to right and wrong actions. If *synderesis* were such a motivating force, it would also be a source of error and sin. He argues further that contraries arise in the same power, and since virtue and vice are contraries, they must originate in the same potency. Virtue, which is the gift of wisdom, would arise from the supreme power of the soul and therefore would originate in *synderesis*. Sin, as virtue's opposite, would then be the contrary originating

---

[53] SDB I, 199, 105–108: Synderesis movet liberum arbitrium dictando bonum et cohibendo a malo et movet in bonum commune quod invenitur in isto bono aut in illo. Non ergo est in bonum particulare secundum se, sed in commune inventum in eo.

[54] SDB I, 199, 109–115.

[55] SDB I, 199, 116–121: Intelligentia autem vocatur illa que est cognitionis. Potentia habitualis dicitur que facilis est ad actum. Et sic synderesis dicitur potentia habitualis, quia non impeditur ab actu suo quantum in se est, sed hoc, scilicet impediri, contingit per inobedientiam rationis. Ipsa ratio dicitur potentia habitualis, sed non in tantum, quia etsi impediri non possit quantum ad actum faciendi quod vult interiori facere, tamen quantum ad actum iudicii in difficilibus.

[56] SDB I, 199, 122–125.

from the same source.[57] Philip, however, resolutely maintains the infallibility of *synderesis*: even if it is understood as the same power of the soul as conscience and desire, it still differs in manner. It helps in producing meritorious actions in the way that inordinate sensuality leads to non-meritorious behavior. If *synderesis* were to be understood differently, so that it is thought to be flexible toward good and evil, then it could lead to meritorious or non-meritorious deeds. If *synderesis* is the same as understanding, or is understanding with a particular habit, then of itself it does not err. It may, however, be clouded by misjudgments and not produce its proper effect on the inferior part of the soul. Error is properly attributed to free choice, when *synderesis* is obscured. Philip clearly maintains that *synderesis* in itself always directs one toward good actions.[58]

In the final discussion concerning the contraries of virtue and vice as the origin of all moral conditions of the soul Philip places the spiritual gifts and the virtues in both reason and the will. The specific location of the gift of wisdom lies in the superior part of reason, where sin may occur when it seems to lack grace and illumination. When wisdom is said to be in *synderesis*, it does not follow that error in itself may also lie in *synderesis*. The soul is deprived of all gifts when it errs through one power. Even if the soul were not to err according to wisdom, it may lose wisdom that is a gift of grace.[59]

Philip provides medieval moral theory with an infallible source of universal principles. The standard of ethical action is no longer the practically wise person, the *phronimos* of the *Nicomachean Ethics*. The habitual potency of *synderesis* displays a universal code of right and wrong actions. Although medieval thinkers had some difficulty in explaining how the individual comes to develop an innate habit such as *synderesis*, they agreed upon its central role in the determination of good and evil actions. The moral syllogism described by Aristotle becomes anchored in the soul's ability to formulate universal precepts, from which the moral agent may deduce particular courses of action. Whether *synderesis* recognizes the dictates of natural law or the commands of the divine will, the human being has an infallible guide to all ethical decisions.[60]

The human conscience arises from the conjunction of *synderesis* with free choice, but it is separate from *synderesis* itself. *Synderesis* is unchanging

---

[57] SDB I, 200, 8–13. [58] SDB I, 201, 30–45. [59] SDB I, 202, 63–70.

[60] Philip gives an example of what is written in *synderesis* as the notion that each one who makes oneself a son of God shall not die: Verbi gratia sicut in synderesi sit scriptum quod omnis qui fecerit filium Dei et non sit morte moritaur. SDB I, 201, 50–51.

in that it always prescribes the good, but the association with what belongs to reason may allow for the selection of evil. *Synderesis*, therefore, with the nature of free choice may allow for a proper, or erroneous, exercise of conscience.[61] Philip asks whether such a power could ever be extinguished. To resolve the question he first distinguishes between the damned and the living. He considers the specific case of heretics and asks whether *synderesis* alerted them to their evil. While conscience may have directed them to accept martyrdom in defense of their faith, the effect of *synderesis* was weakened by a lack of true faith. Their error arose not from *synderesis*, but rather from those actions governed by free choice, or reason. *Synderesis* is not extinguished in them since evil generally remains displeasing to them, as does their specific failing.[62] The damned and the devil retain only one element of *synderesis*, which is the aversion to pain. What they lose is the instinct for goodness and the displeasure arising from the performance of evil.[63]

Philip determines the meaning of reason in three distinct ways. One manner, which is particularly relevant to moral theory, is the way in which reason belongs to the definition of free choice. So understood, it is called a potency by which one may judge good and evil, and what should be done, or not done. In this way reason is a motivating force to action. Reason may be understood as a power that discerns truth or goodness, not with the aim of action, but merely as a cognitive power. Reason may finally be understood as a power according to which a judgment and desire arise as an end or means to an end. Taken in the first manner, reason is a constituent element of free choice, not so much as comprehension, but as the choice itself; in the second way, it designates a cognitive, but not a moving, force; in the third mode, it implies reason not so much as it does choice. The designation 'free' concerning choice, refers to an ability to choose between contraries that belongs to the created free will. 'Reason' is used for such an operation because it orders actions to an end. There is a two-fold order of reason toward the supreme good: through an examination, and performance, of temporal operations, or through the contemplation and love of eternal objects.[64] From this order two elements of reason contribute to virtue and vice, but reason itself does not cause sin, but rather error. Despite his claim that reason does not cause sin, Philip places the origin of mortal transgressions in the superior part of reason: "because there exists only in the superior part of reason the power of sinning mortally, and this is because it has an order to

---

[61] SDB I, 201, 46–56.   [62] SDB I, 203–204, 42–52.   [63] SDB I, 205, 80–85.
[64] SDB I, 210, 49–65.

contemplating and reflecting upon superior things and should act according to eternal laws."[65] Here Philip has implicitly identified the content of *synderesis* as the eternal laws. Those who do not act according to these precepts have failed to act in the pursuit of goodness and have ignored through their free choice the dictates of *synderesis*.

f Human virtues

The distinctions among the powers of reason, deliberation and appetite allow Philip to respond to the question concerning the unity of virtues. If natural appetite and deliberative appetite are common to every virtue, how can one distinguish the virtues of faith, hope and charity?[66] Philip already has provided an answer in his distinction between reason and the appetite: natural appetite is directed toward objects, but virtues are not found in these objects of desire. Virtue arises in the commands of reason and in the unity of the end, but never in the objects themselves. Faith, for example, may be said to consist in truth, but the virtue does not consist in truth, but originates in its tendency toward truth and in its submission to the command of reason.[67]

The treatment of moral virtue begins with an analysis of the meaning of the term, 'good'. The good generally (*in genere*) is so called because of the primary potency; the good from circumstances, or the moral good, is so designated according to an ordered potency; and the good of grace is so termed because of the complete potency.[68] Philip gives a number of definitions of virtue, but prefers the following, which he attributes to Augustine: "Virtue is a good quality of the mind that God works in us without us." This definition actually is found in Peter the Lombard's commentary on the *Sentences*.[69] The notion of virtue that best reflects Philip's own philosophical understanding is: "virtue is desire ordered by reason." Such a definition depends upon his conviction that all virtues reflect the activities of desire and reason. A correct free choice requires both the powers of will and reason, since reason judges concerning true goodness and the will desires properly. Virtue then must be the perfection

---

[65] SDB I, 218, 69–71: . . . quia in superiori parte rationis est tantum potestas peccandi mortaliter, et hoc est quia ipsa est habens ordinem ad superna contemplanda et consulenda et secundum eternas leges operari debet.
[66] SDB I, 227, 141–144.   [67] SDB I, 145–149.   [68] SDB I, 327, 13–15.
[69] SDB I, 361, 12: Virtus est bona qualitas mentis quam Deus in nobis sine nobis. See also O. Lottin, "Les première définitions et classifications des vertus aux moyen âge," *Psychologie et morale*, v. III, 101, n. 2.

of each power to perform properly. If one desires properly and reasons correctly then the ensuing virtue will be the perfection of free choice.[70] Using an analogy drawn from Aristotle's natural philosophy, Philip compares cognition to matter and love to form in certain virtues. In prudence, which is an intellectual virtue in Aristotle's *Ethics*, and in faith, the analogy to matter and form is appropriate, but the essence of virtue comes from desire.[71] Virtue is completely characterized by desire, or by knowledge with desire. Charity, for example is completely voluntary, while prudence and faith, which involve cognition with desire, are called intellectual, and still require the involvement of the will. According to Philip even Aristotle recognized that some virtues are desires of the will (*voluntates*), or at least cannot exist without the will. The difference in the will's involvement determines the different types of virtue.[72] Whatever differences the will contributes to virtue, voluntary activity is essential to good actions.[73]

Philip places both the virtues of faith and prudence in the power of free choice, and characterizes them as both rational and voluntary. Faith follows the rational inclination to action, and has a voluntary desire for the end. Prudence is knowledge within free choice according to that element which is called reason. Some virtues are purely voluntary, such as charity, while others have a cognitive element within motivation, such as prudence. Prudence moves one to action by means of an inclination toward the end.[74] Philip considers the source of the distinction between intellectual and voluntary virtues not to be the work of Aristotle, but rather the writings of Paul:

Just as there are two elements in the soul, the intellect and desire, according to which two ends, truth and goodness, are distinguished from one another, so too the Apostle defines two elements only – of faith which pertains to the intellect, and of charity which pertains to desire.[75]

The introduction of Aristotelian conclusions on the nature of virtue in the early thirteenth century led Philip to a complex understanding of the topic. He argues that virtue can be considered in a number of ways: with respect to the principle from which; with respect to the potency; with respect to the act; and with respect to the end. In the first way, actions are simultaneous and none is the form of another; in the second way the form is said to perfect the potency; in the third way an act is said to be the

---

[70] SDB II, 534–535, 259–268.   [71] SDB II, 538, 353–354.   [72] SDB II, 589–590, 186–198.
[73] SDB II, 596, 22–25.   [74] SDB II, 591, 224–232.   [75] SDB II, 648, 7–9.

principle according to which it proceeds correctly from the potency; in the final way, a virtue is said to be a disposition to the end. When applied to the definition of virtue as a good mental quality that God works in us and without us, the perfection of the potency results from infusion. As a result the principle from which, and the potency in which, are meant, and one virtue is not the form of another, since they flow simultaneously from the same source. As ordered to the end, however, there is priority of one virtue over another, and some virtues may be forms of others.[76] Philip specifies the order of virtues in terms of the cardinal and theological perfections of the soul. The cardinal virtues that regulate dealings with human beings are ordered to the theological virtues that direct all to God. Primary among the first category of virtues is justice, the first among the second group is charity. The primary element of charity is the love of God, which is reflected in the command simply to love God. Faith and hope in God must be qualified since one believes in God incarnate and hopes in God as the giver of eternal life. Charity is like the form of all virtues in its manifestation as the end, and its ability to unite a human being with the divine persons.[77]

Like William of Auxerre, Philip does not distinguish strictly the philosophical ideal of human perfection from the theological one. He views all virtues as directed toward the goal of the beatific vision, which the act of charity primarily causes. Without charity, which unites one to the ultimate moral goal, there can be no merit, not only in defense against vice, but also as conducive to the desired end. Beatitude cannot be granted through an act of faith, or by any other virtue, but by all of them simultaneously. Charity is the only virtue that inclines the will in act and habit to goodness *simpliciter*, while every other virtue is limited to a particular good. In the act of charity one may be granted eternal beatitude.[78] Faith earns beatitude only *secundum quid*, because it gains only a part of beatitude. All virtues simultaneously merit beatitude completely and the ultimate element is charity that supersedes all other acts.[79]

The charity that is appropriate to human life leads to the love of one's neighbor through love of God. Charity that is appropriate to the after-life is loved because of its participation in beatitude. Philip argues that Augustine claims that all four objects of love are so desired because of their relation to beatitude.[80] Philip identifies various causes of charity and its intention in human beings. Its material cause is a certain similitude, or image of God, in

---

[76] SDB II, 701, 105–116. [77] SDB II, 701–702, 116–131. [78] SDB II, 705, 223–236.
[79] SDB II, 706, 243–245. [80] SDB II, 710, 59–63.

the object of love. This similitude is the goodness of the object. God is the
efficient cause of charity insofar as He commands one to love. God is also
the final cause insofar as there is an obligation to love what is loved through
charity. Such an object of love is recognized by its connection to God
or through divine precept, as one's neighbor is loved because he is related
to God.[81]

g Prudence and the unity of virtues

Prudence relates to a proper love that is ordered and originates in virtue
by identifying what and how one should love. Because prudence prevents
human beings from being deceived by apparent goods, Augustine defined
the virtue of prudence as "that love which discerns well those things that
lead to God [and away] from those which impede progress to Him."[82]
Philip does not regard prudence in its relation to love as an intellectual
virtue, but one that rules the appetite as the principle of action. Augustine
in the *De moribus ecclesiae* defined the cardinal virtues through love
because of the requirements of determining how human beings attain
beatitude. In the pursuit of the supreme good love is said to be in all
actions as a motivating cause in relation to the end that moves all to
action. In the order of definitions and of virtues love is assumed to be as
relevant to the higher and lower objects of desire. Because love is simply
in the concupiscible part of the soul the first definition of temperance is
located in the concupiscible element. Because the concupiscible and
irascible powers of the soul pertain to desire, they are the first to be
defined through their connection to love. Motivation through cognition,
which characterizes the virtues of justice and prudence, then follows.
Because prudence has a closer connection to the cognitive power of the
soul and is the most distant from the motivating element it seems to have
the weakest connection with love.[83]

   When Philip moves from a general discussion of the cardinal virtues to a
specific analysis of prudence, he accepts primarily the principles of
Augustine. Aristotle's discussion of *phronesis* in book VI of the NE had
not yet appeared in widely circulated Latin translations. Philip's understanding of Aristotle's theory of virtue develops from his reading of the
Ethica vetus. Philip gives a number of definitions of prudence, the most

---

[81] SDB II, 716, 43–50.
[82] SDB II, 749–750, 159–164. The reference is to *De moribus eccles.*, I, 15, n. 25.
[83] SDB II, 752–753, 37–50.

important of which come from the works of Augustine and appear in other works of this period. Prudence may generally be described as the knowledge of what should be desired and what ought to be avoided. Augustine provides the following two specific definitions of prudence: the love that distinguishes wisely those things that are helpful from those that are impediments; the virtue by which the soul knows what it should do. The citations to Augustine illustrate a persistent question in the early medieval understanding of prudence.[84] Philip must determine whether it is primarily an intellectual virtue and provides a type of knowledge concerning right and wrong, or a virtue primarily of the will that provokes a type of love for what is morally advantageous. Subsequent medieval discussions of prudence often return to the questions raised by the Augustinian designation of prudence as both love and knowledge. As a motivating element of the will, prudence is primarily a moral virtue that directs ethical choices to desired ends. As an intellectual virtue guided by *synderesis* and syllogistic reasoning, it recognizes rationally and logically the means whereby one may best attain a good end. The elements of both desire and understanding are present in Aristotle's notion, but he characterizes *phronesis* as only an intellectual process that functions in moral decisions. The goal of practical wisdom is the attainment of truth concerning good and the direction of human actions. In the former manner it is intellectual; in the latter, moral.[85] The dual nature of prudence leads Philip to identify it with free choice, a power of both reason and the will, since prudence must consist in more than mere knowledge in order to be a true virtue, since virtues must be more than mere awareness (*cognitio*) of right and wrong.[86] He locates prudence within free choice because it has both rational and voluntary elements. Philip takes the various definitions of prudence and again compares them to Aristotle's doctrine of matter and form. He considers the determination of prudence as cognition as analogous to the matter of this virtue. The component of love within prudence is similar to its form. This particular form is related to charity from which all virtues are ultimately derived. Philip concludes that philosophers did not define the cardinal virtues by love because they did not relate them to charity.[87]

---

[84] SDB II, 748, 114–116 and SDB II, 757, 2–4: ... et Augustinus in ln libro *De moribus ecclesiae*: "Prudentia est amor ea quibus adiuvatur ab hiis impeditur sagaciter eligens." SDB II, 757, 4–5: Idem in libro *De anima et spiritu*: "Prudentia est virtus qua anima scit quid debeat facere."
[85] EN 1140b6–8. [86] See M. Tracey, art. cit., p. 275. [87] SDB II, 758, 38–53.

The primary function of moral virtues consists in the choice of the best means to attain a desired end. Such discernment arises from prudence as a type of knowledge that Philip designates as a material disposition to virtue.[88] Judgment concerning action is common both to prudence as a virtue and to a type of prudence that is merely a kind of practical knowledge. The same distinction may be applied to other acts ordered to an end, such as those from knowledge (*scire*) and cognition (*cognsocere*). Philip notes that cognition inclines one toward acting, but implies that action is not a necessary result of knowledge. The primary nature of virtue arises from the ability to choose and not from knowledge alone.[89] Philip further divides prudence as a virtue into moral prudence and the prudence of grace. He argues that when he speaks of moral prudence, which is acquired, grace adds a perfection with respect to the act of discerning between spiritual and carnal goods. If he speaks of moral prudence, which is a moral virtue, then grace will perfect it according to the act of choosing spiritual goods.[90]

Philip regards prudence as a distinct virtue, but also recognizes its close connection with all other virtues. In particular actions every virtue may not be realized according to the proper activity, but each one acts in accordance with the nature of all virtues. Temperance, for example, has the nature of prudence in the ability to act with discernment, and prudence has the nature of temperance in its aptitude for moderation.[91] If one were to speak properly, then one should refrain from saying that temperance imposes moderation onto prudence, since each virtue is a complete habit. We can, however, speak this way by way of appropriation (*per modum appropriationis*) and so temperance is said to impose moderation onto prudence, just as prudence imposes discernment onto temperance. Such notions on the connection of distinct virtues are permitted because there are many essential elements common to virtues. The element may be more or less related to a particular virtue as it actualizes or reinforces the act of that virtue.[92]

Philip emphasizes the connection of prudence and temperance to other virtues. He calls them general virtues and says they are in the nature and act

---

[88] SDB II, 775, 25–27.   [89] SDB II, 776, 31–38.

[90] SDB II, 788–789, 23–29: . . . quod secundum quosdam qui sustinet quod naturalia fiant gratuita prudentia moralis potest fieri prudentia virtus per informationem gratie. Et ad hoc quod sequitur quid superaddat gratia respondet quod si loquimur de prudentia morali que est prudentia acquisita, gratia illa addit perfectionem quantum ad actus discernendi inter spiritualia bona et carnalia, si autem si loquimur de prudentia morali que est virtus moralis, gratia superaddita perficiet eam secundum actum eligendi spiritualia. On the distinction between *prudentia spiritus* and *prudentia carnis*, see M. Tracey, art. cit., pp. 285–286.

[91] SDB II, 864, 78–82.   [92] SDB II, 869, 100–106.

of all other virtues as their matter. One can consider nature here in two ways: either as what is moved by itself, just others are moved by it, namely the irascible and the concupiscible; or as motivating, that is, as moving through itself and by other means. The result of the division is the multiplicity of diverse habits and acts. As something that is moved by itself, the habit is faith and its acts are belief and wisdom. As natures, which motivate and move, the habits are prudence and justice. In motivating two elements are to be considered: discretion and command. When discretion or deliberation concerning what ought to be performed pertain to motivating nature the result is the virtue of prudence. The deliberator is reduced to the efficient cause according to which the command concerning obligation produces justice. The act of believing is the result of the different modes of the three virtues of faith, prudence and justice. The act of belief comes from faith in a different manner than from prudence and justice. It originates in faith as an act similar to this habit and originally and efficiently from this same habit, because it actualizes the habit and is close to the habit. The act or exercise of faith comes not formally or proximately from prudence or justice, but from the former by means of deliberation and from justice through its command.[93]

When Philip identifies the difference in the approach that philosophers and theologians take in regard to virtue, he rightly understands that the philosophers construct an ethical art through formulation of universal propositions, while theologians limit their enquiry to the problem of merit or fault (*demeritum*). Because the philosopher intends to produce an art of living, the moral theorist does not descend to a consideration of corruptible single events, but remains focused upon perpetual universal concepts. The theologian, however, considers specific events and their relation to merit. Philip concludes that moral science proceeds by way of speculation, whereas the theologian's analysis of more specific acts produces an active type of knowledge.[94] Philip's claim that ethics concentrates upon universal propositions and ignores specific actions does not reflect the doctrine of Aristotle. While many of his contemporaries understood Aristotle's notion of happiness to include both theoretical and practical wisdom, they did not limit ethics to a speculative science of

---

[93] SDB II, 948–949, 34–49.

[94] SDB II, 889, 428–436. In his sermons Philip distinguishes the philosophical approach from the theological method because the prophets gain their message from heaven and the philosophers from the earth. The philosophical method depends upon a rational foundation and not upon divine inspiration. J. Schneyer, *Die Sittenkritik in den Predigten Philipps des Kanzlers* (Münster: Aschendorff, 1962), p. 22.

universal propositions. They understood ethics to be both a theoretical
and practical science because it provides universal principles of conduct
and specifies certain individual actions as good. When Philip treats the
virtue of temperance he again raises the question of the relation of
theology to ethics. An obvious difference lies in the philosophical treatment of virtues and vices that originate from free choice and emerge in
proper and inordinate acts. The philosopher has no consideration of
original sin, whereas the theologian must consider not only actual sin
but the corruption of nature that arises from original sin.[95] Here Philip
seems to indicate the ethics do not merely consider universal propositions by way of speculation but includes a practical analysis of particular
actions, virtues and vices. The final difference noted by Philip concerns
habitual virtues that are founded upon the principle of human nature. A
moral philosopher considers to a greater degree virtues that distinguish
the principles of nature and the nature of the objects than the theologian.
Virtues of this kind are habitual concerning which Aristotle noted that
they exist from nature or not beyond nature. A theologian concentrates
upon the operations, means and circumstances by which merit, fault,
reward and punishment result.[96]

The two Summas considered here were written to provide answers to
theological questions on a variety of topics. Their contribution to medieval
moral theory lies in their introduction of the concept of *synderesis* as the
foundation for the recognition of universal moral principles and its role in
the production of prudential wisdom. Their understanding of the virtue of
prudence was limited by their unfamiliarity with the entire text of the NE,
but their discussions on the topics of beatitude, the will, reason and
prudence provided a point of departure for the later, and philosophical
richer, doctrines of their successors.

---

[95] SDB II, 891, 485–492.

[96] SDB II, 893, 532–541. Moralis igitur plus attendit circa virtutes distinguendas principia
nature quam theologus et naturam obiectorum et similia quam theologus, quia huiusmodi virtus consuetudinales est secundum principium nature, de qua dicit Aristoteles
quod nec est a natura nec preter naturam. Theologus autem magis considerat operationes
et instrumenta per que operationes et circumstantias operationum modum, tempus,
locum, secundum quod est maius demeritum vel meritum et iuxta que etiam erunt
pene et premia ... Considerat etiam theologus quod puniendus est homo in eo in quo
deliquit.

4

The earliest medieval Latin commentaries
on the *Nicomachean Ethics*

For more than fifty years we have known from the work of Lorenzo Minio-Paluello that a complete Latin translation of the NE was available in the late twelfth century. René-Antoine Gauthier discovered fragments of this translation in manuscripts from this period, and recently Fernand Bossier identified Burgundio of Pisa as the translator of the entire Greek text into Latin. The appearance of the first fragmentary Latin translation of the NE comprised book II and almost all of book III of Aristotle's work. Then another fragment of the translation, book I of the NE, was available to medieval authors a few years later.[1] For reasons yet unexplained, the earliest Latin commentators on the NE limited their works to the first three books of Aristotle's text, and they referred to book one as the *Ethica nova* and books II and III as the *Ethica vetus*. The theologians of the first half of the thirteenth century, such as William of Auxerre and Philip the Chancellor, were familiar with only the first three books of the NE. An important element in the process of comprehending the meaning and intent of Aristotle's ethics was the practice of careful commentary on

---

[1] L. Minio-Paluello, "Note sull'Aristotele latino medievale, VII," *Rivista di Filosofia Neo-Scolastica*, 44 (1952), pp. 485–495; R.-A. Gauthier, ed., *Ethica Nicomachea, Praefatio in Aristoteles Latinus* (Leiden-Brussels, 1974), XXVI, fasc. 1, pp. xv–xvi; F. Bossier, "L'élaboration du vocabulaire philosophique chez Burgundio de Pise," in *Aux origines du lexique philosophique européen. L'influence de la latinitas. Actes du Colloque international organisé à Rome (Academia Belgica, 23–25 mai 1996)*, ed. J. Hamesse, (Louvain-la-Neuve: Fédération Internationale des Instituts d'Etudes Médiévales, 1997), pp. 81–116; F. Bossier, "Les ennuis d'un traducteur. Quatre annotations sur la première traduction latine de l'*Ethique à Nicomaque* par Burgundio de Pise," in *Bijdragen. Tijdschrift voor filosofie en theologie*, 59 (1998), pp. 406–427; R.-A. Gauthier and Y. Jolif, *L'Éthique à Nicomaque*, Publications universitaires (Paris, Louvain: Béatrice-Nauwelaerts, 1970), pp. 111–114; D. Luscombe, "Ethics in the Early Thirteenth Century," in *Albertus Magnus und die Anfänge der Aristoteles-Rezeption im lateinischen Mittelalter: Von Richardus Rufus bis zu Franciscus de Mayronis*, ed. L. Honnefelder *et al.* (Aschendorff: Münster, 2005), 657–684.

the text of the work itself. From the first half of the thirteenth century, six commentaries on the *Ethica vetus* and/or the *Ethica nova* remain. Despite the existence of the entire translation of the NE, only the first three books of Aristotle's work were the subject of commentary and instruction at the universities in the first half of the century. As recent scholarship has shown, these commentaries reflect the methods of teaching in the newly established universities and attempted to explain the ideas of Aristotle. At times, influenced by the works of Augustine, Boethius, Avicenna and Averroes among others, they were not entirely successful in reporting accurately Aristotle's ideas on human goodness and virtue, but they did help to determine the direction in which the later more comprehensive commentaries followed.[2] In addition to the six known commentaries on the old *Ethics*, a number of other works from this period display an awareness of the NE. They also consider some of the most important topics in moral philosophy and demonstrate a familiarity with contemporary moral deliberations.[3] Although the authors of these works did not have the sixth book of the NE where Aristotle explicitly discussed practical wisdom, they were aware of the

---

[2] In addition to the works of R.-A. Gauthier already cited, see V. Buffon, "Philosophers and Theologians on Happiness: An Analysis of Early Latin Commentaries on the *Nicomachean Ethics*," *Laval théologique et philosophique*, 60 (2004), 449–476, "The Structure of the Soul, Intellectual Virtues, and the Ethical Ideal of Masters of Arts in Early Commentaries on the *Nicomachean Ethics* in *Virtue Ethics in the Middle Ages: Commentaries on Aristotle's Nicomachean Ethics, 1200–1250*," ed. I. Bejczy (Brill's Studies in Intellectual History, 160: Leiden, Boston, 2008), 13–30 and "Happiness and Knowledge in Some Masters of Arts before 1250: An Analysis of Some Commentaries on Book I of *Nicomachean Ethics*," *Patristica et Mediaevalia*, 25 (2004), 111–115; I. Zavattero, "Le Prologue de *Lectura in Ethicam Veterem* du 'Commentaire de Paris' (1235–1240)," *Recherches de Théologie et Philosophie médiévales*, 77 (2010), 1–33 and "Moral and Intellectual Virtues in the Earliest Latin Commentaries on the *Nicomachean Ethics*," in Bejczy, pp. 31–54; M. Tracey, "An Early 13th-Century Commentary on Aristotle's *Nicomachean Ethics* I, 4–10: The *Lectio cum Questionibus* of an Arts-Master at Paris in MS Napoli Biblioteca Nazionale, VIII G 8, ff. 4r–9v," *Documenti e Studi sulla Tradizione Filosofica Medievale*, 17 (2006), 23–70 and "Virtus in the Naples Commentary on the *Ethica nova* (MS Napoli Biblioteca Nazionale, VIII G 8, ff. 4r–9vb)" in Bejczy, pp. 55–76; A. Celano, "The Understanding of Beatitude, the Perfection of the Soul, in the Early Latin Commentaries on Aristotle's *Nicomachean Ethics*," *Documenti e Studi sulla Tradizione Filosofica Medievale*, 17 (2006), 1–22; G. Wieland, *Ethica–scientia practica. Die Anfänge der philosophischen Ethik im 13. Jahrhundert* (Beiträge zur Geschichte der Philosophie des Mittelalters, Neue Folge, 21. Münster: Aschendorff, 1981).

[3] See, for example, G. Dahan, "Une introduction à l'étude de la philosphie: *Ut ait Tullius*," in *L'enseignement de la philosophie au XIIIe siècle: Autour du 'Guide de l'etudiant' du ms. Ripoll 109*, ed. C. Lafleur with J. Carrier, Studia artistarum, 5 (Brepols: Turnhout, 1997), pp. 3–58; C. Lafleur, *Quatre introductions à la philosophie au XIIIe siècle. Textes critiques et étude historique* (Publications de l'Institut d'études médiévales, XXIII: Montreal, Louvain: Vrin, 1988).

inclusion of *phronesis/prudentia* among the intellectual virtues listed by Aristotle at the end of book I. The topics contained in the moral works of the first half of the thirteenth century are limited by the missing books of the NE, but the discussions on moral goodness and virtue are of interest since they reflect the first extensive confrontation between Christian moral theology and Aristotle's moral philosophy.

In an early anonymous commentary on the *Ethica nova*, partially preserved in a Neapolitan manuscript and recently edited by M. Tracey, the author quickly dismissed the identification of happiness and virtue. His conclusion is based upon the tenuous nature of human virtue, which may cease to be exercised for a number of reasons. Since happiness is the end of civic life and is stable and self-sufficient, and the virtuous may cease to practice developed habits, virtue itself is too insecure an activity to constitute happiness.[4] The soul's tripartite division has three corresponding virtues, which arise from the intelligent, rational and desiderative elements within human beings. The speculative intellect seeks truth and goodness, which is best exemplified by the unity of knower and known in the first cause. The intellect is the location of contemplative perfection whose ultimate goal is comprehension of the first cause itself. The commentator claims that the speculative intellect can comprehend only universals, but the rational intellect is able to relate universal perceptions to singular apprehensions and conversely the application of singular perceptions to universal understanding. The irascible and desiderative elements of the soul fall under the direction of the rational part, and in this relation the civic life is regulated.[5]

The master of the commentary argues that happiness must be related to one of the types of lives that originate in the different elements within the soul. He, like his contemporaries, emphasizes the aspect of perfection that is always part of the description of happiness as the supreme moral good. In human life, in which there is always a lack of perfection (*privatio perfectionis*), happiness can never be attained.[6] The idea that the

---

[4] M. Tracey, "An Early 13th-Century Commentary ..." p. 30, ll. 74–81. See also R.-A. Gauthier. "Le Cours sur l'*Ethica* nova d'un maitre ès Arts de Paris (1235–1240)," *Archives d'histoire doctrinale et littéraire du moyen* âge, 42 (1975)[=Le cours], p. 109.

[5] M. Tracey, "An Early 13th-Century Commentary ..." p. 31, ll. 105–116; also, M. Tracey, "Virtus in the Naples Commentary ..." p. 59.

[6] In [omnibus in qubius] est vita cum labore et pena, illa privatur a sua perfectione ... set felicitas est secundum propriam perfectionem, que accipitur secundum propriam virtutem; ergo in hiis in quibus est privatio perfectionis, non est felicitas. M. Tracey, "An Early 13th-Century Commentary ..." p. 31, ll. 120–126.

designation 'perfect', limited the understanding of Aristotle's concept of happiness has been noted by a number of modern scholars, foremost among whom is R.-A. Gauthier, who maintained that it led Latin authors to misread Aristotle's *Ethics* and to create a false harmony with Christian teaching on the ultimate fate of human beings.[7] For this anonymous commentator, Aristotle's notion of the supreme good has three character-istics by which he designates its essence (*quiditatem*): absolutely perfect (*perfectissimum*); always and for itself choiceworthy (*eligibile per se et semper*); and completely sufficient (*sufficientissimum*).[8] He asserts that Aristotle did not prove that there is an end of all actions that will be maximally good, but this assertion is, nevertheless, true and describes the operable good sought in ethics.[9] Human aspirations are never satisfied until they attain what is always and in itself desired. No good can be more perfect than one that fulfills these conditions, and such perfect goodness can only be happiness. Two traditions are apparent in the commentator's concept of perfection: the philosophical ideal whereby perfect is defined by the acquisition of something that is required; the Christian depiction whereby something is held superabundantly and with joy. Since something described according to the first concept does not include superabundance, it may be considered to be less perfect than what is portrayed by the second. The latter understanding of perfection comes from the *De consolatione philosophiae* of Boethius and characterizes the first cause and true happi-ness, which have everything that they should, are exultant, and their perfection flows from its essence to all things related to it. Nothing can be termed more perfect than the first cause that lacks absolutely nothing, but the commentator argues that intelligence may be called perfect in the sense of possessing everything that it should.[10]

Since the rational intellect taken generally is the proper place for the development of human virtue moral goodness is perfected according to reason or understanding. The commentator rightly understands the Aristotelian ideal of intellectual perfection to consist in a continuous union of knower and known, which liberates the intellect from any

---

[7] R.-A. Gauthier, "Trois commentaires 'averroistes' sur *l'Ethique à Nicomaque*," *Archives d'histoire doctrinale et littéraire du moyen âge*, 16 (1947–1948), 187–336: see also M. Tracey, "Virtus in the Naples Commentary ... p. 60 and A. Celano, "The Understanding of Beatitude ..." *passim.*

[8] M. Tracey, "An Early 13th-Century Commentary ..." p. 41, ll. 431–436.

[9] M. Tracey, "An Early 13th-Century Commentary ..." p. 41, ll. 442–444.

[10] M. Tracey, "An Early 13th-Century Commentary ..." pp. 43–44, ll. 530–541; M. Tracey, "Virtus in the Naples Commentary ..." p. 67.

unactualized potency. In this complete actuality the intellect achieves true happiness.[11] The commentator may have understood the Aristotelian intellectual ideal well, but he is certainly unaware of Aristotle's admonition in book X of the NE to remember that such a union is impossible for human beings. The medieval master's designation of perfection as the delight in the union of potency with its act suggests the language of Augustine, who understood human perfection ultimately to exist in the enjoyment (*frui*) of the first being. The commentator implies here that such a perfect intellectual union is possible for human beings: "For he who lives according to the operations of virtue lacks nothing. For such is happiness, etc."[12] The commentator views the relationship of virtue to happiness in the manner of an immediate material disposition in a principle. An analogy to material that is receptive to fire illustrates how just as matter conditioned by material dispositions to burn must receive the form of fire, so too must the soul's virtues lead to the good of happiness. Virtue is like the motivating principle in happiness, since it moves one to the goal of happiness. Another analogy is given when the virtue of the soul is compared to light, which is also a moving cause to the actuality of sight.[13] Although the author of the commentary sees a close connection between virtue and happiness,[14] he, like many of his contemporaries, distinguishes them, just as light is distinct from the act of seeing.

a The commentary of Robert Kilwardby

Another commentary, which was composed slightly later than the one in the Neapolitan manuscript and attributed to Robert Kilwardby, differs in method and interpretation from the other similar works of this era. The commentary on the *Ethica vetus* and *nova* is found in ms. Cambridge Peterhouse 206 (C), ff. 285ra–307vb, and partially in ms. Prague, Czech State Library (*olim* University) III. F. 10 (Pr), ff. 1ra–11vb. While there is no internal designation of authorship in either manuscript, a fourteenth-century table of contents on the flyleaf names Kilwardby as the author. The information from the flyleaf is corroborated neither by the early

---

[11] M. Tracey, "An Early 13th-Century Commentary . . ." p. 47, ll. 631–639.

[12] M. Tracey, "An Early 13th-Century Commentary . . ." p. 58, ll. 994–995: . . . ergo qui vivvit (sic) secundum operationes virtutis nullo indiget. Talis autem est felicitas etc.

[13] M. Tracey, "An Early 13th-Century Commentary . . ." p. 59, ll. 1036–1041.

[14] M. Tracey, "An Early 13th-Century Commentary . . ." p. 68, ll. 1327–1328: Felicitas, ut dictum est, secundum actum virtutis est.

history of the Dominicans, nor by the earliest catalogue of their writings, but there is no compelling reason to doubt the attribution.[15]

The introduction to Kilwardby's commentary provides a cursory summary of the doctrine contained in the various examinations and classifications of philosophy composed in the first half of the thirteenth century. The elementary divisions within the branches of human science represent an initial phase of understanding that led to the deeper and more sophisticated treatises produced by the university masters in the second half of the century. The commentary begins with a statement about the general topic of moral science: "the whole of moral science is primarily and principally concerned with the human good as its subject."[16] Ethics is divided into two parts that correspond to human goodness: the first part concerns the supreme human good, which is happiness; the second treats the 'inferior good', virtue, which is ordered to happiness. As in many writings of this era, the relation of virtue to happiness is a complicated problem for the writers of the thirteenth century. At times, the same author may view virtue as the essential constitutive element of the highest good, and at other times, he may understand it to be an inferior means whereby a person is united to the supreme good. In either case, the commentator claims that once virtue

---

[15] M. R. James, *A Descriptive Catalogue of the Manuscripts in the Library of Peterhouse* (Cambridge: Cambridge University Press, 1899), pp. 245–247. An extensive bibliography is provided by the Stams Catalogue, a list of Dominican authors compiled in the first half of the fourteenth century. Kilwardby is identified as a master in theology with an extensive literary output. The entry for Kilwardby includes many logical commentaries, treatments of all Aristotle's natural philosophy and Aristotle's metaphysics, all the books of the *Sentences* and the *De ortu scientiarum*. Noticeably absent from the accounts of Kilwardby's literary activity is the commentary on the *Ethics*, but the omission is hardly conclusive, since the Stams Catalogue is not always accurate. Fr. Rupertus, natione Anglicus, magister in theologia, archiepiscopus Cantuariensis, scripsit super Porphirium et praedicamenta, perihermenias, sex principia, divisionum, et topica Boethii, super librum priorum, posteriorum, topicorum Aristotelis, super librum elenchorum, super Priscianum minorem; item librum de natura relationis; item sophisticam grammaticalem et sophisticam logicalem; item librum de ortu scientiarum, de rebus praedicamentalibus, de unitate formarum, super libros physicorum, super *metheorum*, super de anima, super de coelo et mundo, de generatione et corruptione, super metaphysicam, et omnes alios libros naturales; item super omnes libros sententiarum: G. Meersseman, ed., *Laurentii Pignon Catalogi et Chronica, accedunt Catalogi Stamensis et Upsalensis Scriptorum O.P.* (Rome: Monumenta Ordinis Fratrum Praedicatorum Historica, XVIII, 1936), p. 57; D. A. Callus, "The 'Tabulae super Originalia Patrum' of Robert Kilwardby O.P.," *Studia Mediaevalia in honorem R.J. Martin* (Bruges: De Tempel, 1948), 244–245. The catalogue's inclusion of a work on meteors may very well be a misreading of the Latin abbreviation in the source. The abbreviation /// eo4 could easily be a variant for iii ethi[c]orum.

[16] C f. 285rb, Pr f. 1rb: *Omnis ars et omnis doctrina* etc. (94a1) Supposito quod tota moralis sciencia sit primo et principaliter de bono humano, sicut de subiecto.

is recognized, it will be desired so much more in order that the goal may be attained.[17]

Kilwardby considers the possibility that one acts for the sake of evil as in the magical arts, but follows the text of Aristotle in rejecting such a notion. One always chooses what is good, or what appears to be so. An action of any type must reflect a desire for what appears beneficial to the agent. The term 'action' (*operatio*) may be understood in two ways: (1) strictly, and refers to an action that is opposed to speculation; (2) more generally and so may include speculative acts. The implication that the human moral good includes both speculative and practical actions, and is not limited to the 'good of *praxis*',[18] is based on an acute understanding of Aristotle's intention. Although Kilwardby did not have the final book of the NE available to him, he rightly assumes that the human actions that cause moral goodness must include theoretical speculation. There is no indication of the doctrine of '*due felicitates*' (political and theoretical happiness) that became the common interpretation of the NE in the later more complete commentaries.[19]

Like his contemporaries, Kilwardby takes quite literally Aristotle's assertion that all things desire the good. In order to maintain Aristotle's claim, he divides the appetite into two types: natural and animal. Natural appetite is the inclination in things to fulfill their nature, which is analogous to the appetitive desire in animals. In the first manner all things are said to seek the good; in the second only animate beings can desire what is beneficial. In the discussion of human goodness, Kilwardby considers the nature of the end and refines his terminology concerning human actions. The end is two-fold: one that is the act (*actus*), just as the end of the potential for sight is seeing, or as the end of military doctrine is military action; the second is the work or effect (*opus*) that proceeds from the act. 'Operatio' is understood here as the finished or accomplished action, as generation may be understood as a thing generated. As an example of such an operation, he says that the end of the art of building is the work produced and the goal of military art is victory. In such practical activities the end or the product is

---

[17] Ibid.: Bonum autem humanum duplex est: scilicet bonum summum sive felicitas, et bonum inferius ordinatumad summum bonum, scilicet virtus.

[18] C f. 285va, Pr f. 1va: Et nota quod operacio dicitur proprie et communiter: proprie autem dicitur operacio actio que opponitur speculacioni; communiter autem dicendo operacio comprehendit actum speculandi racionem proprie dictam. Intelligenda ergo proposicio quando dicit quod omnes sunt operatrices de operacione communiter que se extendit ad operacionem speculacionis; et similiter extendendum est nomen boni ad bonum speculacionis et non solum ad bonum praxis.

[19] A. Celano, "The Concept of Worldly Beatitude in the Writings of Thomas Aquinas," *Journal of the History of Philosophy*, 25 (1987), 215–226.

better than the act itself, since the goal is to produce an effect independent of the activity.[20]

In every art and doctrine there are architectonic principles that lead to the good simply. Kilwardby again relegates virtue to an end that is ordered to the superior goal of happiness. The anonymous commentator on the *Ethica nova* of the mid-1240s at Paris also sharply divides virtue from happiness: "In the first part the author determines happiness; in the second part, about that which is directed to happiness, that is, about virtue."[21] A contemporary of this commentator casts the problem of happiness and virtue in a different light. The 'Pseudo-Pecham' considers the question of human goodness to be primarily a theological problem, even in a commentary devoted to an explication of Aristotle's *Ethics*. In the beginning of his work, he distinguishes goodness into two types: divine, which is received from God and is called happiness; and human, which is attained by human beings through perseverance in pleasurable and painful pursuits.[22] Happiness, the end of the best actions, is merely a means of joining human beings in a certain way to the uncreated good.[23] Virtue is even further removed from the highest good since it is described consistently as a means subordinate to happiness.[24] To the Pseudo-Pecham the philosopher's deliberations remain subordinate to the theological notion of true happiness, for which virtue is merely a means. How virtue may be distinct from happiness is a question untreated by the Pseudo-Pecham. While to a modern reader of Aristotle the strict separation of happiness as the end and virtue as the means may seem contrary to the Philosopher's intention, the early medieval commentators were aware that the exercise of virtuous actions could not satisfy the conditions for their understanding of the nature of happiness. They knew that a person could be virtuous in certain ways, such as courageous in battle or eloquent in

---

[20] C f. 285va, Pr f. 1vb: In quibus ergo finis est opus sive aliquid operatum ipsum opus est melius actu. Hoc autem ad minus in plerisque est verum. Cum ergo opus sit melius actu, patet quod bonum melius est.

[21] "Le cours ...", p. 96: In prima parte determinat auctor de felicitate; in secunda parte determinat auctor de eo quod est ad felicitatem, hoc est de virtute.

[22] Ms. Florence, conv. soppr. G 4.853 (=F), f. 1ra. Bonum autem duplex est: divinum, id est a deo collatum, ut felicitas ... et humanum, id est ab homine (hominis, *ms.*) per rectas operaciones cum delectactione et tristicia et cum perseverancia in hiis adquisitum.

[23] F f. 4vb: ... quia felicitas sive finis optimus operacionum est medium coniungens nos quodam modo bono increato.

[24] F f. 2ra: Sic moralis bonum in operacionibus determinat propter bonum virtutis sive habitus et bonum in virtute considerat prout ordinatur ad felicitatem. F f. 2vb: ergo felicitas prior erit simpliciter virtute. F f. 2vb: virtus ordinatur ad felicitatem. See V. Buffon, "The Structure of the Soul ...," p. 28 and I. Zavattero, "Moral and Intellectual Virtues ...," *passim.*

discourse, but not be excellent in other ways required for eternal happiness. Taken separately, the virtues may be understood merely as means to human goodness. The early commentators lacked the discussion of *phronesis* that allowed for the unifying element in the good person's quest for happiness. Without this central notion of Aristotle's ethical theory, they could easily judge each virtue as a separate step leading to a distinct higher end of happiness. Only when the full work of Aristotle was available did commentators, like Thomas Aquinas, see the close connection between virtue and human goodness described in Aristotle's *Ethics*.

The science of ethics instructs human beings about the four cardinal virtues, which are in Kilwardby's commentary interpreted to be civic virtues instituted for the benefit of the state. Their purpose is thought to be primarily in the interest of the citizens' pursuit of external goods. The cardinal virtues are not viewed here either in the theological manner, or in the traditional way of guiding an individual concerning the moral issues in a lifetime. Fortitude is preeminent in military matters, temperance in economic, justice in legal affairs, and prudence in deliberation about expediency.[25] Prudence does not appear as the primary virtue of practical wisdom in this discussion of the cardinal virtues. The entire section seems peripheral to the central theme of individual moral goodness, as Kilwardby treats the cardinal virtues as political virtues only, as does Hugh of St. Victor in the *Didascalion*.[26]

Kilwardby returns to the question of the relation of virtue to happiness in section I, 6 of his commentary. One might assume virtue to be the end of the civic life, and to be happiness itself, if one were to claim honor to be

[25] C f. 286va, Pr f. 2va: Nota quod in hoc argumento potest haberi ab Aristotile que sit doctrina civilis, quia illa que instruit homines circa quattor virtutes cardinales, scilicet fortitudinem, prudenciam, temperanciam et iusticiam. Per hoc enim quod dicit ipsam preordinare militarem, innuit ipsam instruere homines circa fortitudinem. Per hoc quod ordinat rhetoricam significat ipsam instruere homines circa prudenciam. Per rhetoricam enim intendit provisionem et deliberacionem de expedientibus; et hoc maxime pertinet ad prudenciam, cum sit secundum Tullium bonarum et malarum rerum utrarumque sciencia. Et iste virtutes sunt civitatis et civium respectu extraneorum. Per hoc autem quod dicit ipsam ordinare yconomicam, significant ipsam instruere circa temperanciam que est in ordinacione hominis ad se et ad propriam familiam. Per hoc autem quod dicit ipsam ordinare legem, significat ipsam instruere de iusticia que exhibet unicuique quod suum est secundum legum precepcionem; et hoc consistit in ordinacione hominis ad suos concives. Ex hiis videtur haberi que sit doctrina civilis secundum Aristotilem.

[26] *Didascalion*, ed. C. Buttimer, *Hugonis de Sancto Didascalion. De studio legendi* (Washington: Catholic University Press, 1939), ii, 19, p. 38. See also Robert Kilwardby O.P. *De ortu scientiarum*, (=DOS) *Auctores Britannici Medii Aevi*, 4, ed. A. Judy (Oxford, Toronto: The British Academy and The Pontifical Institute of Mediaeval Studies, 1976), #356, p. 126.

such an end. Virtue, however, cannot be happiness according to the earliest commentators for two reasons: virtue is in imperfect beings and happiness is not; the virtuous may cease to act virtuously, since they are not constant beings.[27] The commentators of this period were misled by Aristotle's description of happiness as a perfect act. Concentrating on the word 'perfect', they argued that human virtue is subject to a variety of limitations and consequently could not be happiness. Rather than argue that virtue is the perfection in act of the soul's potential, they understood Aristotle's description of happiness to be a perfect continuous act.

Kilwardby refines his understanding of the imperfection of virtue by listing three possible defects associated with human virtue. One might cease the actions proceeding from a good habit. Sleep, which inhibits the actual exercise of virtue, is not an evil, but is a condition of the material aspect of a human being. The natural demands of corporeal nature prevent the continuous exercise of virtuous activity and prohibit the identification of virtue with happiness. The Pseudo-Pecham gives a similar response to the question: "then he [Aristotle] shows that virtue is not happiness and the reason is this: virtue is characteristic of imperfect beings, happiness is not; virtue, therefore, is not happiness."[28] The later commentators developed a more accurate reading of Aristotle, when they realized that he was describing a perfect act within the limits of a particular being's potential.

The commentary of Kilwardby concludes this discussion by claiming that the virtuous person can only be called happy in the same way as one taking medicine is called healthy. For just as he is healthy in the sense of progressing toward health, so too is the virtuous person happy in the sense of moving toward happiness.[29] The question of the contemplative life is reserved for subsequent discussions on the meaning of happiness.

---

[27] See "Le cours ..." p. 118: quod aliud est esse virtutem, aliud est secundum virtutem; quamvis enim felicitas est actus perfectus secundum virtutes, non ideo [sequitur] quod virtus et felicitas sint simul, immo virtus est ... disponens ad felicitatem. In the commentary of Kilwardby: Secundo ostendit ipsam non esse felicitatem per duas raciones, quarum prima talis est: virtus est in inperfectis; felicitas non est in eis; ergo etc. Huius racionis primo ponit maiorem, et hoc est: *videtur autem* (95b32). Secundo declarat, dicens quod virtuosi videntur se[s]cedere et dormire et non operari in vita, quamvis scilicet possint operari et non impediantur. Iste autem condiciones sunt inperfectorum; quare habentes virtutem possunt esse inperfecti, et hoc est: *videntur autem* (95b32). C f. 288ra, Pr f. 4ra.

[28] F f. 11rb: Deinde ostendit quod virtus non est felicitas, et est racio talis: virtus est inperfectorum, felicitas non; ergo virtus non est felicitas.

[29] C f. 288rb, Pr f. 4rb: ... addit quod virtuousus non est dicendus felix, nisi sicut dicitur sanus qui utitur pocione; sicut enim hic est in via ad sanitatem, sic virtuosus est in via ad felicitatem, et hoc est: *nisi pocionem* (1096a2:). Si autem sit ibi posicionem, tunc hec est sentencia: nullus dicit virtuosum esse felicem ....

Kilwardby does not wish to introduce this topic to his analysis of the first book of the NE. He concentrates rather on the habitual virtues and understands moral virtues to be a precondition for the higher activity of contemplation. Moral virtue then contributes most to a secondary type of happiness. This reading of Aristotle is similar to the position of Albert the Great, who clearly distinguishes between *felicitas civilis* and *felicitas contemplativa* in his commentaries on the *Ethics*.

The medieval commentators could not completely reject the relevance of a separate universal good to moral philosophy, since they realized that Christian moral theology offers a vision of union with God as the ultimate human goal. The Pseudo-Pecham formulates this moral doctrine succinctly in his analysis of the *Ethica nova*: "Happiness, or the best end of actions, is a means joining us in some way to the uncreated good."[30] No matter how a medieval author understood Aristotle's definition of happiness, the universal uncreated good remained part of the supreme human activity. Most often the universal good was considered to be the external end toward which all human endeavors were directed. For Thomas, it was the *finis cuius*, and for the Pseudo-Pecham it was the *bonum divinum*.[31] Whatever the formulation, the commentators understood Aristotle's description of the *summum bonum hominis* to include God as the ultimate object of human desire. In their interpretations they were not wholly incorrect, since Aristotle makes the highest form of contemplative activity to be consideration of the nature of the first cause. Kilwardby limits his discussion to the analysis of Aristotle's treatment of Plato's position, and refrains from a consideration of the broader theological considerations. He does, however, admit that the Platonic view must be at least partially true. Aristotle did not reject the idea that the supreme good is separate from any particular good, and did not attack the concept of separate forms, which the commentators say necessarily preexist in the divine mind for all created objects. Kilwardby merely dismisses the possibility that an ideal good is predicable of particulars since it remains always distinct from them. He rejected the idea of a separate good because nothing univocal is predicated

[30] F f. 4vb: Felicitas sive finis optimus operationum est medium coniungens nos quodam modo bono increato.

[31] For Thomas, see A. Celano, "The 'Finis Hominis' in the Thirteenth-Century Commentaries on the *Nicomachean Ethics*," *Archives d'histoire doctrinale et littéraire du moyen age*, 53 (1986), 23–53. The Pseudo–Pecham argues: Bonum autem duplex est: divinum, id est a deo collatum, ut felicitas ... et humanum, id est ab hominis per rectas operaciones ... ergo veritas que est obiectum speculativi intellectus prius erit bono quod est obiectum practici. F f. 1ra.

of all categories, but 'good' may refer to all things in a non-univocal manner. If 'good' were univocal then it would refer in the same way to God, the intellect and all other categories. God would not be distinguished substantially from other beings. As a result Aristotle criticized Plato's position. If there were one idea of goodness, then there would be one science of all things said to be good. Since there are many doctrines concerning good things, there cannot be a separate idea of goodness. If there were one separate idea of good, there would necessarily be only one definition of goodness, and a perpetual good would be no better than a temporal one. Such an understanding is impossible, so there can be no univocal idea of goodness.[32]

Kilwardby accepts Aristotle's admonition that a discussion of an ideal separate good may be appropriate to another branch of philosophy. He adds that, in the *Metaphysics*, Aristotle demonstrated that the first cause pertains to all things as the efficient and final cause, but the understanding of the universal good provides little help in the practical arts. A doctor does not consider a universal theory of health, when only one diagnosis pertains to his patient. Even a general understanding of health may have to be adjusted to suit particular cases. Medicine concerns health theoretically, but a good practitioner adapts the theory to meet particular demands.[33]

Kilwardby explains more precisely Aristotle's notion of happiness. If happiness is indeed the end of all actions, moral science must determine which kinds of acts are most appropriate for its attainment. In a general sense, those actions must endure throughout the entirety of an active life. Happiness must also be that act (*opus*) which is proper to a human being *qua* human. One cannot advocate a life of uninterrupted contemplation as a proper definition of happiness since it lies outside the potential of any human being. He then clarifies the terminology that is used to translate the text of Aristotle. He says that an act (*opus*) may be understood as the thing done (*res operata*); while action (*operatio*) may signify the deed (*actum*) in which the act unfolds. The act may be taken as duty (*officium*) and *operacio* may refer to the deed that results from that duty.[34]

The Pseudo-Pecham analyzes the *summum bonum hominis* in a similar manner. Although he does not distinguish the terms '*opus*' and '*operatio*', he considers the relation between action and habit. He claims that Aristotle

---

[32] C f. 288va, Pr f. 4va.   [33] C f. 289rb, Pr f. 5rb.

[34] C f. 289rb, Pr F. 5rb: Et potest per opus intelligi res operata, et per operacionem, actum in quo procedit opus; vel potest per opus intelligi officium; per operacionem, vero actum illius officii.

divided the end into one that is an act and one that is an operation.[35] In some ways the action or operation does not seem better than the act or habit, since the habit perfects the potentiality. The action, however, is a means whereby the potentiality is perfected. As a result, the habit is deemed better than the resulting act.[36] Because Aristotle defines happiness as an action or operation, the Pseudo-Pecham compromises in his conclusion by stating that happiness is both a habit and an operation: ". . . a habit is called an end. And so he [Aristotle] wishes to say that there is a certain end that is only a habit such as virtue; and another end that is not only a habit but also an action, such as happiness."[37] The complex relation between virtue and happiness, habit and operation seems to have caused great difficulty for the earliest commentators on the NE, and not until Albert's great commentary did the Latin authors come to a better understanding of Aristotle's moral terminology.

Kilwardby notes that Aristotle identifies a function for each part of a human being, and therefore it is reasonable to assume a proper operation for a person taken as a whole. This operation must certainly arise from the soul, which is the primary principle of humanity. What is specific to the human species is not life or desire, but rather rationality. The particular human function is to be found in the rational element of the soul, which may obey reason or be in itself rational or intellectual. The latter operation is that which is most properly human. Happiness must concern a rational operation of the soul, which endures throughout a lifetime. The rational soul is both practical and speculative in its operations. Kilwardby claims with some justification that *praxis* takes precedence over speculation.[38] The proper action (*opus*) of human beings must be in accordance with reason, since every human action must conform to reason, or at least not expressly contradict it. He adds that when Aristotle speaks of the action of the soul as a certain type of life, he is not referring to the hylomorphic union of form and matter, but rather to the soul's perfection as living and acting well. This phrase is his basic understanding of Aristotle's concept of

---

[35] F f. 4rb. Item dividit hic finem in finem qui est actus, et in finem qui est opus, et queritur cum opus actus sit quomodo pro diversis accipitur . . .

[36] F f. 4rb: . . . dicit quod in quibusdam est melius opus quam actus sive habitus. Hoc non videtur quia habitus perficit potenciam; opus autem est mediante quo potencia perfectionem acquirit. Unde semper habitu melior quam opus.

[37] F f. 4rb. . . . habitus finis dicitur. Et per hoc vult dicere quod quidam est finis qui est habitus solum, ut virtus; quidam est finis qui non est habitus, sed opus, ut felicitas. F f. 4va.

[38] C f. 290ra, Pr f. 6ra: In prima dicit quod cum anima racionalis duplex sit, scilicet speculativa et practica, ponendum est felicitatem esse circa eam que practica est. Principalior enim est praxis speculacione . . .

happiness. The human good is to live and act well; all other determinations concerning the nature of happiness stem from this definition.[39]

b The cause of happiness

The question of prosperity's role in happiness leads Kilwardby to consider the specific cause of human goodness. Prosperity comes from chance, which is one possible source of happiness. Virtue comes from knowledge and custom, which are human efforts. The third possibility, which every medieval commentator on Aristotle's *Ethics* considered carefully, is divine providence. Kilwardby quickly deflects the question of divine causality by arguing that although to assume happiness to be a divine gift is reasonable, the divine role is better left to metaphysical or theological discussions. He avoids the question of divine causality because he views Aristotle's intention to be limited to the human contribution to happiness. If happiness is not wholly and immediately from a divine source, and is indeed the result of virtue, learning and care, it still is divine and proceeds from God.[40] One should note that Kilwardby, when speaking of habitual virtues, never claims them to constitute human perfection. The role of divine causality remains a topic in all medieval discussions of human perfection, since the prevailing understanding determined union with God to be the supreme good for human beings. Since no person could attain such an end through natural means, God must somehow be the cause of human perfection.[41]

The Pseudo-Pecham regards the problem of divine causality as linked to the question of the two types of happiness. The first way to judge happiness is according to its essence, and so in no way does it depend on human acts, but rather on the first cause alone. The second manner considers happiness insofar as it is the act by which one is made happy or perfect, and then this act belongs to all who possess it as an efficient cause. Even as efficient cause, this act depends on us only insofar as it is received and disposes us through

---

[39] C f. 290rb, Pr f. 6va: Prima enim est ex coniunctione anime cum corpore; secunda autem perfectio anime secundum bene vivere et bene operari. Secundo manifestat quod circa operacionem hominis studiosi est felicitas, dicens quod bonum uniuscuiusque perficitur secundum eius operacionem; quare cum felicitas sit bonum et perfectio anime perficitur secundum operacionem anime, et si plures fuerint eius operaciones, perficietur secundum optimam et perfectissimam . . .

[40] C f. 291vb, Pr. 8ra. In prima dicit quod cum quicquid inest hominibus insit a doctrina, racionale est felicitatem a deo datam esse, cum deus sit causarum optima et felicitas sit bonorum humanorum optimum; sed utrum sic sit vel non alterius scrutacionis est quam civilis, sicut forte metaphisice vel theologie . . . C f. 291vb, Pr. 8ra.

[41] A. Celano, "The Understanding of Beatitude . . .," esp. pp. 8–14.

good actions.[42] The Pseudo-Pecham does not wish to attribute happiness to human actions because he understands it to be the perfection not of the composite being, but only of the separate soul.[43] Since happiness is distinct from virtue, human operations can only dispose one to receive happiness from an external source.[44]

In the anonymous guide for students at Paris the question is succinctly put: "Are we entire cause of good, as we are the entire cause of evil?" The answer seems simple, since the will is the principle of good and evil. There are, however, two ways of providing an answer to this question. The philosophical response is that we are the total cause of good and evil, but the theological position claims we are not because we need an infusion of divine grace, which the theologians call *synderesis*.[45]

A similar resolution is found in Arnoul of Provence's *Divisio scientiarum*. There he claims the good that is the end and perfection of the soul is two-fold: virtue, which is accomplished by human beings, and happiness, which cannot be attained by their actions, but it is something to which we are joined. Arnoul argues that Aristotle speaks of the latter good in the *Ethica nova*.[46] For these early commentators, who understood happiness to be the perfection of the separate soul or a type of Christian beatitude, human causality could never be a sufficient response to the question of its cause.

---

[42] F f. 17ra-b: Quod de felicitate est loqui dupliciter secundum suam essenciam et sic nullo modo dependet ab opere nostro, sed solum a prima causa; vel quo ad eius actum qui est felicitas vel perficere hominem. Sed tunc sciendum est quod actus ille est alicuius, sicut efficiens, et sic predicatur commune, et sic non dependet a nobis, vel sicut recipientis, quia sic non recipitur in aliquo nisi disponatur per operaciones bonas.

[43] F f. 17rb: Virtus est anime proprie in coniuncto secundum philosophum, sed felicitas proprie est anime separate . . . ergo non sunt idem.

[44] F f. 17vb: Cum virtus disponat ad felicitatem, in eodem debet esse virtus et felicitas. Sed in libro sequenti auctor volens ostendere quid sit virtus, enumerat ea quae sunt in anima, non in coniuncto.

[45] C. Lafleur with J. Carrier ed., *Le 'Guide de l'étudiant' d'un maitre anonyme de la faculté des arts de Paris au XIIIᵉ siècle. Édition critique provisoire du ms. Barcelona, Arxiu de la Corona d'Aragó, Ripoll 109, fol 134ra–158va* (Québec: Faculté de Philosophie, Université Laval, 1992), pp. 66, #119 (Hereafter, Le Guide): Utrum nos sumus tota causa boni sicut sumus tota causa mali. Et videtur quod sic . . . quia voluntas est in nobis ut principium utriusque. –Ad hoc quod dicimus quod loquendo philosophice sumus tota causa utrius-que. Loquendo tamen theologice, non sumus sufficienter ad bonum, sed oportet gratiam in nobis a Deo infundi, que a theologis sinderesis appelatur.

[46] C. Lafleur, *Quatre introductions . . .*, p. 335: Nam bonum quod est finis est perfectio anima in hac [parte] maxime consideratur. Bonum autem illud duplex est: quoddam enim est quod est ab homine operabile . . . et huiusmodi bonum est virtus; aliud est bonum quod non est ab homine operabile, set tamen per bonas operationes sibi unibile, quod est felicitas, de qua determinatur in *Nova ethica* . . .

Kilwardby now considers the preliminary discussions on happiness to be complete and now is ready for the final determination concerning its nature. Some human goods, such as external benefits of good fortune, cooperate in the production of happiness. Such instruments are useful, but not necessary, for its attainment. What is necessary for happiness is the best action of the human soul. Happiness, then, is the act of the rational practical soul, consisting in the good and most perfect actions. Act may be understood as the form or perfection of the soul to which it is ultimately ordered, or as the actual actions of the soul in accordance with virtue.

In the examination of the conditions of happiness Kilwardby claims that no irrational being can be rightly called happy, because it does not participate in the civic activities that are part of the supreme moral good. He then considers the proper age of one who can be called happy. What seems to be an elementary problem becomes more complicated with the additional consideration of the effects of fortune on happiness. A child is dismissed from consideration since a young person cannot perform civic duties. The real question, however, involves the effect of misfortunes on a good person. Young adults well on the way to a good life may be affected by such tragic occurrences that they would be unable to actualize their potential for virtue. Even one who has lived virtuously for many years, like Priam, is not immune from the type of disaster that can destroy the good life. Kilwardby sees in the example of Priam a fundamental problem about the nature of the human condition. Can one truly be 'blessed', while one lives, or should judgment about the quality of a life be reserved until death, when the body separates from the soul, and is safe from the disasters that chance may bring in the material world? Kilwardby rejects the possibility that happiness, which is in accordance with a good and perfect activity, could occur after death. 'Human' activity ceases at death, and so it would be incongruous to claim that the perfection of human potential occurs after the human being ceases to be.[47]

Kilwardby is careful to distinguish the philosophical ideal of happiness from the religious notion of perfect beatitude. He indicates that one seeks death only for the sake of another good, which must itself be beatitude, while happiness is never desired for anything other than itself. He concludes, therefore, that happiness cannot come after death. We should note that he correctly uses the term 'beatitude' to refer to a state beyond evils

---

[47] Cf. 292rb, Pr f. 8va: ... felicitas dicitur a nobis esse secundum actum quemdam, scilicet bonum et perfectissimum; sed talis actus non videtur esse in morte vel post mortem; inconveniens est ergo felicitatem esse in morte vel post mortem.

and misfortunes. Whether it is the imperfect beatitude of the happy man blessed by good fortune, or the perfect beatitude of the eternal life, the 'beatus' enjoys constant good fortune.[48] The dilemma presented by human misfortune may extend to the judgment of a person after death. The possibility of catastrophic events occurring to one's friends and relatives may affect the judgments concerning the happiness of those deceased. The response that a living person who bears calamity well would not apply in such cases. Kilwardby is reluctant to respond, but claims it is unlikely that such remote changes can alter the fate of the dead.[49]

The final discussion on the cause of happiness considers a widely circulated variant of the *Ethica nova*. The Greek text concludes the discussion of fortune with the assertion that human beings can be blessed, but only as humans (μακαρίους δ'ἀνθρώπους: NE 1101a2021). In several manuscripts of the *Ethica nova*, this phrase is translated not as "*beatos ut homines*," but rather as "*beatos autem homines ut angelos.*"[50] The idea that human beings could be blessed as angels led many early commentators to reformulate the interpretation of the NE in a decidedly un-Aristotelian manner. They discussed the possibility that the human moral good may be the perfection of the separate soul. The anonymous examination guide asks whether the body is able to receive happiness as does the soul, for the body seems to merit it as well. The resolution is a theological response:

Because it is true that the body receives happiness, since the theologians assert that the soul reunites with the body after death. This is more miraculous than natural. For this is simply unnatural and so it is not asserted by the philosophers. And therefore since happiness is after death, as the author [Aristotle] demonstrates [*NE*, 100a11], and the philosophers do not claim the soul after death is joined to the body, then happiness naturally belongs properly to the soul alone and not to the body.[51]

---

[48] Secundo inquirit an sit post mortem, et procedit sic: primo dat racionem per quam posset videri felicitatem inesse post mortem talem; ille necessario beatus est, qui est extra mala et infortuna.

[49] C f. 292ra, Pr f. 8vb: Inconveniens eciam erit si bona vel mala nepotum in ullo tempore redundent ad parentes, ut circa eos faciant transmutacionem; et in hoc videtur significare quod mortuus non sit felix.

[50] *Ethica Nicomachea, Ethica nova*, ed. R.-A. Gauthier, *Aristoteles Latinus* (Leiden: Brill, & Brussels: Desclée de Brouwer, 1972), v. 26, 1–3 (fasc. 2), p. 88, l. 14.

[51] *Le Guide*, p. 59, #94: utrum corpus sit natum recipere felicitatem sicut anima ... Et ita videtur corpus mereri sicut anima. – Ad hoc dicimus quod secundum theologos hic habet veritatem, quia ponunt animam reiungi corpori post mortem. Sed hoc est plus per miraculum quam per naturam. Simpliciter enim hoc est innaturale, et ideo non ponitur a philosophis. Et propter hoc cum felicitas sit post mortem, sicut probat hic auctor, et non ponunt philosophi animam post mortem coniungi corpori, ideo proprie felicitas per naturam debetur solum anime et non corpori.

The Pseudo-Pecham considers the text in a similar manner: "He [Aristotle] says that men should be called blessed as angels; and so since a man is not like an angel except by reason of the soul, there should be a determination about the soul itself."[52] Despite the corruption of Aristotle's text, the Pseudo-Pecham does not think Aristotle attributed beatitude to the separate soul itself, and correctly judges happiness to occur to the soul disposed by good actions.[53] While the Pseudo-Pecham denies that Aristotle attributed happiness to the separate soul, he makes a distinction between the philosophical and theological determinations of the human good: "The soul's virtue properly belongs to the composite according to the Philosopher, but happiness properly belongs to the separate soul; virtue and happiness, therefore, are not the same."[54] Virtue is dispositive only and certain virtues that are most important for happiness are characteristic of the separate soul. He implies a distinction within virtues and subsequently within moral theory as well. Habitual virtues belong to the composite and the intellectual virtues, which comprise happiness, and are proper to the separate soul.[55]

Kilwardby, although aware of the corruption, does not think Aristotle considered the possibility of beatitude for the separate soul. He reads 'beatos ut angelos' not as a reference to immortal life, but rather as an indication of perfection within the realm of human potentiality. Just as angels are perfect according to their being, so too are humans in theirs. There is no discussion of eternal beatitude, or happiness, for the separate soul. Such topics are not pertinent to the science of ethics, and Aristotle did not determine such a question in any way at all.[56] Kilwardby's response

[52] F f. 17vb: Item inferius dicit quod homines beati dicendi sunt ut angeli, ergo cum homo non sit ut angleus nisi ratione animi determinatio erit per se anime.
[53] F f. 18ra: . . . quod homines beati dicuntur esse sicut angeli, non quia beatitudo sit hominis ratione anime ut est separate. See also G. Wieland, Ethica–*scientia practica*, p. 168, n. 168: anima enim per se non est cui conferatur felicitas, sed anima disposita per bonas operationes.
[54] F f. 17vb: Virtus est anime proprie in coniuncto secundum philosophum, sed felicitas proprie est anime separate . . . ergo non sunt idem.
[55] F f. 17vb: Cum virtus disponat ad felicitatem in eodem debet esse virtus et felicitas; sed in libro sequenti auctor volens ostendere quid sit virtus enumerat ea que sunt in anima, non in coniuncto ut per hoc habeatur quid est virtus, quare virtus est anime non coniuncti, ergo et felicitas.
[56] C f. 293va, Pr9vb: Et addit qualiter dicemus eos beatos, ut angelos; et hoc sic intelligendum est non quia homines viventes inmortales sint sicut angeli, sed quia perfecti sunt in ordine suo, sicut angeli in ordine suo; sicut enim intelligencie non licenciantur ad malum, nec declinant a bono, similiter huiusmodi homines nunquam ad malum declinant bonum relinquentes . . . Habemus ergo determinacionem prime questionis: scilicet utrum vivens felicitabitur vel non; et videtur Aristotiles determinasse iam quod sic. Et

became the standard explanation of the text, '*beatos ut homines*', and despite the corruption of his own text, he provided an insightful and accurate analysis of Aristotle's intention.[57]

c The relation of virtue to happiness

Kilwardby now discusses one of the most interesting questions in the early commentaries on Aristotle's *Ethics*: the relation of virtue to happiness. The Aristotelian position perplexed the earliest commentators, who failed to realize the essential contribution of virtue to happiness. Despite his earlier remarks about virtue, Kilwardby claims here that virtue is an inferior good ordered to happiness. He reiterates Aristotle's definition of happiness as an act of soul according to perfect virtue and concludes that virtue needs to be considered. 'Act', he argues, is to be understood as perfection. Although he views happiness as the perfection or actuality of the soul's potentiality, Kilwardby does not realize that the very act of perfection is the exercise itself of virtue. He subordinates virtue to happiness and makes it a means to a superior end. Kilwardby distinguishes human virtue, which concerns the soul, from happiness, which perfects the soul. As a result of the distinction, the moral philosopher must consider carefully the nature of the soul as it relates to the way in which virtue is acquired.

The anonymous guide for students differentiates between happiness and virtue as well. Virtue, said by some to be the primary subject of ethics because it is the means by which happiness is attained, is subordinate to happiness, the end for which all actions are performed. Happiness is the most perfect good among all particular goods.[58] The author of the guide makes his position clear when he asserts that virtue is a means through which happiness is acquired.[59] As R.-A. Gauthier has shown, the early medieval commentators on the NE saw the distinction between happiness

hoc dico de illa felicitate de qua locutus est in hoc libro, quam ipse semper et ubique vocat actum perfectum secundum virtutem. Unde forte non intendit de illa felicitate nisi que dicitur vita secundum modum doctrine civilis; nec debuit forte doctrina civilis de felicitate alia pertractari. Utrum enim post mortem felicitetur anima vel totus homo forte non pertinet ad ipsam, nec hoc determinat Aristotiles.

[57] See Thomas Aquinas, *Sententia libri Ethicorum* (=SLE), ed. Leon., 47, 1–2, (Rome, 1969) p. 60, ll. 215–225. DOS, p. 124, #352: Et [Aristoteles] locutus est ipse de virtutibus consuetudinalibus tantum non de theologicis.

[58] *Le Guide*, p. 54, #77:

[59] *Le Guide*, p. 55, #79: ostendit quod de virtute dicendum est et quare, quia virtus est medium per quod acquiritur huiusmodi felicitas. Also p. 58, #90: Sed si probantur passiones [virtutis], hoc non est propter se, sed prout est principium ad felicitatem vel medium.

and virtue as the rationale for the division between the *Ethica nova* and *vetus*. Virtue, which humans accomplish through their own means, is treated in the *Ethica vetus*; happiness, to which they can only be united, is discussed in the *Ethica nova*.[60]

The Pseudo-Pecham claims that happiness will be simply prior to virtue, and that virtue is ordered to happiness as its prize. Virtue can only be a disposition to the supreme good.[61] He tries to provide a rationale for his strict separation between virtue and happiness by arguing that an end, which is a habit alone, differs from one that is both habit and act. Virtue is the former and happiness, the latter, as was shown above. An act and habit together are superior to a habit alone; happiness, therefore, is a separate end superior to virtue.[62] Like his contemporaries, the Pseudo-Pecham recognized the supreme end desired by human beings to be God. No virtuous activity was sufficient to attain such an end, and so Aristotle's *Ethics* had to be reinterpreted to allow human actions to be directed toward an uncreated good.[63] He concludes that Aristotle's position on the role of virtue in happiness is poorly constructed. Aristotle, he claims, will say later that happiness is not present (*inest*) according to virtue; since it is nobler than any human good it is not present (*inest*) according to any good of man. Aristotle, therefore, demonstrates badly that it is present according to virtue or a good action of the soul.[64] The function of virtue in the production of happiness is merely to dispose the soul so that happiness may be united to it. The young do not have sufficient good habits to allow for the dispositive and mediating process of virtue to begin; happiness, therefore, cannot be united to them.[65]

---

[60] R.-A. Gauthier, "Arnoul de Provence et la doctrine de la 'fronesis', vertu mystique suprême," *Revue du Moyen Âge Latin*, 19 (1963), 146. Again Gauthier notes this position is certainly not that of Aristotle.

[61] F f. 2vb: . . . ergo felicitas prior erit simpliciter virtute; Moralis philosphus principaliter intendit de felicitate, et de ea primo determinat, et quia virtus ordinatur ad felicitatem. F f. 2ra: Est autem felicitas bravium virtutis, unde virtus est disposicio ad optimum.

[62] F f. 4va: Et per hoc vult dicere quod quidam est finis qui est habitus solum, ut virtus; quidam est finis qui non solum est habitus, sed [eciam] opus, ut felicitas.

[63] F f. 4vb: Felicitas sive finis optimus operacionum est medium coniungens nos quodam modo bono increato.

[64] F f. 19va: De primo sic: Aristotiles in parte sequenti dicet quod felicitas non inest secundum virtutem; immo cum sit nobilius quolibet bono humano ostendit quod non inest secundum aliquid bonum hominis. Male ergo ostendit hoc quod inest secundum virtutem sive secundum anime bonam actionem.

[65] F f. 25vb: Quod felicitas unitur anime mediantibus dispositis, scilicet per habitus bonos disponentes ad eius inceptionem et mediantibus operacionibus bonis quibus, quia caret puer, non potest uniri felicitas.

The rational part of the soul acts in accordance with rational commands and thus participates in reason when acting. The implication, according to Kilwardby, is that human inclinations tend toward the irrational and must be restrained by reason. Rational actions are most obvious in courageous and honest persons than in any others because in them the sensitive part is most disposed to obey reason. Honesty is wholly consistent with reason, probably because its effects are usually detrimental to the corporeal desires of the agent.[66]

Virtues of the wholly irrational part of the soul are irrelevant to ethics, but the concupiscible and irascible elements need the dictates of reason, just as some people listen to the advice of friends and relatives. Such virtue is not deduced as a mathematical formula, but is the result of experience and practical judgments. Only reason can judge an act that proceeds from sensitive desires, while human virtue principally concerns the part of the soul that has of itself reason. Kilwardby describes the activity whereby reason rules sensitive desires as a three-fold process: One must perceive (*videre*) and understand what reason shows; one must then discern (*discernere*) its significance; finally, one must choose (*eligere*) what reason proposes (*deprecatur*).[67]

The division within the soul gives rise to a corresponding division into intellectual and moral virtues. The former are wisdom, *fronesis* and intelligence; the latter are liberty and honesty, although earlier in the commentary they were identified as honesty and courage. The intellectual virtues perfect the soul through the activities of speculation and understanding. The habitual moral virtues perform and inform the intellect in action. Intelligence is defined as cognition only, but wisdom is cognition with delight. *Fronesis* is a certain type of prudence and is a choice of what is previously known and desired. Honesty and liberty are not an exhaustive list, but merely examples of moral virtues.[68]

---

[66] C f. 294vb, Pr f. 11rb: Et addit quod magis subiecta est sensitiva racioni secundum quod est hominis fortis et honesti quam secundum quod est cuiuslibet alterius, quia in honesto et forti est sensitiva magis disposita ad obedienciam racionis. Honesta enim omnino consonant racioni . . .

[67] C f. 295ra, Pr f. 11rb: . . . et magis forte ad intencionem Aristotilis quod sensitiva debet primo videre et intueri que ostendit racio; postea vero discernere circa ea, sicut discernit racio; ultimo vero eligere ea que deprecatur racio.

[68] C f. 295ra, Pr f. 11va: Et patet sufficiencia huius divisionis considerando divisionem intellectus per practicum et speculativum. Intellectuales enim perficiunt speculativum; morales vero practicum. Per intelligenciam autem intellige cognicionem tantum; per sapienciam cognicionem cum delectacione; per fronesim, que prudencia quedam est, electionem prius cognitorum et amatorum. Et ex hiis patet sufficiencia trium

Unlike Arnoul of Provence or the Pseudo-Pecham, who elevate *fronesis* to a supreme virtue, by which a human being is united to God,[69] Kilwardby does not consider it to be superior to the other intellectual virtues. While his contemporaries understood happiness to consist in a union with the uncreated good, Kilwardby limits his discussion here to the concept of living and acting well. He is unaware of the central role practical wisdom (*phronesis*) has in the psychology of the moral act, since he does not have Book VI of the NE available to him. He sees no need for a supreme intellectual virtue uniting man to God. Kilwardby understands prudence (*fronesis*) to be both an intellectual and practical virtue, despite Aristotle's description of it as an intellectual virtue only. He thinks that Aristotle's classification unduly limits the scope of prudential decisions. Moral virtues pertain to more than mere speculation and the designation, 'intellectual', must be understood in relation to the object of thought. Intelligence, wisdom and prudence, when directed toward understanding of the first being are termed intellectual; when they consider inferior objects they are not.[70]

Kilwardby argues that the moral virtues direct human actions with respect to inferior things and are located in the rational, not the sensitive, part of the soul. He indicates also that a consideration of three intellectual virtues is sufficient for Aristotle's purposes. He describes these virtues in a way that was common at Paris in the 1240s: intelligence is the recognition of the first being; wisdom adds the aspect of love to recognition; and *fronesis* allows the human being a measure of participation in what is already recognized and loved. As Gauthier notes, the commentators of this era had not yet fully comprehended the aim of Aristotle's *Ethics*.[71] Still greatly influenced by theological traditions, but also by Aristotle's praise of the contemplative life, they viewed the intellectual virtues as a philosophical expression of their own assumption that the primary goal of ethics was the unification of man with God. The examination guide for students summarizes these views:

Intellectual virtue exists through the contemplation and investigation of divine matters, whereby one is brought to love the first being above all. Thus, such virtue does not have to be known through some actions, but is totally spiritual, and so

intellectualium quas ponit: per libertatem autem et honestatem non intendit sufficientem divisionem virtutum moralium, sed magis explanacionem exemplarem . . .

[69] R.-A. Gauthier, "Arnoul de Provence . . .", p. 152.

[70] Cf. 295rb, Pr f. 11vb: Similiter et fronesis, cum sit prudencia in eligendo prius cognita et amata; aut hoc est in comparacione ad hec inferiora, aut ad primum. Et secundo modo est virtus intellectualis, primo modo non.

[71] See R.-A. Gauthier, "Arnoul de Provence . . .", pp. 150–151.

STEVENS, TIM, 1973-

CYBER SECURITY AND THE POLITICS OF TIME.

                              Cloth   269 P.
CAMBRIDGE: CAMBRIDGE UNIV PRESS, 2016

AUTH: ROYAL HOLLOWAY, UNIV. OF LONDON. REVISED
DISSERTATION. EXAMINES ISSUES OF TIME/TEMPORALITY.
LCCN 2015016413
  ISBN 1107109426   **Library PO#** FIRM ORDERS
                                    List   99.99 USD
  8395 NATIONAL UNIVERSITY LIBRAR   **Disc**   14.0%
  App. Date   3/30/16 SOPS   8214-08 **Net**   85.99 USD

SUBJ: TECHNOLOGY & INTERNATIONAL RELATIONS.

CLASS JZ1254   DEWEY# 327.1028558   LEVEL ADV-AC

YBP Library Services

STEVENS, TIM, 1973-

CYBER SECURITY AND THE POLITICS OF TIME.

                              Cloth   269 P.
CAMBRIDGE: CAMBRIDGE UNIV PRESS, 2016

AUTH: ROYAL HOLLOWAY, UNIV. OF LONDON. REVISED
DISSERTATION. EXAMINES ISSUES OF TIME/TEMPORALITY.
  LCCN 2015016413
  ISBN 1107109426   **Library PO#** FIRM ORDERS
                                    List   99.99 USD
  8395 NATIONAL UNIVERSITY LIBRAR   **Disc**   14.0%
  App. Date   3/30/16 SOPS   8214-08 **Net**   85.99 USD

SUBJ: TECHNOLOGY & INTERNATIONAL RELATIONS.

CLASS JZ1254   DEWEY# 327.1028558   LEVEL ADV-AC

there is no such recognition or knowledge of its properties. Or such virtue can be said to be in those in whom divine grace is most inspired.[72]

While the author does not consider the intellectual virtues merely as a different way to express the need for grace, he still understands them as steps leading to love and knowledge of God.

d The habitual virtues

In the commentary on the *Ethica vetus* contained only in the manuscript from Cambridge, Kilwardby examines topics that are less contentious than the opinions on the nature and cause of human happiness. He considers generally the topic of habitual virtues. His first assertion is that they do not arise from nature. He again distinguishes habitual virtue from intellectual virtues by stating that intellectual virtues are generated by teaching, which requires time and experience. His argument is not very convincing, since the habitual virtues would also require time and experience to develop. Still he correctly recognizes that the principles of the intellectual virtues cannot be deduced without a range of experiences over a lengthy period of time.[73] Habitual virtues are not created by nature, but by repeated actions. The genesis of moral virtue depends upon the relation of act and habit. The relation is not that of prior and posterior, but rather a reciprocal one. The act of virtue precedes the habit, and virtue is generated by human choice and action. The acquisition of habitual virtue is comparable to a mechanical or technical skill. There is a traditional aspect to such areas in that a skilled practitioner teaches others the best way to act effectively. Kilwardby shows a perceptive understanding of Aristotle's concept of virtue when he recognizes the importance of traditional practices. Virtue, while partially dependent on human nature, can only be learned by the observation of those who are virtuous. Without benefit of the discussion of *phronesis*, Kilwardby understands that human beings learn virtue best from others. The acquisition of habitual virtue is a process like the development of a skill. Just as one is not a carpenter who cuts a piece of wood properly, one is not honest who tells the truth occasionally. The truthful responses are the material from which a habit is built. Only when the acts

---

[72] *Le Guide*, pp. 60–61, # 101.
[73] C f. 295va: Item quia huiusmodi fit ex doctrina, ideo indigat experimento et tempore; huiusmodi enim virtus non sit [consuetudinalis]; universale autem non habetur sine experimento. Item experimentum precedit cogniciones sensitive et memorie que sine mora temporis fieri non possunt . . .

proceed from the habit is the virtue realized. The duty of legislators is to assure that good actions are performed within their city. In this way, the transmission of the moral virtues, which comprise the political tradition, is handed down from one generation to the next.[74]

When considering the origin of habitual virtue, Kilwardby knows the process is more complicated than the normal relation of cause and effect. Habits of action are in a way the material cause of virtues, since they precede, and are in potency to, the actual virtuous states. They are also the efficient causes as well, since they move and actualize the soul's potential to virtue.[75] The genesis of virtues is always a complicated process because the actions generate the habits, and these habits determine further good actions of the same kind.

The science of ethics is not merely an intellectual pursuit, but its goal is to "make us good." The practical considerations lead to a flexibility in doctrine that must consider the various circumstances affecting right decisions.[76] The primary consideration is the common principle of acting according to right reason. Right reason cannot prescribe specific responses, but rather it is itself good or the soul's potency infused by good. As such, reason leads lower virtues toward the human good and away from evil. Kilwardby is not entirely satisfied with Aristotle's explanation of right reason, and seems to think it vague. He wonders whether there is a fuller explanation of the idea in the books unavailable to him. He does, however, realize the importance of choice (*proheresis*) in right reason. He finally accepts right reason as a good intention and choice.[77]

---

[74] C f. 295vb.

[75] C f. 295vb Per hoc enim quod dicit ex eisdem significat quodammodo ipsas materiales esse ad virtutem. Precedunt enim et sunt in potencia respectu complecionis que est virtus. Per hoc quod dicit *et per eadem* (1103b7) significat easdem in racione efficientis aliquo modo; movent enim et operantur quod fit virtus [et] ad ipsam finaliter ordinantur.

[76] C f. 295vb: ... non enim scrutatur de virtute ut sciamus quid est virtus ibi statum faciendo, sed ut boni fiamus. Hoc autem non potest fieri, nisi per operacionem sub debitis circumstanciis operatas; ergo necesse [est] considerare si[c] circumstancias operacionum per quas fiamus boni. C f. 296ra.

[77] C f. 296ra: quia cum sic dicendo rectam racionem, non videtur esse circumstancia in operando, potest dici quod recta racio sit idem quod proheresis de qua determinat vel in tercio, vel quod fit intencio bona in operando que forte non est aliud a proheresi; et tunc potest dici quod non determinatur de recta racione in aliquo librorum quos habemus in tercio. A similar understanding of the nature of ethics is offered by the Pseudo-Pecham: Dico quoniam civilis determinans bonum optimum per bona sensibilia quia determinat ipsum ut boni fiamus quid sit. Et illa bona sensibilia causa sunt ex parte nostra quare bonum optimum in nobis acquiratur. F f. 7va.

The theological *Summae* and the commentaries on the NE from the first half of the thirteenth century were instrumental in the development of moral thought in the Middle Ages. William of Auxerre identified natural law as the expression of reason and the source of universal moral principles. He also recognized an implied connection between *synderesis* and natural law and emphasized the imperative function of the virtue of prudence. Philip the Chancellor discussed extensively philosophical topics concerning prudence, *synderesis* and moral choice in a theological treatise. He elevated *synderesis* to a supreme moral power that leads to perfect goodness. For him all ethical actions must ultimately lead to perfect beatitude. In the commentaries on the text of the NE and in the various treatises on the sciences that appeared before 1248 the authors attempted to understand the intent and meaning of Aristotle's moral thought. Although not entirely successful, they identified the main questions and troublesome passages in Aristotle's work. Their treatment of issues on the nature of goodness, the meaning and cause of happiness and the definition of virtue provided a basis upon which subsequent, more gifted, theologians, such as Albert, Thomas and Bonaventure could build their theories. The two approaches to ethical questions, one theological, the other philosophical, become unified in the deeper and richer philosophical and theological products of later thirteenth-century authors, but the earlier contributions constitute an important phase in the understanding of Aristotle's ethics in medieval moral theory.

5

The early moral works of Albert the Great

The work of Albert the Great marks a significant development in the understanding of ethics in the thirteenth century. The beneficiary of the new translation of the entire text of the NE with the accompanying Greek commentaries, Albert produced two extensive commentaries on the entire text of Aristotle. The first commentary, the *Super Ethica*, completed shortly before 1250, was, together with the *Summa theologiae*, I–II and II–II of Thomas Aquinas, the most influential work on Ethics in the Middle Ages.[1] Before he was able to analyze the entire range of Aristotelian moral questions, Albert addressed topics that reflected the state of moral enquiry in the first half of the century. His first works on ethical topics, the *De bono, De natura boni* and the so-called *De homine*, rely heavily on the partial translation of the NE that was available before Grosseteste's translation. In all his works Albert accepts the main idea that all human actions are directed toward a single end, which he and his contemporaries accepted as happiness. How such a goal was attained is the thread that unites all his writings on ethics. His main early work on the topic is the *De bono*, which begins with questions concerning goodness in general, the convertibility of goodness with being and truth, and dependence of all good on the supreme being. In this work Albert describes all being as good insofar as it participates in the transcendental divine goodness. This divine good is "the divine intellect, [which is] the efficient, formal and final cause, as well as the origin and the preserving principle of being, and the final goal of all created

---

[1] R.-A. Gauthier, "Trois commentaires 'averroistes' sur *l'Ethique à Nicomaque*," *Archives d'histoire doctrinale et littéraire du moyen âge*, 16 (1947–1948), 187–336; Introduction to R.-A. Gauthier and Y. Jolif, *L'Éthique à Nicomaque, trans. et comm.* (Louvain: Publications universitaires, 1970), pp. 120–124.

good."[2] Despite these complicated metaphysical and epistemological topics, Albert quickly turns his attention to a concentration of human moral goodness. He makes his interest clear when he accepts Aristotle's definition of goodness as that which all seek, a passage taken from the opening lines of the NE. Even in discussions on goodness in general, Albert tends to investigate the way in which the human appetite should desire appropriate ends. After a cursory discussion of the more general topics concerning goodness, Albert turns his attention to the specific subject of moral goodness (*De bono*, tr. I, q. 2, a.4). The first division is into goodness that results from habit or custom, and that which proceeds from grace. Habitual goodness is usually divided further into general goodness, circumstantial goodness and the goodness of political virtue.[3]

The primary subject of morality, which provides the conditions for praise and blame, falls under the heading of general goodness. In other words, the general good involves virtue and vice, which arise from a voluntary act involving choice and deliberation, since one must choose between contrary demands.[4] The conditions accompanying an act do not constitute the act as act, but rather convey the nature of what is proper or blameworthy. Circumstances may be external to the act, but they are integral to its worth,[5] and provide a certain modality that is essential to the nature of virtue and vice.[6]

The introductory questions on political virtues contain a distinction between happiness and virtue common in the first half of the thirteenth century. Happiness is seen as a state of perfection distinct from virtue. Although many early commentators repeat Aristotle's definition that happiness consists in the exercise of virtue, they seem to view happiness as an achievement that comes from virtues, but is distinct from them.[7] The end in ethics is two-fold, just as the end in nature. The natural end, maintained in one act, is form; the end maintained in many acts is what Albert calls the perpetuity of nature whereby one is assimilated to the divine being. In

[2] H. Anzulewicz, "'Bonum' als Schlüsselbegriff bei Albertus Magnus," in *Albertus Magnus zum Gedenken nach 800 Jahren: Neue Zugänge, Aspekte und Perspektiven*, ed. W. Senner *et al.* (Berlin: Akademie Verlag, 2001), p. 116.

[3] *De bono* in *Alberti Magni Opera omnia* 28, ed. H. Kühle *et al.* (Münster: Aschendorff, 1951), tr. I, q. 2, a. 4, p. 28, ll. 11–16.

[4] *De bono*, tr. I, q.2, a. 4, p. 29, ll. 42–49.   [5] *De bono*, tr I, q. 3, a. 2, p. 38, ll. 7–20.

[6] *De bono*, tr. I, q. 3, art. 2, p. 38, ll. 48–50.

[7] *De bono*, tr. I, q. 4, Introduction, p. 43, ll. 3–5. See A. Celano, "The Understanding of Beatitude, the Perfection of the Soul in the Early Latin Commentaries on Aristotle's *Nicomachean Ethics*," *Documenti e Studi Sulla Tradizione Filosofica Medievale*, 17 (2006), 1–22.

morality the motivating potency in one act according to matter moves by specifying and distinguishing the will existing in act. Virtues and vices take their specific nature according to this end. A second end, which is not attained in any one act or virtue, is beatitude or happiness.[8] The motivating power of the will allows human beings to be responsible for their own virtuous or vicious states. Human beings have an innate ability to produce virtue according to a 'natural potency'. This power is not completely material, but is the product of an act and the consequent operations of correct choice and desire. Albert agrees with the philosophers who argue that the natural power for virtue results from both the material and efficient potencies.[9] The philosophers claim that operations develop the habits that produce virtues and vices, and actions in accordance with right reason create the proper operations. Theologians, however, concede that only with divine teaching and assistance can true goodness result. God may grant certain gifts without any human cooperation, such as the effects of grace, but human beings must contribute to habitual and natural operations.[10]

Albert compares intellectual principles to those that govern moral actions, and concludes with Aristotle that while universal principles exist naturally in the intellect they are not the same as moral principles. Since the latter principles are wholly related to human acts, they cannot be actually within the soul naturally. Citing a passage from book two of the NE, Albert concludes that one has an innate ability to begin the process toward virtue, but needs habituation to perfect it.[11] The intellectual principles are complete in the intellect because they are merely to be known through cognition. Even after the moral principles are recognized, they must govern actions in order to produce a virtuous habit. To know them only is not sufficient for moral virtue, whereas knowledge alone is the end in the intellectual sphere. The will governs choice in the moral act, and it may direct one to abide by, or ignore, moral principles. Choice is constituted by the following three components. The first involves the object that must be subject to deliberation (*consiliabile*). Deliberation, as Aristotle explains, never considers the end of action, but only the means that are useful in the acquisition of the desired end. The second aspect of choice arises from the potency that is understood as desire. This desire can be thought of as a certain wish that chooses one alternative as leading to the end. The third component of choice is the act that lies within human power.[12]

---

[8] *De bono*, tr. I, q. 4, a. 1, pp. 44–45, ll. 76–11.   [9] *De bono*, tr. I, q. 4, a. 2, p. 49, ll. 3–17.
[10] *De bono*, tr. 1, q. 4, a. 2, p. 49, ll. 48–53.   [11] *De bono*, tr. I, q. 4, a. 2, p. 49, ll. 70–78.
[12] *De bono*, tr. I, q. 4, a. 6, p. 61, ll. 15–31.

Aristotle, in Albert's view, distinguished between what is voluntary and the will that directs choice. Voluntary actions are a more general category than those of choice (*prohaereticum*) in that the former are actions governed by the appetite motivated by imagination or intellect. In this way children and animals are thought to have voluntary actions. The will refers only to a more limited class of actions that use reason.[13] If one were to claim that the will at times precedes reason and acts without its counsel, Albert responds that such a process does not truly reflect human choice. Albert insists that true choice always involves the use of deliberative reason. When he considers the question whether choice is an act of will, he cites Aristotle's claim that not every act of will is a true choice, but only those which seek the attainment of an end. Choice always involves reason and intellect deliberating about the desired goal. Such an understanding of choice led Aristotle to align choice closely with the act of will according to Albert's reading of the NE.[14]

John Damascene defined deliberation as inquisitive appetite since the appetite is the general principle of motivation. In the form of the appetite all motivating powers are united. As a result, practical reason may be reduced to the appetite that pursues what should, or shuns what should not, be done. In a stricter understanding of appetite, which is divided into desire and will, reason should not be understood as the appetite it self or even part of it.[15] A good act is absolutely voluntary and undetermined, and depends upon deliberation and choice to direct one to the proper end. Deliberation and choice select the appropriate means to the desired end.[16] In response to the question whether the will is the entire cause of virtue, Albert cites Aristotle's distinction between habit and virtue. Human beings control operations from beginning to end when they are aware of the relevant particular facts that contribute to the operation. Although the moral agent controls the beginning of habits, particular elements may arise that cannot be foreknown. Since human power allows a variety of actions, habits may be termed voluntary, which seems contradictory, since many use habitual behavior to excuse them from responsibility. Albert, however, understands Aristotle's distinction to mean that operations are entirely voluntary, but habits are voluntary only in their principle, which Albert understands to be those operations that lead to the formulation of habits.[17]

---

[13] *De bono*, tr. I, q. 4, a. 6, p. 61, 39–47.   [14] *De bono*, tr. I, q. 4, a. 6, p. 61, ll. 83–90.
[15] *De bono*, tr. I, q. 4, a. 7, p. 63, ll. 65–74.   [16] *De bono*, tr. I, q. 4, a. 8, p. 65, ll. 64–69.
[17] *De bono*, tr. I, q. 4, a. 8, p. 66, ll. 1–15.

In the *De bono* Albert accepts four different definitions of virtue, two of which come from the works of Augustine, and the other two from the writings of Cicero and Aristotle. Augustine, as Peter Lombard remarks, defined virtue as a good mental quality by which one lives rightly, which no one misuses, and which God works within us without us. Augustine's second definition makes virtue the correct order of love. For Cicero virtue is a mental habit in harmony with nature, moderation and reason. Aristotle defines virtue as a voluntary habit consisting in a mean relative to us, as reason determines, and as a wise person will decide.[18] Albert accepts all these definitions and uses them at various times to ascertain the nature of human excellence, but unites them all in his own succinct rendering of virtue as the perfection of the motivating powers of the soul. His definition leads him to consider various opinions on the nature of the four cardinal virtues, which Albert initially calls political. Albert, like Philip the Chancellor, distinguishes the virtues according to the principal acts of the potencies, and not by the mental powers themselves. Temperance develops from the constraint of desire by reason; courage comes from an irascible act directed to the overcoming of difficulties; justice is an act of reason discerning and rendering what is owed to another; prudence is an absolute act of reason that distinguishes good from evil as they relate to each individual person.[19] Another way to divide virtues arises from the law of reason and the law of nature. The law of reason consists in the ability to discern good from evil, which is the task of prudence. The law of nature is found in the ability to do what is personally useful, or to distribute what is owed to others. In accomplishing good one becomes temperate, and in overcoming evil, brave. In giving what is due to others one achieves justice.[20]

a Prudence, an intellectual cardinal virtue

In his own understanding of the virtues as the motivating powers of the soul, Albert distinguishes between an ordering, and an ordered, potency. The former is reason, while the latter category is found in both irascible and concupiscible potencies. The order of reason that leads to the best actions is determined by the intention to do good. Such an order manifests itself either with respect to a mean that lies in the operations or passions, or with regard to someone else to which the operation or passion is referred. In the first way, prudence displaying the mean is the perfection of reason; in the

---

[18] *De bono*, tr. I, q. 5, a. 1, p. 67, ll. 6–18.   [19] *De bono*, tr. I, q. 6, a. 1, p. 79, ll. 22–31.
[20] *De bono*, tr. I, q. 6, a. 1, p. 79, ll. 53–63.

second way, its perfection is justice directing action in accordance to what is owed to another. The ordered powers of the soul are perfected by temperance and courage.[21] These cardinal virtues are so named because all others that are comprised of operations and passions relative to a mean are reduced to the primary virtues. They are also termed political or civic virtues because the state perfects itself in the exercise of the cardinal virtues.[22]

Whatever order one may ascribe to the development of the cardinal virtues, prudence is the principle that governs choice. If one were to consider the virtues from the perspective of the soul's powers, then prudence and justice, as the manifestation of reason, are prior to courage and temperance. Because choice determines operations, prudence is prior to all other virtues in indicating the best course of actions. If, however, one were to consider the virtues in relation to habituation, prudence is generated last, since it originates more from experience and teaching than from habituation alone.[23] The combination of the intellectual and habitual aspects makes prudence slower in development than the other cardinal virtues.

The analysis of the four cardinal virtues comprises the greatest part of the *De bono*. The examination of prudence begins with definitions taken from both Christian and ancient sources, which concur in designating prudence as a virtue essential to human integrity.[24] To those who preclude prudence from the list of virtues because of its intellectual nature, Albert cites Aristotle's claim that all willing exists in reason in such a way that the will is the moving element (*motor*) of reason, and thereby is antecedently ordered to reason. As a result, the voluntary act of reason is caused. Prudence, as a virtue, consists in reason, and is a voluntary habit that responds to both praise and blame. It is not merely an intellectual process of deductive reasoning.[25] Since something is freely willed, or at least willed in conjunction with reason, the act of prudence is not merely the final premise of syllogistic reasoning or some other intellectual process.

The specific nature of the prudential habit harmonizes with reason in a natural way, and not in the manner of art. Insofar as prudence is a virtue, it does not consist in reason, except as it is moved antecedently by the will. As

---

[21] *De bono*, tr. I, q. 6, a. 1, p. 80, ll. 21–41.

[22] *De bono*, tr. I, q. 6, a. 2, p. 80, ll. 75–80: Principales autem dicuntur ista virtutes, eo quod aliae, quae sunt in operationibus et passionibus consistentibus in medio, ad ipsas habent reductionem. Politicae vero, idest civiles, dicuntur, eo quod in ipsis et in operibus earum perfectionem habet res publicae secundum optimum statum civium.

[23] *De bono*, tr. I, q. 6, a. 3, p. 81, ll. 28–64.

[24] *De bono*, tr. IV, q. 1, a. 1, p. 218, ll. 82–84: Dicendum, quod in veritate prudentia virtus est et pars honestatis ut dicunt sancti et philosphi.

[25] *De bono*, tr. IV, q. 1, a. 1, pp. 218–219, ll. 82–08.

a result the habit generated does not originate in reason alone, but simply from the will producing the habit; it originates in reason only as a subject. The prudent person may know the nature of actions, but is inclined to do them, just as in other virtues, only as the habit and its power directs one to goodness. In the *De bono* Albert insists that virtue results more from the will's desire for goodness than from the dictates of reason.[26]

Like his contemporaries, Albert views prudence not merely as an intellectual virtue, but also as a habitual or moral one. Prudence is generated from experience and action, since it has characteristics of both knowledge and virtue. Albert cannot conceive of any virtue in which the will is not the primary motivating element (*motor primus*). Just as the will produces acts in the moving element of the sensible soul, so too are its acts in the same part of the rational soul. As a result, in every act and passion there remains something of habitual virtue that belongs to prudence. The specific action of prudence is the ability to choose what is needed for life according to right reason. In its operations and passions prudence has formally the nature of virtue; in its origin from study and learning it is materially the knowledge of such actions.[27]

To resolve the problem concerning the nature of prudence as science or virtue, Albert distinguishes between Aristotle's description of *phronesis* and the *phronimos*. Prudence designates both knowledge and virtue: when it signifies knowledge there is an equivocal reference to the habit of knowing alone, and another reference to the habit of acting that is acquired through study and learning. Albert actually misrepresents Aristotle's description of the *phronimos* despite his use of citations from the moral works. Albert believes Aristotle to have identified the *prudens* with the *sapiens*.[28] Despite the citation to Aristotle's description of the prudent person as one who seeks as much precision as the inquiry demands (NE 1094b25–27), Albert does not yet have the benefit of the discussion of the *phronimos* in book VI of the NE where Aristotle describes the moral excellence of the practically wise person. Prudence may be a virtue that combines intellectual and moral pursuits, but it does not make practical wisdom (*phronesis*) the same as theoretical wisdom (*sophia* or *sapientia*).[29]

The question that directly addresses the nature and substance of prudence begins with a number of definitions taken from ancient and patristic

[26] *De bono*, tr. IV, q. 1, a. 1, p. 219, ll. 15–41.
[27] *De bono*, tr. IV, q. 1, a. 1, p. 219, ll. 49–75.
[28] *De bono*, tr. IV, q. 1, a. 1, p. 220, ll. 22–24: Et Aristoteles loquitur ibi de prudente secundum quod convertitur cum sapiente.
[29] *De bono*, tr. IV, q. 1, a. 1, p. 220, ll. 17–44.

sources. The first two citations to Cicero reinforce the notion of prudence as knowledge or the discovery of truth.[30] According to Macrobius prudence is contempt for the world and directs the mind toward contemplation of the divine. Augustine gives two very different definitions of prudence: (1) It is love choosing what is useful and avoiding what is harmful; (2) it is a virtue by which the soul knows what it should do.[31] Augustine's doctrine influences the early thirteenth-century understanding of the nature of prudence more than the writings of Aristotle, since the writers of this period could not comprehend how a virtue included by Aristotle among intellectual activities could also direct moral choice. The combination of love and knowledge could, however, account for the dual force of prudential reasoning. Love governs choice, and the awareness of the right course of action is deduced intellectually from moral principles. Albert notes the tension in the tradition when he discusses the question whether prudence consists in speculative or practical knowledge. It cannot be speculative, he says, because such knowledge is not a virtue, or part of a virtue, which is always directed to action. Cicero, however, extended the domain of prudence to include the understanding of truth. Since the recognition of truth is the function of the speculative intellect, prudence must also be a type of speculative knowledge.[32]

In his response Albert claims that prudence is not a type of speculative knowledge. Such knowledge is involved in prudential decisions, but only accidentally. Speculation does not generate prudence, but does contribute to its act in two ways. Cicero understood prudence broadly insofar as it relates to the nature of what is knowable, which is identical, or nearly identical to the subject matter of prudence. Albert compares the broader sense of prudence to the way in which the subject of theology, ethics, civil and canon law may be termed the science of what to do and not to do. Such theoretical knowledge contributes much to the act of prudence, but does little to accomplish it. Theory does not produce prudence by generating its act, but rather by way of teaching and persuasion. The second way speculative knowledge contributes to prudence is more remote in that it, like every science, contributes to the discernment of what is to be chosen. One who can see truth in one area is more likely to recognize it in another.

---

[30] Gauthier and Jolif, I, p. 267 note that Cicero, who designated *phronesis* to be both wisdom (*sapientia*) and practical knowledge (*prudentia*), contributed to uncertainty concerning the exact nature of the virtue in the earliest Latin commentaries on the NE.

[31] *De bono*, tr. IV, q. 1, a. 2, p. 221, ll. 39–65.

[32] *De bono*, tr. IV, q. 1, a. 2, p. 222, ll. 12–26.

Cicero merely tried to show how theoretical sciences help to promote the act of prudence.[33]

The virtue of practical wisdom may be thought to have connections with the Christian ideals of humility, poverty and contemplation of the divine being, but the rejection of the world is characteristic of humility and poverty rather than of prudence. Contemplation of the divine does not seem to fall within the range of prudential decisions that proceed from reasons taken from human law. Contemplation of God then must result from the gift of wisdom that affects the intellect. In his response to these questions Albert declares rejection of the world must be understood under different aspects. A humble person condemns the world through a con-sideration of his unfitness (*inidoneitatis*) for the world because of feelings of unworthiness of earthly praise and honor. Poverty of the spirit rejects the world by considering the connection to Christ's poverty. The prudent person condemns the world by recognizing its vanity when it is compared to a truer and more stable good. Prudence, considered as a habit of the will tending to action, functions in accordance with human law; as an essential part of happiness, however, prudence recognizes the need for contempla-tion. The gifts of intellect and wisdom contemplate divine objects differ-ently than the prudential process. The former lead to contemplation because of the worthiness of the divine objects; the latter because the end of the act of happiness is divine.[34]

Albert neatly dissolves the tension between the ideal of Aristotle's *phronimos,* who is completely engaged in the affairs of the *polis,* and the notion of the Christian *prudens,* who condemns the world and turns to the higher goal of contemplation of God. The understanding of prudence in the *De bono* persists throughout all the moral works, as Albert develops his theory of two distinct types of happiness (*due felicitates*). Albert does not unite the political and contemplative lives, because he considers civic virtues as a preparatory stage calming the passions in order to make contemplation possible.[35] Even in his early works Albert has little interest in attempting to provide a vision of how the virtuous person unites all the different aspects of human activity.

The limits of prudence are made clear when understood as a political virtue. It cannot direct every thought toward the divine being. To do so is a function of supreme perfection that surpasses political virtue. Prudence

---

[33] *De bono,* tr. IV, q. 1, a. 2, pp. 224–225, ll. 78–26.
[34] *De bono,* tr. IV, q. 1, a. 2, pp. 226–227, ll. 75–02.
[35] A. Celano, "The Concept of Worldly Beatitude . . .", pp. 217–220.

then can only indicate the means to an end and not the end itself.[36] Albert refers again to Cicero, who identified the acts of prudence to be deliberation about justice in order to live well, and to be also the pursuit of knowledge. Prudence cannot merely be knowledge about God, but leads better to contemplation about divine objects. While it may be true that political virtue does not belong to the supreme perfection, prudence is determined according to the state of perfection, which is happiness, and not according to its essential nature. Considered in its essence and with reference to its act, prudence is defined accurately by Cicero, who recognized both its primary and secondary natures. As it relates to happiness, prudence involves only the act of one who is happy in the truest and best way.[37]

Augustine's definition of prudence as love refers to its connection to charity, or perhaps to another disposition. If it signifies charity, then prudence itself is charity because such love falls under its definition through just acts. If it refers to another disposition, then prudence belongs to a potency whose principal act is to desire or love, or may belong to some other disposition. If taken in the first way of desire, then prudence would consist in the disposition of desire, which Albert considers false. If prudence consisted in another disposition, then it could not be love except as an inclination of the potency with respect to its proper object. Then all virtue and vice would be love, which again cannot be true.[38] What Augustine truly meant is that prudence as love refers to charity. Charitable love may be understood in one of two ways: (1) in itself, and as such, tends toward the first good that is the general form and mover of virtues; (2) as not distinct from those virtues that it informs, and that are not sought for themselves, but are desired on account of God. Charity in the second way is not distinguished from the virtues but predicated in their definitions. The example of one who acts prudently and charitably because of God shows that one need not be first moved by an act of charity and then by acts of prudence and chastity. Rather one need only to have the habit of charity in order to direct all one's actions

---

[36] *De bono*, tr. IV, q. 1, a. 2, p. 223, ll. 35–41: Praeterea, omnen animi cogitationem in sola divina dirigere non convenit prudentiae, quae est virtus politica consistens in medio. Omnem enim animi cogitationem in sola divina dirigere summae perfectionis est. Item virtus politica non dirigit ad finem, sed potius ad medium.

[37] *De bono*, tr. IV, q. 1, a. 2, p. 227, ll. 3–12: ... quod bene verum est, quod hoc est summe perfectionis, et prudentia etiam sic diffinita est determinata secundum statum summe perfectum, qui est felicitas, et non est sic diffinita per essentiam ... quod prudentia, considerata essentialiter et ad actum, in his versatur principaliter vel secundario, ut dicit Tullius, sed secundum statum felcitatis, in quo est determinata, versatur tantum circa actum verissime et optime felicis.

[38] *De bono*, tr. IV, q. 1, a. 2, p. 223, ll. 54–64.

to be done for the sake of God. Charity causes only the form and perfection of virtues in their performance. In this way prudence may be considered a type of love.[39]

Albert's resolution attempts to unite as many different definitions of prudence as possible, since he believes they satisfactorily illuminate the different facets of the virtue. Cicero's definition of prudence as science refers to its genus and proper subject that occur in every voluntary act. Cicero spoke appropriately because '*scientia*' limited to its subject matter supposes that which formally and substantially is part of prudence. Science, which motivates one to do good and evil, can only be voluntary. What remains to reason is consequently ordered to voluntary choice. Cicero implies a type of voluntary science, but he does not designate a science of good and evil because they are not considered in themselves. The science of good and evil truly refers to a consideration of what is true of the passions concerning moral matters. That which is formally in the virtue of prudence is clearly part of science, insofar as it is a correct habit.[40] Cicero's broad concept of prudence as science helps to discern its proper subject. The extension of practical wisdom occurs in two ways. (1) By the nature of the knowable, which is the same, or nearly the same, as the subject of prudence in the way that theology, ethics and law dictate what ought to be done. Such knowledge conveys much to the act of prudence, but does little to produce it, since it advances the virtue only by way of teaching and persuading. (2) Another, and more remote, way that science aids in the prudential act is the manner whereby the exercise of every science contributes to the process of choice.[41]

The source of the dichotomy between the theoretical and practical aspects of prudence originates in the understanding of its goal. There is a distinction between the act, and the end, of prudence. The true end of prudence is sought for its own sake, and its act is exercised in order to

---

[39] *De bono*, tr. IV, q. 1, a. 2, p. 227, ll. 24–49.
[40] *De bono*, tr. IV, q. 1, a. 2, p. 224, ll. 39–52.
[41] *De bono*, tr. IV, q. 1, a. 2, p. 224, ll. 78–93: ... dicendum, quod Tullius large accipit prudentiam, scilicet inquantum extendit se ad materiam secundariam, ut adiuvetur ex illa ad discernendam materiam propriam. Et hoc contingit duobus modis, scilicet per rationem scibilis, quod idem est vel fere idem cum materia prudentiae, sicut est scibile theologicum et scibile ethicum et scibile iuris civilis vel canonici, ut summatim dicatur, omnis scientia in qua agitur de faciendis vel non faciendis. Hoc enim scire multum confert ad prudentiae actum, licet parum proficiat ad prudentiam. Non enim proficit per modum generantis ipsam, sed potius per modum docentis et suadentis. Alio autem modo est materia secundaria omnis scientia et hoc remotius, quia exercitium cuiuslibet scientiae valet ad discretionem eligibilium.

discover truth in actions. Such truth results from an intellectual process, but another end *in alio* permits the discovered truth to order and rule all other powers and virtues pertaining to the human community. The latter aspect of prudence is the domain of justice, as Cicero rightly indicated.[42] This distinction foreshadows Albert's strict division between political and contemplative happiness that is a prominent feature of his later moral works. He could not accept the Aristotelian notion that *praxis* encompasses all human activity and that the practically wise person would make decisions that align all virtues with the pursuit of individual happiness. Albert remains constant in his conviction that moral practices are always the means to a superior life.

Albert limits prudence to the discovery of goodness in the practical realm. Its final act is an assent to a practical particular action. Such recognition of the particular operation is a feature of practical, and not of theoretical, science, even if one were to accept the claim that prudence recognizes truth in the nature of goodness.[43] Albert's interpretation of Aristotle is accurate in ascribing to prudence the governance of practical decisions, but too restrictive in excluding the choice to engage in contemplation from its domain. Although Albert realizes that Aristotle designated *phronesis* as an intellectual virtue, it functions in Albert's ethics as a practical exercise in directing one to the higher end of contemplation.[44] The prudential person knows how to subordinate all temporal pursuits to those which are superior.[45] As he noted in his general discussions on virtue, Albert indicates that choice must be a free act that is essential to practical reason. Prudence, therefore, must consist in reason ordered to the will. Only such reason moves one to action, since Albert argues in both the *De bono* and *De homine* that reason and intellect can only motivate one by means of the appetite that functions in both reason and will. Reason moves through appetite because one has to choose an alternative to which one is disposed by cognition.[46]

Both the sciences of law and morality concern what should be performed by human beings. As such, they are ordered closely to the act of prudence, but do not generate its habit. This habit is voluntary, and like all virtuous habits it is generated from an assent to acts that follow the will. In the *De bono* Albert insists upon the primacy of the appetite in motivating one to action. To cherish something is not an act of concupiscence, and to detest

---

[42] *De bono*, tr. IV, q. 1, a. 2, pp. 225–226, ll. 90–02.

[43] *De bono*, tr. IV, q. 1, a. 2, p. 226, ll. 52–57.

[44] *De bono*, tr. IV, q. 1, a. 2, p. 226, ll. 61–69.

[45] *De bono*, tr. IV, q. 1, a. 2, p. 226, ll. 70–74.

[46] *De bono*, tr. IV, q. 1, a. 2, p. 227, ll. 51–61.

something is not an act of irascibility because both have their origins in an act of will that first moves, and by virtue of which reason functions. Albert cites the *De anima* as support for his position that the intellect, or reason, cannot motivate one, unless the appetite is involved. The appetite in reason is the will which antecedently reflects the nature of what to do.[47]

Albert, unlike Aristotle, makes prudence itself subordinate to the will, just as all other motivating powers within the human soul are. Again the *De anima* is the source for the claim that Aristotle himself wanted to unite all motivating forces within the appetite. Even in science there is first an appetite tending toward the assent for the deed, and then the intellect accepts the knowledge of the deed in its inquiry and deliberation. Science, therefore, follows the appetite that is made in the will functioning in a rational act. Albert believes that Aristotle ordered both knowledge and reason to the will.[48] Ethics differs specifically from other sciences because no one is inclined to act through the will in purely theoretical fields of knowledge. There is no regard for what should be done or desired in sciences other than the moral ones. Theory pursues an act of learning or reflection rather than one directed by the will. Since the object of theoretical sciences is not voluntary their end falls under the power of the speculative intellect.[49]

Another element that was never part of the philosophical examination of virtue is included in Albert's discussion of prudence: the effect of the gift of knowledge conveyed by the Holy Spirit. Albert distinguishes between the science of actions governed by the gift of knowledge and that knowledge ruled by civic prudence. The gift of science arises from inspiration that leads to spiritual works. This gift involves the perfection of the active life as it is ascribed to the Holy Spirit. As such, it implies a spirituality and sanctity that remove one from worldly affairs. Prudence, however, rests upon the nature of human honesty and integrity, and reflects the spiritual life only secondarily insofar as human affairs are connected to spiritual ones. The gift of science reflects *per se* the spiritual interaction among human beings, and indicates decency in civic affairs, as the spirit directs external acts to a norm of internal dispositions.[50] The gift of spiritual knowledge recalls the idea of poverty and humility that Albert considers marks of the truly moral Christian. The view of ethics as the absolute perfection of the soul leads

---

[47] *De bono*, tr. IV, q. 1, a. 2, p. 228, ll. 23–33.
[48] *De bono*, tr. IV, q. 1, a. 3, pp. 230–231, ll. 75–08.
[49] *De bono*, tr. IV, q. 1, a. 3, p. 231, ll. 9–21.
[50] *De bono*, tr. IV, q. 1, a. 2, pp. 227–228, ll. 99–15.

Albert to restrict the range of prudential decisions to those that affect the public domain. Since no human power can perfect the soul, then natural powers can only rule human beings within a limited arena. What remains for prudence is the disposition to receive a higher gift from a superior force. Even when Albert determines human goodness in his later fuller commentaries on Aristotle's ethical works, he limits prudence to the political life.

The question on the specific subject matter of prudence in the *De bono* contains many traditional views and problems concerning practical wisdom. Albert gives three arguments that consider Cicero's designation of the subject of prudence as truth. Cicero distinguished the truth of prudence from the other cardinal virtues that regulate civic affairs. If Cicero is correct in his understanding of prudence, then it should be a type of intellectual cognition, and the remaining virtues are marked by community, magnanimity and moderation, which correspond to justice, courage and temperance.[51] Albert recognizes the seemingly conflicting accounts of prudence in the writings of the classical authors. He cites the *De anima* (III, 427b 24–27), where Aristotle mentions the perceptual differences arising from science, opinion and practical wisdom. Since *prudentia* is a species of rational and intellectual perception it certainly considers truth. Albert quickly notes that Aristotle asserts that all practical sciences exist for the sake of action. As practical knowledge, prudence must not merely seek truth, but it must also produce an act. Its subject matter is the good discovered concerning an act.[52] Cicero transmitted the Greek terms for wisdom and practical wisdom to the Latin world. Albert's understanding of practical wisdom stems from passages in the *De officiis*:

The first among all virtues is wisdom (*sapientia*) itself, which the Greek call *sophia*. We understand prudence, which the Greeks called *phronesis* as something different, which is the knowledge (*scientia*) of what to seek and to avoid. This wisdom, which we say is primary, is the knowledge of divine and human affairs in which the community of gods and their society are contained.[53]

---

[51] *De bono*, tr. IV, q. 1, a. 3, p. 228, ll. 35–62.

[52] *De bono*, tr. IV, q. 1, a. 3, p. 228, ll. 63–81.

[53] *De bono*, tr. IV, q. 1, a. 2, pp. 228–229, ll. 82–04: Item, Tullius in fine I De officiis: 'Princeps omnium virtutum illa sapientia est, quam Graeci sophiam vocant. Prudentiam enim, quam Graeci phronesim dicunt, aliam quandam intelligimus, quae est rerum expetendarum fugiendarumque scientia. Illa autem sapientia quam principem diximus, rerum est divinarum et humanarum scientia, in qua continetur deorum communitas et societas inter ipsos'. Ex hoc accipitur, quod prudentia non est idem quod sophia vel sapientia et quod non est circa cognoscibilia quaecumque, sed circa expetenda ad opus vel fugienda. Ergo materia prudentiae est bonum ordinabile ad appetitum operis. F.-B. Stammkötter observes how the poor translation of the *Ethica nova* forced Albert to interpret a latinized

From this description Albert distinguished prudence from wisdom since the former considers what is known to govern actions while the latter does not. Cicero also argued that action does not follow from contemplation. Since prudence has the complete nature of virtue, it lacks nothing with respect to human action that necessarily follows from it. Its true subject can only be the operable good.[54] Aristotle also separated the practical from the speculative intellect. The former reasons about something other than its own cognition, and what it considers is an act. Since prudence is in the practical intellect, its subject must also be an act.[55]

After considering the opinions of the ancients, Albert specifies the subject of prudence to be what is chosen to produce a correct action. The truth that Cicero says prudence seeks is the true nature of a good that is chosen and performed. Such truth has to be determined by reason of law, justice and expediency. Albert uses an analogy to speculative reasoning, which his student, Thomas Aquinas, will later make a prominent feature of his own notion of practical wisdom. Albert argues that the speculative intellect has certain instruments at its disposal, by which it comes to knowledge. They are the first propositions and principles that regulate scientific understanding. Prudence and practical wisdom employ an analogous method of adopting natural moral principles that lead to an understanding of the operable and desirable good. All such principles are taken from law and justice in order to perform fitting actions.[56]

In one of his earliest work on moral philosophy Albert has correctly grasped the mechanism whereby prudence operates: the deduction of a particular action through syllogistic reasoning. What will soon change from Aristotle's concept of *phronesis* in the medieval reading of *Ethics* is the process of identifying moral principles. Albert indicates in the *De bono* that prudence takes the principles from law; in his later works he specifies that law to be eternal and divine. Albert considers Aristotle's claim that prudence is an intellectual process to reflect a general understanding of the way both the practical and speculative intellect comprehend necessary and probable conclusions. For Aristotle to say that comprehension has every truth as its matter does not imply that prudence's primary subject is intellectual truth. Prudence is merely a part of comprehension, and differs

---

Greek concept (*phronesis*) as a branch of its Latin cognate (*prudentia*). "Die Entwicklung der Bestimmung der *Prudentia* in der Ethik des Albertus Magnus," in W. Senner, p. 307.

[54] *De bono*, tr. IV, q. 1, a. 3, p. 229, ll. 8–21.

[55] *De bono*, tr. IV, q. 1, a. 3, p. 229, ll. 22–28.

[56] *De bono*, tr. IV, q. 1, a. 3, p. 230, ll. 3–18.

from, or is less than, total understanding that is divided in three ways: (1) necessary truth ordered to speculation that is the subject and end of science; (2) practical truth ordered to acting by reason of a just and useful good that is the subject of prudence; (3) probable truth in both speculative and practical inquiry that is the subject of opinion.[57] By means of legal, just and useful reasons prudence chooses whatever it selects, as Paul indicated in I *Corinthians*: "All things are permitted to me, but not all are helpful; all things are permitted, but not all are constructive." In Albert's paraphrase of Paul he emphasizes the legal and useful effects of the actions that prudence commands.[58]

The act of prudence has different aspects, one of which occurs *secundum se*, and another which commands movement and action. The act *secundum se* may be divided further into the antecedent process, which is compared to a disposition and potency to virtuous works, and the consequent act, which is like a perfection in a ruling element that can bring the action to completion. The antecedent element is further divided: it first regards through reason what is to be done, then it examines what to do through legal, useful and just reasons, and subsequently it deliberates how to proceed, and finally commands. The consequent aspect is choice itself: "Such an act whereby it commands action is an opinion about what ought to be done. Prudence and practical reason have the very same acts because reason gives the act and prudence informs it through law, expediency and justice."[59] While Aristotle does not have such a complicated process of prudential reasoning, he would not have objected to Albert's close association of prudence and practical reason with the directive force of reason that considers the importance of law and justice in making practical decisions.

With his distinctions in place Albert can respond to the different opinions of the authorities concerning the prudential act. When Basil asserts that prudence makes us aware of good, evil and neutral actions, he is referring only to the first act of prudence that is the consideration of what to do. When Cicero calls prudence a separate action (*actio discreta*), he considers the last act of prudence, which is opinion about an act through legal and proper reason. Through this opinion an action becomes prudent and distinct. Some may argue that prudence is to be defined by its act of deliberation about what to do, especially with reference to right and wrong.

---

[57] *De bono*, tr. IV, q. 1, a. 3, p. 230, ll. 42–55.
[58] *De bono*, tr. IV, q. 1, a. 3, p. 230, ll. 56–66.
[59] *De bono*, tr. IV, q. 1, a. 4, p. 234, ll. 18–36.

As such, prudence is a type of revealing, because in deliberation what is hidden in an act comes forth in imitation or avoidance. This description pertains only to the prudential act itself.[60]

When one argues that discernment may be correct, but incorrect choice is a different act, Albert sees a distinction between speculative discernment and prudential reasoning. In speculation, discerning by means of the speculative habit may be useful to the prudential act through conformity to what is known, as in legal, moral and theological knowledge. In such reasoning, however, one who discerns properly may choose incorrectly. There is also discernment in prudential knowledge that follows the will. Albert views such discernment as always necessary and prior to choice and action. If a choice is truly prudential, then discernment cannot lead to an evil decision.[61]

Macrobius's notion of prudence as a virtue by which one is joined to happiness appears often in the works on moral philosophy in the early thirteenth century. Albert argues that acts of political virtues understood according to the state of happiness are not regarded as ordered to the end according to the subject of the end or its act, but rather according to the conditions of the end. Just as courage leads one to persist in goodness despite danger, prudence permits one to envision goodness that the prudential act chooses. Macrobius's definition does not refer to virtues in this way, but rather to the manner in which they are joined to happiness, the perfection of the soul according to perfect virtue. This view does not characterize prudence by discernment that occurs in provoking deliberation and doubt. Perfect virtue is free from all doubt and leads to certainty. Prudence in this context teaches one to reject the world whose goods produce doubt; it also leads to contemplation of the immutable and certain good, which is God. Only in this way can one understand prudence as the virtue that produces union with God.[62]

In its act prudence does not consist in a mean, as Albert correctly notes. He ascribes the difference between prudence and other virtues to the logical function of prudence that determines rationally its own subject matter. Since every mean derives its subject in word or deed by an innate or produced passion, prudence cannot limit itself to some mean. The more deliberative it is, the better the logical virtue will be.[63] When Albert

---

[60] *De bono*, tr. IV, q. 1, a. 4, p. 234, ll. 47–56.
[61] *De bono*, tr. IV, q. 1, a. 4, p. 234, ll. 57–70.
[62] *De bono*, tr. IV, q. 1, a. 4, p. 234, ll. 76–95. See also c. 2, n. 30.
[63] *De bono*, tr. IV, q. 1, a. 4, p. 235, ll. 1–14.

discusses the Aristotelian definition of political virtue as a voluntary habit consisting in a mean, he says that not every virtue consists in the mean in the same way. Virtues may be described as a mean, insofar as they have a specific subject and they may determine a mean for themselves. Since logical virtues are not determined by the subject matter, they do not have a proper mean. As they posit their subject matter determined by reason they recognize a mean in another area. The mean, therefore, relates to logical virtues only accidentally, and not properly.[64] To clarify further the relation between prudence and the mean, Albert regards the definition of virtue as a mean in different ways. The science of prudence is determined in those acts that have a mean, but science in itself is not. The substantial element in prudence is not the mean *per se*, but the mean according to what is knowable by prudence.[65] The general definition of prudence identifies the virtue as practical knowledge (*scientia*) ordered to the will that chooses wisely what is helpful and avoids what is harmful. For Albert it is primarily a political virtue and secondarily it may be termed wisdom (*sagacitas*) or shrewdness (*sollertia*) because it discovers the particular or universal good in any subject.[66]

Intelligence as an intellectual and logical virtue is a power of prudence, since it is a type of discernment and light that arises in the mind from the subtle penetration of circumstances surrounding the deed. Intelligence allows the practically wise person to choose what should be pursued or avoided.[67] Cicero's definition of intelligence as the ability to see things that are does not refer to a habit of the speculative part of the soul. Cicero distinguishes practical intelligence from speculation when he refers to the power of the mind. Mind in Cicero's definition signifies a practical element, which motivates and acts, so that intelligence is a part of the practical soul. Speculative intelligence, however, understands those things that exist without reference to time, while practical intelligence regards what is relevant to the business at hand. Cicero does not designate intelligence by pure abstraction, but rather by a comparison to memory and foresight.[68]

---

[64] *De bono*, tr. IV, q. 1, a. 4, p. 235, ll. 29–40.
[65] *De bono*, tr. IV, q. 1, a. 4, p. 235, ll. 41–49.
[66] *De bono*, tr. IV, q. 1, a. 5, p. 239, ll. 17–26.
[67] *De bono*, tr. IV, q. 2, a. 3, p, 252, ll. 56–64: Dicendum, quod intelligentia virtus est logica et intellectualis, potestativa autem pars prudentiae. Intelligentia enim est discretio et lumen, quod nascitur in animo ex penetratione subtili eorum quae circumstant praesens negotium. Ex hoc enim prudens efficitur potens ad eligendum id quod est operandum vel fugiendum. Unde patet, qualiter complet secundum aliquem modum potestatem prudentiae et ita est pars ipsius.
[68] *De bono*, tr. IV, q. 2, a. 3, p, 252, ll. 65–88.

This type of intelligence is similar to providence since it permits one to foresee the consequences of actions. It differs from foresight because of its more limited view.[69] Speculative intelligence abstracts from all temporal conditions and understands universal propositions. Practical intelligence considers the actual circumstances that surround the action to be performed. Since its goal is a particular act that is connected to time it does not abstract the temporal condition from its consideration.[70]

When Albert examines the intellectual virtues treated by Aristotle at the end of the first book of the NE, he notes two important problems with the division of virtues into practical and intellectual. He says that Cicero in *De officiis* explicitly calls *phronesis* wisdom (*sapientia*). If Cicero is indeed correct then *phronesis* does not differ from *sapientia* at all. A second problem arises from the translation of the *Ethica vetus*. Albert asks why Aristotle does not list *prudentia* among the intellectual virtues, as he does in the *De anima*. Since *phronesis* is left untranslated in the Latin text of the *Ethica vetus*, Albert lists the intellectual virtues as *sapientia, intelligentia* and *phronesis*.[71] In his solution Albert argues first that Aristotle touches upon the general habits of intellectual virtue in the same way, i.e. that reason generally is a potency reflecting all moral elements, or in the way that they are ordered to the concupiscible or irascible part of the soul. In his judgment wisdom in the civic sphere refers only to the habit of morals with an awareness of the final moral cause. Albert clarifies his position by noting that wisdom always aims to designate a type of knowledge that exists through the first cause, but in ethics such wisdom is found in the final cause of happiness and justice. *Phronesis* in the strict sense taken by Aristotle is called a habit of morals with knowledge of natural and positive law. It also determines right and wrong. As a result *phronesis* contains a greater cognition of morals than is needed in *prudentia*. The latter may have knowledge of the reason 'because' (*quia*) while *phronesis* and *sapientia* determine the 'why' (*propter quid*). *Phronesis* knows the reason why by recognizing what is required and obligated by law; *sapientia* by recognizing the end itself. Intelligence indicates the same things as prudence that leads to the simple awareness of what to choose for a particular act.[72] Cicero's identification of *phronesis* with wisdom depends upon his broad interpretation of both practical and theoretical wisdom. For Cicero

[69] *De bono*, tr. IV, q. 2, a. 3, p, 253, ll. 3–8.   [70] *De bono*, tr. IV, q. 2, a. 3, p, 253, ll. 9–20.
[71] *De bono*, tr. IV, q. 2, a. 6, p, 257, ll. 29–34 and 57–62. The editors of the *De bono* note that Cicero calls *phronesis sophia*. Albert then is not wrong in ascribing the association of *phronesis* with *sapientia* to Cicero.
[72] *De bono*, tr. IV, q. 2, a. 3, p, 257, ll. 66–87.

practical wisdom proceeds from divine and human reasons that allow for knowledge of particulars pertaining to action. Cicero then classifies *phronesis* as a type of wisdom and understanding, even if Aristotle did not.[73]

b *Synderesis* and natural law

Unlike Philip the Chancellor, Albert does not introduce the concept of *synderesis* into his discussion of Aristotle's doctrine concerning prudence, but does consider it when treating the meaning of natural law. Citing Basil, who placed an awareness of the universal principles of law within a natural ability to judge, and Paul, who claimed the act of law to be written in the heart, Albert accepts the idea that universal legal principles should direct human action. Like William of Auxerre, Albert understands Paul's text to allow for the introduction of the idea of *synderesis* into the discussion on correct moral laws. In them there can be no error or doubt, since the natural ability to judge is formed by reason and *synderesis*. So formed, the critical faculty of judgment knows what to do.[74] Such universal principles are clearly expressed in the decalog, and individual tenets are the belief in one God, to honor one's parents, not to kill, and the like. These commands are universally taken from natural and written laws (*scripta*), and are comprehended by that power that responds to reason. Albert compares the process of acting in accordance with natural law to the process whereby the speculative intellect is perfected. The intellect contains a two-fold power before it receives an act of knowledge: a potency to know the instruments of knowledge, and the power of knowledge itself. The instruments of knowledge are the first principles of science. The same process holds for the development of a habit of the practical intellect that directs actions. In the knowledge of law the first potency is directed toward its universal principles. Albert argues that before the moral habit can develop there must be knowledge of the terms of the universal imperatives. He says that the knowledge of principles, such as do not steal or commit adultery, is acquired *per accidens,* that is, through recognition of terms. Because there is no prior understanding, knowledge of such terms is instilled naturally and acquired by subsequent recognition. The meaning of Basil and Paul on

---

[73] *De bono*, tr. IV, q. 2, a. 3, pp. 257–258, ll. 89–04.

[74] *De bono*, tr. V, q. 1, a. 1, p. 263, ll. 19–26: Dicendum, quod, ut dicit Basilius, universalia iuris sunt in naturali iudicatorio, et similiter Apostolus ad Rom. (II, 15): 'Ostendunt opus legis scriptum esse in cordibus suis'. Et vocantur universalia iuris illa dirigentia nos in opere, in quibus non est error neque dubium, in quibus naturale iudicatorum rationis vel synderesis informatum accipit, quid faciendum sit vel non faciendum.

the topic is that justice is known by the form of justice impressed upon all those whose life and actions conform to the dictates of the universal commands. In this way one develops a habit of natural law.[75] Natural law may be a habit, but not one that in itself is sufficient to produce action. Augustine's definition of a habit as that by which someone acts as desired refers to a complete habit that has no trace of potency. This type of habit is not one of principles, by whose possession one is led to action. The innate cognition of the imperatives of natural law leads only potentially to corresponding actions that need to be aligned with the dictates of right reason. The potency of the natural habit is actualized when specified by the particulars of human positive law.[76]

When discussing what this force of nature that law actually is, Albert maintains that it is doubtlessly the light of the agent intellect. This light is a type of intelligible species that leads to an awareness of terms that comprise the first principles of the agent and practical intellects. To assent to such principles of knowledge and actions requires no proof or demonstration.[77] This natural power is common to both the speculative and practical intellects because the light of the agent intellect is proportional to each by means of the principles, and through these principles one is led to proper conclusions. Albert does not give a definitive response to the question on the source of natural law, but he does say that it arises from reason or even *synderesis*. In either case it is not its own cause, since the agent intellect does not receive any species, or any habit, whether natural or acquired. The natural light may be described as a habit of that which is essentially a form that illustrates and conveys intelligible being through its act, just as the light of the sun is related to all colors in transmitting visible being.[78] In a strict sense natural law is an innate power as defined by Cicero. The results of this law are the universal moral precepts that the conscience dictates from the very nature of goodness. In a more general sense natural law refers not to human deliberation or reason, but to what is commanded by God according the seeds of law

---

[75] *De bono*, tr. V, q. 1, a. 1, p. 263, ll. 31–83. See also *De homine* (=DH) in *Alberti Magni Opera omnia* 27/2, H. Anzulewicz and J. Söder, ed. (Münster: Aschendorff, 2008), q. 71, a. 1 and *De bono*, tr. V, q. 1, a. 1, p. 264, ll. 63–70.

[76] *De bono*, tr. V, q. 1, a. 1, p. 264, ll. 33–43.

[77] *De bono*, tr. V, q. 1, a. 1, p. 265, ll. 58–67: Si autem quaeritur, quae sit illa vis naturae, dico, quod absque dubio illa naturae vis est lumen intellectus agentis, cuius lumen est species specierum intelligibilium … Illud enim lumen distinctum ad species terminorum, quae sunt in principiis primi intellectus agentis et practici, facit per se, hoc est sine probatione et demonstratione, asssentire principiis primis scientiarum et operationum.

[78] *De bono*, tr. V, q. 1, a. 1, p. 266, ll. 4–22.

(*semina iuris*) that are implanted in the human heart. In this way the law, prophecies and the gospels are derived from natural law.[79]

In another early work, *De homine*, the literary style and its biographical sketch indicate a product of Albert's teaching activity before the completion of his theological degree. The *De homine* is part of a larger consideration of all creation and was certainly composed before 1246 and more specifically *circa* 1242.[80] This early treatise is very important for the understanding of Albert's views on the mechanism of human moral action, and contains specific discussions devoted to the definition and function of *synderesis*. While Albert scarcely mentions the concept of *synderesis* in his other works on moral philosophy, he devotes an entire section to its importance for moral action in the *De homine*. He takes the claim of Basil that the soul has the natural ability to judge good from evil as his point of departure. This power of the soul naturally has the innate seeds (*semina*) of judgment from which truth may be cultivated. From Basil's understanding of *synderesis* its definition may be expressed as a "virtue of the soul having in itself the fixed and innate seeds of judgment by which we separate evil from good." Two other conclusions follow from this definition: (1) *synderesis* is a natural judgment of the soul: (2) it is a potency and not a habit of the soul.[81] The second conclusion is that of Philip the Chancellor who was instrumental in introducing the notion of *synderesis* into the discussion on moral action in the thirteenth century, and preferred the designation of *synderesis* as a habitual potency. Albert does not identify *synderesis* completely with reason, which does not have the natural judgment, but is rather discursive. Reason also lacks innate seeds of justice and acquires them through custom and the teaching of prudence. Albert does not claim that the principles of *synderesis* are learned, but rather that reason comes to recognize them through teaching and practice.[82] Another source for the doctrine of

[79] *De bono*, tr. V, q. 1, a. 1, p. 266, ll. 39–55 and 67–73.
[80] *Albertus Magnus, Über den Menschen, De homine*, ed. and tr. H. Anzulewicz and J. Söder (Hamburg: Felix Meiner Verlag, 2004) Intro. p. XXIX and XXXII.
[81] DH, p. 527, ll. 9–20: Dicit Basilius . . . 'Quoniam quidem habemus ipsi naturale quoddam animi iudicium, per quod mala segregamus a bonis. Quae virtus animi habens in se naturaliter sibi insita et inserta semina iudicandi, si vere huius iustitiae eruditionibus excolatur, directum et aequum tenebit iudicii ac discretionis examen'. Ex hoc accipiuntur tria de synderesi est diffinitio synderesis, scilicet quod ipsa est 'virtus animi habens in se sibi insita et inserta semina iudicandi, per quam mala segregamus a bonis'. Secundum est quod ipsa est 'naturale animi iudicium'. Tertium est quod est potentia animae et non habitus, ut quidam dixerunt. C. Trottmann notes that Albert views Augustine's term *'naturale iudicium'* as the Latin translation for the Greek, *synderesis*. Art. cit, p. 262.
[82] DH, p. 527, ll. 21–26.

synderesis is Augustine, who wrote that the universals of law were naturally written in the innate ability to make judgments. Since Augustine determined habits to be in the potency or virtue of the soul, *synderesis* must also be a habit.[83] Albert identifies Jerome's *Gloss on Ezechiel* to be another source for the understanding of *synderesis*, and cites in his work a passage where Jerome introduces a fourth element into the Platonic division of the soul. In addition to rationality, concupiscence and irascibility the soul possesses *synderesis*, which is the inextinguishable spark of the conscience. Albert understands Jerome's *Gloss* to place *synderesis* within the genus of the soul's potencies. As the spark of conscience it cannot exist apart from its corresponding habit. This reading of Jerome is in harmony with the definition given by Basil. *Synderesis* exists through every mode and apart from any organ, and is superior to reason, desire and irascibility. Finally, it is not a potency mixed with other motivating forces, but rather corrects errors in them.[84]

Albert considers also the argument that *synderesis* may be a certain power (*vis*) in the soul, but quickly gives opposing arguments supporting the claim that it is a habit. From its etymology, the combination of σῦν and αίρησις, one understands it to be opinion or knowledge abiding through reason within a human being. According to its Greek roots *synderesis* indicates a habit rather than a potency. Another argument claims that what always leads one to evil is a habit termed incitement (*fomes*). What is opposed to such a habit inclines one always to good, and must be a contrary habit. *Synderesis*, therefore, will be a habit. The third argument considers two circumstances of deliberative will which contribute to free choice. Incitement comes from the inferior part of the soul and inclines one to evil; the other, *synderesis*, arises from the superior part of the soul and assists in the commission of good. Since nothing can assist or inhibit a potency, *synderesis* must then be a habit.[85] These arguments later influence Thomas Aquinas's final determination of *synderesis*.

If one accepts the idea that *synderesis* is without doubt a potency with a habit, then further questions arise. The first of which considers whether it denotes one or several potencies, or perhaps even something joined to several potencies. *Synderesis* seems also to be identical with the practical intellect. Albert says that Aristotle indicated that it was a habit when he asserted that the practical intellect is always correct. Since such invariable rectitude also is the characteristic of *synderesis*, it seems to be substantially

---

[83] DH, p. 527, ll. 27–32.   [84] DH, pp. 527–528, ll. 23–28.   [85] DH, p. 528, ll. 50–66.

the same as the practical intellect.[86] Others, who view *synderesis* as a habit, potency or power, identify it with reason itself, or the practical intellect. Jerome and other Christian authors argued that *synderesis* may differ from reason or may be many potencies, and not merely one. Finally Albert recognizes that no philosopher placed *synderesis* among the motivating powers of the soul, even though most Christian moralists did so.[87]

Albert's extensive discussion of the various positions concerning the nature of *synderesis* summarizes the philosophical-theological deliberations on the topic in the first half of the thirteenth century. In his own determination he accepts the notion that *synderesis* is a special power of the soul, in which, as Augustine argued, the universal dictates of natural law are displayed. Albert sees a direct connection between the principles of *synderesis* and those of the speculative sciences. Both have principles and values that human beings do not learn, but are led to truth through their direction. In practice certain universals direct actions through which the practical intellect gains assistance in distinguishing right from wrong in all ethical decisions. As in theory, one does not learn such principles, but, as Jerome says, they are the natural law written on the human spirit. Augustine specifies further the universal commands and gives examples, such as avoid fornication, do not kill, show compassion for the sick, and others. Those commands comprise the subject matter of *synderesis* and are the immutable principles of moral actions.[88]

What the Greeks called *synderesis* Augustine designated as natural ability to judge because human beings have the ability to discern universal principles without deception. The eagle in Ezechiel symbolizes *synderesis*, since it perceives the most elevated ideas that are in harmony with divine

---

[86] DH, p. 529, ll. 1–9: Si propter hoc dicatur quod sine dubio synderesis dicit potentiam cum habitu, tunc quaeritur, utrum dicat unam vel plures vel aliquid coniunctum pluribus potentiis. Videtur autem quod sit idem cum intellecto practico. Supra enim habitum est a dicto Philosophi quod intellectus practicus semper est rectus. Cum igitur hoc attribuatur synderesi, et quaecumque sunt eadem proprio, sunt eadem etiam substantia, videtur synderesis idem esse quod intellectus practicus.

[87] DH, p. 529, ll. 10–60.

[88] DH, p. 529–530, ll. 61–08: Sine praeiudicio dicimus quod synderesis est specialis vis animae, in qua secundum Augustinum universalia iuris naturalis descripta sunt. Sicut enim in speculativis sunt principia et dignitates, quae non addiscit homo, sed sunt in ipso naturaliter et iuvatur ipsis ad speculationem veri, ita ex parte operabilium quaedam sunt universalia dirigentia in opere, per quae intellectus practicus iuvatur ad discretionem turpis et honesti in moribus, quae non discit homo, sed secundum Hieronymum sunt lex naturalis scripta in spiritu humano. Et dicuntur ad Augustino universalia iuris, sicut est non esse fornicandum, et non esse occidendum, et afflicto esse compatiendum, et huiusmodi; et subiectum illorum synderesis est.

justice, but does not apply them to particulars. The application of universal commands to specific acts is the function of reason. The directive force of *synderesis* is similar to understanding in speculative knowledge, although reason and knowledge govern inferences and conclusions.[89] *Synderesis* is a power of the soul, but Basil's description of it as a potency refers to the seeds of justice and the dictates of natural law that lead to invariable rectitude when cultivated by instruction or justice. Basil called *synderesis* a potency when the universal principles of law are applied to particular cases through positive law. Positive law may be discovered by reason in particular cases that concern justice.[90] Jerome's authority led to Albert's acceptance of the claim that *synderesis* is a force of the soul with a habit of the principles of natural law. Jerome called it a spark of conscience because conscience follows from *synderesis* and reason. While *synderesis* can never err, reason may sometimes be deceived, a failing which Albert treats in his question on conscience.[91] When one calls *synderesis* a habit, one does not mean a simple habit, but rather designates a potency with a habit. A mere habit could never incline one to good, but a potency with a habit could. The combination of potency and habit makes *synderesis* a true power with the human soul.[92]

To respond to the question whether *synderesis* is identical to the intellect or to reason, Albert distinguishes between the general and specific meanings of intellect. The intellect generally signifies every power of the soul that moves with cognition, and so *synderesis* would be one of its parts. Specifically it is divided into reason and *synderesis* because the latter power considers common principles and the former particular conclusions. Reason depends upon repetition while intellectual understanding does not.[93] Other writers, such as John Damascene, generally understood reason to denote every motivating power that accompanies cognition, but Augustine divided reason into superior and inferior parts. His division arose from his perception of the differences between wisdom and knowledge. In his general way of understanding reason, Augustine includes *synderesis* in its meaning; in the specific way he does not.[94]

Albert considers *synderesis* to be a unique power despite its desire for the good about which it makes its judgments. Because of the restrictions to universal judgments, its appetite will not be determined even when it

[89] DH, p. 530, ll. 8–17. [90] DH, p. 530, ll. 18–25. [91] DH, p. 530, ll. 27–33.
[92] DH, p. 530, ll. 55–61: Ad id quod obicitur quod synderesis sit habitus, dicendum quod non est simplex habitus, sed nominat potentiam cum habitu . . . Licet enim potentia per se non iuvet potentiam vel inclinet ad bonum, tamen potentia cum habitu iuvat et inclinat.
[93] DH, p. 530, ll. 62–70. [94] DH, p. 530–531, ll. 70–06.

rejects evil, since there can be no motivating force without appetitive desire. This understanding of the psychology of the human action led Aristotle to argue that the intellect moves, insofar as it is a certain appetite and by means of appetite. Appetite, however, is not some special power, but rather a general passion for all motivating desires.[95] *Synderesis* is not some power united to the other faculties of the soul. Albert thinks that while other powers may be completely, or partially, corrupted, corruption cannot be a principle of actuality. What is the cause of error is the failure of the potency to attain its perfection. *Synderesis* is a part of the soul, more removed from the corruption of desire than any other of the soul's components. Its distance from corruption allows it to remain unconquered, although some may claim it to be part of the primary rectitude in all the powers of the soul.[96] Philosophers ignored *synderesis* because they distinguished potencies according to general objects. When they considered actions they did so from the perspective of human law. Christian thinkers, however, made more specific classifications and added the universal principles of divine law to that of human justice. As a result, they applied *synderesis* to principles and the superior part of reason. *Synderesis* allowed for contemplation of divine justice in accordance with eternal standards. The philosophers did not posit any such eternal ideals.[97] In this explanation Albert has given an accurate depiction of the difference between the philosophical and theological explanations of moral principles.

Theological arguments dominate the question whether *synderesis* is able to err or sin. If one is condemned to eternal damnation then every human element must thereby be punished. The logical conclusion would be that every potency has sinned. If a human being is wholly corrupted by sin, then *synderesis* must also bear the stains of error. Like Philip the Chancellor, Albert wonders whether heretics and pagans, who persist in error, are examples of those whose *synderesis* has become corrupted. Basil, however, wrote that the mind's natural judgment always accepts what is praiseworthy and rejects evil. Such a power can never consent to sin. John Chrysostom speaks of the incorruptible judgment of conscience, which

---

[95] DH, p. 531, ll. 9–19.   [96] DH, p. 531, ll. 24–36.

[97] DH, p. 531, ll. 36–47: Ad id quod quaeritur ulterius, quare philosophi non fecerint mentionem de synderesi, dicendum quod philosophi distinguunt potentias secundum obiecta generalia; et si considerant operabilia, faciunt hoc secundum rationes iuris humani. Sancti autem specialius distinguunt secundum ius divinum et humanum, et secundum principia iuris et particularia inventa; et ideo sancti ponunt synderesim ad principia et portionem superiorem rationis, quae inhaerescit iustitiae divinae contemplandae secundum rationes aeternas, quarum neutram ponunt philosophi.

Albert takes to mean the spark of *synderesis*.[98] Albert agrees with Basil and John Chrysostom that *synderesis* never errs because it involves only innate universal principles. Reason is the source of error when it applies universals to particular decisions, and errs because it is a lower faculty than *synderesis*. The Christian authors do not elevate reason to the same level as the Greek philosophers did.[99] Even the condemnation and damnation of the whole person because of sin does not destroy the power to reject evil. In heretics and unbelievers error originates not in *synderesis*, but rather in reason's application. *Synderesis* commands only that faith requires defending, or that faith and justice should inform a life. The particular applications concerning what constitutes faith and justice come from reason, which may lead to error.[100]

Conscience is the final element in the moral process that results from the practical syllogism. Albert defines conscience generally as the conclusion of practical reason that follows from the general premise of *synderesis* and the minor premise of reason. O. Lottin considers Albert's treatment of *synderesis* and conscience to be similar to a modern theory of the norm of morality.[101] When someone asks why the conscience dictates that something is to be done, the response is because that something is good. If one persists and asks for what reason is something good to be done, the answer is that every good should be performed. These simple questions form the following syllogism: Every good is to be done; this is good; it, therefore, should be done. The major premise depends upon *synderesis* whose task is to direct one to good through universal principles (*rationes*). The minor comes from reason that aligns the particular with the universal. The conclusion to act arises from conscience, which recognizes the connection between the two premises.[102] The practical syllogism approximates the process of theoretical reasoning, since the principles of *synderesis* provide premises known *per se*. The premise that should be evident through reason often is overlooked because experience is lacking. As a result, error creeps into the particular conclusion.[103] *Synderesis*, rather than reason, is called the spark of conscience because the former provides immutable rectitude, while the latter may fall into the darkness of error.[104] While conscience

[98] DH, pp. 531–532, ll. 50–29.   [99] DH, p. 532, ll. 30–38.   [100] DH, p. 533, ll. 58–62.
[101] O. Lottin, "Le rôle de la raison dans la morale Albertino-Thomiste," *Psychologie et morale aux XIIᵉ et XIIIᵉ siècles* (Louvain, Gembloux: Abbaye du Mont César, Duclot, 1942-1949), v. III, pp. 543-544. C. Trottmann notes that prudence is insufficient for morality without intuition of principles. C. Trottmann, "La syndérèse selon Albert le Grand," in Senner, p. 261.
[102] DH, p. 535, ll. 48–53.   [103] DH, p. 536, ll. 12-19.   [104] DH, p. 536, ll. 38–41.

may at times cause moral error, Albert often indicates that the more common source of moral evil lies in a false conclusion of reason. Conscience may sometimes err when both the dictates of *synderesis* and the direction of reason may not coincide.[105]

Albert distinguishes *synderesis* further from the other motivating human powers in his question on the possibility of conscience being extinguished. He says that an image belongs primarily to the rational soul according to the mind. So that this statement may be fully understood one should know that the motivating powers are either ordered to God alone, or to what is human. If ordered to God, the powers are simply ordered to God under the guise of truth and goodness placed by nature. If they are operable powers they reflect their practicality through universal principles alone, or through reasons applied in particular cases. If the former, then *synderesis* will be the simplest power consequent to the images in the mind. If the latter, i.e. reasons applied to particulars, then the motivating power functions either with cognition and is science, or is only a function of the appetite. Practical science may be understood in three ways. The acts are sought according to the deliberation of eternal and divine law, and such seeking is the function of the superior part of reason. The acts are pursued according to human positive law, which is the province of the inferior part of reason. Finally actions may be practiced indifferently under the nature of choice, which is the motivating power as the basis of free choice. If the power exists only with appetite, it may issue commands, be commanded, or both. If it commands, it is the will; if commanded it sends signals to the body; if both, it is concupiscence, irascibility and sensuality. As an informing power the practical intellect according to right reason simply considers good and evil. It may also provide information about good and evil in particular circumstance and is called the motivating phantasm. As an imperative force, it functions either with respect to goodness simply, and is the will following the practical intellect. If it acts with respect to a particular good, it is an irascible or concupiscible power. This division is the doctrine of the Christian authors, since the philosophers simplify the psychology of the act by dividing it into the practical intellect and the motivating image. If the soul commands with respect to the good simply, this power is the will that follows the practical intellect; if it commands with respect to particular goods, it is the function of the irascible or concupiscent power of the soul.[106] Albert stresses the importance "of introducing into the practical syllogism an infallible source of the major premises capable always of

---

[105] DH, p. 537, ll. 42–43 and ll. 53–55.   [106] DH, pp. 554–555, ll. 44–15.

envisioning the sovereign good; towards this end it directs action. Such is the role of *synderesis*."[107]

In a series of questions composed about 1250 Albert again raises the question of the meaning of *synderesis*, first in an article on the powers of reason. The writings of Augustine provide the inspiration for Albert's findings. The nature of justice and other virtues, he argues, may be considered universally according to the universal principles of right. In this way there can be no error because of the power of *synderesis*. Even a heretic recognizes the universal principle that one should believe what is necessary to believe, but is deceived in believing a particular doctrine.[108] The content of *synderesis* is contained in the universal principles of law that are written in the natural ability to judge. This natural ability is the true meaning of *synderesis*, which Albert believes Augustine determined.[109] Albert responds to the question whether *synderesis* is a potency or habit initially with the simple statement that it is a rational potency. But this answer demands more explanation. *Synderesis* is a moving power in that it directs one to a proper end, either actually or potentially, but it is also a directive power because it involves universal principles, which function similarly to those in intellectual knowledge. Just as the recognition of intellectual principles guides one to knowledge, the apprehension of moral imperatives leads to correct action.[110]

Synderesis is not a simple potency because it has innate content and elements of both cognition and appetite. A pure potency would only have actuality when some causality acts upon its development. As a result of such considerations Albert again refines his notion of *synderesis* and calls it a certain motivating potency through a habit of the universals of rectitude (*quaedam potentia motiva per habitum universalium iuris*). While it includes aspects of cognition and appetite it inclines more to the cognitive side, since the practical intellect always repels evil to a greater degree than the will that may be led by desire to incorrect action.[111] The habit associated with *synderesis* is innate (*inditus*) or natural, but is called natural not because it specifically or individually preserves its own nature, but rather because it is part of the endowment of human nature. Albert says even if

---

[107] C. Trottmann, "La syndérèse selon Albert le Grand," p. 261.

[108] *Quaestiones* in *Alberti Magni Opera omnia* 25/2, ed. W. Kübel and H. Anzulewicz (Münster: Aschendorff, 1993), pp. 227, 38–45.

[109] *Quaestiones*, p. 232, ll. 25–26: . . . sicut dicit Augustinus, universalia iuris sunt scripta in naturali iudicatoris, quod est synderesis.

[110] *Quaestiones*, p. 234, ll. 14–22.

[111] *Quaestiones*, p. 234, ll. 29–35. For a diagram of the cognitive and apprehensive powers of the soul in Albert's moral thought, see C. Trottmann, "La syndérèse selon Albert le Grand," p. 268.

this habit is considered essentially natural, it comes from God in its creation.[112]

The term 'potency through a habit', refers to the complicated status of *synderesis*. It cannot be a pure potency since it has content and a type of actuality before any activity whatsoever; it cannot be a true habit since it exists without any repetitive measures to develop it. Like the attainment of the principles of scientific knowledge, the actualization of *synderesis* seems to need some individual experiences before its possessor recognizes its universal principles. Just as a person needs to see triangles to know the principle that all triangles are three-sided, so too does one need to encounter the expression of the imperatives of natural law in order to recognize its truth. The principles are imparted in the creation of the human soul, but do not operate immediately and without some apprehension. A potency perfected by a natural habit can produce its act without any further activity, but *synderesis* is a potency perfected by a habit of universal principles in practical acts. As such, the potency awaits application in particular circumstances.[113] Albert concludes that *synderesis* must be a motivating cognitive potency of the rational soul that is perfected by a natural habit. Its inflexibility comes both from the nature of the potency and also of the habit. Its steadfast nature could not come from the nature of the potency alone because then no motivating potency of the soul could err, which is clearly false. Its rigidity cannot arise from habit alone since a habit is something imperfect in its being, and so it would lack the power in which it exists, and through which it acts. The only conclusion left to Albert is that *synderesis* exists in a union of both potency and habit, even if it takes its nature more from the habit that perfects the potency. There are habits that perfect the motivating potencies of the rational soul, and some of these habits wholly complete the potencies by determining them necessarily to one course of action, such as the habit by which one knows infallibly the imperatives of law. A true understanding is this type of habit, which is always correct, as Aristotle had determined in the *De anima* and the *Nicomachean Ethics*. This necessary and correct understanding is for Albert the true meaning of *synderesis*.[114]

For a modern interpreter of Albert the association of the habit with the potency preserves the infallibility of *synderesis*, and the perfection that

---

[112] *Quaestiones*, p. 234, ll. 44–49.

[113] *Quaestiones*, pp. 235–236, ll. 69–01: Potencia perfecta per habitum naturalem potest per se sine aliquo adveniente producere suum actum, sed synderesis est potentia perfecta per habitum universalium principiorum in operabilibus.

[114] *Quaestiones*, p. 237, ll. 10–27.

comes primarily from the habit determines the potency to the individual act.[115] C. Trottmann here clearly recognizes the dilemma that introduction of *synderesis* into the understanding of Aristotelian ethics presents. If one knows infallibly the principles of right action, then human moral choice must always be determined to what is right. But the potency lies dormant until it is perfected by the natural habit that pursues the correct paths of action. *Synderesis* is neither an ordinary potency nor an ordinary habit because each requires the presence of the other in order to function properly. The seemingly complex theory concerning the meaning of *synderesis* is Albert's attempt to preserve the innate rectitude of the cognitive function as well as the freedom of the appetitive one. He, like his medieval contemporaries, provides primarily a basis for universal codes of conduct despite their endeavors to preserve voluntary liberty.

In itself, *synderesis* can never err, but despite its rule over other powers, moral error can occur. Albert compares such error to a soldier who may fall from his horse through no fault of his own, but because the horse missteps. The fall from rectitude is ascribed to *synderesis* only with respect to the effect, just as the horseman's fall is produced by his mount.[116] Albert distinguishes *synderesis* as a rational potency 'as nature' from a rational potency 'as reason'. 'As nature', it is understood as that which provides for a human being those things that preserve human nature. Such a concept of nature prevents *synderesis* from being turned from its purpose because it is perfected in those principles imparted by its very creation. It should not be thought to act 'as nature' in the sense that the potency is determined to one effect only, as the nature of heavy bodies that always fall downward.[117]

Albert in composing these early discussions on the nature of moral reasoning prepares himself for the task of reconciling the entire text of Aristotle's NE with the Christian ideals of perfect beatitude and natural law. In his later works he provides a thorough commentary on Aristotle's thought, which greatly influenced his successors. In the next chapter we will consider the treatments on beatitude, happiness and prudence and their relation to the process of moral decision making.

---

[115] C. Trottmann, "La syndérèse selon Albert le Grand," p. 270.

[116] *Quaestiones*, p. 237, ll. 35–41: Unde patet, quod synderesis per se non potest praecipitari, sed tamen [secundum] quod est in aliis viribus ut regens in recto, potest praecipitari, sicut aliquando miles cadit non sui vitio, sed casu equi. Et ita praecipitari erit synderesis quantum ad effectum, quem non consequitur in libero arbitrio, quod est quasi suus equus.

[117] *Quaestiones*, p. 237, ll. 47–56.

6

Happiness, prudence and moral reasoning
in the later works of Albert the Great

Albert's commentary on the complete text of the NE, known as the *Super Ethica*, is an important contribution to the history of moral philosophy. Albert was the first medieval author to benefit from the translation of the entire text of Aristotle and the accompanying Greek commentaries. The work, which reflects Albert's teaching at Cologne, includes questions and commentaries on every topic in Aristotle's text. Thomas Aquinas attended the lectures on the *Ethics* at the Dominican House of Studies, and benefitted greatly from Albert's careful exposition of Aristotle's text.[1] Modern scholars such as G. Wieland and L. Sturlese regard this work as a comprehensive foundation of a philosophy independent of theology and based on reason entirely free of the religious domination of the age.[2] Other scholars deny so radical a departure from theological doctrines in Albert's first commentary on the NE,[3] but in either case this commentary had an enormous influence on subsequent discussions on topics concerning human goodness, happiness and moral virtue in the Middle Ages.

In the general introduction to the commentary, Albert lists three topics in ethics: the subject, the end and the use. Its subject, as described by

---

[1] A. Pelzer, "Le cours inédit d'Albert le Grand sur la morale à Nicomaque recuilli et rédigé par S. Thomas d'Aquin," *Revue néoscolatique de philosophie*, 24 (1922), pp. 331–361, 479–520: *Super Ethica Commentum et Quaestiones* (=SE), *Alberti Magni Opera omnia*, 14.1&2, ed. W. Kübel (Münster: Aschendorff, 1968–1987), Introduction, pp. V–VI.

[2] G. Wieland, "Albertus Magnus und die Frage nach menschlichen Glück–zur ersten Kölner Ethikvorlesung," Albert der Große in Köln (Kölner Universitätsreden, H. 80), ed. J. Aertsen, *Albert der Große in Köln. Gehalten auf der Feierstunde zur 750sten Wiederkehr der Einrichtung des Kölner Generalstudiums der Dominikaner am 6. November 1998* (Köln, 1999), p. 26; L. Sturlese, *Die deutsche Philosophie im Mittelalter. Von Bonifatius bis zu Albert dem Großen (748–1280)* (Munich: Beck, 1993), p. 333.

[3] J. Söder, "Die Erprobung der Vernunft. Vom Umgang mit Traditionen in *De homine*," *Albertus Magnus zum Gedenken nach 800 Jahren: Neue Zugänge, Aspekte und Perspektiven*, ed. W. Senner *et al.* (Berlin: Akademie Verlag, 2001), pp. 1–13.

Ptolemy, is a type of discipline that leads to knowledge or conduct (*morum*). Conduct studied in ethics consists in the actions of a human being *qua* human, and concerns the question of right and wrong. This discipline complements the intellect, since Aristotle describes the practical intellect as that element that motivates by means of knowledge gained by reason. According to Aristotle the greatest delight is found in the consideration of truth, which alone has no contrary and produces no regret. One of its uses produces gratitude from others who recognize justice. By means of such recognition a foundation for true friendship is laid.[4] In the first question of the commentary, which asks whether there can be a science of ethics, Albert sketches a response that influences many subsequent commentators. He notes that every science considers what is necessary, but one may argue that there is no necessity associated with conduct.[5] If one were to consider the intent and nature of conduct, however, its reasons are necessary and produce a science. Just as in a science that considers generation and corruption from contingent causes, but attains the status of science according to universal reasons for such changes, so too does such a basis for moral science exist. These universal reasons become an important part of medieval moral theory.[6] The use of ethical theory may lead to specific actions, but its doctrine is found in universal reasons. Such reasons, which Albert places under the heading of *ethics docens,* also have a significant role in *ethica utens,* since the former aims at knowledge, while the latter seeks to make a person good. They are not really distinct ends, since in a practical science knowledge should be carried out in practice.[7]

a Civic and contemplative happiness

In the prologue to the SE, Albert offers another idea that becomes a central theme in his understanding of human goodness. He asks how there could be one science that determines the perfection of the speculative and the moral intellect. He argues that the perfection of the speculative intellect does not fall under moral science, insofar as it is speculative, but rather as it produces pleasure. It derives pleasure from the will's choice of speculation as something desirable. In this way its perfection becomes part of moral

---

[4] SE, p. 1, ll. 1–55.   [5] SE, p. 1, ll. 58–60.   [6] SE, p. 2, ll. 11–19.
[7] SE, p. 2, ll. 16–22. See G. Wieland, "Ethica docens – ethica utens," *Sprache und Erkenntnis im Mittelalter,* ed. J. P. Beckmann *et al. Miscellanea medievalia,* 13 (Berlin/New York: W. de Gruyter, 1981), II, pp. 593–601.

science[8] and pertains to what Albert terms the double human good (*duplici bono humano*).

In the preliminary discussions on the subject of ethics, Albert raises questions that persisted throughout centuries of commentaries on the NE: the relationship between virtue and happiness; and whether the goal of ethics is virtue or happiness. He says that neither intellectual nor moral virtues seem to be part of the essence of happiness since divine beings, which are supremely happy, are neither brave nor prudent. Aristotle, however, does consider both happiness and virtue, but not consistently throughout the entire NE. In his solution, Albert compares the manner of regarding the subject of metaphysics to that of ethics. The subject of science may be that which is principally intended, such as God in first philosophy, whose conclusions aim at knowledge of the divine being. There may be that which is commonly determined in a discipline, such as being in metaphysics. In ethics happiness is indeed its principal subject and virtues are considered in their relation to it. Albert says that one may also regard human voluntary choice as the subject of ethics since it is a consideration within every ethical decision. Insofar as the form of the choiceworthy and deliberation of the will fall under complete or moral happiness, they fall within the scope of moral science.[9]

The first part of the commentary contains a division of ethics into two parts. Since there are two types of perfection, moral and contemplative, Aristotle first considered moral happiness and then moral virtue.[10] Albert recognizes immediately that such an interpretation of Aristotle may be controversial since he places virtue under the definition of happiness. It falls within the definition, however, not as formally different, but as materially different. Because the end is the most important cause in ethical action, Aristotle determined the question of happiness before all others.[11] The distinction between happiness according to its essence and happiness in its supreme possibility (*in maximo suo posse*) appears early in the SE. The former state cannot be easily lost since it consists in an internal good, but the latter may be subject to misfortunes, such as the loss of wealth or friends. This distinction permits Albert to resolve neatly the questions concerning the stability of human happiness. Happiness in its essence is extremely stable, but in its supreme possibility it depends upon many

[8] SE, p. 3, ll. 18–24.   [9] SE, p. 3, ll. 54–76. See also SE, p. 5, ll. 56–63.

[10] SE, p. 5, ll. 21–25: Quia cum in consideratione huius scientiae veniat perfectio moralis et contemplativa, primo determinat de morali secundo de contemplativa . . . Prima dividitur in duas. Primo determinat de felicitate morali, secundo de virtute morali.

[11] SE, p. 5, ll. 27–32.

external factors.[12] The commentary of Eustratius provides support for such a division. According to Albert, the Commentator believes Aristotle to have considered the necessity of health for happiness in its supreme possibility, which encompasses all necessities for the human organism. Health is needed in order to perform civic duties. Good health may not be the supreme good in the practical order, but it does provide the end for all medical actions that contribute to the supremely happy life.[13]

The modifier, 'supreme' (*summum*), refers to goodness, (*bonum*), in two ways: simply, and so there is only one supreme good, which is God; or supreme with respect to something (*alicui*), which is that end to which all operations proper to it are ordered. What Aristotle seeks to identify is a supreme good that belongs to a human being *qua* human. Human nature depends primarily upon the nature of the soul that must be understood in two ways: in itself and so it is rational; according to its highest part by which it attains theoretical understanding. Reason is created in the shadow, and on the horizon of, the intellect. Eustratius says that the soul is intellectual by participation, and the intelligible forms are grasped by an act of the intellect. There must, therefore, be a two-fold order in human acts: one that is ratiocinative, and the principle of external actions, since reason considers contingent events; another that is contemplative insofar as one attains intellectual understanding. The former's end is civic happiness, and the latter's goal is contemplative happiness. The two human supreme goodnesses (*summe bona hominis*) have an order in that civic happiness is directed toward contemplation. Civic excellence permits a peace of mind that helps one better contemplate.[14]

---

[12] SE, p. 22, ll. 37–43: ... dicendum, quod felicitas secundum essentiam non potest aliquo modo auferri; sed quantum ad actus exteriores, secundum quod est in maximo suo posse, ut non solum se regat, sed domum vel civitatem, per multa infortunia aufertur, sicut est amissio rerum et amicorum quibus indiget ad regimen aliorum.

[13] SE, p. 31, ll. 38–53.

[14] SE, pp. 32–33, ll. 74–15: Dicendum, quod summum dicitur dupliciter: vel simpliciter, et sic est unum tantum, quod est deus; et sic non quaeritur hic. Vel summum alicui et hoc est, ad quod ordinantur omnes operationes propriae illius rei; et sic quaeritur hic summum bonum hominis, et ad quod ordinantur omnes operationes propriae quae sunt eius, inquantum est homo non autem operationes communes vel aegritudinale. Natura autem animae rationalis, per quam homo est homo, potest dupliciter considerari: aut secundum se et sic est rationalis, aut secundum suam summitatem qua attingit intellectum, quia ratio creatur in umbra et horizonte intelligentiae, et sic est intellectualis; unde Commentator dicit, quod anima est intellectualis participatione, intelligentiae vero sunt intelligibiles per essentiam. Et secundum hoc est duplex ordo in actibus suis propriis, quia inquantum ratiocinativa, sic est principium exteriorum operum, quia ratio est contingentium; et sic est optimum eius civilis felicitas. Inquantum autem attingit intellectualitatem, sic actus eius est contemplatio, et sic finis eius et optimum est contemplativa felicitas. Et sic secundum duos ordines duo sunt

Happiness is supreme in its own order, but may also be directed to a higher end, that which is what is simply best for a human being.[15] According to Albert there are two supreme goals for a human being, with each the best in its own order, but not supreme simply.[16] Civic happiness is termed 'perfect' in its genus and a perfect good in the order of political affairs. In itself, it encompasses all the nobilities of its genus and the corresponding virtues.[17] The assertion that contemplative and civic happiness constitute two distinct ends for human beings will become the dominant reading of Aristotle in subsequent commentaries on the NE in the Middle Ages.[18] Although civic happiness is ordered to contemplative, it may be considered superior in one sense. It is more useful since it leads to a communal good, and provides a peaceful environment.[19] All good human actions will ultimately lead to true beatitude, which is unattainable in a human life or through purely human efforts.

The question of what types of actions produce happiness leads to a consideration of prudence in relation to happiness itself. If prudence is exercised in order to contribute to other virtues, Albert concludes that it may be subordinated to them. If it is so subordinate, then happiness could not consist in prudential virtue, since it is not an end in itself. Because Aristotle identifies wisdom as the most perfect intellectual virtue, he must have thought happiness to consist in wisdom and not in prudence. Prudence may be thought of as the perfection of reason, but how can it be complete, if it contributes to other practical virtues? Since every form of ruling is directed to that which it governs and the act of prudence is to rule itself and others, then the ruling acts of prudence must seek a goal more worthy than itself, which can only be happiness itself.[20] These arguments seem to exclude prudence from the definition of happiness, but Albert distinguishes reason into that which acts according to its own object, and that which governs other actions. Only what perfects itself in acting in accord with its own object can order other actions. In this way prudence is more perfect than other virtues and completes reason by choosing what is beneficial. It perfects itself not in theoretical thought alone, but also as it

summe bona hominis, quorum tamen unum ordinatur ad alterum, scilicet civilis ad contemplativam, quia omne regimen, quod est per civilem, quaeritur propter quietem, in qua libere possit esse contemplatio. Et sic finis eius et optimum est contemplativa felicitas, quia una est materialis et dispositiva ad alteram. Et sic relinquitur, quod tantum sit poni unum optimum hominis.

[15] SE, p. 33, ll. 31–34.   [16] SE, p. 33, ll. 41–47.   [17] SE, p. 34, ll. 23–30.

[18] A. Celano, "The End of Practical Wisdom: Ethics as Science in the Thirteenth Century," *Journal of the History of Philosophy*, 33 (1995), pp. 225–243.

[19] SE, p. 35, ll. 31–40.   [20] SE, p. 41, ll. 28–48.

identifies the mean in every virtue. Both Socrates and Eustratius saw a connection between all virtues and prudence, and in its function as a ruling element prudence is the most perfect achievement of reason and is essential to happiness.[21]

Prudential judgments may produce other virtues, but they are not ordered to them as something separate from the desired ends. Prudence includes in itself the end, and conveys its grasp of the end to other operations, just as celestial motion may be said to be ordered to the generation of inferior bodies. While the production of inferior objects may be the task of celestial motion, inferior bodies cannot be said to direct such motion.[22] Wisdom (*sapientia*) belongs to a different order from prudence, one that concerns the perfection of the intellect and not of reason. It pertains to contemplative happiness, which is simply superior to the type of civic happiness that results from prudential judgments.[23] Prudence does not perfect reason insofar as it deliberates contemplatively, but as it leads to action and maintains its rectitude in an act.[24] Prudence does not rule when it produces its best function, such as disposing one to an end, since it causes more perfectly in containing, and directing one to, the end.[25]

Happiness, as described by Aristotle, must be that which is most perfect in a human being within the limits of a human life. It must contain a combination of all virtues steadfastly practiced over a lengthy period of time. Prudence may be viewed as if (*quasi*) a form of all these virtues because it rules the process that discovers the mean and determines choice according to right reason. Albert accepts Aristotle's claim that one who has prudence does indeed have all other virtues, but emphasizes its role in the practical arena. He does note that happiness arises according to prudential action that rules itself and other acts, and joins all virtues in the happy person.[26] Prudence is

---

[21] SE, p. 41, ll. 53–66.   [22] SE, p. 41, ll. 75–79.

[23] SE, p. 41, ll. 80–84: ... dicendum, quod sapientia est de alio ordine, scilicet de perfectione intellectus, non rationis, et pertinet ad felicitatem contemplativam, quae melior est quam civilis, quae est secundum prudentiam.

[24] SE, p. 41, ll. 84–87: ... dicendum, quod prudentia non perficit rationem, secundum quod est tantum in contemplatione ut consilians, sed secundum quod immiscet se operi et in opere retinet suam rectitudinem.

[25] SE, p. 42, ll. 1–4.

[26] SE, pp. 42–43, ll. 84–03: Dicendum, quod prudentia est quasi forma aliarum virtutum, quia in omnibus datur medium et eligibile secundum rationem rectam, quadirigit prudentia. Et cum prudentia non sit tantum in speculativa, sed secundum quod tenet rectitudinem rationis in opere: oportet ad hoc, quod simpliciter sit prudens, quod sit rectus in omni opere et qui habeat prudentiam, habeat omnem virtutem. Et ideo qui est tantum castus, est prudens secundum quid et non simpliciter. Et quia felicitas est secundum operationem prudentiae, qua aliquis regit se et alios, oportet, quod felicitate congregentur omnes virtutes.

present in other virtues when its actions are correct and when it produces habits from the corresponding acts. Happiness should not be understood as a congregation of results, but rather as a simple state resulting from the many actions that lead to it. Happiness is the end in the sense of a formal cause, perfecting all that is directed to it.[27]

The various ancient opinions on happiness concur in the idea that it consists in living and acting well (*bene vivere et bene operari*), but such a vague designation led to different doctrines concerning its essential nature. Albert eliminates virtue from the possible definitions of happiness when he says virtue cannot be the essence of happiness because the supreme human good is an operation. An operation, however, may be reduced to virtue as a cause, just as any effect exists in harmony with its cause.[28] Virtue, as a habit, will not comprise the substantial nature of happiness, except as a cause. The substance of happiness encompasses possession, operation and use. Possession is a stable state; operation is its true substance; and use is the custom of acting. Operation may refer to the act of virtue, which is a principal component to happiness. Human goodness may be viewed as it is in itself, or as it is diffused through others. The operation of prudence, through which happiness results, belongs to one person, insofar as one rules oneself through proper actions and passions that are communicable to others. Happiness, as a function of individual prudential decisions, requires no external goods. What is more divine and perfect pertains to an entire community and requires prudential decisions to extend to the rule of many. In the best possible state of extended happiness external goods are needed for acts that go beyond personal pursuits. A prudential person who directs attention to the community must understand the effect of external goods for the society's welfare.[29]

Albert merely mentions in passing the problem of the exact nature of happiness in the SE. He notes that, as Aristotle says, some claim happiness to be the same as virtue, and that no one asks whether virtue is acquired by operations. Albert concludes that Aristotle designated happiness, or contemplative virtues, as something that could be learned (*discibile*); whereas he thought the moral virtues needed habituation (*assuescibile*); the act of external rule he thought must be exercised (*exercitabile*).[30] Albert limits the question of the relation of virtue to happiness to the consideration of the cause of human goodness. He does not devote a separate question to the role of virtue in producing happiness, but rather considers the role of

---

[27] SE, p. 43, ll. 19–27.   [28] SE, p. 47, ll. 48–52.   [29] SE, pp. 51–52, ll. 94–18.
[30] SE, p. 54, ll. 1–7.

divine causality in its production. Human actions are the cause of the type of happiness that Aristotle describes, and while God may be the first cause from which all goodness proceeds, Albert considers here only the proximate cause of happiness.[31]

Like some modern commentators, Albert concentrates upon the political and communal aspects of human goodness in his exposition of book I of the NE. He discusses the specific topic of contemplative happiness in his commentary on book X. He defines civic happiness as the operation of prudence, and this operation enters into the substance of the other virtues of lower potencies when it furnishes the mean to them. This operation does not occur in the separate power of the soul that contemplation perfects.[32] While Christian writers argue that virtue remains after death by means of different acts, the philosophers deny such a possibility. The Christian idea develops from the notion of the meritorious power of grace, which permits attribution of virtuous acts after death. Philosophers, however, consider the virtuous acts as they have the mode of virtue only from the actions themselves. As a result, they do not posit meritorious acts of virtue.[33] Virtue is generated from actions directed toward its production and acts proceeding from the developing habit. The repetition of good actions removes vice and purifies the natural power. When the last operation induces a perfect habit the result will be a state of happiness. Operations that precede virtue have a dominant role in producing happiness in the manner of a remote cause; the operations that result from virtue function as a proximate cause. The operations of perfect virtue have the most dominant role, since they are the essential element to the production of happiness.[34]

In the commentary on book I Albert has several opportunities to discuss the state of the separate soul and its fate after death, but he refrains from any discussion of such topics. When analyzing Solon's warning to call no one happy until death, he rightly uses the term '*beatus*' rather than '*felix*' in order to indicate the possibility of the benefits of good fortune that may enhance the life of the *felix*. Both he and Thomas Aquinas often use the term '*beatus*' in order to describe one who enjoys the benefits of chance, or

---

[31] SE, p. 55, ll. 44–49.

[32] SE, p. 59, ll. 3–8: Dicendum, quod felicitas civilis est operatio prudentiae, secundum quam intrat in substantiam aliarum virtutum quae sunt in potentiis inferioribus, determinans eis medium; et ideo in anima separata non potest esse talis felicitas, etsi felicitas aliqua, scilicet contemplativa.

[33] SE, p. 59, ll. 28–36.   [34] SE, p. 64, ll. 67–78.

one who attains eternal bliss.[35] Albert claims that no one should believe that any life can be called totally blessed. Aristotle's phrase, μακαρίους δ'ἀνθρώπους, translated into Latin as *beatos ut homines*, indicates that there is always some defect in human life, which does not affect the contemplative perfection of divine purely spiritual beings. Albert's use of *angelos* in connection with this passage recalls the earlier commentators who had before them the corrupted text of the NE, where *beatos ut homines* was rendered *beatos ut angelos*.[36]

The state of the soul after death cannot be sufficiently understood through philosophy. If philosophers were to suppose that the soul does indeed survive death, they could say nothing about its status and its relation to the living. Only through the infused supernatural light of faith could one answer such question. Albert adds that what contradicts faith cannot be rationally demonstrated, because faith is not *contra rationem*, and there can be no discord within truth.[37] Philosophers realize that once the soul is freed from its union with the body, it cannot exercise any operations that originate in the powers joined to the organs of the body. There must be another process of understanding than the method of abstraction by the soul of an intelligible species through mental images (*phantasmatibus*).[38]

Happiness is not a certain general beatitude or an arrangement of the entire soul according to every potency, as the theologians maintain, but rather an operation according to a particular virtue, prudence, and according to a particular potency, reason. The order of reason and the judgment of prudence affect the lower psychic powers and inform every virtue. The perfection of reason according to prudence affects the entire person, even when the particular virtue of prudence and the specific power of reason have their own proper objects.[39] Aristotle's definition of happiness as an operation according to virtue leads Albert to distinguish the state of human goodness from virtuous accomplishment. He recognizes an element of circularity in Aristotle's notion of happiness, since happiness is posited in the definition of virtue. Aristotle terms virtue a disposition of the perfect to the best, but such a description also applies to happiness. If virtue is

---

[35] For the difference in meaning between *beatitudo* and *felicitas* see A. Celano, "The Concept of Worldly Beatitude in the Writings of Thomas Aquinas," *Journal of the History of Philosophy*, 25 (1987), pp. 215–226.

[36] SE, pp. 69, 39–42: Et ne credatur, quod quis possit in vita esse omnino removet hoc dicens: hos dicimus esse 'beatos ut homines', in quibus necessario est aliquis defectus non ut deos ut angelos. See above c. 4, p. 87.

[37] SE, p. 71, ll. 73–83.   [38] SE, pp. 71–72, ll. 91–06.   [39] SE, pp. 75–76, ll. 72–11.

placed within the definition of happiness then the same thing will be both prior and posterior. In other words, virtue produces happiness, but happiness consists in the continued exercise of virtue.[40] To answer this criticism of Aristotle's position, Albert distinguishes between happiness, which is simply prior as a principle, and virtue, which is prior with respect to the actions of human beings. Happiness is prior by priority of the end and virtue prior through its efficient causality. Virtue elicits the operations by which one acquires happiness, and so it can be both prior and posterior to happiness, since its relation is not strictly as cause to effect.[41] How the operation of happiness differs from those virtuous actions that produce it is not explained by Albert. The process of developing virtue occurs as follows: a virtuous habit arises from an operation that is directed to virtue, ruled by reason and measured according to the appropriate circumstances. Everything that is measured is done so with respect to something else, and that to which any operation is measured is the mode or rectitude of reason. The type of habit produced in this way reflects the type of operations that lead to the development of habitual virtue.[42]

The intellectual virtues are generally contemplative and closer to the ultimate end than the moral one. The soul may be perfected in two ways, since the ultimate act of the speculative intellect is contemplation of truth, and the final act of the motivating element of the soul is the operation of good.[43] Prudence functions as a mid-point between intellectual and moral virtues. Aristotle described it in such a way that its material aspect pertains to the genus of intellectual activity, but the formal element finds its order in the genus of morality.[44] When defining the mean in virtues relative to the moral agent, Albert understands right reason to be that very mean in prudence. While some may choose more than they should and others less, the prudent person holds to the middle way. Because prudence is not only a particular virtue but also governs others, it maintains the mean in actions outside prudence's primary domain, as in courage and temperance.[45]

One may do wrong by making a choice that is somehow based in ignorance, but ignorance does not constitute the reason for choice, because an evil person may know the proper reason, but choose to act improperly. An appetite for something contrary to good may overwhelm a person to the extent that one cannot rightly apply the universal reason to a particular act. One is not unaware of the universal proposition, but is deceived in the

---

[40] SE, p. 75, ll. 63–67.   [41] SE, p. 76, ll. 29–36.   [42] SE, pp. 77–78, 88–06.
[43] SE, p. 90, ll. 85–88.   [44] SE, p. 91, ll. 3–6.   [45] SE, p. 120, ll. 48–54.

application of the minor premise or conclusion.[46] The wrongdoer has knowledge of the action that he chooses to commit, but remains ignorant of the rectitude of reason, as it is applicable to a particular act through choice.[47] Such ignorance of evil removes the practical knowledge that regulates action, but does not destroy theoretical knowledge that characterizes consideration and the syllogistic process.[48] The universal propositions of moral science are naturally impressed upon all human beings. Just as in the theoretical sciences there are certain common principles from which one proceeds to specific conclusions, so too in moral science are there similar imperatives that rule actions, such as do not steal and the like. All people are bound, and able, to know them, because all have a path to them provided by reason itself. Such principles are called natural law, and are not determined by the process of reason. Other principles are called common law, as they are reflected in written laws. Ignorance of such laws displays a lack of awareness of the universal. Albert does not think we determine universal principles by the reasoning process because they are innate.[49]

The will whose object is goodness does not determine the good, but rather is made good by the pursuit of what is simply good. Albert here follows the doctrine of Cicero, who calls simply good actions honorable or proper (*honesta*) because they attract and compel one by their intrinsic force, and not merely by their appeal to the human will.[50] Interior goods derive their goodness from their similarity to the first good. Albert claims that there is a substantial likeness, but these goods are closer to the supreme good by a formal similitude.[51] The perfect measure of moral rectitude originates in the habit of virtue by which one directly attains the mean. Albert correctly notes that Aristotle places the external measure of moral decency in the morally upright person (*studiosus*), and not in a separate standard. Just as the virtue of a horse is tied to equine nature, the rectitude

---

[46] SE, p. 146, ll. 16–25.   [47] SE, p. 146, ll. 36–39.   [48] SE, p. 146, ll. 40–44.

[49] SE, p. 146, ll. 72–82: Dicendum, quod sicut in speculativis sunt quaedam principia communia ex quibus proceditur ad particulares conclusiones, ita etiam sunt in morablibus quaedam principia communia quibus regulatur ad operationes, sicut non esse furandum et huiusmodi. Et haec quilibet tenetur scire et potest, quia habet ad haec viam rationis. Et haec dicuntur ius naturale, secundum quod sunt non determinate in ratione. Dicuntur etiam communia iuris, secundum quod determinata per ius scriptum. Et horum ignorantia dicitur ignorantia universalis.

[50] SE, pp. 165–166, ll. 85–02.

[51] SE, p. 166, ll. 19–24; see also J. Müller, *Natürliche Moral und philosophische Ethik bei Albertus Magnus* (Beiträge zur Geschichte der Philosophie und Theologie des Mittelalters: Texte und Untersuchungen, Neue Folge, 59: Münster, Aschendorff, 2001), pp. 183–186.

of reason in the good person is the perfect measure and rule of morally good actions. All human beings because of the nature of reason have the capacity for moral integrity, but only those who have developed the proper moral habits are said to have achieved perfectly moral rectitude.[52]

In his commentary on book III of the NE Albert views the question on the cause of good actions as an opportunity to discuss both philosophical and theological responses. He indicates that Aristotle maintained without reservation that human beings are the sole cause of voluntary good actions, but religious doctrine claims that beatitude results from good actions, but such virtue requires the assistance of grace.[53] Some say that human beings are unable to perform any good act without the infusion of some divine grace. If they mean that divine grace is truly the natural good bestowed by God then Albert agrees; if, however, they insist that infused grace added to natural gifts are necessary to cause political virtues, they are wrong. For Albert free will, which may choose between alternatives, is the source of good human actions.[54] Like most Christian moralists, Albert accepts the idea that the human being cannot be perfected because of its material nature, but some human aspects are not wholly material. They may be perfected as virtue formed *in semine*, which in itself is imperfect, but may become complete in the development of true virtue.[55] The end of virtuous actions, which is civil or contemplative happiness, is a topic for the philosophers, and they indicate how it results from human natural acts, and not meritorious ones.[56] Moral virtue's immediate genus lies in the middle way, and more specifically, is the mid-point in a habit or a middle habit (*habitus medius*).[57]

Virtues may be divided into moral and intellectual ones, but they still have a connection to the will. Albert views the role of the will in producing virtue in two ways. It may follow the intellect and, as such, is receptive to a concept that moves the will. What is in the intellect in this way will be ordered to something else, and is not desired in itself. If one speaks in this manner, knowledge, art, wisdom or any other perfection of the intellect cannot truly be a virtue. If one regards the will as preceding the intellect and as the motivating power of the soul's potentials, then the will orders the

---

[52] SE, p. 166, ll. 62–70.   [53] SE, pp. 169–170, ll. 96–06.   [54] SE, p. 170, ll. 9–18.
[55] SE, p. 170, ll. 19–27.
[56] SE, p. 170, ll. 65–70: ... dicendum, quod beatitudo civilis vel contemplativa, de qua considerant philosophi, est in potestate nostra, quia acquiritur per operationes nostras. Sed obiectio procedit de futura beatitudine, quam per opera meritoria meremur, in quae non possumus ex nobis.
[57] SE, p. 178, ll. 25–30.

intellect, and commands the act of superior powers. Just as the perfections of inferior powers are virtues because they are acquired by voluntary acts, so too are the perfections of the intellect itself. An important difference between the moral and intellectual virtues arises from the development of intellectual virtue as the supreme power of the soul. The more the superior power develops, the greater the virtue will be, as wisdom is greater than knowledge (*scientia*), which is greater than art. A moral virtue is one that perfects human beings in a way that allows for the accomplishment of acts that display themselves in external words and deeds.[58] The truth that regulates human practice falls under three general headings: the truth pertaining to justice, the truth of doctrine, and the truth of life. What these truths have in common is that they are all ruled by the divine law to which legal knowledge, religion and proper conduct are directed. The truth about which Aristotle speaks in the NE is civic truth that rules the words and deeds in public affairs.[59]

Justice differs from right (*ius*) because justice is determined not only with reference to an act, but also to the idea of right, from which the just action is derived. Right is both human and divine, and the former ideal derives its exemplars from the latter. When it follows divine exemplars, human right is called perpetual justice, but when it finds its exemplars and confirmation in the will, it is designated as constant right. Other virtues do not have such a direct relation to external right.[60] All law and all just acts have fairness and legitimacy either from their substance or nature, which is natural law, or they derive their virtue from custom, which is legal justice. The former type of justice prohibits actions, whereas the latter understands them to be evil.[61] Natural justice arises from its connection with human nature as characterized by reason. Reason is the principle of human actions, insofar as they are human.[62] Albert understands the ideal of natural justice in two ways, the first of which he claims is found in Plato's *Timaeus*. Justice exists in natural things, as a type of rectitude that aligns such things with an exemplar. Such a doctrine belongs either to metaphysical or natural science. Another kind of natural justice arises from an innate principle of human nature. The latter type of justice is moral in subject and pertains thereby to the science of ethics.[63] Natural law itself

---

[58] SE, pp. 284–285, ll. 79–09.   [59] SE, p. 285, ll. 56–70.   [60] SE, p. 348, ll. 48–57.
[61] SE, p. 356, ll. 1–8.
[62] SE p. 357, ll. 2–7: Dicendum, quod iustum naturale dicitur hic a natura speciali, quae est hominis, inquantum est homo, scilicet a ratione, non inquantum est forma dans esse, sed inquantum est principium operum humanorum, inquantum sunt humana.
[63] SE, p. 357, ll. 8–22.

may be understood according to a naturally innate habit, and is therefore not acquired. In this way the principles of natural law are similar to the first premises of speculative sciences. Examples of what may be innately known are commands, such as do not harm others, or respect one's parents. The principles direct moral actions as they are applied to specific circumstances.[64]

Natural justice has vigor and equity from its very substance, traits that are in themselves consistent with reason and effective in attaining human good-ness. This type of justice is applied in particular cases through custom and acceptance of law. Albert understands both of Cicero's descriptions of natural law to be included within Aristotle's understanding of the concept of natural law. Both the claim that the beginning of law comes from nature and that certain things come into use by reason of utility fall under Aristotle's description of natural law. A third type of law is enacted by a wise person in order to direct human behavior.[65] The principles of natural law can never vary essentially, but their use may differ when they are applied to particular cases.[66]

b Albert's analysis of prudence

Albert begins the examination of the intellectual virtues in book VI of his commentary on the NE almost as if he were starting an entirely new work. He cites Alkindi, who defines philosophy as order in the soul, and claims that disorder comes from confusion within the potencies. Such confusion is the result of the imperfections within human psychic powers. A soul's potency may be perfected primarily through habit, or secondarily through action. The soul's operation is two-fold: according to intellect or desire. The first action results in speculation, and the second in practice. The division within the soul produces the two main areas of human accomplishment, which are speculative and practical science. Ethics becomes perfected in each because it includes the ends of both theory and practice, which are civic and contemplative happiness. Since the soul is perfected by the intellectual contemplation of truth and the performance of moral virtues, ethics reflects the order in the soul better than any other area of philosophy.[67] Albert understands the sixth book of the NE to be the beginning of the examination of the ideal of contempla-tive perfection, and as distinct from the treatment of moral virtues and

---

[64] SE, p. 357, ll. 58–65.   [65] SE, pp. 357–358, ll. 90–24.   [66] SE, p. 359, ll. 79–90.
[67] SE, p. 391, ll. 4–30.

civic happiness.[68] In Albert's reading of the NE, Aristotle first determines what leads to the goal of contemplation, then considers the intellectual virtues and friendship, and finally describes the supreme end of human activity. When the intellectual virtues refer to the perfections of the soul's potencies, they have the nature of virtue, are moved by the will, and are worthy of praise. In these ways the will involves itself in the supreme act of the intellectual being, and thereby renders intellectual virtue a proper subject of ethics.[69] Although speculation and civic activity are unified within the genus of human goodness, their specific differences lead Albert to consider them distinct ends of human action. Political or moral excellence remains a disposition to the superior achievement of contemplating eternal truth.[70]

Prudence belongs to the intellectual virtues by means of its subject, which is essentially the perfection of the mind or reason. It falls under the intellectual virtues because it, like wisdom, requires time and experience to develop. With respect to its object it becomes a moral virtue, since it has the nature of choice that leads to action. Prudence has a special place among the virtues because of its common traits with both intellectual and moral excellence.[71] Albert raises a particularly insightful question on the nature of Aristotelian ethics when he asks whether one can have moral virtues without intellectual ones. While a modern moralist may claim that intellectual accomplishment may have little, or no, connection to moral goodness, Albert has a different view. He argues that for every deed that has rectitude in attaining the appropriate end, there is a continuation of the process to something that is right in itself. What is right *per se* informs the will and the intellect of the moral agent. Albert connects the action of every nature to the operation of the prime mover because of a continuity of the first mover's acts through mediate causes. This continuity proceeds from the first to the last act, and indicates the desire of anything for its proper end. Moral virtues do not continue on to natural causes, but rather to something right in itself that directs them and that remains a directive force in any moral virtue. The directive intention is perfect right reason, and without the presence of intellectual virtues there could be no moral ones.[72]

The moral virtues may be determined without the involvement of the intellect, but they are formally completed through intellectual cognition.

---

[68] SE, p. 391, ll. 31–34: Postquam ergo determinatum est de moribus et felicitate civili, quae est finis ipsarum, in hoc sexto incipit agere de his quae pertinent ad contemplationis perfectionem . . .
[69] SE, p. 392, ll. 65–73.   [70] SE, p. 394, ll. 4–13.   [71] SE, p. 394, ll. 31–46.
[72] SE, pp. 394–395, ll. 78–08.

The lower potencies of the soul understood materially are distinct from reason, but taken formally as they participate in reason, they are the subject of moral virtues.[73] The intellectual virtues are simply worthier than the moral ones, but the latter can be more useful, as almsgiving to the needy is more useful and choiceworthy than philosophizing. The intellectual life attains a more complete good than moral actions, since intellectual goodness is purified of its contrary and does not include any objectionable characteristic. Moral virtues permit regret at times because they do not include the supreme goodness of contemplation. All virtues, including temperance and prudence, are directed toward the enjoyment of the contemplative life.[74]

Prudence, as an intellectual virtue, is ruled by both divine and human law. Because philosophers do not consider rules prescribed by divine law, 'divine' refers here to what is naturally impressed upon the soul and is grasped by the intelligence. The directive power of law allows prudence to attain wisdom and makes prudence more perfect, despite its greater uncertainty than other intellectual virtues. Prudence is closer to wisdom (*sapientia*) than it is to knowledge (*scientia*) in that it prepares the soul for contemplative happiness by removing impediments to speculation.[75] Prudence need not govern intellectual virtues because they already exist in what Albert calls a regulatory potency; they, therefore, require no other ruling virtue. Albert believes that Aristotle's description of prudence as constituted with true reason is the best of all classical designations because it refers to the governing power in its act. Every operation needs something that directs it. Even if the purpose of prudence is to govern contingent choices, such choices have a determination by reason that allows for the selection of the best alternative. This choice reflects a type of truth that is not necessary, but holds for the most part, since the choice follows from universal principles. Contingent choices do not reflect truth in themselves or through their causes, but are ordered to reason and the understanding of the end. Reason, order and will determine the actions directed to the

---

[73] SE, p. 395, ll. 9–18.   [74] SE, p. 396, ll. 18–37.

[75] SE, p. 417, ll. 53–79: ... dicendum, quod prudentia regulatur iure divino et humano, et dicimus divinum, non quod divina lege traditum est, quia hoc non consideraverunt philosophi, sed quod impressum est naturaliter animae, secundum quod exacta est ab intelligentia, et secundum quod hoc iure regulatur, attingit sapientiam et sic est perfectior quam scientia ... Prudentia autem, quamvis magis recedat a sapientia quantum ad formam medii quam scientia, tamen quantum ad ea circa quae est prudentia, maxime propinqua est sapientiae, inquantum praeparat animam ad sapientiam, et felicitatem contemplativam removendo impedimentum contemplationis ...

attainment of the proper end.[76] Aristotle's notion of prudence includes its subject matter 'concerning human goods', its act, its genus as habit, and the governing function of true reason.[77] The active habit of prudence is substantially identical with true reason because both habit and reason, which remain distinct according to reason, are united in the virtue of prudence. Prudence is a habit existing in reason that allows for both the choosing and rejection of actions that pertain to human life. From the part whereby it achieves reason, prudence has true reason as its ruling element; from the part whereby it is ordered to an act, it has an active element. Aristotle implies this distinction when he uses the phrase, 'with true reason'.[78]

In the discussion on prudence as an active habit, Albert raises the question concerning its rule over an entire life. Since prudence is the directive force through deliberation over the complete life, which must include both action and contemplation, then prudence must also rule the intellectual virtues. Albert then asks why prudence should be described as an active virtue rather than a contemplative one. Albert's response to this question is disappointing, since he does not address the more complex and interesting aspects of the problem, or consider the possibility that Aristotle's ethics does indeed elevate practical wisdom to the primary moral virtue controlling all human decisions. He merely states that life may be characterized as pleasurable, political or contemplative. He quickly limits prudence to control over civic action and the political life: "Prudence directs only acting and living in a civic life."[79] Albert never doubts that Aristotle restricted the operation of prudence to the moral virtues only, even if he describes it as an element between intellectual and moral excellence.[80]

The limitation of prudence to human goodness leads to a discussion of Cicero's claim that prudence considers everything that can be known by human beings. As such, it investigates more than human affairs. As an intellectual virtue it extends to every theoretical idea and transcends mere human concerns. If deliberation is the act of prudence, then one may deliberate about more than human achievements.[81] Despite these arguments from Cicero's position, Albert continues to limit prudence to human goodness, and more specifically to the good moral actions within the span

[76] SE, pp. 436–437, ll. 65–05.   [77] SE, p. 437, ll. 51–57.   [78] SE, p. 437, ll. 58–69.
[79] SE, pp. 437, ll. 80–84: ... dicendum, quod est triplex vita ... scilicet voluptuousa et civilis et contemplativa. Prudentia autem non dirigit nisi tantum ad agere vel vivere civilis vitae.
[80] SE, 438, ll. 10–12: ... sed Philosophus considerat hic prudentiam, secundum quod operatur in materia moralium virtutum; est enim media quodam modo inter intellectuales et morales, et ideo diffinit per actum.
[81] SE, p. 439, ll. 3–22.

of a human life.[82] For Albert, Cicero's definition of prudence that encompasses providence, memory and understanding is too broad. Aristotle described the virtue properly when he distinguished it from all others.[83] Like the other cardinal virtues, prudence derives its nature from the preeminence of its act. It is the principal intellectual virtue not because it is superior to other virtues and encompasses all of them, but because of the superiority of its act. As such, it does not involve itself in every intellectual pursuit, but its deliberation concerns itself simply with its own proper subject matter and not with every kind of deliberative process.[84]

The judgment that occurs within the prudential act is not the same as the virtue itself, but is the inducement to action. This incitement to action is expressed in a command, expressed as a major proposition, such as do not fornicate, or in the minor premise and the particular circumstances, such as to lie with this person is fornication. The final element in prudential reasoning is the conclusion, which is to know in acting that something should, or should not, be done. Intemperate delight does not destroy the habit of prudence, but it does corrupt its command. Immoderate pleasure does not affect the major proposition, but partly corrupts the minor, and destroys completely the conclusive command when it blinds reason.[85] Aristotle's choice of Pericles as the *phronimos* reinforces Albert's belief that prudence functions only in the practical areas of human life. Pericles was accomplished in civic decisions that governed his household and his city.[86]

Prudence cannot be simply and totally forgotten, although the prudent person may be less able to apply its principles to a particular act, if distracted by passion. Albert argues against the possibility of forgetting the virtue, since the universal innate principles of law are always present. In these principles prudence substantially exists. Because the principles must be applied to particular acts, a flexible rule that time and experience construct guides a prudent person.[87] Prudence must always include knowledge of both universals and particulars. Since it aims at an action that consists in a particular choice, it requires universal, particular and active knowledge. Albert considers the nature of prudence to be more active, since it may produce correct particular actions without true knowledge of universals, especially in the early stages of its development when one imitates the good actions of wise persons.[88] Any action requires knowledge

---

[82] SE, p. 439, ll. 23–26: Dicendum, quod prudentia est tantum circa humana bona, et dicuntur humana bona operationes virtutum moralium, quae sunt circa humanam vitam.
[83] SE, p. 439, ll. 27–33.   [84] SE, p. 439, ll. 27–49.   [85] SE, p. 441, ll. 21–39.
[86] SE, p. 443, ll. 39–45.   [87] SE, p. 445, ll. 21–39.   [88] SE, p. 467, ll. 16–33.

of the universal principle and its application to a particular choice, since no act can occur except particularly.[89] Since prudence applies the universal principle to a particular choice, Albert says that it is midway (*media*) between the moral and intellectual virtues, and cannot be a purely intellectual process.[90] Reason perfected to its best state consists in knowledge of universals, but perfection in its directive capacity comes from particular awareness, which produces what Albert calls the inferior virtues. Prudence perfected in the second manner is the guide to all moral virtues.[91]

Prudence and politics are in actuality the same habit with respect to their subject, but differ in their manner or nature. Prudence is associated with the governing aspect of reason, but politics is more concerned with the act. Politics is related to prudence as that which follows from the governing principle.[92] Albert does not claim that everyone acts from knowledge of infallible principles, since one could operate from the false premise that an act of adultery is an expression of voluntary freedom. In such a case freedom is understood as a good, but the identification of adultery and freedom is erroneous. As a result, a stated rule may be false, although the good person would recognize true principles and reject false ones.[93]

Albert again recognizes a type of circularity in Aristotle's formulation of the practical syllogism. Unlike the order of speculative science, practical reasoning arises from the particular that is desired and intended in action. The particular is the foundation for the subsequent elements in the syllogism. The order in the practical syllogism is the reason why Aristotle says that the motion of the appetite is circular. The appetitive power is passive and cannot be perfected except by the species of the object acting upon it. Desire provoked by the appearance of the desirable object moves the power in the muscles and nerves. These physical movements lead to the attainment of the object, and so the process ends with that which began the process.[94] The particular object of desire is the motivating principle in action despite its placement in the practical syllogism as the minor premise, which states this object is desirable. Its motivating force makes it more effective in producing action than the first principles, but also allows for greater uncertainty in practical reasoning.[95] Actions that comprise a good life are naturally innate in the manner of a planting bed (*seminaria*) of law. Experiences through which common principles are determined present

---

[89]   SE, p. 467, ll. 34–38.
[90]   SE, p. 467, ll. 40–42: . . . dicendum, quod prudentia inter intellectuales et morales; unde non est pure intellectualis.
[91]   SE, p. 467, ll. 44–50.   [92]   SE, p. 467, ll. 78–86.   [93]   SE, p. 482, ll. 37–51.
[94]   SE, p. 491, ll. 56–72.   [95]   SE, p. 491, ll. 75–87.

themselves to all since they live in accordance with the human way of existence. These innate abilities need nurturing through time and by experience and as they mature they end the fluidity of youth.[96]

c Happiness and virtue

In nature one good may be ordered to another, as both civic and contemplative happiness are human goods, but for a human being the former is directed to the acquisition of the latter in its function as a disposition removing impediments to contemplation. Albert distinguishes the contemplative virtues from the contemplative activity when he says they are ordered to contemplation. Civic happiness also is directed to the final good of contemplation in Albert's understanding of human purpose.[97] Albert's separation of contemplative happiness from the intellectual virtues once more provokes the question how does happiness differ from the virtues themselves. What further state of excellence beyond the virtues does Albert envision happiness to be? Does he consider happiness merely to be a general term that Aristotle uses for convenience rather than to list intellectual activities, or does happiness imply a state of perfection that transcends the various operations of the intellect? One explanation for Albert's insistence upon the hierarchy of operations that lead to one ultimate goal is his belief that ultimate goodness leads one to a union with God. Since this union is the overriding purpose of all intellectual and moral actions and cannot be achieved by human causality, then happiness must then be a state that differs in some manner from the virtues themselves.

Albert addresses this question specifically when he asks whether Aristotle reasoned falsely when he made virtues parts of happiness. Albert's response includes three elements that he claims are ordered to happiness. What is essential is virtue whose operation characterizes happiness (*virtus, cuius est operatio felicitatis*). Albert does not identify virtue and happiness here, although he could have very well formulated the sentence with the nominative case for *felicitas*, and identified virtue and happiness. Despite his insistence that virtue is essential to happiness, Albert remains reluctant to make them identical. In addition to virtues happiness encompasses dispositions and instruments. Civic happiness he calls again the substantial operation of prudence, and all other moral virtues are directed to the dispositions to the perfect prudential act. Contemplative happiness similarly is substantially the act of wisdom, because, as Averroes claims, human flourishing consists in

---

[96] SE, p. 492, ll. 47–62.   [97] SE, p. 496, ll. 12–22.

speculative wisdom that all other virtues serve.[98] Again Albert is reluctant to identify happiness with virtue, but comes close to doing so when he makes prudential and sapiential virtue substantially the same as happiness. His strict dichotomy between two types of happiness restricts prudence to the active life, and undermines a unified notion of happiness. No longer is the human good a complex life of varied accomplishments; it has become the quest for intellectual contemplation. The political involvement that is integral to Aristotle's ideal is abandoned for the life of contemplation.

Aristotle's assertion that virtue makes the intention right leads to Albert's conclusion that a certain nature tends toward its end in the way a heavy body falls down. To make the intention right does not have the nature of the end, but does direct and incline action toward its proper goal. Moral virtue is specifically sufficient for the understanding of the end, but prudence is needed for the means to attain it.[99] Happiness is described as perfect virtue of which individual virtues comprise the parts. Albert seems to use '*felicitas*' as a general term that denotes the acts of complete virtue within a particular area of action: "Since wisdom is a part of perfect virtue whose operation is happiness itself, through its end and acting, it makes one happy."[100] The term 'happiness', refers to perfection in different types of action, since theory and practice are separate areas of endeavor in Albert's moral theory. The identity of end and act is common to all intellectual pursuits, but prudence has a special mode in directing choice in external acts toward civic happiness. In this way it resembles a moral virtue and by producing results beyond an internal state, prudence demands special consideration in moral philosophy.[101] Whereas Aristotle asserts that with *phronesis* all virtues will be given, Albert adds the qualifier, 'moral,' to modify the virtues.[102] One may consider the virtues that comprise human excellence according to their perfection and so they would all exist simultaneously. In perfect virtue prudence would also appear perfectly in conjunction with all moral virtues. Someone may also be imperfectly prudent and be accomplished in one area of virtuous activity, but not

---

[98] SE, p. 499, ll. 31–46.   [99] SE, p. 500, ll. 23–43.

[100] SE, p. 503, ll. 28–30: Cum enim sapientia sit *pars* perfectae virtutis, cuius operatio felicitas ipsa, per suum finem *et* per suum *operari facit felicem*. Italicized words are from the text of the NE.

[101] SE, p. 503, ll. 30–36: Et hoc quidem commune est omnibus intellectualibus, sed prudentia speciali modo se habet ad felicitatem, inquantum dirigit in operibus exterioribus ordinatis ad felicitatem civilem, sicut etiam moralis virtus specialiter, inquantum exsequitur opera illa; et ideo specialis et dubitatio et solutio debet esse de prudentia.

[102] SE, p. 505, ll. 65–66.

in others. Albert implies that the first way of perfect virtue would be essentially identical to happiness, since with the presence of perfect virtue one would necessarily be happy.[103]

The insistence upon order that underscores all moral, political and metaphysical understanding leads to Albert's assertion that all actions derive their meaning from one supreme good. All human beings are naturally ordered to participate in one good so that they are ruled by one goal, just as every conclusion of any art is determined by one habit. Such order was placed in human beings as the natural light of reason through which this good might be obtained. Before sin darkened this light, reason directed one to the attainment of the ultimate end, so that anyone could immediately perceive the divine rule. The darkness affected people differently so that some who saw more clearly than others were fit to govern. The clarity of vision in some is the reason why the many remain subject to the rule of one.[104] Albert's acceptance of a natural hierarchy leads him so far as to prefer tyranny over democracy: "Democracy simply is worse than tyranny because in tyranny order to one superior at least remains, as well as an order of power, even if it may be abused. But in democracy nothing remains because the whole order of civility is brought to disorder . . ."[105] While tyranny may be bad *secundum quid* by reason of its opposition to a greater good, democracy is simply worse due to its complete lack of order.

Order in every aspect of human life contributes to knowledge of how to respond to conflicting demands. Aristotle raised the question in the *Topics* whether to sacrifice one's father is an honorable act. Albert recasts this problem as one concerning the priority of obedience to law or of the duty to filial devotion. Augustine had answered the question properly when he maintained that one always owes greater obedience to a superior authority. One should obey an emperor rather than a consul, but obey God above all. Aristotle did not consider the question in terms of obedience to God, but only with respect to the different levels of authority in human communities. One should heed the commands of a prince in civic affairs, a father in domestic matters, and a doctor in medical proceedings. While all these figures are primary in their respective fields, God is first in all things, and has influence over life, health, and ultimately all things. To God, therefore,

---

[103] SE, p. 511, ll. 9–22.   [104] SE, p. 636, ll. 13–35.

[105] SE, p. 632, ll. 16–21: . . . dicendum, quod democratia est simpliciter peius quam tyrannis, quia in tyrannide saltem manet ordo ad unum superiorem et manet ordo potestatis, quamvis ille abutatur. Sed in democratia nihil manet, quia totus ordo civilitatis confunditur . . . See also, SE, p. 637, ll. 72–78.

the greatest obedience is due.[106] Albert locates every act and pursuit in its proper place according to an ascending order. The moral virtues, for example, derive their fullest meaning when serving to calm the mind for the supreme state of contemplation.[107]

The commentary on book X of the NE is the culmination of Albert's theory on the meaning and goal of human morality. He begins the section with a citation to Boethius, who summarized well the purpose of the last book of Aristotle's great work in *Ethics*:

> Felix qui potuit boni   Happy is he who has been able
> fontem visere lucidum   to gaze upon the clear font of goodness;
> felix, qui potuit gravis   happy is he who has been able to loosen
> terrae solvere vincula   the chains of heavy earth.

Despite some translations that render the auxiliary verb '*potuit*', in the present tense, Boethius's clear use of the past tense denotes his under-standing that happiness comes only after the physical world has been left behind. Only after loosening the earthly bonds can one become truly happy, an idea that Albert clearly accepts. Both Aristotle and Boethius in Albert's view consider the primary moral concept to be the good *per se* to which all other goods are ordered. In moral terms this good is the parti-cular perfect operation of the speculative intellect, or contemplative happi-ness. The source of such happiness is the divine intellect that emits the light of awareness toward all cognitive beings. Imitation of the activity of the divine intellect brings happiness because the ultimate perfection of human nature consists in that which is the most desirable object of knowledge. Albert takes the intellectual activity of the divine being to be the model for all those endowed with an intellect. Following Averroes, he understands divine activity to consist in self-contemplation, and in knowing itself the divine intellect comprehends all things. This accurate rendering of a metaphysical conclusion of Aristotle leads Albert to compare human activity to divine perfection. Albert understands Boethius's first two lines as a reference to contemplative happiness whereby one sees the font of goodness unclouded by any darkness. The earthly chains of Boethius's verse represent corporeal delights by which a human being falls from the heights of nature to its depths. When one loosens the material chains, one can truly enjoy (*fruitur*)

---

[106] SE, p. 659, ll. 24–46.

[107] SE, p. 668, ll. 23–26: ... Philosophus loquitur hic de virtuoso, qui est perfectus in vita contemplativa, cui virtutes morales subserviunt ad optimum statum contemplationis.

authentic intellectual pleasure. The use of the term 'enjoy', unites the passage of Boethius with the moral thought of Augustine.[108]

Only one human operation can be considered sufficiently perfect or final in Albert's understanding of moral goodness – the contemplation of supreme substances. The many other morally good acts have their meaning in the ability to contribute to the single ultimate end. Cognitive human power allows the knower to enjoy one final pleasure to which all other delights are directed and contribute.[109] Albert also distinguishes life itself from happiness, because he thinks that life, morality and even contemplation are ordered to the supreme good. Happiness, the final operation of human nature, is not directed to any higher end.[110] In contemplative happiness there is one certain good, wisdom, that elicits the act of contemplating the divine being. In such wisdom happiness is maximized with the help of the other intellectual virtues that contribute to knowledge, and with the assistance of the dispositive effects of the moral virtues.[111]

---

[108] SE, p. 708, ll. 4–35: Boethius dicit in libro *De consolatione philosophiae*:

> 'Felix qui potuit boni
> fontem visere lucidum,
> felix, qui potuit gravis
> terrae solvere vincula'

In quibus verbis trahitur et tangitur tota materia huius decimi libri; bonum enim maxime est illud quod per se bonum est et ad quod alia ordinantur, et hoc praecipue est perfecta operatio intellectus speculativi, quae dicitur felicitas contemplativa. Huius autem fons est divinus intellectus, qui profundit lumen cognitionis in omnia cognoscentia et per cuius imitationem est felicitas contemplativa, quia perfectio ultima omnis nostrae contemplationis est in eo qui est maxime desideratum ad sciendum. Et haec est quaestio de divino intellectu, ut dicit Commentator in XI Metaphysicae; ipse autem deus intellectum suum perfectissime contemplatur et intelligendo se intelligit omnia alia. Et ideo contemplativa felicitas est quaedam imitatio divini intellectus, et sic per contemplativam felicitatem videt aliquis fontem boni, qui dicitur lucidus, quia 'tenebrae in eo non sunt ullae'. Et sic tangitur per primum versum materia huius libri quantum ad secundam partem, quae est de felicitate contemplativa. Vincula autem terrae gravis sunt corporales delectationes, quibus deorsum homo iungitur ab altitudine suae naturae ad infimum ipsius; quae quidem vincula perfecte solvit, qui veris intellectualibus delectationibus fruitur.

[109] SE, p. 742, ll. 7–16.

[110] SE, p. 744, ll. 46–51: Dicendum, quod felicitas est, ad quam ordinatur humana vita, et maxime contemplativa, et ipsa non ordinatur ad aliquid aliud. Et ideo oportet quod felicitas sit operatio, quae est ultima perfectio humanae naturae.

[111] SE, p. 748, ll. 31–40: . . . dicendum, quod in felicitate contemplativa est quoddam bonum ut eliciens actum, et hoc est unum, scilicet sapientia, cuius est contemplatio divinorum, in quibus contemplandis est summa haec felicitas, quaedam autem sicut adminiculantia sicut aliae intellectuales virtutes, quibus in tali operatione iuvatur intellectus ex

d Albert's paraphrase of the NE

In 1262, Albert composed a second commentary on the *Nicomachean Ethics* that has come to be known as the *Paraphrase*. The name often leads to a dismissal of the work as inferior to, and less important than, the *Super Ethica*, but J. Müller has argued that the later work can only help to enrich our understanding of Albert's positions on the nature and breadth of ethical science.[112] In this commentary Albert considers again the nature and end of moral science. He accepts Aristotle's position that one studies ethics not for the sake of contemplation, but in order to make us good (*ut boni fiamus*).[113] What makes human beings good as human is the attainment of their perfection and ultimate end. Such an accomplishment manifests itself in the cultivation of just and proper actions in all people. Although not specifically discussed, the doctrine of *synderesis* lies behind the assertion that all human beings have the ability to attain moral perfection because they have, as Boethius stated, the innate seeds of virtue that they can develop.[114] The primary good in a moral genus, and the source of all other subordinate goods, is the voluntary act that is determined to the proper subject (*ad propriam materiam*) by reason. Albert specifies these goods as feeding the hungry and assisting the poor. Such actions, which have the first potency to goodness, are also the primary subjects of goodness, even if they may be conditioned by circumstances.[115] Reason analyzes all the factors that contribute to the attainment of the desired goal. One may view reason in its quest for truth or in its ability to lead to just actions. In the first way, a human being is perfected according to the mode of humanity that is superior to the moral ability to overcome the inclination of passions. Again Albert maintains the hierarchy of human goals and makes the purely intellectual life the supreme achievement of the soul.[116]

The specific topic of ethics is not goodness in a general way, but rather the good that relates to humankind. True goodness for anything occurs when in both being and possibility something can perform whatever

---

posterioribus in priora revolvendo deveniens, et quaedam sicut disponentia sicut virtutes morales et ordinata ad ipsas . . .

[112] J. Müller, "Ethics as a Practical Science in Albert the Great's Commentaries on the *Nicomachean Ethics*," W. Senner *et al.*, pp. 275–276.

[113] See G. Wieland, "Ethica docens – ethica utens," pp. 593–601.

[114] *In X Ethicorum*, in *Opera omnia, v. 7*, ed. A. Borgnet (Paris: Vives, 1891), I, tr. 1, c. 6, p. 14 (critically edited by J. Müller in *Natürliche Moral und philosophische Ethik bei Albertus Magnus*, pp. 353, ll. 5–13).

[115] *In X Eth.* I, tr. 1, c. 6, p. 14, Müller, pp. 353–354, ll. 14–02.

[116] *In X Eth.* I, tr, 1, c. 6, p. 15, Müller, pp. 354–355, ll. 3–20.

conforms to its nature.[117] No potency perfects itself, but relies upon a natural, or acquired, habit in order to attain its actuality. Human goodness comes from the perfection of the soul's potencies, which Albert lists as desiderative, rational, mental and intellectual. He considers happiness, the ultimate perfection, as the general designation for human goodness, while he calls virtue the perfection of certain human potencies. As in his other works on ethics, Albert separates happiness from the virtuous activities and orders the latter to the former.[118]

Every discipline intends to produce a good result, and prudence has particular relevance for moral doctrine, since it is reason perfecting choice. Albert says that prudence may be understood as the virtue that chooses, or as a type of doctrinal wisdom that indicates the best paths to choice. Prudence does not have a special perfection beyond its role in choice and instruction. Art and instruction seek rationally particular goods, but prudence does not.[119] Moral teaching aims at producing the highest good of happiness, which Albert defines in the last commentary as a perfect act according to every virtue of the mind.[120] The combination of Aristotle's definition of happiness (act according to every virtue) and Boethius's description as perfect leads Albert to conclude that all ends and human powers must be directed toward a supreme good that is achieved by the highest human power. For the specifically human powers and life, civic science or politics contains the supreme good. Politics encompasses all practical disciplines and enacts laws concerning what to pursue and to avoid. In encompassing all human ends civic happiness is human goodness.[121] Albert attributes this doctrine to Aristotle's *Magna Moralia* where he describes happiness as a good composed of all subordinate goods. Albert understands this composite good to signify happiness in a collective sense, since it contains each element separately. Happiness does not integrate all parts into a whole, but denotes parts ordered to one good. The general concept of happiness denotes the whole in which the potencies of virtues are realized and perfected.[122] The lack of integration of the human condition precludes a state of perfection, as the variability and errors of human lives demonstrate. Albert notes that different people may judge differently about justice and chastity. There are variations in different societies and right seems to exist in legislation only, and not in nature. Since nature and its

[117] *In X Eth.* I, tr. 2, c. 7, p. 27.   [118] *In X Eth.* I, tr. 2, c. 7, p. 28.
[119] *In X Eth.* I, tr. 3, c. 3, p. 34.
[120] *In X Eth.* I, tr. 3, c. 10, p. 42: Cum autem felicitas actus sit secundum omnem virtutem animi perfectus, nec perfectio possit esse si aliquod subserventium desit.
[121] *In X Eth.* I, tr. 3, c. 13, p. 48.   [122] *In X Eth.* I, tr. 5, c. 1, p. 58.

foundation are the same for all, one must seek that which is the same good for all.[123] Albert clearly understands the tension in Aristotle's ethics since it allows for diversity among different societies, but true goodness demands universal moral principles. For Albert the variations in practical affairs characterize the mortal world, but universal principles transcend human limitations and bring a type of singular perfection, since they are rooted in the divine order.

The uncertainty and variety that characterize ethical behavior give rise to many different opinions on the meaning of happiness. Albert examines the same positions on happiness as Aristotle did in the NE, but his most interesting discussion considers the identification of virtue with the supreme good. Albert admits that virtue is preserved essentially in beatitude and contributes substantially to happiness. Still virtue is less perfect than the supreme good and its inferior status manifests itself in two ways. The first sign of its inferiority is its nature as a habit, which, as Averroes says, is a quality perfecting a potency whereby one does what one decides. The final perfection consists not in a habit, but in action, since a habit may allow for further development in its act. Such a state cannot be the ultimate good. The second sign of virtue's lower status is the possibility of the coexistence of virtue and misery in the same subject. Happiness allows no such possibility and cannot, therefore, be identical with virtue. As an example, Albert provides the case of a chaste pauper. A virtuous person may still be subject to misfortune, which makes him wretched and unhappy. One cannot be simultaneously both happy and unhappy; a virtuous person then is not necessarily happy.[124]

After a quick dismissal of the position identifying virtue with happiness, and a longer analysis of the Platonic theory of moral goodness, Albert offers his own interpretation of Aristotle's concept of human happiness. The good of any operation or art is found in that end for the sake of which all other actions are done. The final end to which all operations and acts are directed can only be the supreme final good. These elements must be part of the definition of happiness. The instinctive powers of the soul cannot bring happiness, since the animal powers in human beings are subject to the ruling intellect. People master their actions because of the liberty provided by the intellect. The intellect itself may turn toward the agent intellect from which illumination flows, or to the inferior potencies that need intellectual guidance. Because of the intellect's two aspects there must

[123] *In X Eth.* I, tr. 4, c. 2, p. 52.   [124] *In X Eth.* I, tr. 5, c. 9, pp. 68–69.

be two corresponding ends of operations and thought. The perfection of
the practical potencies employ what Albert calls purgative virtue, which
prepares one for the attainment of the ultimate goal of contemplative
happiness.[125] Albert maintains the medieval position that happiness is a
telos in that its primary characteristic is unchanging perfection, rather a
completion or fulfillment of a potency or nature: "We will see that happiness is the best of all endeavors, if we discover what is most perfect."[126]
What is best seems to be something perfect (*perfectum quid*). Albert's
primary understanding of *perfectum* is an immutable psychic state. The
ideal of actualizing a variety of human potentials that directs Aristotle's
discussion of the human *telos* has been subsumed under the ideal of
perfect beatitude of the soul. Such is the meaning of Boethius's definition
of beatitude as a perfect state with the accumulation of all goods. No one
is perfected by collecting different goods, so Boethius's definition takes
on a more subtle significance. Perfection may refer simply, or according
to a certain status (*secundum statum*). Perfect simplicity in which nothing is lacking can only refer to God. Perfection *secundum statum* may refer
particularly or universally. In the first sense it means the perfection in
the attainment of a proper end without impediments to its obligatory acts.
Such perfection also lacks nothing that is ordered to its end. In this way
one might speak of a perfect carpenter or doctor. In the universal sense of
perfection *secundum statum*, we speak of something that lacks nothing
required for the end that simply is the final for human beings. The last
sense of perfection lies behind Boethius's statement since everything
related to the human end without exception is meant. This perfect state
is specified as beatitude, which includes every good performed by a
human being.[127]

Albert's last commentary on the NE contains an entire treatise devoted
to Boethius's definition of human goodness, which Albert identifies with
his own concept of *felicitas secundum posse*. He first treats the problem of
the effect of external goods on happiness. Albert juxtaposes Aristotle's
definition of happiness as a human operation with his variation of
Boethius's understanding of happiness as a state or an act with an accumulation of all goods.[128] If one were to accept Boethius's definition strictly,
then every possible external good must be attained; one might, however,

[125] *In X Eth.* I, tr. 6, c. 1, p. 85.
[126] *In X Eth.* I, tr. 6, c. 2, p. 86: Videbimus enim quod felicitas optimum operatorum est, si
invenerimus quod perfectissimum est ...
[127] *In X Eth.* I, tr. 6, c. 2, p. 87.   [128] *In X Eth.* I, tr. 7, c. 1, p. 105.

consider happiness only according to its essential nature. In this way one needs external goods, such as friends, wealth, and beauty in order to avoid contaminating the state of beatitude. The sadness produced by external deficiencies is a source of pain, and one cannot be perfect with respect to the best actions. Albert unifies the two concepts of happiness by associating Boethius's declaration of it as perfect state with Aristotle's description of the essence of happiness.[129] Happiness is essentially an activity that does not wish to be impeded.[130] External goods contribute instrumentally to the perfect state described by Boethius, but are always subject to fortune. Virtues, however, act upon happiness essentially, although they do not bring happiness themselves.[131]

Albert challenges the Platonic identification of virtue and wisdom. Socrates, according to Albert, did not sufficiently distinguish wisdom and prudence because he assumed that prudence was a type of science of action. Since wisdom involves contemplation of the supreme and most divine beings, Socrates identified virtue in all things with the supreme and most divine good. Albert says that virtue cannot be totally the result of learning, and that moral virtue is not learned in the same way as wisdom is.[132] While moral virtue receives the form of the mean from nature and not from reason itself, reason does indicate the natural mean. Socrates was led into error because he thought that what indicated the form of the mean was the same as that which gives that very form.[133]

In the analysis of Solon's dictum Albert posits a variation of his distinction between happiness *secundum esse* and happiness *in maximo suo posse*. He argues in the *Paraphrase* that the benefits of good fortune make a life more blessed, while misfortune disturbs and torments the blessed person. Tribulations do not in themselves turn one away from good deeds. The language of the later work indicates a more accurate interpretation of Aristotle's text than that in his earlier works. Aristotle implied a type of human beatitude that comes from divine favor and good fortune. With the benefits of favor one can be called blessed by external causes, but happiness still depends primarily upon the internal dispositions of human beings.[134] A happy person cannot be made wretched through calamities, since the

---

[129] *In X Eth.* I, tr. 7, c. 1, pp. 106–107.

[130] *In X Eth.* I, tr. 7, c. 1, p. 107: Felicitas autem operatio est quae non impedita vult esse.

[131] *In X Eth.* I, tr. 7, c. 2, p. 108: Et quia exteriora operantur ad felicitatem organice, et illa subjacent fortunae: virtutes autem operantur ad felicitate essentialiter.

[132] *In X Eth.* I, tr. 7, c. 3, p. 109.   [133] *In X Eth.* I, tr. 7, c. 3, p. 110.

[134] *In X Eth.* I, tr. 7, c. 12, pp. 124–125. See also A. Celano, "The Concept of Worldly Beatitude . . ."

essential constituents of human goodness, whereby one is made formally happy, differ from external factors.[135]

Happiness may be wholly attained before death, and worldly beatitude may also be achieved during a life. What Solon meant was that the judgment concerning the state of happiness requires the persistence of a life in accordance with goodness. Albert notes that 'perfect' refers to something that has everything that belongs to its essence and potency; it does not refer to every possible good thing.[136] He does not understand Solon's admonition to refrain from judging living men happy as a reference primarily to the benefits of good fortune, but views Aristotle's response to Solon as concentrating upon the essential activities of virtue that fortune could not easily destroy. Happiness is the activity of the soul according to perfect unimpeded virtue, which is not subject to the impediment of contrary states. Happiness cannot then be affected by the passions that are subject to the forces contrary to virtue.[137] When philosophers speak of perfection, or the beatitude of human beings, they do not mean a divine or celestial existence. The use of perfect virtue refers to the relation among virtues and the participation in reason. Human virtues participate somehow in reason through persuasion and obedience to the rational power, but they are not perfect in rationality. Prudence may be the perfect human virtue, but only as a person exercises it in the human manner.[138] Something perfect in all things provides form and order; in civic affairs this formative and ordering power is prudence. In its determining function prudence is more perfect than all other human virtues. Only prudence contemplates, rules and orders all other actions, insofar as they are directed toward human goodness. For this reason Cicero erred when he elevated justice over prudence.[139]

Aristotle's discussion of the effect of the living on the status of the dead gives Albert an opportunity to introduce his ideas on the perfection of the separated soul. He asserts a Peripatetic doctrine that the intellect is distinct from the sensible world as the incorruptible is different from the corruptible. Since happiness exists according to the incorruptible part of the soul, death does not seem to affect the incorruptibility of the intellect. Rather than destroy happiness death enhances it, since the loss of the body removes impediments to operations of reason and intellect.[140] This account of the soul is reasonable because the rational soul has only two

---

[135] *In X Eth.* I, tr. 7, c. 13, p. 126. [136] *In X Eth.* I, tr. 7, c. 14, p. 127.
[137] *In X Eth.* I, tr. 7, c. 14, p. 128. [138] *In X Eth.* I, tr. 7, c. 15, p. 129.
[139] *In X Eth.* I, tr. 7, c. 15, p. 129. [140] *In X Eth.* I, tr. 7, c. 17, p. 133.

operations: one related to the intellectual light of the first cause and the other connected to the body. No one doubts that the best is capable of what is supreme according to its highest element. What is best in the soul comes from its connection to the intellectual light. What is primary in this regard is capable of the highest form of happiness in accordance with the intellect. What is separate from corruption is nobler and better than what is united to it; one will, therefore, be happy more nobly after death. This is why Averroes claimed that the end for the fortunate soul occurs after death in its union with the prime mover.[141] All the Peripatetics accept the position that intellectual perfection is at the root of immortality. The intellect's contemplation of the supreme truths of theoretical knowledge brings the most powerful type of happiness, as Aristotle himself stated. The souls that achieve this intellectual understanding through virtue and understanding must clearly enjoy happiness after death.[142]

Despite the distinction made between virtue and happiness, virtues contain a dominant element and lead to a principle of happiness. Perfect contemplative happiness follows the virtues, since one does not reach this state until every virtue is realized in its supreme perfection. Civic happiness, the perfect operation according to prudence, is the principle and form of all other political virtues.[143] Again Albert struggles with the question of the relationship between virtue and happiness. The perfect state of happiness, despite requiring the dominant contribution of virtue, does not come to one through virtuous activities, but only after them. Even if one were to accept the relegation of moral and civic virtues to a preparatory state in the genesis of human goodness, one would still find it difficult to distinguish intellectual virtue from contemplative happiness, and maintain Aristotle's conclusions on *eudaimonia*. In his summary of Book X, of the NE Albert arranges the virtues according to the differences in potencies. Some are intellectual because of the intellectual potency related to speculative and practical potency; others are moral because they are determined and ordered to the form of reason. Wisdom, understanding and knowledge are the intellectual virtues according to the speculative intellect. Prudence and art have a special status since they are intellectual excellences according to the practical intellect.[144]

The human soul does not naturally produce virtue, but does have a susceptibility to virtue by way of inception, or, as Albert says, through the mode of a certain seed. The instruments by which the seed grows are within

---

[141] *In X Eth.* I, tr. 7, c. 17, p. 133.   [142] *In X Eth.* I, tr. 7, c. 17, p. 133.
[143] *In X Eth.* I, tr. 9, c. 1, p. 139.   [144] *In X Eth.* I, tr. 9, c. 7, p. 147.

the soul, as is clear in the case of intellectual excellence, whose first seeds are the intellectual lights proceeding from the first intellectuality (*ab intellectualitate prima*). The instruments are the first principles that are the common conceptions of the intellect. As Boethius says, any hearing of the first principles demonstrates their validity. If they were not within the soul no one could become wise or know through any study whatsoever.[145] The same process also directs the moral virtues. To produce virtue from the natural seeds within the soul five qualities must characterize virtuous operations: (1) they must be done in accordance with right reason; (2) what is needed to produce goodness is present; (3) the operation is directed to a mean; (4) the operation produces and sustains virtue; (5) the operation always produces either pleasure or pain in the moral agent. With these five conditions the natural ability to become virtuous actualizes itself into the necessary corresponding habits.[146]

Moral error may be the result of ignorance, since one can be unaware of the meaning of either the major or minor proposition. Ignorance of the practical syllogism differs from that of the contemplative, since in the practical syllogism the major premise, if known, determines action, and the minor comes from the elective appetite leading to the impulse to act. The conclusion is the choice of the better alternative. There is no error from the major premise that contains the universal principles directing action. These principles may come from natural or positive law, or may be determined by the rule of reason in the absence of any authority. Elective desire features both choice and appetite. Evil results from the error and ignorance that appetite may produce. Appetite unrestrained by reason produces evil, but choice has dominion over desire and may produce good in accordance with the principles known through reason.[147] When Aristotle claimed that there can be no deliberation about the ends of actions Albert understands him to refer to certain and self-sufficient principles.[148] Although Aristotle does not expressly identify the ends of moral action that require no deliberation, Albert's identification of the ends and principles is not entirely wrong. Albert will, however, go further than Aristotle when he specifies in book V of his commentary such first propositions to be the dictates of natural and divine law.

---

[145] *In X Eth.* II, tr. 1, c. 2, p. 152.   [146] *In X Eth.* II, tr. 1, c. 5, p. 156.

[147] *In X Eth.* III, tr. 1, cc. 9–10, pp. 206–207.

[148] *In X Eth.* III, tr. 1, c. 18, p. 223: Et quidem circa eas disciplinas quae in suis principiis certae sunt et per se sufficientes, non est consilium.

The will is simply the appetite of the rational soul and is directed to the end only.[149] The pivotal virtues of the soul are called 'cardinal' because they are the ones around which an entire human life revolves. Prudence has the principal place among all moral virtues in ordering the passions and determining the mean. Prudence is materially a moral virtue in its consideration of practice, but formally it belongs to intellectual virtues because of its recognition of universal principles.[150] Simple natural justice has no measure of legal justice since its principles are universally assumed and accepted, and has a universal power to obligate. For this reason, Cicero claimed justice to arise from nature, since opinion does not generate it, but rather it is innate in all. This justice may be generally considered in itself or determined *sub specie*. If understood in itself, justice functions according to reason, but obligates through a natural instinct, and not by the application of justice. In this way one speaks of the natural justice of the union of male and female, procreation, repelling force and the preservation of life.[151] Specific natural justice (*sub specie*) is that by which reason informed by rational principles alone formulates commands. Such principles are not discovered by enquiry or discussion. Cicero speaks of natural obligations of this kind and lists them as religion, piety, grace, and truth, among others.[152]

Natural law requires veneration of God, and despite civic laws demanding religious observance, political justice is not the same as natural justice. The preservation of the city may be an example of natural justice, since it conforms to the demands of reason, but specific laws are not natural. Likewise, the command to honor one's parents is an individual precept of natural justice, but the manner of its performance is not, just as particular ways of worship are not prescribed by nature.[153] Truly natural principles are immediately apprehended and do not emerge from study and discussion that produce the dictates of habitual justice.[154] The principles of natural justice are so compelling they demand immediate acceptance, while their negations must be rejected. Reason tells all to venerate the divine beings, to honor parents, to socialize with equals and to respect superiors. Albert extends the

---

[149] *In X Eth.* III, tr. c. 2, p. 226: Voluntas autem quae simpliciter est appetitus animae rationalis, finis est tantum . . .

[150] *In X Eth.* III, tr. 2, c. 1, p. 235.

[151] *In X Eth.* V, tr. 3, c. 3, p. 367. Cicero specifies these obligations in *De officiis* I, iv, 11–13.

[152] *In X Eth.* V, tr. 3, c. 3, p. 367.   [153] *In X Eth.* V, tr. 3, c. 3, p. 367.

[154] *In X Eth.* V, tr. 3, c. 3, p. 368: Cum igitur dicitur quod justum naturale verum habet eamdem potentiam, hoc intelligendum est quantum ad prima principia justi naturalis, et non quantum ad ea quae per studium vel discussionem ex talibus emergentibus eliciuntur, et non naturae.

list of natural precepts to include the recognition of one God, the prohibition against perjury and bearing false witness and the bans against adultery, theft and murder.[155]

Moral virtues that consist in a mean require the agent not only to discover the mean, but also to attain it through action. Reason determines the mean as it rules and orders the appetite and discovers the particular mean as the wise person determines. A wise person does not accept the principles of determination through appetite or passion, but rather from the nature of the mean with respect to the agent.[156] In the commentary on Aristotle, Albert insists that despite the determination of the mean by reason, the will is still free to choose good or evil. The will, however, never proceeds to a volitional act until the end has been judged by reason. Without reason's information there can be no will, but only what Albert calls a certain confused appetite. Albert believes that Aristotle had located the will in the rational soul.[157] Just as there is no perfection in appetitive powers unless they are regulated by reason, so too nothing in the moral virtues is perfected until reduced to the intellect or the rational potencies, since a human being is human only by means of rationality.[158]

The goal of all virtues of the speculative intellect is truth with the exceptions of prudence, whose end is practical, and art, whose aim is production. The act of both the practical and speculative intellect is the determination of truth or falsity, but practice does not formulate truth simply. Practical truth is related to correct desire or appetite, and is an operable truth to which right desire is always connected, just as a good servant clearly and devotedly follows the commands of his lord. This truth considers the means to an end, and does not regard the end itself.[159] The origin of choice lies in the appetite and in practical reason that determines truth not for its own sake, but to produce an action. Reason begins and arranges actions while the appetite completes them.[160] Without the appetite the determination of reason cannot move anyone to act. Choice is deliberative appetite and its deliberation concerns only what lies within the agent's power.[161] The intellect commands the appetite toward practical ends only, since the mind in itself, or the speculative intellect, is not a motivating power. But the mind, which determines truth for the sake of particular actions, is a motivating power, and, as such, is the practical intellect. Whether choice is

---

[155] *In X Eth.* V, tr. 3, c. 3, p. 368.   [156] *In X Eth.* VI, tr. 1, c. 1, pp. 391–393.
[157] *In X Eth.* VI, tr. 1, c. 2, p. 395.   [158] *In X Eth.* VI, tr. 1, c. 3, p. 395.
[159] *In X Eth.* VI, tr. 1, c. 6, p. 403.   [160] *In X Eth.* VI, tr. 1, c. 6, p. 403.
[161] *In X Eth.* VI, tr. 1, c. 6, p. 404: Electio autem appetitus consiliativus: consilium autem non nisi de operabilibus per nos.

called intellectual appetite or appetitive intellect is of no consequence for
Albert because in either case the elements of mere choice are the recognition and desire for the end.[162]

e The analysis of prudence

The specific discussion on prudence in Albert's last commentary on the NE
begins with an astute and accurate description of the virtue:

> The act of a prudent person seems to be the ability to deliberate well about those
> things which are, or bring, good to the person, or which are useful not in part,
> but universally according to everything which confers [goodness], and is useful,
> to a life.[163]

The deliberative aspect concerning contingent events led Aristotle to place
prudence as a mid-point among the intellectual virtues. The rational mind,
unaffected by the images of sense objects, cannot perform the individual
actions that are the true measure of prudence. Prudence achieves both
moral and intellectual reason and is therefore both types of virtue.[164]

Knowledge is a perfect demonstrative habit because it comprehends
eternal and necessary propositions. Since prudence considers contingent
events, it cannot be identified completely with knowledge. It is best called
an active habit of human beings with true reasoning concerning the good
to be chosen and evil to be avoided.[165] The three most important singular
active principles in the production of actions are "who, how and for the
sake of which." The last is most important since it denotes the end. It may
be corrupted by pleasure or pain that may entice one to act against all right
reasons.[166] From his analysis of deliberation and the causes of action Albert
redefines prudence as an operation or active habit with true reason concerning human goods. Prudence acts with reason because only reason can
qualify acts as human acts, and true reason refers to the ability to judge

---

[162] *In X Eth.* VI, tr. 1, c. 6, p. 404: Propter quod electio vel est appetitivus intellectus, vel
appetitus intellectivus: et tale principium operum suorum per talem electionem inter
omnia est solus homo.

[163] *In X Eth.* VI, tr. 2, c. 9, p. 417: Prudentis autem opus videtur esse posse bene consiliari
circa quae sunt bona sibipsi et conferentia sive utilia non secundum partem quidem, sed
universaliter secundum omne id quod conferens et utile est ad vitam.

[164] *In X Eth.* VI, tr. 2, c. 9, pp. 417–418. F.-B. Stammkötter claims that in his last commentary on the NE Albert no longer understands prudence as an intermediary (*Vermittlerin*)
between the ethical and intellectual virtues, but rather he emphasizes above all the
connection between theory and practice. "Die Entwicklung der Bestimmung der
Prudentia in der Ethik des Albertus Magnus," W. Senner, p. 310.

[165] *In X Eth.* VI, tr. 2, c. 10, p. 418.   [166] *In X Eth.* VI, tr. 2, c. 11, p. 419.

correctly concerning ends.[167] Prudence is an operative habit because every human operation involves choice. Choice allows for the ability to do, or to refrain from, an act. Without freedom virtue loses its essential quality. Speculative reason does not involve choice since it is contemplative and not active, and no one chooses not to understand. Pure reason does not comprise prudence whose reason is primarily practical. Good practice is the end of both moral virtue and prudence as well.[168]

The prudential process involves the intellectual and opinionative (*opinativa*) parts of the rational soul. The virtue of each part is similar to a disposition of what is perfect to what is best. Opinion considers contingent occurrences and is an important part of prudential reasoning. Opinion, however, is not a result of intellectual reason and so prudence must be more complex than a purely rational habit. One may forget intellectual arguments, but one does not really lose an awareness of prudence.[169] The complexity and classification of prudence remain much discussed topics throughout the thirteenth century. The intellect recognizes the necessary and ennobling first principles, but the intellect has other ways of knowing, as in the moral virtues. Prudence and art derive their principles from imitation and similitude, as Aristotle had recognized.[170] The principles of prudence are primarily political, but they do not constitute wisdom. If they did, prudence and politics would form a type of transcendent immutable knowledge that would preclude variety and difference in societies. To say that politics falls under the heading of wisdom is clearly incorrect and prudence, as a type of political science, must also differ from *sapientia*.[171] Prudence may describe the cleverness of animals and the ability of different types of beings to adapt to changing circumstances, but human wisdom remains the same under all conditions.[172] In more technical terms, prudence is the ability to deliberate well, but deliberation considers only that which has the possibility of change. The purpose lies always outside prudential reasoning, which determines only the appropriate means to attain its goal. While the restriction of prudence to means alone is a common feature of the medieval interpretation of the NE, Aristotle seemed to have indicated a greater role for prudence in understanding the end of actions. Wisdom, however, considers only what is immutable and beyond practice, and superior to merely human affairs.[173]

---

[167] *In X Eth.* VI, tr. 2, c. 11, p. 419.   [168] *In X Eth.* VI, tr. 2, c. 12, pp. 420–421.
[169] *In X Eth.* VI, tr. 2, c. 13, p. 422.   [170] *In X Eth.* VI, tr. 2, c. 18, p. 434.
[171] *In X Eth.* VI, tr. 2, c. 21, p. 437.   [172] *In X Eth.* VI, tr. 2, c. 21, p. 438.
[173] *In X Eth.* VI, tr. 2, c. 22, p. 440.

Since human decisions end in particular actions the prudent person must know both universal principles and particular conclusions drawn from them. True prudential reason goes beyond the universal maxims of practical knowledge and results in a type of expertise comparable to medical skill. A good doctor knows both universal scientific theorems and their particular applications, since the former are ineffective without the latter. Both are present in the prudent person who uses the universal rule to govern the particular application. The universals are always theoretical and architectonic; the individual conclusions are always useful and practical.[174] Only experience can provide knowledge sufficient enough to align particular choices with the dictates of universal principles.[175] The lack of a necessary connection between the universal and individual experience may produce error in one of two ways: (1) in the process of deliberation one may overlook the relation of the universal to the end; (2) the lack of proper experience may lead to particular errors.[176] Prudence does not consist in the intellectual understanding of terms, definitions and principles that are immediately grasped, but rather uses a common sense experience (*sensus communis*) that unites, divides and judges individual events.[177]

The ultimate goal of all human endeavors is happiness, and what is not directed to it must be considered without use. Some may argue that prudence regards what is beautiful, just and good, but as an intellectual virtue, it may be viewed as an activity that is good itself, and not merely useful for attaining a higher goal. Albert notes that if this account of prudence were correct, then it would contribute nothing to happiness.[178] To answer this question Albert considers the relation of prudence to wisdom, and concludes that the former is inferior to the latter virtue because it involves inferior objects.[179] Wisdom is the end of the speculative intellect while prudence is the end of the practical. Without the practical perfection of prudence the intellect's potency for rationality could not be actualized. Both prudence and wisdom are desirable in themselves as ends of the particular powers of the soul.[180]

---

[174] *In X Eth.* VI, tr. 2, c. 23, p. 440. J. Müller sees in *prudentia singularium* and *universalium* a reflection of the distinction between *ethica utens* and *ethica docens* in "Ethics as a Practical Science in Albert the Great's Commentaries on the *Nicomachean Ethics*," p. 283, n. 33.

[175] *In X Eth.* VI, tr. 2, c. 25, p. 442.   [176] *In X Eth.* VI, tr. 2, c. 25, p. 444.

[177] *In X Eth.* VI, tr. 2, c. 26, p. 444.   [178] *In X Eth.* VI, tr. 4, c. 1, p. 454.

[179] *In X Eth.* VI, tr. 4, c. 1, p. 455: prudentia enim deterior est quam sapientia, eo quod circa deteriora est.

[180] *In X Eth.* VI, tr. 4, c. 1, p. 455: Sapientia igitur est finis speculativi intellectus, et prudentia finis practici, sine quibus ipse intellectus non habet rationem nisi in potentia: sunt ergo desiderativa in se.

Albert regards the virtues as the soul's goods (*bona*) and as the formal constituents of human happiness, but places them in order to one good. The moral virtues are ordered to prudence whose completely perfect act is happiness. This happiness with all its virtues is directed to the intellectual virtues from which it receives its reality (*certitudinem*). All of these acts are further ordered to wisdom whose final and completely perfect act is contemplative happiness. Since beatitude is a perfect state with the accumulation of all goods, it cannot exist without wisdom. Beatitude transcends the practical intellect and prudence because without wisdom they cannot find a proper order to what is best in a human being.[181] Three types of virtue are needed for happiness: speculative, which are wisdom, understanding and knowledge; practical, which are art and prudence; and those which participate somehow in reason and are courage, temperance and justice. Without these virtues no human being can attain the perfection of the potencies that bring happiness.[182]

Prudence is related to moral virtues, and employs their potencies to perfect its habit. One such potency is what Albert calls *deinos*, that which greatly influences the practical intellect in attaining its intention. Prudence is not the same as the dinotic potency, but needs its contribution. As Albert often maintains no subject can develop a habit unless its seeds are naturally present. The dinotic potency is nothing other than the confused seeds of prudence that experience and learning develop into prudential reasoning. Such development does not occur without moral virtue, which Albert asserts is naturally evident. For the practical syllogism, which prudence employs in deliberation, a principle, which is the cause of action and to which deliberation is directed, is needed. This principle is a certain optimal end in accord with the intent of the deliberator, and will generally be any end in accord with any moral virtue. Virtue makes the intention correct and orders all propositions in the syllogism to prudence. The seeds that exist naturally develop into correct moral reasoning through the moral virtues and prudence.[183] Prudence needs the moral virtues in order to derive its operative principles from the desired end that the virtues determine.[184]

In his two commentaries on the NE Albert makes no mention of the concept of *synderesis*, most likely because it does not appear in Aristotle's text. Albert notes that such a notion is not properly a philosophical consideration, but he does imply in his discussions on natural law that universal principles of conduct are impressed upon the human soul. He

---

[181] *In X Eth.* VI, tr. 4, c. 1, p. 456.   [182] *In X Eth.* VI, tr. 4, c. 1, p. 456.
[183] *In X Eth.* VI, tr. 4, c. 2, p. 458.   [184] *In X Eth.* VI, tr. 4, c. 2, p. 458.

cites only Boethius's discussion of the common concepts of the human intellect and omits any references to Paul, Augustine or Jerome, which appear in his earlier works. Albert locates these concepts of universal imperatives in the active intellect whose connection to individual human souls provides the basis for the recognition of universal moral principles. Albert's great student, Thomas Aquinas, agrees fundamentally with his teacher's description of the manner in which all human beings are aware of eternal laws of moral action. Albert's interpretation of Aristotle's moral philosophy had enormous influence on later medieval commentaries on Aristotle. His division of happiness into two distinct types is almost universally accepted after the appearance of the *Super Ethica*. His restriction of prudence to the realm of moral virtue constitutes a reinterpretation of Aristotle's primary virtue of practical wisdom. Although Thomas rejected Albert's understanding of 'two happinesses', he did accept Albert's limits to prudential reasoning. It is to these doctrines in Thomas's works that we now turn.

Thomas Aquinas and Bonaventure on the understanding
of moral goodness

In his moral theory, Thomas Aquinas constructs a hierarchy of human achievement that has its foundation in the intellectual and rational powers of the soul. At the pinnacle of human accomplishment is perfect beatitude, which consists in the intellectual union of the separate soul with the first being. Although such a union is not possible for the composite human being, a living person may attain a type of beatitude on earth through virtuous actions and good fortune. The quest to attain supreme beatitude is the directive principle behind all human choices according to Thomas, since every moral act derives its goodness in relation to its contribution to the realization of beatitude. As a result Thomas begins his treatment of human morality in the *Summa theologiae* with a basic question: what is the ultimate goal of a human life (*de ultimo fine hominis*)? Although Thomas discusses this topic in many other works, his most complete treatment appears in the *Primae secundae* of the *Summa*. Thomas introduces the question guided initially not by Aristotle, but rather by John Damascene, who considers human beings with their intellect, volitional freedom and elective power to reflect the image of God. Thomas indicates immediately that despite his admiration for Aristotle's moral deliberations, he considers the topic from a number of different points of view. The citation to Damascene demonstrates his intention to place moral questions within a theological context. Like Albert he will freely employ Aristotelian thought when helpful, but criticizes and supplements the Philosopher's conclusions with arguments taken from Scripture and its interpreters.

The first question on the topic identifies the human end as beatitude, which Thomas considers in a general way. In order to determine whether all human beings act for the sake of an end, Thomas distinguishes between truly human actions and other types of acts that fall within human ability. When reason and will rule one's actions, one performs truly human

170

operations. What is most fully human is an act that proceeds from the will informed by deliberation.[1] Since every action takes its nature from the corresponding potency directed to its proper object, and the object of the will is the end and goal of action, all proper human operations exist for the sake of an end. What does not proceed from reason's deliberations cannot be a specifically human act, since it has only a type of imagined end (*quasi finem imaginatum*), and not one displayed by reason.[2] Those who possess reason also have the ability to pursue ends because they control their actions by means of their free choices that arise from the cooperation of the will and reason.[3] The proper objects of the will are the end and goodness understood in a universal sense. Those beings that lack reason and understanding are incapable of truly voluntary decisions because of their inability to apprehend universal principles. They must depend upon the divine will to direct them toward goodness.[4] Because the goal of all beings is God, and human beatitude is union with God, Thomas asks whether there is one and the same end for all creatures. He responds by citing Aristotle's distinction within the end itself which in Latin is expressed as the 'end of which' (*finis cuius*) and the 'end by which' (*finis quo*). The *finis cuius* is that very thing in which the nature of goodness is found, and the *finis quo* is the use or attainment of that end. The avaricious person pursues money as the object of desire (*finis cuius*) and its possession as its use (*finis quo*). If one speaks of the final human end as the object desired, then God is the same end for all beings, both human and non-human. If one speaks of the attainment (*consecutio*) of the goal, then the human end cannot be proper to irrational beings that are incapable of knowing and loving God. They achieve this end insofar as they are able to participate in some similitude to God in their lives.[5]

Beatitude is the perfect good that satisfies the appetite completely; otherwise it could not be the ultimate end for all human beings, since something else would remain to be desired. Only the universal good could end the quest for perfection, since the human appetite desires participation in the complete goodness of the first being.[6] The identification of beatitude with the actualization of potency shows the influence of Aristotle on Thomas's doctrine of moral goodness. Human beatitude, as something

---

[1] S. th. I–II, 1, 1.   [2] S. th. I–II, 1, 1, ad 3. See also S. th. I–II, 1, 3.   [3] S th. I–II, 1, 2.

[4] S. th. I–II, 1, 2, ad 3.

[5] S. th. I–II, 1, 8. See A. Celano, "The 'Finis Hominis' in the Thirteenth-Century Commentaries on the *Nicomachean Ethics*," *Archives d'histoire doctrinale et littéraire du moyen âge*, 53 (1986), pp. 23–53.

[6] S. th. I–II, 2, 7.

created, must necessarily be an operation because anything is perfected insofar as it is in act. Beatitude is the operation as a moral agent's ultimate act that arises from the essential nature of humanity.[7] Aristotle had defined the very essence of beatitude when he demonstrated how one gains a blessed state through a certain operation. Boethius's definition of beatitude as a perfect state expresses a different understanding of human excellence. For Aristotle human moral goodness is a dynamic condition of constant human operations; for Boethius it is a completed state of absolute perfection. Both notions inform Thomas's doctrine of human moral goodness.[8]

The specific operation that perfects human nature is one that unites the soul with God. Living beings cannot enjoy a continuous intellectual union since human acts are subject to interruption and cessation. Like Aristotle, Thomas ascribes true perfection to superior beings whose existence is identical to their activity. Separate substances have a similar existence in that their essences are characterized by a single eternal operation, but the object of their desire differs from themselves. God, however, can only take delight (*fruitur*) in Himself.[9] Aristotle knew the difference between imperfect and perfect beatitude when he notes that we call humans blessed only 'as men' (*ut homines*). The more continuous and unified the operation, the greater it participates in the nature of perfect beatitude. The most constant and self-sufficient activity is contemplation, which seeks one object, truth.[10] Human beatitude consists essentially in the union with the uncreated good.[11] This union cannot consist essentially in a voluntary action because beatitude is the actual attainment of the desired end. The will is brought to this end which it does not possess, and then the will delights in its attainment. The desire for the end is not its attainment, but rather the impetus toward the goal. Another act must present the end to the will, and so the essence of beatitude consists in the intellectual operation, and the ensuing delight is the operation of the will.[12]

Thomas claims that imperfect beatitude attains the nature of beatitude because of its participation and similitude to the perfect state. Perfect beatitude consists in the vision of the divine essence that would satisfy all elements of human desire. The perfection of the intellectual potency occurs when it comprehends the supreme intelligible. As Aristotle says in the *De anima*, the object of the intellect is that which is (being), or the essence of

---

[7] S. th. I–II, 3, 2.   [8] S. th. I–II 3, 2, ad 2.   [9] S. th. 3, 2, ad 4.   [10] S. th. I–II, 3, 2.

[11] S. th. I–II, 3, 3: Nam beatitudo hominis consistit essentialiter in coniunctione ipsius ad bonum increatum, quod est ultimus finis, ut supra ostensum est, cui homo coniungi non potest per sensus operationem.

[12] S. th. I–II, 3, 4.

the thing perceived. The knowledge of the essential nature of things perfects the intellectual capacity. Since human knowledge begins with an awareness of effects and then proceeds to cognition of causes, only an understanding of God as the first cause can completely fulfill the intellectual potency. True beatitude requires the intellect to reach the very essence of the first cause. In the union with the divine object of the intellect perfect beatitude is found.[13]

Since beatitude is not merely an intellectual achievement, but also a moral perfection, Thomas insists that the rectitude of the will is needed both antecedently and concomitantly. The will requires antecedent correctness, because its integrity exists in its required order to the end. The end for the will is similar to form, and the means to an end are like the matter in a physical object. Just as matter cannot follow form without a proper disposition, the end cannot be reached without proper order. The will's rectitude ensures the proper relation of all means to the end. The will that perceives the divine essence would love all things in relation to their order to God. Even those who do not discern the divine essence would still love what is right from the perception of the general nature of goodness. The will's correctness becomes a concomitant element of beatitude.[14]

Material goods contribute nothing to intellectual perfection, but they provide the instruments that make imperfect earthly beatitude possible. Both contemplative and practical virtues require some goods in order to provide the opportunities to exercise such virtues, such as money for the exercise of generosity. Even contemplation needs the necessities to maintain life. Because contemplation approximates the perfect intellectual existence of the separated soul it requires fewer material goods than the active life.[15] The contemplative life participates in beatitude (*aliqualis beatitudinis participatio*), but the human condition subject to misfortune and mutation prevents anyone from attaining true perfection on earth. Despite the desire for a permanent state of goodness all human beings are transitory creatures, and the Christian vision of true beatitude requires the soul to be separate from the body.[16] Imperfect beatitude may be lost in a number of ways since contemplation may yield to confusion, the will may turn one from virtue, or grave misfortune may destroy the ability to enjoy life. Thomas, like his contemporaries, knew that Aristotle's vision of happiness could be destroyed by the vagaries of temporal existence.[17]

[13] S. th. I–II, 3, 8. [14] S. th. I–II, 4, 4. [15] S. th. I–II, 4, 7. [16] S. th. I–II, 5, 3.
[17] S. th. I–II, 5, 4.

In Thomas's own time his commentary on the NE, while a careful exposition of Aristotle's text, exerted less influence on his contemporaries than the exposition of his teacher, Albert the Great.[18] While Thomas agrees with many interpretations of Albert, especially concerning the nature and process of prudential decisions, he does not accept Albert's notion of 'two happinesses' as a correct reading of Aristotelian doctrine. While Albert views the potentialities of reason as so distinct that their actualities result in two distinct types of perfection, contemplative and practical, Thomas judges Aristotle to have intended both moral and intellectual virtue to be complementary elements within human happiness. Thomas's reading of Aristotle may be accurate, but Albert's understanding of this idea influenced every known commentary on the NE in the late thirteenth century, since they all include the idea of two distinct kinds of human happiness. Only Boethius of Dacia in his short treatise, *De summo bono*, agreed with Thomas, and claimed that Aristotle spoke of only one form of happiness that encompasses both moral and intellectual excellence.[19] Perfect beatitude exceeds not only the nature of human beings, but also that of all creatures.[20] Rectitude of the will may be required for true beatitude, but this condition does not mean that some human operation must precede the attainment of perfection. Thomas claims that God could make the will seek the end simultaneously with its acquisition, just as He can simultaneously dispose matter and induce the corresponding form. Since divine causality is always involved in the production of perfect beatitude, necessity on the human side need not be presumed.[21]

a Choice and the practical syllogism

A theologian considers human actions as they are ordered to beatitude. Everything that has order to an end should be proportionate to that end according to a proper measure (*commensuratio*), which results from the required circumstances. A theologian judges the human act as it has the nature of good or evil, or is meritorious or blameworthy. Voluntary actions depend upon the agent's state of knowledge, which all moral theologians

---

[18] A. Celano, "Act of the Intellect or Act of the Will: The Critical Reception of Aristotle's Ideal of Human Perfection in the 13th and Early 14th Centuries," *Archives d'histoire doctrinale et littéraire du moyen âge*, 57 (1990), pp. 93–119. R.-A. Gauthier, "Trois commentaires 'averroistes' sur l'Ethique à Nicomaque," *Archives d'histoire doctrinale et littéraire du moyen âge*, 16 (1947–1948), pp. 187–336.

[19] A. Celano, "Boethius of Dacia on the Highest Good," *Traditio*, 43 (1987), pp. 199–214.

[20] S. th. I–II, 12, 4.   [21] S. th. 5, 7.

must consider.[22] For an act to be truly human it must be voluntary, since
the motivation for the will is the end itself. The most important circumstance of human actions is that which the end provides, 'that for the sake of
which' (*cuius gratia*).[23] The will, as rational appetite, can only pursue what
is good, but an appetite that arises from perception may tend toward
perceived goodness that may not be truly good.[24] The will's proper act,
or its intention, can only be for the sake of the end, since the means follow
from the desire for the end.[25]

Moral choice follows a judgment that functions as a conclusion in the
practical syllogism. The end in all practical decisions functions as a first
principle and not as a conclusion. The end insofar as it is an end does not fall
within the elective process (*electio*). Just as nothing prevents a speculative
principle of one science from being a conclusion in another, no end in one
decision is prohibited from being ordered to a further goal. In medicine, for
example, health is the end about which no doctor deliberates. The physician
intuits the goal of restoring or maintaining health and selects the proper
means. Bodily health, however, may be ordered to the good of the soul, and
one entrusted with care of the soul may at times have to sacrifice corporeal
health for a superior end.[26] No one can choose what lies beyond one's
abilities or power to accomplish. The will is the bridge between the intellect
and the external operation, since the intellect proposes its object to the will,
which in turn is the motivating force to action. The intellect, which comprehends something as good in the universal sense, drives the will to action.
The perfection of the voluntary action develops according to the order
leading to the operation by which one strives to attain the object of desire.
The voluntary act's perfection results from the performance of some good
that lies within the agent's power.[27]

The will can choose freely, since it may decide to act or not to act. Only
beatitude, which reason recognizes as perfect, involves a certain necessity,
since no one could prefer misery over blessedness. Because the will's
choices concern the means to beatitude, it may reject any particular good
as not conducive to this end.[28] Everything that has intellective cognition
has an appetite proportionate to this awareness. This type of cognitive
appetite is the will. The will as appetite is not proper to the intellectual
nature, but rather is related to it only as it depends upon the intellect. The

---

[22] S. th. I–II, 7, 2.   [23] S. th. I–II, 7, 4.   [24] S. th. I–II, 8, 1.
[25] S. th. I–II, 8, 2 and 3. See M. Perkams, "Aquinas on Choice, Will and Voluntary Action,"
Aquinas and the Nicomachean Ethics, ed. T. Hoffmann, J. Müller and M. Perkams
(Cambridge: Cambridge University Press, 2013), pp. 72–90.
[26] S. th. I–II, 13, 3.   [27] S. th. I–II, 13, 5, ad 1.   [28] S. th. I–II, 13, 6.

intellect itself is that which determines an intellectual being. Happiness consists substantially and principally in the act of the intellect rather than in the act of the will.[29] The intellect moves the will *per se* and primarily because it presents the perceived good to the voluntary potency. The will moves the intellect as if accidentally (*quasi per accidens*) in that what is understood as good is desired by the will. The intellect must act in order for the will to desire by presenting the object as good.[30]

Choice presupposes deliberation about matters that have some measure of uncertainty. If there are fixed ways to determined ends as in certain arts, there can be no deliberation at all. A scribe does not deliberate concerning the structure of letters because the scriptorial art determines the manner in which he writes. Choices that affect minimally the acquisition of the end require no deliberation, since reason pursues the best course to the desired goal.[31] For such reasons no one deliberates about beatitude, which moral science proposes and reason accepts immediately as the proper end for all endeavors.[32] The will's goodness depends upon the object that reason proposes. The will has the ability to aim at the universal good that reason comprehends, and so the will depends upon reason as it depends on its object.[33] Human reason becomes the measure of the will by which its goodness is calculated because of the eternal law of divine reason. The light of reason in human beings as it displays goodness and rules the will depends upon the reflection of the divine countenance. The goodness of the human will clearly depends more upon eternal law than upon human reason. Where human reason fails there must be a turn to eternal reason.[34] As it exists in the mind of God the eternal law is unknown to human beings, but it can be known somehow either by natural reason or through revelation.[35]

The intention to attain a proper end ultimately leads the will to the supreme good, which is God. A requirement for voluntary goodness is the order that leads to this good. Since the first element in any genus is the measure and rationale for all subsequent elements, what is right and good is judged in relation to the principle of all goodness. As a result the human will can be good insofar as it conforms to, and imitates, the divine will.[36] Human beings can know the divine will in a general way (*secundum rationem communem*) because whatever God wills He does so under the nature of goodness. No one, however, can know what God wills

---

[29] SCG III, 26, 8.   [30] SCG III, 26, 22.   [31] S. th. I–II, 14, 4.   [32] S. th. I–II, 14, 6.
[33] S. th. I–II, 19, 3.   [34] S. th. I–II, 19, 4.   [35] S. th. I–II, 19, 4, ad 3.
[36] S. th. I–II, 19, 9 and ad 1.

particularly.[37] In voluntary actions the proximate regulative principle is human reason, but the supreme principle is the eternal law. Whatever human act proceeds to the end according to the order of reason and to the eternal law is right. Actions that do not proceed in this way are always wrong.[38] Thomas does not envision any conflict between the regulatory forces of reason and the eternal law, since their principles are identical.

b Prudence and right reason

Prudence presupposes the rectitude of the appetite and is called right reason of what is to be done. Prudence requires that the agent must be well disposed concerning the end that depends on correct appetite. Prudence does not convey the rectitude to the appetite, but rather moral virtue governs the desire for the proper end.[39] Thomas's claim that prudence is necessary to an entire human life seems, like Albert's assertion, to refer to the life of moral virtues alone.[40] Thomas views prudence primarily in its relation to the need for living well (*bene vivere*). To live well consists in right actions, which require that both what is to be done and how something is performed be in accordance with right reason. Correct choices concerning appropriate moral actions require the proper end and the corresponding means. What disposes one to the end is virtue, which perfects the appetitive part of the soul, whose object is goodness. To order the means effectively, one must be directly disposed by the habit of reason to make deliberation and choice rational acts. The rational process requires an intellectual virtue by which reason is perfected, and this virtue can only be prudence.[41] Thomas does not include the other aspect of happiness, which is the knowledge of God (*cognitio Dei*) in his discussion of prudence, since he most likely understood prudence to govern the moral virtues.

Truth for the practical intellect differs from that of the speculative intellect, since the latter kind of truth consists in the conformity of the intellect to the object of knowledge. Because the intellect cannot conform infallibly to the object in contingent judgments no necessary intellectual habit of contingent events can be developed. The truth for the practical intellect consists in its conformity to correct appetite. This conformity does not admit necessity, for then the will could not be free. Conformity to right

---

[37] S. th. I–II, 19, 10 ad 1.   [38] S. th. I–II, 21, 1.   [39] S. th. I–II, 57, 4.

[40] S. th. I–II, 57, 4 ad 3: Ad tertium dicendum quod prudentia est bene consiliativa de his quae pertinent ad totam vitam hominis, et ad ultimum finem vitae humanae. See also *De virtutibus*, q. 5, a. 2.

[41] S. th. I–II, 57, 5.

appetite occurs internally concerning contingent actions (prudence), or in the production of some external object (art).[42] Prudence has a connection to both the speculative and practical powers within the intellect. In actions three rational operations, deliberation, judgment and command, act together. The first two acts are functions of the intellect, but command leads to action, and, as such, belongs properly to the practical intellect. It is the principle of action to which all others in the process are ordered. In prudence, whose primary act is to command, the action of the practical intellect directs the deliberative processes of the speculative intellect.[43] Thomas calls prudence an intellectual virtue according to its essence, but it belongs to the moral virtues according to its subject, since it is right reason in actions.[44] Prudence is needed for all moral virtues because it determines the proper means to the desired end and issues appropriate commands. Despite its classification as an intellectual virtue it functions in the moral realm. It does, however, comprehend the naturally known moral principles and deduces correct actions from them.[45]

While other intellectual virtues may exist without moral virtue, prudence cannot because it requires right reason in both universal and particular judgments. Right reason presupposes a comprehension of principles from which particular actions may be deduced. These principles are known by a natural understanding whereby one knows that no evil should be performed. Although these principles direct action, they do not translate immediately into action, since passion may corrupt their commands. Just as the disposition to act rightly concerning principles comes from natural understanding or the habit of knowledge, so too do habits concerning natural judgments concerning ends arise from moral virtue. Natural virtue displays the proper end in particular choices in accordance with the natural knowledge of universal imperatives.[46]

Because the object of reason is truth and truth also presents itself in contingent moral decisions, only one virtue, prudence, can have directive force. The object of appetitive virtue, the desired good, is diversified according to different circumstances affecting the moral agent.[47] Certain virtues may construct a bridge that creates a kinship with a divine being, and are called purgative. Prudence may be considered purgative when it

---

[42] S. th. I–II, 57, 5 ad 3.   [43] S. th. I–II, 57, 6.
[44] S. th. I–II, 58, 3 ad 1: Ad primum ergo dicendum quod prudentia, secundum essentiam suam, est intellectualis virtus. Sed secundum materiam, convenit cum virtutibus moralibus, est enim recta ratio agibilium, ut supra dictum est. Et secundum hoc, virtutibus moralibus connumeratur.
[45] S. th. I–II, 58, 4.   [46] S. th. I–II, 58, 5.   [47] S. th. I–II, 60, 1 ad 1 and ad 2.

proceeds from a reflection of mundane affairs to contemplation of the divine being.[48] Virtue perfects human beings by ordering them to beatitude, which can be proportionate to human nature and attained by human means. Another kind of beatitude exceeds human nature and is reached by divine virtue only. This beatitude consists in a certain type of participation in the divine being and exceeds any human potency. Some additional principles must be divinely granted to a person, by which one is granted supernatural beatitude. These infused principles are the theological virtues that have God as their object. Such virtues are revealed only through scriptures.[49]

Virtue has a natural component, since human rationality knows naturally innate principles of science and action. Like Albert, Thomas designates these principles as a type of fertile ground (*seminaria*) for intellectual and moral virtues. The will also has a natural desire for goodness in harmony with reason. Individual material differences explain why certain people seem to have a disposition toward developing virtues more completely than others.[50] Specific measures determine goodness and because there are two ends for human existence there must be two distinct measures: divine law and human reason. Because the former is superior to the latter it extends further and rules all human actions. Human virtue ordered to the good regulated by reason can have its origin in human acts as they proceed from reason itself. Virtue ordered to the good regulated by divine law cannot originate in human operations whose principle is reason, but are caused only by a divine operation.[51] Thomas has the opportunity here to accept the Ciceronian unification of Platonic and Aristotelian ethics, whereby the eternal law is subject to the interpretations of the wise person, but he chooses to keep the two moral ends separate because reason can never unite the two.[52]

No moral virtue can exist without prudence, just as prudence cannot exist without moral virtues, since the virtues direct one properly to the ends by which the nature of prudence proceeds. For the true nature of prudence there is a greater requirement for the proper relation to the final end, which is made by charity, than to other ends that are made by moral virtue. The relation of charity to the final end is similar to right reason in speculative sciences that need the prime indemonstrable principle of non-contradiction. What Thomas calls infused prudence cannot exist without charity, as can no other virtue that orders a human being to the ultimate end.[53]

[48] S. th. I–II, 61, 5.   [49] S. th. I–II, 62, 1.   [50] S. th. I–II, 63, 1.   [51] S. th. I–II, 63, 2.
[52] Cicero, *De officiis*, ed. M. Winterbottom, *M. Tulli Ciceronis De Officiis* (Oxford: Oxford University Press, 1994), I, 5.
[53] S. th. I–II, 65, 2.

Thomas views the question concerning the supremacy of the virtue of wisdom with respect to its relation to prudence. He notes in his preliminary arguments that since prudence directs human action to happiness it seems to rule over wisdom. In his response Thomas understands the specific character of any virtue in relation to its object. Since wisdom's object is the supreme cause of all things, God, it must take the preeminent position among all virtues. Wisdom can make valid judgments concerning all other intellectual virtues, and therefore orders all theoretical pursuits in an architectonic hierarchy.[54] Because prudence is limited to human affairs it cannot be superior to the wisdom that considers the highest cause. Thomas unites Aristotle's claims that man is supreme on earth with Paul's assertion that "what is spiritual judges all things and is judged by no one." According to Thomas prudence is not involved in the objects of wisdom, although it may govern actions that lead to it. Prudence ministers to wisdom in preparing the way just as a courtier serves a king.[55]

Thomas devotes six questions to the topic of prudence in the *Secunda secundae* of the *Summa theologiae*, and begins with a consideration of three well-known definitions. The first two are taken from Augustine and the third comes from Aristotle. Thomas cites Augustine's designations of prudence as love (*amor*) and knowledge (*cognitio*), as well as Aristotle's description of prudence's function in art as the deliberate choice of error. He later adds Isadore of Seville's depiction of prudence as a type of foresight (*porro videns*), which demonstrates that prudence pertains to the cognitive powers of the soul. Prudence's vision allows one to predict future events from past and present experiences.[56] Thomas interprets Augustine's description of prudence as love in terms of how the will moves potencies to act. Since the first act of appetitive virtue is love, prudence may be called love, insofar as love moves one to action. Augustine refined his definition by adding the element of discernment that helps one to makes correct choices that lead to God.[57] Prudence pertains most properly to deliberation, but since all choice involves deliberative judgment, prudence may be also attributed to the art of choosing.[58]

Thomas understands Aristotle's opening line on the topic of prudence, "it is characteristic of the practically wise person to be able to deliberate well," to pertain to the ability to exercise right reason over choices that lead to desired ends. Such ability is the mark of practical reason.[59] In any area the wise person considers the absolute highest cause, and in human actions

---

[54] S. th. I–II, 66, 5.   [55] S. th. I–II, 66, 5 ad 1.   [56] S. th. II–II, 47, 1.
[57] S. th. II–II, 47, 1, ad 1.   [58] S. th. II–II, 47, 1, ad 2.   [59] S. th. II, 47, 2.

the supreme cause is the universal end for every life. It is this to which prudence directs actions, since the one who reasons well about a completely good life (*totum bene vivere*) is absolutely prudent and wise in human affairs. Thomas's choice of the phrase, *bene vivere*, demonstrates his intention to limit prudence to the practical world of human interactions, whose mastery makes one humanly wise, but does not result in unqualified wisdom.[60]

Thomas accepts Aristotle's depiction of prudence's ability to know both universal principles and individual applications. For Thomas both the consideration of reason and its application to an act leading to an end are features of prudence. No one can apply one thing to another unless a person knows both applications. Because operations consist in individual choices the *prudens* knows both the universal principles of reason and the individual operations that result from them.[61] The combination of the right consideration of reason and the rectitude of the appetite required of prudence places it among both the intellectual and moral virtues.[62] Prudence, however, is distinguished from other intellectual virtues by the material diversity of the objects, since wisdom, knowledge and understanding consider necessity. Prudence's objects are actions within the moral agent and allows for variations according to circumstances and abilities. Prudence differs from moral virtues according to a formally distinct nature of the powers of the intellect and the appetite. Prudence takes a special place in the list of human virtues because of its affinity for both kinds of virtue.[63]

c *Synderesis* and natural law

In the discussion on prudence Thomas refers obliquely to the concepts of *synderesis* and natural law. He argues that because the good for the soul exists according to reason the ends of moral virtue necessarily preexist in reason. The method of understanding ends is similar to the immediate apprehension of scientific axioms. The moral principles naturally known are the ends of the moral virtues, but they differ from scientific laws in that they lead to action.[64] Thomas makes the implied reference explicit in his response when he claims that "natural reason, which is called *synderesis*,

---

[60] S. th. II–II, 47, 2 ad 1.   [61] S. th. II–II, 47, 3.   [62] S. th. II–II, 47, 4.

[63] S. th. II–II, 47, 5.

[64] S. th. II–II, 47, 6. For a recent study of this topic, see D. Farrell, *The Ends of Moral Virtues and the First Principles of Practical Reason in Thomas Aquinas* (Rome: Gregorian and Biblical Press, 2012).

displays the end in moral virtues"[65] and thereby moves prudence itself.[66] For Aristotle virtue displays the end in moral decisions, but Thomas makes the process less flexible when he makes *synderesis* the moving force of reason. Like his medieval predecessors who sought to place the principles of moral practice on a foundation more secure than the choices of a good person, Thomas chooses to introduce a measure of ethical certitude in the innate habit of *synderesis*. In his early work, the commentary on Peter Lombard's *Sentences* Thomas considers the state of human beings before Adam's fall from grace, and then discusses the human natural power to avoid sin. In these questions the concept of *synderesis* has an important role in directing human beings to choose what is good. After a treatment of the problem of free choice Thomas abruptly introduces the question whether *synderesis* is a habit or a potency. In the preliminary arguments he notes that a habit can only be attributed to a potency, but Augustine says that the universal precepts of law are written in the natural judgment, which is *synderesis*. Since there is a habit of the universal precepts of law, *synderesis* may seem to be a potency to which the habit is attributed. Thomas's adroit answer to the question is less important here than his unqualified acceptance of Augustine's assertion that the precepts of law are collected in an innate habit, and form the unshakeable foundation for proper moral choices.[67]

In the commentary on the *Sentences* one finds a position that directs many subsequent conclusions throughout Thomas's career: the notion that order and reason are derived from a single principle. Thomas compares the process of reasoning in practical science to that of theoretical sciences:

Just as in the motion of natural things all motion proceeds from an unmoved mover ... every dissimilar relation comes from one relation that is similar in some way, so too does the process of reason function. Since reason has a certain variety and is mobile in some way insofar as it deduces conclusions from principles, in the process it is frequently deceived, all reason must proceed from some cognition by which it has a certain uniformity and stasis. This does not occur by a discursive investigation, but is offered immediately to the understanding, just as reason in speculative [sciences] is deduced from some principles known in themselves whose habit is called understanding.[68]

---

[65] S. th. II–II, 47, 6 ad 1: Ad primum ergo dicendum quod virtutibus moralibus praestituit finem ratio naturalis quae dicitur synderesis, ut in primo habitum est, non autem prudentia, ratione iam dicta.

[66] S. th. II–II, 47, 6, ad 3.   [67] *In II Sent.* d. 24, q. 2, a. 3.

[68] *In II Sent.*, d. 24, q. 2, a. 3: quod sicut est de motu rerum naturalium, quod omnis motus ab immobili movente procedit, ... et omne dissimiliter se habens ab uno eodemque modo se habente; ita etiam oportet quod sit in processu rationis; cum enim ratio varietatem quamdam habeat, et quodammodo mobilis sit, secundum quod principia in conclusiones

The principles of action are known immediately and include the command to avoid evil and obey the laws of God. The resulting habit is *synderesis*, which differs from practical reason, not by the substance of the potency, but because it is an innate habit. *Synderesis* is somehow innate because of the very light of the agent intellect, just as this light provides immediate comprehension of statements, such as the whole is greater than any part. In the commentary on the *Sentences*, as in the later works, Thomas does not seem to concern himself greatly with a precise designation of *synderesis*: "And so I say that *synderesis* designates a habit alone or a potency subject to an innate habit in us."[69] This natural habit can never be lost, as is evident from the habit of recognizing principles of speculative sciences that a human being always retains.

Later in the commentary Thomas again appeals to the argument from order as a basis for his theory about *synderesis*. Divine wisdom, as Dionysius claimed, unites the first elements of lower things to the last elements of higher ones, and in the order of creation what follows must be similar to what precedes. Their similarity is the result of participation in perfection, and so an inferior creature participates by means of its similitude to the superior one. In the order of creatures the angelic nature is first and is followed by those with a rational soul. But the soul is united to a body, and its knowledge then arises from sensation, which leads by inquisition to understanding. Angelic incorporeal beings require no inquisitive process to apprehend truth because angelic nature is purely intellectual, while the embodied soul is properly called rational. Because the rational soul is close to the angelic nature, it can participate in intellectual virtue and apprehend certain truths without discursive reason. Such truths include the first principles of speculative and practical sciences. In practical inquiry the immediate apprehension of first principles is the habit of *synderesis*. Thomas refers to this ability as a spark, since just as a spark is a small bit flying out from the fire, so too is this power (*virtus*) a certain modest participation in the intellectuality that characterizes angelic beings. This spark is the supreme element in rational natures, which is why Jerome depicted it as an eagle soaring above

---

deducit, et in conferendo frequenter decipiatur; oportet quod omnis ratio ab aliqua cognitione procedat, quae uniformitatem et quietem quamdam habeat; quod non fit per discursum investigationis, sed subito intellectui offertur: sicut enim ratio in speculativis deducitur ab aliquibus principiis per se notis, quorum habitus intellectus dicitur.

[69] *In II Sent.*, d. 24, q. 2, a. 3: Et ideo dico, quod synderesis vel habitum tantum nominat, vel potentiam saltem subjectam habitui sic nobis innato. O. Lottin, "Syndérèse et conscience aux xiie et xiiie siècles," *Psychologie et Morale aux XIIe et XIIIe siècles* (Louvain, Gembloux: Abbaye du Mont César, Duclot, 1942–1949), II, pp. 101–349.

all other creatures. It is *synderesis*, which cannot be extinguished and always repels anything that contravenes natural principles.[70]

The most extensive treatment of the topic of *synderesis* appears in the disputed questions on truth (*De veritate* 16, articles 1, 2 and 3). Thomas begins with the usual question whether *synderesis* is to be considered a potency or a habit. In the preliminary arguments two important comments on *synderesis* emerge: (1) the universal principles of law are said to be attributed to *synderesis*; (2) in the natural ability to judge (*synderesis*) there are certain true immutable rules and the 'lights' of virtue.[71] However Thomas may resolve the question of what *synderesis* is, he maintains these features of *synderesis* throughout his discussions. The resolution to the question includes a cursory summary of contemporary opinions, including that of Albert. In his own response Thomas again connects human rationality with the angelic nature. Human beings can recognize those truths that produce all subsequent knowledge without discursive investigation in both the speculative and practical areas.[72] Thomas again uses Albert's term in claiming that such innate knowledge is similar to fertile ground (*seminarium*) for subsequent conclusions, just as natural seeds must preexist subsequent vegetation. This type of knowledge must be habitual so that it will be ready for use when needed. As the first principles in the theoretical sciences direct all subsequent conclusions, so too in moral reasoning a certain natural habit of the first principles of action must exist as the universal dictates of natural law. This habit, says Thomas, pertains to *synderesis* and exists in no other potency than reason.[73] Lottin claims that the definitions of natural law and *synderesis* may be made more precise by referring to the former as that which is formally constituted by the first principles of the moral order, while the latter may be considered as the innate disposition that expresses them.[74]

---

[70] *In II Sent.*, d. 24, q. 39, a. 1.
[71] *De veritate*, q. 16, a. 1, arg. 5: Praeterea, habitui non inscribitur aliquid, sed potentiae tantum; sed universalia principia iuris dicuntur inscribi synderesi. *De veritate*, q. 16, a. 1, arg. 9.
[72] *De veritate*, q. 16, a. 1.
[73] *De veritate*, q. 16, a. 1. See also R. McInerny, "Action Theory in St. Thomas Aquinas," *Thomas von Aquin Werk und Wirkung im Licht neuerer Forschung*, ed. A. Zimmermann, Miscellanea Mediaevalia, 19 (Berlin, New York: de Gruyter, 1988), pp. 19–20: ". . . as the first principles of demonstration are to speculative reason, so too are the precepts of natural law to practical reason. The similarity lies in the fact that in both cases the principles are *per se nota*."
[74] O. Lottin, "Le Rôle de la Raison dans la Morale Albertino-Thomiste," *Psychologie et morale . . .* III, p. 569.

Thomas never provides a precise determination of the habit of *synderesis*, since he says "this term, *synderesis*, either designates absolutely a natural habit similar to the habit of principles, or designates the very power of reason with such a habit, and whichever of these makes little difference because it produces doubt only concerning the meaning of the term."[75] *Synderesis* refers generally to what Thomas calls both superior and inferior reason. The habit of universal legal principles contains certain precepts that reflect eternal commands, such as obedience to God. It also indicates lower precepts, such as living in accord with reason. *Synderesis* refers to immutable commands that can never change, but it also has relevance to mutable beings that are bound by the necessity of truth. Just as the whole will always be greater than any part even though the whole may change, so too must mutable human beings live always according to reason. *Synderesis*, therefore, implies both objective and subjective necessity.[76] Without eternal principles a human being could never overcome moral uncertainty and chaos, since nature always intends what is good. In all natural acts the eternal immutable principles preserve moral rectitude. Aristotle's assertion that principles must endure is the foundation for stability and certitude in all endeavors.[77] The first principles can never admit error, for then all subsequent information could be doubted. To ensure moral rectitude the permanent principle against which all acts are measured is *synderesis*, whose task is to resist all evil and assent to all good. All subsequent moral conclusions follow from this command.[78]

Thomas again compares *synderesis* to the light of the active intellect when he responds to the question whether *synderesis* may be extinguished. With reference to the habitual light of *synderesis* it can never be lost, just as the human soul may never be deprived of the light of the agent intellect. This light arises from the intellectual nature of the soul that always displays the good. *Synderesis* may be thought to be lost only by some organic impediment that interferes with the intellectual ability, or in the particular choice that strays from the universal principle.[79] In the *Summa theologiae* Thomas is more emphatic in his designation of *synderesis* as a habit: "*synderesis* is not a potency but a habit, although some say *synderesis* is a certain potency higher than reason; some say it is reason itself, not as it is

---

[75] *De veritate*, q. 16, a. 1: Restat igitur ut hoc nomen synderesis vel nominet absolute habitum naturalem similem habitui principiorum vel nominet ipsam potentiam rationis cum tali habitu, et quodcumque horum fuerit non multum differt, quia hoc non facit dubitationem nisi circa nominis significationem.

[76] *De veritate*, q. 16, a. 1 ad 9.   [77] *De veritate*, q. 16, a. 2.   [78] *De veritate*, q. 16, a. 2.

[79] *De veritate*, q. 16, a. 3.

reason, but as nature."[80] Just as there is no special potency to know theoretical principles, but only a particular habit of understanding, so too is there no special potency to comprehend practical principles but rather only the particular natural habit of *synderesis*.[81] True and perfect prudence requires correct deliberation, judgment and command about what leads to a good end for an entire life. Such prudence cannot be found in sinners, because, as Aristotle said, it is not possible to be prudent and not to be good. One may say that an evildoer has a type of prudential similitude as he organizes his actions to attain a corrupt end. One may speak of a 'good' thief, but only in the sense that the thief successfully executes his crime, but he cannot be designated as good in a moral or human sense.[82]

The essential action of the contemplative life pertains to the intellect, and its essential motivation pertains to the will. Because the will moves all other human potencies it must also move the intellect to act.[83] Since truth is the end of contemplation, it possesses the nature of an appetible, desirable and delightful good.[84] Thomas views contributions to the contemplative life as essential or dispositive, and moral virtue is not an essential part of the contemplative life, since it does not have much power to contribute to truth, as Aristotle explained in the NE (1178a9). Thomas, like Albert, does identify moral virtue with 'active' happiness, since it produces traits that calm the passions so that one may turn to contemplative pursuits.[85] Thomas does not, however, separate the two virtuous lives to the extent that they produce two distinct human perfections. All human endeavors should ultimately lead to contemplation of divine truth, which is the true end of all intellectual life. Thomas notes that contemplation of God will be perfected after death when one will 'see' God 'face to face'. On earth one attains only imperfect awareness of divine truth, as if through a glass darkly. Such imperfect contemplation creates in us a certain beginning in beatitude that ends in the afterlife.[86] All truths perfect the intellect as they are ordered to divine truth, which is the ultimate perfection of the intellect.[87]

Thomas believes Aristotle limited prudence to active happiness, which arises from the activities of moral virtue.[88] He argues that anything that is

---

[80] S. th. I, 79, 12: Respondeo dicendum quod synderesis non est potentia, sed habitus, licet quidam posuerint synderesim esse quandam potentiam ratione altiorem; quidam vero dixerint eam esse ipsam rationem, non ut est ratio, sed ut est natura.

[81] S. th. I, 79, 12.   [82] S. th. II–II, 47, 13.   [83] S. th. II–II, 180, 1.

[84] S. th. II–II, 180 ad 1.   [85] S. th. II–II, 180, 2.   [86] S. th. II–II, 180, 4.

[87] S. th. II–II, 180, 4, ad 4.

[88] S. th. II–II, 181, 2, arg. 3: Sed contra est quod philosophus, in X Ethic., prudentiam pertinere dicit ad felicitatem activam, ad quam pertinent virtutes morales. NE 1178a9 and 16.

ordered to another as end, especially in moral matters, is drawn to the species of that to which it is ordered; for example, he who commits adultery in order to steal is called a thief more than an adulterer. Prudential cognition has order to the operations of moral virtues as to an end according to its definition as "the right reason of actions." The ends of moral virtues are the principles of virtue as Aristotle indicates in the NE (1140b20). Prudence functions directly in the active life by providing guidance in the moral virtues. Thomas, like Albert, judges the proper function of prudence in contemplative happiness as a preparatory stage. Taken more generally prudence is involved in the contemplative life, since it involves a certain type of cognition. Cicero noted the cognitive function of prudence when he claimed that "he who most acutely and swiftly can see what is true and explain its nature is the one who rightly can be considered most prudential and wise."[89] The ends specify the moral operations, but the cognition that has the end in the perception of truth pertains to the contemplative life. The cognition involved in prudence has its end in the act of the appetitive virtue and is relevant only to the active life.[90]

Prudence seems to be able to deliberate well concerning appropriate goods and instruments not for a particular pursuit, but rather what is good and useful for an entire life.[91] Prudence must be directed toward a good end, since Thomas, like Kant, considers the possibility that a clever thief may pursue an evil end successfully, but remains evil.[92] Despite its appearance among the intellectual virtues prudence cannot be considered true knowledge (*scientia*) because science is demonstrative knowledge proceeding from necessary principles. Since prudence is primarily deliberative, and deliberation considers possible actions, it cannot proceed in the manner of immutable science, which is a demonstrative habit concerning necessity.[93] Prudence is an active habit with true reason concerning good and evil for a human being.[94] For Thomas, Aristotle's example of Pericles as the *phronimos* relates only to political prudence and has relevance only to domestic and political domains.[95] Thomas emphasizes the connection between

---

[89] S. th. II–II, 181, 2. *De officiis* I, 5. On the relation of prudence and wisdom in Cicero and its effect on medieval thought, see A. Celano, "*Phronesis*, Prudence and Moral Goodness in the Thirteenth Century Commentaries on the *Nicomachean Ethics*," *Mediaevalia Philosophica Polonorum*, 36 (2007), pp. 5–27.

[90] S. th. II–II, 181, 2 ad 1. See also S. th. II–II, 182, 1 ad 2 and 182, 3 where Thomas describes the active life as subservient to the contemplative life.

[91] SLE, p. 345, ll. 16–23.   [92] SLE, p. 345, ll. 24–39.   [93] SLE, p. 345, ll. 51–76.

[94] SLE, p. 346, ll. 77–79: ... prudentia sit habitus cum vera ratione activus ... circa bona et mala ipsius hominis.

[95] SLE, p. 346, ll. 100–110.

politics and prudence because he sees a connection in their dominant function of governing. Since prudence is essentially self-governance, it closely resembles the political virtue that rules a state. Thomas places prudence on the same level as politics when he distinguishes it from the supreme science that considers subjects that are superior to human beings.[96] Prudence and politics are substantially the same habit because both have right reason in common concerning what is to be done. They differ in definition since prudence considers individual goodness, while politics concerns the good of the entire community. Thomas views the relation between politics and prudence as similar to the connection between law and virtue.[97] He extends prudence in a general way to domestic, legal and administrative governance, since prudence is a central feature of all decisions that affect human government.[98]

Synderesis always proposes the proper principles of action to the intellect, just as the mind immediately intuits the major premises in scientific demonstrations, but the pursuit of pleasure may corrupt the judgment of reason. As a result, the true end of action may be obscured and the estimation of the true end may be lost through desire.[99] Moral virtue ensures the rectitude of judgment concerning prudential principles that appear to the intellect as ends of action. Thomas argues that moral virtue in its role of preserving principles has a type of necessity, which is the deduction of correct individual acts when reason functions properly.[100] In its subject matter prudence does not follow necessarily because it requires the rectitude of the appetite. Since practical decisions require alternatives, prudence is placed most properly in the 'ratiocinative' or 'opinionative' part of the soul.[101]

The prudential process can admit error in two ways: failure to recognize the universal, as one might not recognize the principle that heavy water is bad; or an inability to apply or recognize a particular instance, such as this water is stagnant.[102] The principles are not subject to a rational process, but rather to one of understanding (*intellectus*), which immediately grasps the universal premises of the moral syllogism. Prudence also must understand the final premise in action that necessarily leads to activity. Prudence does not achieve the same level of certainty as science, since its final term is not proved by reason, but rather an interior perception by which one apprehends images (*imaginabilia*) in the manner of a mathematician recognizing

---

[96] SLE, p. 352, ll. 23–44 and p. 353, ll. 82–90.
[97] SLE, p. 356, ll. 23–32. Cf. NE 1130 a 10–13.   [98] SLE, p. 357, ll. 70–102.
[99] SLE, p. 346, ll. 127–145.   [100] SLE, p. 347, ll. 156–164.   [101] SLE, p. 347, ll. 179–188.
[102] SLE, p. 359, ll. 215–221.

a triangle.[103] Thomas differentiates the type of understanding (*intellectus*) in practical decisions from that involved in theoretical comprehension. Practical understanding must grasp the significance of singular and contingent elements that are not immediately apparent. Singular apprehensions lead to the formulation of universals, for example, certain herbs are conducive to health. Sense experience must be operative in both the construction of the major premise as well as in the conclusion of the practical syllogism. The internal awareness that certain herbs produce health may be a universal, but is not useful until one recognizes that particular plants belong to the category of producing health. Both types of understanding are needed in order for the syllogism to function properly.[104]

The two principal virtues leading to happiness are wisdom and prudence, and both Aristotle and Thomas perceive a need to demonstrate how they contribute to the good life.[105] Thomas views the relation of the two virtues in much the same way as his teacher, Albert. In comparison to wisdom prudence is inferior in dignity, even though it may seem superior because of its ability to command action. At this point in his commentary on the NE Thomas might have departed from Albert's interpretation and provided a theory closer to a unified notion of happiness, but he quickly returns to a hierarchical ordering of virtues. Thomas argues that the possible superiority of prudence is offered only in the manner of a question (*per modum dubitationis*).[106] The usefulness of the two primary virtues lies in their capacity to perfect the rational parts of the soul. Even if they were to contribute nothing to happiness, they would be desirable as perfections, but they, of course, do comprise a great part of happiness. Happiness is in fact the perfection of the soul, and prudence and wisdom, therefore, must be elements of human moral goodness. One who possesses both wisdom and prudence, and who acts in accordance with their habits, must be happy. Thomas says this conclusion is especially true for wisdom, "because in its operations consists a more powerful happiness (*potior felicitas*)."[107]

Like Albert, Thomas identifies prudence's function to be the selection of the appropriate means to ends to which moral virtue directs the appetite. In the virtuous act moral virtue perfects the appetite and participates in reason, while prudence contributes by perfecting reason.[108] Thomas also detects an element of circularity in the Aristotelian doctrine, since there can be no prudence without moral virtue and no moral virtue without

---

[103] SLE, p. 359, ll. 238–255.   [104] SLE, p. 367, ll. 164–185.   [105] SLE, p. 370, ll. 6–30.
[106] SLE, p. 371, ll. 90–104.   [107] SLE, pp. 371–372, ll. 122–138.
[108] SLE, p. 372, ll. 151–162.

prudence. Both are needed since moral virtues require an operative principle that constructs ways that lead to the end. This principle is called
'dinotic' and is like a certain ingenuity or industry that permits the realization of the intention. Prudence contributes to the dinotic potency by
directing one always to moral goodness, although ingenuity and industry
may be directed to evil goals.[109] Thomas avoids a more difficult question
concerning the relation of moral virtue and prudence. If one needs moral
virtue to be prudent and prudence leads to moral virtue, it is difficult to
explain how either may be generated. One must ask how moral virtue may
display the end to one who is not already virtuous. If one has moral virtue
then prudence would not be developed, but comes simultaneously with the
perception of the moral ends. Certainly this understanding of virtue
neither Aristotle nor his medieval commentators accepted, and the difficulty
may have led the medieval authors to introduce the idea of *synderesis* as the
innate ability to recognize the proper principles of action. Once they are
known, then the experience required in the development of prudence may
proceed according to a correct path. With the goals recognized, the good
person develops practical wisdom through a variety of experiences concerning the best means to the appropriate ends. Thomas sees some indication of
this type of reasoning in Aristotle's claim that a natural disposition to virtue
seems to exist in some persons. Unlike Aristotle, who identified some as
naturally prone to specific virtues, such as courage and generosity, Thomas
adds natural dispositions that come from both reason and the will. Human
reason naturally recognizes first principles of action, such as one ought not
to harm another. The will has a natural inclination to virtue in that it is
moved by a good perceived as its appropriate object. The sensitive intellects
of composite human beings differ according to individuals, and are the
reason why certain people are prone to specific virtues and vices. Since the
will and reason are common to all, the first two dispositions to virtue are
universal.[110]

Aristotle's claim that no one can be good without prudence and
Socrates's view that all virtues were facets of wisdom Thomas recasts into
a discussion on the moral virtues only. For Thomas, Socrates erred when he
thought all virtues to be forms of prudence (*prudentias*), and so he did not
recognize that moral virtue and prudence originate in different parts of the

---

[109] SLE, pp. 372–373, ll. 169–253.
[110] SLE, p. 375, ll. 22–51. For the relation of conscience and *synderesis*, see T. Hoffmann,
"Conscience and Synderesis," *The Oxford Handbook of Aquinas*, ed. B. Davies and
E. Stump (Oxford, New York: Oxford University Press, 2012), pp. 255–264.

soul. Socrates was correct, however, in thinking that *moral* virtue could not exist without prudence.[111] According to Thomas, Aristotle argued that perfect happiness consists in speculative virtue and that he preferred such virtue to that which consists in actions.[112] One seeks through the political life a higher type of existence that consists in contemplation. The entire civic life seems to be ordered to speculative happiness since it brings the peace necessary for the contemplation of truth.[113] Intellectual contemplation never aims at a superior end, endures throughout a lifetime, and brings the type of perfection that is possible to a human being.[114] The moral life that prudence governs makes one happy only in an inferior way, especially in comparison to the perfection of contemplative happiness. Thomas compares the relation of wisdom and the intellectual virtues to that of prudence and the moral ones:

> Just as speculative happiness is attributed to wisdom which encompasses in itself the other speculative habits as existing more principally, so too active happiness which exists according to the operations of the moral virtues is attributed to prudence, which perfects all moral virtues.[115]

Although prudence is an intellectual virtue, it is joined to moral virtue through a certain affinity, since the principles of prudence are received through moral virtues whose ends are prudence's principles. Prudence conveys the rectitude of moral virtues, since it makes the choice concerning the means to an end right. Since moral virtue and prudence control the emotions that arise from the composite being they both concern the union of body and soul, rather than the intellect alone.[116] Thomas maintains a strict division between human life and the divine element in the soul:

> the virtues of the composite properly speaking are human, insofar as a human being is composed of body and soul; the life according to them, that is, according to prudence and moral virtue is human, which is called the active life. Consequently the happiness that consists in this life is human, but the contemplative life and happiness which is proper to the intellect is separate and divine.[117]

---

[111] SLE, p. 376, ll. 107–124. [112] SLE, p. 583, ll. 59–66. [113] SLE, p. 587, ll. 44–51.

[114] SLE, p. 587, ll. 60–77. SCG III, 25, 9.

[115] SLE, p. 590, ll. 11–16: Sicut enim felicitas speculativa attribuitur sapientiae, quae comprehendit in se alios habitus speculativos tamquam principalior existens, ita etiam felicitas activa, quae est secundum operationes moralium virtutum, attribuitur prudentiae, quae est perfectiva omnium moralium virtutum.

[116] SLE, pp. 590–591, ll. 39–53.

[117] SLE, p. 591, ll. 53–61: ... unde patet, quod tam virtus moralis quam prudentia sunt circa compositum. Virtutes autem compositi proprie loquendo sunt humanae, in quantum homo est compositus ex anima et corpore, unde et vita quae secundum has, id est secundum prudentiam et virtutem moralem, est humana, quae dicitur vita activa, et

This reading of Aristotle does not necessarily include a concept of eternal beatitude, but Thomas's characterization of speculative happiness as separate and divine allows for its possible attainment in accordance with Aristotelian moral theory.[118]

Since prudence regulates those actions that produce moral virtues and since happiness does not consist in the acts of moral virtue, happiness cannot consist in the act of prudence.[119] Prudence does not consider the perfect objects of the intellect or reason, and it does not regard necessary objects of knowledge. Since the supreme human act proper to human beings exists in its relation to its most perfect objects, the ultimate happiness cannot consist in prudential operations.[120] For true happiness certain conditions, such as the acts of moral virtue, by which impediments to contemplative happiness are removed, must preexist. They calm the mind from the influence of passions and the disturbances of the external world. The true act of virtue that completes happiness is the act of reason or the intellect: "Contemplative happiness is nothing other than the perfect contemplation of supreme truth; active happiness is the act of prudence by which a human being governs oneself and others."[121] The acts of the speculative intellect are closer to ultimate happiness than the habits of the practical intellect by way of similitude, although the habits of the practical intellect are closer by way of preparation or merit.[122] Merit does not preclude knowledge, since Aristotle argued that no one can knowingly err in art or science. Although Thomas speaks of two happinesses here, he views them as two complementary elements to human goodness, as does Aristotle in the NE, and considers civic happiness alone to constitute human goodness only in a secondary way. For true happiness a human being must actualize both the intellectual and rational potentialities within the soul.

In his discussions on *synderesis* and prudence Thomas does not specify the commands that originate in the habit of *synderesis*, but his identification of the dictates of natural law and the principles of *synderesis* provide

---

    per consequens felicitas, quae in hac vita consistit, est humana. Sed vita et felicitas
    speculativa, quae est propria intellectus, est separata et divina.
[118] SCG III, 25, 16.
[119] SCG III, 35, 2: Actus enim prudentiae est solum circa ea quae sunt moralium virtutum.
    Non est autem in actibus moralium virtutum ultima hominis felicitas. Neque igitur in
    actu prudentiae.
[120] SCG III, 37, 7; *De virtutibus*, q. 1, a. 5, ad 8.
[121] *De virtutibus*, q. 1, a. 5 ad 8: Nam felicitas contemplativa nihil aliud est quam perfecta
    contemplatio summae veritatis; felicitas autem activa est actus prudentiae, quo homo et
    se et alios gubernat.
[122] *De virtutibus*, q. 1, a. 7, ad 4.

explicit direction in prudential decisions. While very little guidance arises from the admonition to do good and avoid evil, Thomas constructs a hierarchy of duties within the natural law.[123] Thomas makes the close connection between *synderesis* and natural law clear in the *Summa theologiae*: ". . . *synderesis* is called the law of our intellect insofar as it is a habit containing the precepts of natural law, which are the first principles of human acts."[124] Thomas asks whether natural law contains different formulations or only one general principle. In his answer Thomas compares the principles of natural law to those of any demonstrative science. In each there are more than one principle that are known in themselves. Principles are known in themselves in two ways: (1) according to themselves (*secundum se*) and (2) according to the state of the knower. Thomas does not really distinguish the principles objectively, but rather according to the state of the subject:

Something is said to be known in itself in two ways, in one way according to itself; in another way with respect to us. According to itself a certain proposition is said to be known in itself whose predicate comes from the definition of the subject; it does happen, however, that such a proposition will not be known in itself to one ignorant of the subject. As in this proposition, 'man is a rational being', it is known in itself according to its own definition because he who says 'man' says 'rational being', and yet to one ignorant of what a man is, this proposition is not known in itself.[125]

Just as being and the principle of non-contradiction are the primary concepts for theoretical wisdom, goodness and its function as the end of action direct practical knowledge. Practical wisdom's basis in the concept of goodness produces the primary legal precept that good should be done and evil avoided. All other legal commands that human reason apprehends have their foundation in this simple precept. As there is an order of natural inclinations, there is also one for legal precepts. The basic inclination of human nature is the desire for its own preservation. Then follows the natural desire to communicate with other living beings, which leads to

[123] For a discussion on how the relation between the principles of natural law and the virtue of prudence departs from the moral thought of Aristotle. see P. Payer, "Prudence and the Principles of Natural Law: A Medieval Development," Speculum, 54 (1979), pp. 67–68; T.-H. Deman, *Saint Thomas d'Aquin, Somme théologique. La prudence: 2a-2ae, questions 47–56, traduction françaises, notes et appendices* (Paris: Desclée & Cie, 1949), pp. 426–428; T. Hoffmann, "Prudence and Practical Principles," *Aquinas and the Nicomachean Ethics*, pp. 165–183.

[124] S. th. I–II, 94, 2, 1 ad 2: Ad secundum dicendum quod synderesis dicitur lex intellectus nostri, inquantum est habitus continens praecepta legis naturalis, quae sunt prima principia operum humanorum.

[125] S. th. I–II, 94, 2.

the natural consequences of the union of male and female, the education of the young, and similar practices. The third natural inclination is the desire to know the truth about God, to live in society and to avoid offending others in the community.[126]

All virtuous acts insofar as they are virtuous pertain generally to the law of nature because the natural law considers everything to which a human being is inclined naturally. The rational soul determines human nature and therefore human beings tend to act according to reason, which is the determining factor of virtue. All virtuous acts come from the natural law, since reason naturally directs everyone to act virtuously.[127] This natural inclination to act rationally is common to all human beings, regardless of political, religious or geographical differences. The variety of moral practices that arise in different societies does not originate in any common precepts of natural law, but rather in the reasoning process to particular choices. With respect to universal principles, whether speculative or practical, there is the same truth or rectitude that can be known by all.[128]

The common principles of natural law can neither be changed nor abolished, although they may be negated in a particular action when passion or desire may impede its application to the particular act. Thomas does allow for some variability in secondary precepts of natural law that are derived from universal principles, such as the acceptance of thievery by some Germanic tribes. This contravention against the natural law Thomas attributes to depraved customs and corrupt habits.[129] The failure to recognize the prescription against thievery occurs from the inability to connect a derived precept (do not steal) from the universal principle (do not harm another).[130] The natural law is a reflection of eternal law, which, in turn, reflects divine wisdom. Divine wisdom is evident in every created thing because "the nature of divine wisdom moving everything to its proper end achieves the nature of law. The eternal law, therefore, is nothing other than the nature of divine wisdom that directs every act and motion."[131]

[126] S. th. I–II, 94, 2.
[127] S. th. I–II, 94, 3. See M. Rhonheimer, *Natural Law and Practical Reason: A Thomist View of Moral Autonomy*, tr. G. Malsbary (New York: Fordham University Press, 2000), pp. 80–81.
[128] S. th. I–II, 94, 4. For a contemporary view of Thomas and natural law. see J. Finnis, *Natural Law and Natural Rights*, 2nd ed. (Oxford: Clarendon Press, 2011).
[129] S. th. I–II, 94, 4. I would like to thank Tobias Hoffmann for calling my attention to these passages.
[130] S. th. I–II, 94, 6 ad 1.
[131] S. th. I–II, 93, 1: … ita ratio divinae sapientiae moventis omnia ad debitum finem, obtinet rationem legis. Et secundum hoc, lex aeterna nihil aliud est quam ratio divinae sapientiae, secundum quod est directiva omnium actuum et motionum.

d Perfect and imperfect beatitude

No philosophical thinker could proceed in the manner of a theologian, as Thomas indicates in the *Summa theologiae*: "... this science exceeds all speculative sciences, according to certitude, because other sciences have certitude from the natural light of human reason, which can err. This [science] has certitude from the light of divine knowledge (*scientia*), which cannot be deceived ..."[132] Theology, which is primarily a speculative science about God, extends also to practical areas, since a human being is ordered to God as to an end that exceeds rational understanding.[133] The challenge for Thomas, as for all theologians, is to align the rational conduct of life to the supra-rational method by which one may be united to the divine being. Thomas's view of the relation between philosophy and theology is complex, and is much studied, but there has been general agreement on his opinions regarding the compatibility of Aristotle's moral conclusions with those of Christian belief.

This common understanding derives from Thomas's notion of beatitude, which he distinguished into perfect and imperfect blessedness. Rarely, however, are the means by which they are related examined thoroughly.[134] In the thirteenth century, the translation of the NE provoked a reexamination of ideas concerning human purpose and goodness. For Aristotle the goal of life lies in a human activity in accordance with virtue, and he ignored in his ethical writings the ideal of a transcendent eternal good. Even if such a good were to exist, Aristotle thought it would contribute nothing to human moral endeavors (NE 1096b28–35).[135] Thomas's commentary on the NE attempts to understand the nature of human goodness as conceived by Aristotle, but Thomas cannot abandon the idea of a unique separate good for all. He argues that for anything to be termed 'good' it must have a similarity to, and participate in, the supreme good. Through participation all things are rightly thought to seek this identical goal.[136] For Thomas and all medieval theologians the identity of the supreme good with God is obvious and accepted

---

[132] S. th. I, 1, 5.   [133] S. th. I, 1, 4.

[134] For a discussion of perfect and imperfect beatitude, see D. Bradley, *Aquinas on the Twofold Human Good* (Washington: Catholic University of America Press, 1997). See also J. Müller, "*Duplex beatitudo*: Aristotle's Legacy and Aquinas's Conception of Human Happiness," *Aquinas and the Nicomachean Ethics*, pp. 52–71.

[135] See also J. Owens, "The KALON in Aristotelian Ethics," *Studies in Aristotle*, ed. D. J. O'Meara (Washington: The Catholic University of America Press, 1981), p. 272.

[136] SLE p. 5, ll. 175–182. For the identification of the good and the end. See S. th. I–II, 1, 4 ad 1 and T. Aquinas, *De divinis nominibus*, ed. C. Pera (Turin, Rome: Marietti, 1950), p. 75, #227: Bonum habet rattionem finis; finis autem, primo, habet rationem causae.

without much discussion.[137] Like other medieval commentators Thomas understood Aristotle's criticism of Plato's idea of separate goodness not to be a denial of its existence, but rather as a statement of its irrelevance to moral investigation.[138]

A particularly difficult problem that arose from the reading of the NE in the thirteenth century was the relation between the philosopher's ideal of happiness and the theologian's notion of beatitude. The question's main focus is the possible connection between the two ends, since one may attain beatitude gratuitously without the exercise of any philosophical virtues whatsoever. Many medieval authors, including Thomas, raised this question when considering the case of the good thief (Luke 23, 42), who is granted salvation after a single act of recognition of the divinity of the crucified Christ.[139] While the fate of the thief may illustrate the Christian belief in the power of the theological virtues, especially hope, it does provoke serious doubts about the necessity for the development of the habitual moral virtues. Thomas is very careful when considering this case and the relation between happiness and beatitude. The association between the two depends upon the idea of an end that all seek and that produces a certain participation of happiness in perfect beatitude. This participation, however, depends not on human actions, but rather upon the object to which they are directed. A passage in Aristotle's *De anima* (414b20–21) provides the foundation for the distinction within the end itself. There Aristotle distinguished between the meaning of 'that for the sake of which' or the end (τό οὗ ἕνεκα): the first is the end to achieve (τό τε οὗ); the second is that in whose interest anything exists, or is done (τό ᾧ). As was discussed above, the Latin translation of the two senses of the end are simply the *'finis cuius'* and the *'finis quo'*.[140] Averroes clarified the distinction within the end when he commented upon the text of Aristotle: "And the *propter quid* is said in two ways: one of which (*finis cuius*) is that which is the end itself; and the other (*finis quo*) is that in which there is the end."[141] In the first

[137] A. Celano, "The 'Finis Hominis' in the Thirteenth-Century Commentaries on the *Nicomachean Ethics*," AHDLMA, 53 (1986), pp. 34–35.

[138] SLE, p. 29, ll. 26–34.

[139] A. Celano, "A Question of Justice: The Good Thief, Cain and the Pursuit of Moral Perfection," *Medieval Philosophy and Theology in the Long Middle Ages: A Tribute to Stephen F. Brown*, ed. R. Friedman, K. Emery and A. Speer (Studien und Texte zur Geistesgeschichte des Mittelalters, 105: Leiden, Boston: Brill, 2011), pp. 321–350.

[140] Averroes, *Commentarium magnum in Aristotelis de anima libros*, ed. F. S. Crawford, *Corpus commentariorum Averrois in Aristotelem*, VI, I (Cambridge, MA: The Medieval Academy of America, 1953), pp. 183–184 and 173, n. 11. See above, pp. 171–172.

[141] Ibid., p. 184.

sense the end is the object desired, and in the second the end is the activity by which this object is attained.

In his commentary on the NE Thomas makes no mention of the two senses of the end, but in his commentary on the *Sentences* he describes the supreme human achievement as *beatitudo imperfecta* and calls it a modest (*modica*) participation in that human perfection that a person may expect after death.[142] Thomas in the *Summa theologiae* also considers the meaning of perfect and imperfect beatitude when he asks whether a living person may be called blessed. Thomas states "that some type of participation in beatitude may be attained in this life."[143] True beatitude, however, which consists in the vision of the divine essence, can never be attained by the living, whose corporeal nature prevents them from having complete cognition of God.[144] Thomas accepts two ways by which one may call the living 'blessed': "through the hope of attaining perfect beatitude; or through a certain type of participation in beatitude according to some kind of enjoyment of the supreme good."[145]

The second manner of designating the living blessed demands further clarification, and Thomas is careful to call the human participation in beatitude imperfect. In one way, imperfection results from the object of beatitude, since God can never be viewed in His essence. In another way, imperfection comes from the participant, who can attain this object only insofar as is capable to the human being. A living person attains the vision of God only imperfectly, which is proper to human nature. Thomas maintains that the true nature of beatitude comes from the object (*finis cuius*) that specifies the acts, and does not arise from the subjects who perform them.[146] Thomas concludes with the observation that human beings believe there to be some beatitude in their lives because of a type of similitude to true blessedness.[147] The belief in such participation or similitude is not without foundation, since the *finis cuius* is identical in both

---

[142] In *IV Sent.*, d. 49, q. 1, art. 1, sol. 4. *Opera omnia* (Paris, 1874), II, p. 463: Sed secundum perfectam rationem beatitudo non est possibilis homini accidere; sed possibile est hominem esse in aliqua participatione ipsius, licet modica, et ex hoc eum dici beatum; et ideo non oportet hominem beatum esse perpetuum et immutabilem simpliciter, sed secundum conditionem humanae naturae.

[143] S. th. I–II, 5, 3: Dicendum quod aliqualis participatio in hac vita haberi potest.

[144] S. th. I, 12, 2.

[145] S. th. I–II, 5, 3 ad 1: . . . vel propter aliquam participationem beatitudinis, secundum aliqualem summi boni fruitionem.

[146] S. th. I–II, 5, 4, ad 2.

[147] S. th. I–II, 5, 3, ad 3: Ad tertium dicendum quod homines reputant in hac vita esse aliquam beatitudinem, propter aliquam similitudinem verae beatitudinis. Et sic non ex toto in sua aestimatione deficiunt.

perfect and imperfect beatitude. The difference in the two ideals of human agency lies in the distinct natures of the type of cognition by which the divine essence is apprehended.

When Thomas discusses the meaning of beatitude in the context of a human life, he refers implicitly to the distinction within the end, and adds that the object or the end truly specifies beatitude:

> It should be said that the participation in beatitude can be imperfect in two ways. First from the object itself of beatitude, which is not seen according to its essence. And such imperfection removes the nature of true beatitude. In another way it can be imperfect from the participant itself, who attains the very object of beatitude, namely God, according to itself, but imperfectly with respect to the manner by which God is enjoyed by the [participant]. And such imperfection does not remove the true nature of beatitude because the true nature of beatitude is considered from the object which gives the species to the act, and not from the subject, even if beatitude is an operation, as previously said.[148]

Thomas's use of the distinction within the end can be summarized as follows. The ultimate *finis cuius* for a human being is the supreme object of contemplation, God, both in the philosophical pursuit of intellectual perfection and in the religious quest for the beatific vision of the separate soul. The *finis quo* is constituted by the individual actions by which one attains the desired end. This distinction allows for medieval authors to posit a single universal end for all (*finis cuius*), while maintaining individual differences and levels of attainment (*finis quo*) in the composition of both earthly happiness and eternal beatitude. In the *Summa* Thomas relates Aristotle's ideal of *eudaimonia* and the Christian concept of perfect beatitude by means of the intellectual union of the human intellect to the divine being. Thomas praises Aristotle for describing well the natural perfection within human existence, which can be considered similar to the perfect vision of God, which those perfected by grace receive. The bliss (*fruitio*) of the contemplative intellectual life differs from that of eternal perfection in the continuity and the clarity of the act of understanding. The object in both intellectual activities remains the same, since in both the desired goal is an intellectual understanding of the first being.

The two ends of human morality may be united by the identity of the object sought, but serious questions arise concerning the relationship between the activities leading to this end. One may ask whether the philosophical virtues described so thoroughly by Aristotle contribute anything at all to that act whereby the soul perfected by grace is united to God.

---

[148] S. th. 5, 3 ad 3.

Thomas indicates the differences by the very language he uses, since he describes Aristotelian virtues mainly in the active voice of verbs, and prefers the passive when describing Christian moral ideals. Thomas argues that the ultimate human end is something created existing in a human being as the attainment or enjoyment of the end (*finis quo*). If understood as the cause or object of this achievement, beatitude cannot be something created.[149] What is created in human beatitude must be a human action (*operatio hominis*), since perfection requires something in act.[150] The connection between perfect and imperfect beatitude clearly exists for Thomas in the identity of the *finis cuius*. The operation by which one is united to God differs both in quality and in its causes. Thomas claims that the operation of the human senses, which is necessary for the attainment of any human type of knowledge, does not pertain essentially to beatitude because it cannot permit one to be perfectly united to the ultimate end. Human sensory experience contributes antecedently only to imperfect beatitude, since human intellectual activity requires the formation of mental images (*phantasmata*) that come only from sense organs.[151] While the human organism may be perfected after the resurrection of the body, the human soul's union with God does not depend upon any sense activity whatsoever.[152]

Thomas explicitly rejects the idea that human abilities can produce the vision of the divine essence in which perfect beatitude exists. To see God in His essence exceeds the nature of any creature, which naturally knows in accordance with its substantial nature.[153] The human intellect may not be capable of attaining beatitude, but human nature provides humanity with free choice, "by which one may be turned to God, who makes one blessed."[154] The will alone, however, cannot produce beatitude because a rational creature needs divine help to attain complete perfection.[155] In a remarkable passage Thomas compares the gift of beatitude to miraculous events, such as the raising of the dead and the restoration of sight to the blind. Human nature is incapable of causing such miracles, just as it is inadequately equipped to produce its own moral perfection. The human involvement in miraculous events is entirely passive and receptive, and Thomas implies the same level of involvement in the genesis of

---

[149] S. th. I–II, 3, 1.   [150] S. th. I–II, 3, 2.   [151] S. th. I–II, 4, 5.

[152] S. th. I–II, 3, 3. See also S. th. I–II, 62, 1; *Summa contra Gentiles* c. 52 and 147; *In III Sent.* d. 27, q. 2 a. 2 and *In IV Sent*, d. 49, q. 2 a. 6.

[153] S. th. I–II, 5, 5.

[154] S. th. I–II, 5, 5, ad 1: Sed [natura] dedit ei liberum arbitrium, quo possit converti ad Deum, qui eum faceret beatum.

[155] S. th. I–II, 5, 5 ad 2.

beatitude.[156] Thomas allows only the possibility that in the order of the universe one might be aided by angelic creatures in the attainment of the ultimate end, but only with certain preconditions by which one is disposed to its reception. The end, however, is achieved only through the first agent, which is God.[157]

Thomas tries to maintain some measure of human agency in the production of beatitude and finds support for his efforts in a passage from the Gospel of John: "If you know things, you will be blessed, if you will do them" (*John* 13, 17). Thomas asserts the rectitude of the will to be necessary for beatitude because it is the proper order of the will to the ultimate end. Its contribution to beatitude lies in the required disposition of the matter to the attainment of form (*ad consecutionem formae*). Thomas, however, is quick to add that this disposition does not mean that any human activity must precede beatitude. God could make the disposition of matter and the reception of form simultaneous, if He so chooses. Normally the order of divine wisdom prevents such simultaneity, but does not necessitate it.[158] While God may grant beatitude without any human disposition, Thomas argues that one normally attains it through many prior operations that are called meritorious. This is why even Aristotle called beatitude "the prize of virtuous actions."[159]

Thomas has reached the problem that every Christian expositor of Aristotelian philosophy faces, who must ask what benefit does a life of moral and intellectual virtue, as described by Aristotle, provide for the expectation of perfect beatitude. Thomas merely hints at the response in the sections on beatitude in the *Prima secundae* of the *Summa*, but his ideas on the will's rectitude and the importance of love (*caritas*) have little in common with Aristotle's moral thought. His solution to the question concerning perfect and imperfect beatitude considers a number of theological topics that would lead far from the analysis of the importance of practical wisdom for the moral life, but it does merit some discussion. Thomas certainly considers philosophical arguments useful to the theological determination of the question and would not separate the fields of inquiry so sharply as do modern thinkers. He denies the human ability, however, to order oneself to perfect beatitude that exceeds the proportion of human nature. Some principles must be added to human endeavors by God, and these theological principles have God as their object and order all to Him. They are the infused virtues that are granted by God alone and

[156] S. th. I–II, 5, 6.   [157] S. th. I–II, 5, 6 ad 1.   [158] S. th. I–II, 5, 7.   [159] S. th. I–II, 5, 7.

known only by divine revelation.[160] Here the shift from philosophical
ethics based on human practice is complete, and the principles by which
one attains moral perfection are divinely decreed, and the virtues based on
these principles are infused by God alone (*a solo Deo*). However Thomas
views the relation of the ethical life to the soul's perfection he offers no way
by which the former leads inexorably to the latter. The two moral lives run
parallel and there is no bridge between the two, since no action can
condition God to produce the necessary virtues within any human soul.
Tertullian's famous question, what has Athens to do with Jerusalem, is
particularly relevant here, since one may fairly conclude that one life has
little to do with the other, as is indicated by the salvation of the good thief
or by those who convert to Christianity on their deathbed. Even when
Thomas tries to maintain human efficacy in the production of moral
perfection in stating that reason and will order one naturally to God, he
adds that they cannot do so sufficiently.[161]

Thomas's final solution clearly offers a vision of human purpose and of
the moral end that differ from that of Aristotle.[162] Thomas, like his
medieval contemporaries, has ultimately rejected the ethics of practical
wisdom for a religious morality based upon eternal divine principles.
Whereas Aristotle locates the origins of ethical behavior in the innate
ability to imitate the best practitioners of virtues, Thomas grounds moral
behavior in "certain principles naturally known ... which are the certain
seeds of the intellectual and moral virtues" and in the will's natural appetite
to recognize these principles as good.[163] The transition from an ethics of
practical wisdom is complete, since prudence according to medieval
authors demands logical deductions from universal principles to specific
conclusions. In the moral theory of Thomas Aquinas the man of practical
wisdom can no longer determine the best life to pursue, since the commands of natural law have been determined innately in every human being.
The function of prudence is to follow in individual decisions the order of
law. As Lottin rightly observes, Thomas calls prudence right reason
because it is the *imperium* of practical reason. This command can be
viewed as correct only insofar as it conforms to the principles that ultimately are the norms of morality because of their participation in the

---

[160] S. th. I–II, 62, 1.   [161] S. th. I–II, 62, 1 and 3.
[162] P. Payer rightly asks "what does prudence provide which enables one to judge the moral
quality of these [human] actions?," and concludes "that the actual criteria which emerged
color the concept of prudence with a specifically medieval character." art. cit., p. 60.
[163] S. th. I–II, 63, 1.

eternal law, or *ratio divina*.[164] The ability of Aristotle's *phronimos* to determine new courses of action and better modes of conduct differs from the virtue of the Christian *prudens* who accepts eternal commands and aligns the will according to their dictates. As a result, the hierarchical order of human actions determines infallibly the proper choices leading to the perfection of the soul. The practical life is subjugated to the intellectual, but all actions must be in accord with love for God. No human being can determine the relative importance of particular pursuits, since divine and eternal law decrees how all should act. The flexibility and practicality of Aristotle's ethics has given way to the universal codes of Christian morality.

e Bonaventure's understanding of moral goodness

When Bonaventure raises the specific question concerning moral goodness, he does so in terms of the relation of the will to its desired good. Like many Franciscan masters, Bonaventure overcomes the gulf between the created intellect and the divine essence by attributing their ultimate union to the will rather than to the intellect.[165] The mystical union of a human soul with God can only occur through love, and C. Trottmann describes the process of eternal beatitude, the ideal of human knowledge as consisting in the love of charity, which resides in the will.[166] Such a union transcends the natural order and is the result of the infusion of grace. Bonaventure's suspicion of the claims of philosophers and his conviction about the inadequacy of natural virtues are well known, and he insists upon the reception of the gifts of the Holy Spirit for moral perfection. Bonaventure clearly offers a moral theology distant from that of medieval masters more receptive to the *Ethics* of Aristotle.[167]

Bonaventure argues that charity renders an act good, insofar as the good is related to supreme goodness. Without the assistance of charity no effect or act can have a sufficient relation to the highest good. Charity makes the final end more cherished than all other goals and permits one to be content in its attainment.[168] The end may be understood in one of three different

---

[164] O. Lottin, "Le Rôle de la Raison dans la Morale Albertino-Thomiste," *Psychologie et Morale* III, pp. 569 and 573.

[165] C. Trottmann, *La vision béatifique, des disputes scolastiques à sa définition par Benoît XII* (Bibliothèque des ecoles françaises d'Athènes et de Rome, 289, Rome: Ecole française de Rome, 1995), p. 197.

[166] Ibid., p. 198.

[167] See E. Gilson, *The Christian Philosophy of St. Bonaventure*, tr. I. Trethowan and F. Sheed (Patterson: St. Anthony Guild, 1965), esp. ch. 13.

[168] *Commentaria in quatuor libros Sententiarum* II, d. 38, a. 1, ad 3 in *Opera omnia* (Quaracchi, Ad claras aquas, 1885), v. 2.

ways: the end in which (*in quo*) the act ceases, or the end by which (*quo*) it ceases; the latter sense of the end may be considered simply (*simpliciter*) or specifically (*ut nunc*). In each of these meanings charity remains the end for the good will. What Bonaventure calls uncreated charity, God, is the end in which all acts terminate. Created and complete charity (*caritas creata et consummata*), such as the love for the afterlife, is an end whereby an act finishes simply in God. Inchoate charity, such as love of the journey to the afterlife, is an end whereby the acts ceases in God in a specific moment.[169] True charity, which is God, one enjoys as the object of desire, while that charity, which is a habit, one cherishes as a disposition.[170] All actions are unified in their goodness because of a single principal end. The solitary supreme goodness fulfills all human desire, and directs the good will in its rectitude.[171]

Despite the moral force of charity and its direction toward the end, the will may become more depraved in its act than any other power. Bonaventure also considers moral error in terms of the human conscience, which John Damascene defined as the law of the intellect.[172] Bonaventure understands Damascene's definition to indicate the nature of the human conscience as a cognitive habit, rather than as a voluntary one. But he limits the power of the conscience to the practical intellect alone, which does not extend to speculative understanding. Bonaventure says that Damascene's definition refers to the conscience as that which 'knows' (*conscitur*), and as such is the law of the intellect. This law then moves the conscience, which may be understood as the knowing potency (*potentia conscientia*) of the natural law that is written therein.[173]

f The natural ability to judge first principles

When Bonaventure considers the conscience itself he asks whether it may be an innate or acquired habit. As support for the first position he cites Paul's Epistle to the Romans in which the law is said to be written in the hearts of all, even those who do not have the benefit of Scripture.

---

[169] II *Sent.* d. 38, a. 1, q. 2.
[170] II *Sent.* d. 38, a. 1, q. 2, ad 3: Nam caritate, quae Deus est, fruimur sicut obiecto; caritate, quae habitus est, fruimur sicut dispositivo.
[171] II *Sent.* d. 38, a. 1, q. 3.
[172] II *Sent.*, d. 39, a. 1, q. 1, arg. 2: Damascenus dicit, quod 'conscientia es lex intellectus nostri', sed lex intellectus non dicitur nisi Scriptura, quae directe respicit intellectum. The reference to Damascene is *De fide orthodoxa*, IV, c. 22.
[173] II *Sent.*, d. 39, a. 1, q. 1.

Bonaventure also calls upon the work of Augustine and Isadore of Seville to defend the idea that the human mind has an innate natural ability to know moral principles.[174] Bonaventure immediately realizes that an inherent awareness of moral principles prior to any experience is certainly not part of Aristotle's philosophy. He refers to the *De anima* where Aristotle argues that the "created soul is like a blank slate on which nothing is depicted." He also acknowledges Aristotle's explanation for the acquisition of knowledge in the *Posterior Analytics* wherein knowledge, which is a cognitive habit, is determined to be acquired. The conscience by extension, which is a directive habit in actions, must also be acquired.[175] Bonaventure has succinctly presented the conflicting views on moral epistemology: the Christian sources maintain an innate element within the mind that can recognize natural moral principles; for Aristotle all knowledge, whether theoretical or practical, depends upon some type of individual experience.

Bonaventure's resolution to the question recognizes Aristotle's and Augustine's criticism of the Platonic theory that all habits of knowledge are wholly intrinsic, but notes that all agree that acquired virtues (*virtutes consuetudinales*), just like cognitive habits, are both innate and acquired. Bonaventure claims that the way they are both innate and acquired varies according to different virtues. He argues that some use Aristotle's distinction within the intellect to support the theory that virtues are inherent in the agent intellect and are acquired with respect to the possible intellect. He judges this interpretation to be un-Aristotelian and false. He then asks why the agent intellect would not communicate such knowledge without the assistance of inferior senses, if it were to have such innate habits. If the agent intellect were to have such knowledge, then the mind in its present state would not ever be ignorant. Bonaventure also rejects Boethius's neat resolution of the question that asserts cognition of universals to be inherent and awareness of particulars to be learned, because it, like the first argument, contradicts the opinions of Aristotle and Augustine, as well as the truth. Bonaventure concludes that cognitive habits of conclusions, principles and particulars are both innate and acquired.[176] His resolution depends upon a comparison to the theory of sense knowledge, which requires both the presence of what is to be known and of light by means

---

[174] II *Sent.*, d. 39, a. 1, q. 2, arg. 1, 2, and 3.   [175] II *Sent.*, d. 39, a. 1, q. 2, contra 1 and 4.
[176] L. T. Somme, "The Infallibility, Impeccability and Indestructibility of Synderesis," *Studies in Christian Ethics*, 19 (2006), pp. 403–416, esp. 413; C. Trottmann, "*Scintilla synderesis*. Pour une auto-critque mediévale de la raison la plus pure en son usage pratique," *Geistesleben in 13. Jahrhundert*, ed. J. Aertsen and A. Speer (*Miscellanea Mediaevalia*, 27, Berlin, New York: de Gruyter, 2000), pp. 116–130.

of which one judges the perceived object. Cognitive habits require an inborn light of the mind as well as an apprehension by reason of the species. Both Aristotle and Augustine agree upon a type of innate illumination of the cognitive potency, which is called the natural ability to judge; the species and the likenesses to objects are attained through the mediation of the senses.[177]

This light, which Bonaventure identifies as the natural ability to judge rightly, directs the mind in discerning both speculative truths and practical courses of action. Like many of his contemporaries, Bonaventure attributes the cognition of first principles to the power of this innate illumination. He does, however, note the need for some experience in beginning the process of recognizing their truth. Like Thomas and Albert, he compares the process of deducing practical truths to that of scientific deduction. Without some natural awareness of evident principles the deductive process would not be possible.[178]

The conscience also possesses a directive innate habit that governs human judgment with respect to actions. The internal moral habit functions regarding those ideas that reflect the first natural commandment (*de primo dictamine naturae*). Conscience operates like other intellectual powers in that its habit is acquired through an innate natural potency and subsequent experience. E. Gilson observes that the conscience "like science, belongs to the intellect and arises from our faculty of knowing, but it does so not by contemplating objects of knowledge but by deciding upon principles of action."[179] The conscience's natural light leads to obedience to parents, the prohibition against harming neighbors, and experience indicates those who are parents and neighbors.[180] This inherent habit shows what is good and functions as a fertile ground (*seminarium*) for the cultivation of other habits. Conscience is not an act, but rather a cognitive habit, partly innate and partly acquired. It concerns both first principles and particular conclusions. *Synderesis*, however, is not part of practical reason, but rather pertains to the will itself.[181] Bonaventure understands Aristotle's analogy of the soul as a blank slate to refer to those things that have existence in the soul by an abstract similitude. He says that they are said to be in the soul in the mode of writing. Aristotle claimed that in the soul nothing is written, not because

---

[177] II *Sent.*, d. 39, a. 1, q. 2. [178] II *Sent.*, d. 39, a. 1, q. 2.
[179] E. Gilson, *The Christian Philosophy of St. Bonaventure*, p. 378.
[180] II *Sent.*, d. 39, a. 1, q. 3.
[181] C. Trottmann, "La syndérèse, sommet de la nature humaine dans l'Itinerarium mentis in Deum," *Dionysius*, 18 (2000), pp. 129–150 and L. T. Somme, art. cit., p. 413.

there is no knowledge in it, but rather because there is no image or abstract similitude naturally in it.[182]

Bonaventure specifies the power that contains the innate principles of action as *synderesis*. His sources for the position are those commonly cited in the thirteenth century. He refers to *Romans* 8, 8 and 8, 26, but correctly identifies the origin of the doctrine to be the gloss of Jerome:

> By the *consort of adolescence* understand the natural law written in the heart, *spirit* is not rightly called the animal part which does not perceive the things of God, but the rational; this he calls *synderesis*: and so *synderesis* seems to pertain to reason or cognition.[183]

While considering the various opinions on *synderesis*, Bonaventure recounts the position that orders the superior part of reason to God. This rational element that is found in the act of *synderesis* considers both God and fellow human beings, as is indicated in the natural law. *Synderesis*, however, indicates that which is a stimulus to good and must therefore pertain also to the desiderative component within the soul.[184] Its function also moves the conscience as does the will in provoking reason to action.[185] The proper nature of *synderesis* is that of a potency of the will, but only insofar as it moves the will naturally with respect to good and evil. It may also be considered a habit, but not in the sense of a virtue or vice, which reflect free choice and the will through deliberation. The meaning of the innate natural characteristic of *synderesis* continues to present difficulties in the medieval attempts to identify its specific constitution.[186]

The relation of *synderesis* to conscience is similar to that of charity to faith, or a habit of desire to the habit of the practical intellect. Natural law is related in a general way to both *synderesis* and conscience because it indicates a mental habit. Since natural law provides instruction and proper order, it is termed a habit that encompasses both the intellect and desire. In

---

[182] II *Sent.*, d. 39, a. 1, q. 3.
[183] II *Sent.*, d. 39, a. 2, q. 1, contra: Glossa Hieronymi: "Per uxorem adolescentiae intellige legem naturalem scriptam in corde, spiritus vero dicitur non animalis pars, quae non percipit ea quae Dei sunt, sed rationalis"; hanc autem vocat synderesim: ergo videtur, quod synderesis se teneat ex parte rationis sive cognitivae. See also D. Langston, *Conscience and Other Virtues: From Bonaventure to Macintyre* (University Park, PA: Pennsylvania University Press, 2001), pp. 29–37.
[184] II *Sent.*, d. 39, a. 2, q. 1, contra: Dico enim, quod synderesis dicit illud quod stimulat ad bonum; et ideo ex parte affectionis se tenet.
[185] II *Sent.*, d. 39, a. 2, q. 1, ad 3: Unde sicut ratio non potest movere nisi mediante voluntate, sic nec conscientia nisi mediante synderesi. See also L. T. Somme, "The Infallibility . . .," p. 414.
[186] II *Sent.*, d. 39, a. 2, q. 1, ad 4.

this way it is relevant to both *synderesis* and conscience. Natural law may also be understood as a collection of commands of natural rectitude, and thereby denotes the object of the dictating power of conscience and the judging power of *synderesis*. *Synderesis* proposes actions that are desired or rejected and conscience dictates the commission of the acts. Bonaventure understands natural law more properly as a mental habit and *synderesis* as a desiderative potency (*potentia affectiva*), since the latter power naturally tends to the good. Conscience denotes truly a habit of the practical intellect and natural law indicates the object of both *synderesis* and conscience.[187]

Bonaventure, unlike many of his contemporaries, rejects the idea that *synderesis* is an intellectual habit and prefers its designation as a desiderative power. In moving the soul naturally and rightly it does not differ essentially from other potencies, but is distinct in the method of moving one to act. Although it is a desiderative power in the manner of motivating action, it always moves correctly and justly. If error is to occur, it will originate in the conscience, rather than in *synderesis*.[188] Almost a decade after the composition of his commentary on the *Sentences*, Bonaventure in the *Iter mentis ad Deum* describes *synderesis* as one of the six levels (*gradus*) of the soul's powers that lead one to God. These powers allow the soul to rise from temporal objects to eternal ones. The highest level of the mind (*apex mentis*) is *synderesis*, is naturally implanted in the soul, and, like the other powers, is ultimately perfected by wisdom.[189]

For Bonaventure as for his contemporaries the act of *synderesis* may be impeded, but *synderesis* itself can never be extinguished because it is part of human nature.[190] No natural power like *synderesis*, can be entirely lost, even in sin because it cannot err deliberatively. It may be impeded in the process leading to good actions when reason and the will deviate from it. Bonaventure attributes such deviance in reason to the blindness of error and in the will to the obstinance of impiety. These failings may lead one to claim that *synderesis* errs, since its effects and rule are inhibited in the deliberative powers.[191] *Synderesis* judges universally and not in specific cases of good and evil. While it provides a method for avoiding particular evil, it does so in recognizing its general character as evil. Bonaventure

---

[187] II *Sent.*, d. 39, a. 2, q. 1, ad 4.
[188] II *Sent.*, d. 39, a. 2, q. 1, ad 4: Synderesis autem nominat <u>potentiam</u> affectivam, secundum quod movetur <u>naturaliter</u> et <u>recte</u>; et ideo non distinguitur ab illis potentiis secundum essentiam potentiae, sed secundum modum movendi; et quia secundum illum modum movendi semper movet recte . . . See also D. Langston, *op. cit.*, pp. 35–37.
[189] *Iter mentis ad Deum* I, 6 in *Opera omnia* (Quaracchi, Ad claras aquas, 1891), V.
[190] II *Sent.*, d. 39, a. 2, q. 2.   [191] II *Sent.*, d. 39, a. 2, q. 3.

attributes moral failure to conscience, which may accept improper courses of action.[192] In his final words on the topic Bonaventure again reminds his readers that *synderesis* like all natural powers is, of itself (*de se*), always moved rightly. What is acquired in moral deliberation, however, may have the characteristics of right or wrong. Even with the correct functioning of *synderesis* the conscience may be either right or wrong.[193] Like almost all medieval theologians, Bonaventure coordinates "the effort of the intellect with the act of faith and maintain[s] the beneficent influence of the habit of faith upon the operation of the intellect."[194]

The theories of moral action differ greatly in the works of Thomas Aquinas and Bonaventure, but they agree in the assumption of the innate human ability to recognize universal principles of conduct. Bonaventure's well-known suspicion of the conclusions of philosophers does not prevent him from criticizing those who erroneously attribute a notion of innate moral principles to Aristotle. Bonaventure's preference for Scripture and for the conclusions of theologians does not mean that he did not read the works of Aristotle carefully. Thomas, who produced a number of careful examinations of Aristotle's philosophical works in his academic career, ultimately rejects the human measure of moral conduct in favor of divine and eternal laws. Both of these thirteenth-century theologians accept the idea of Paul, explained by Jerome, that all human beings have an innate power to recognize universal moral laws. This ability is the foundation for a moral theory that applies universally and eternally. Despite great differences in the understanding of the nature of moral actions, all medieval theologians accept such a basis for human conduct.

---

[192] II *Sent.*, d. 39, a. 2, q. 3. ad 4. As a natural power, *synderesis* can never err and in its natural function it is not subject to other potencies, such as free choice. II *Sent.*, d. 39, a. 2, q. 3, ad 6.
[193] II *Sent.*, d. 39, a. 2, q. 3. ad 4.
[194] E. Gilson, *The Christian Philosophy of St. Bonaventure*, p. 449.

8

Two commentaries on the *Nicomachean Ethics*
in the late thirteenth century

A number of commentaries on the NE began to appear in the late thirteenth and early fourteenth century. The authors of many of these works remain unknown and most of the commentaries are preserved only in manuscripts. The practice of explaining carefully Aristotle's text became part of instruction in the medieval university as well as in the *studia generalia* of various monastic and mendicant orders. Although certainly not as philosophically significant as the ground-breaking work of Albertus Magnus and Thomas Aquinas, these commentaries provide a fuller picture of the state of moral philosophy in the Middle Ages. In order to examine some aspects of the medieval interpretation of important Aristotelian concepts, such as happiness, practical wisdom and moral reasoning, two representative commentaries from the end of the thirteenth century are examined in the following pages: the anonymous questions of a manuscript in Erfurt and the commentary most likely written by Radulphus Brito.

a The anonymous commentator of Erfurt
on the nature of happiness

The anonymous questions of Erfurt are preserved in ms. Erfurt, Bibliotheca Amploniana, F (ca 2) 13 E, ff. 75r–119v, and were copied most likely in the first part of the fourteenth century. These questions have provoked little interest in themselves and have been examined primarily in comparison to other works in the late thirteenth century.[1] The author of

---

[1] R.-A. Gauthier, "Comptes Rendus," *Bulletin Thomiste*, 8 (1947–1953), p. 81; O. Lottin, "Problèmes de morale," *Psychologie et morale aux XIIe et XIIIe siècles* (Louvain, Gembloux: Abbaye du Mont César, Duclot, 1942–1949), t. 4, v. 2, p. 537; R. Hissette, "La date de quelques commentaires à l'Éthique," *Bulletin de Philosophie Mèdièvale*, 18

this commentary displays a good understanding of the basic moral thought of Aristotle and follows closely the interpretation of the text by Albertus Magnus. He, like many commentators of this period, is perfectly willing to sacrifice originality of thought for what he believes to be an accurate explanation of Aristotle's moral doctrines. In his prologue the author considers the nature of goodness which, he claims, cannot be perfected without knowledge of divine and human beings. This division between divine and human spheres of activity produces the dual nature of knowledge, which is speculative and practical. The prologue also includes a careful consideration of the nature of practical moral knowledge. Inspired by the *Politics* of Aristotle, the commentator argues that practical moral science considers human acts directed toward an end. This science may be viewed as 'necessary', since the particular good consists in both the end and the means, or operations that lead to this end. According to the commentator's reading of Aristotle, these two elements, when perceived correctly, prevent error in moral science. As a result moral philosophy may be rightly termed a science.[2] At the end of the prologue the author understands Aristotle's intention in a manner that recalls the interpretation of the earliest Latin commentators when he claims that the primary purpose of book I of the NE is to inquire about the best end to which a human being *is ordered.* He implies that the human good, happiness, is a separate state in which all other goods participate. The commentator finally identifies this simple good as God Himself.[3]

This happiness to which a person is ordered may be either contemplative or practical. The author argues that the first type of happiness is not characteristic of human beings, insofar as they are human, but rather because of a divine element within them.[4] The end of such happiness is truth itself, but practical happiness has action for its end. The commentary here displays the older term '*opus*' to designate the activity of happiness,

(1976), pp. 79–83; I. Costa, *Le* questiones *di Radulfo Brito sull'* 'Etica Nicomachea' *Introduzione e testo critico* (=Questiones), Studia Artistarum, 17 (Turnhout: Brepols, 2008), pp. 146–153.

[2] E, f. 85rb.

[3] E, f. 85va: In primo ergo huius intendit philosophus de fine optimo ad quod homo est ordinatus tamquam ad finem sibi proprium qui est felicitas; et debet homo appetere istum finem tamquam bonum suum immediatum et sibi prorpium mediante quo erit participans illius communis et excellentissimi boni quod est bonum simpliciter, [quod] est ipse deus a quo omnia facta sunt, qui est rex regum . . .

[4] E, f. 85rb: Et tractat de felicitate contemplativa que non est hominis secundum quod est homo, sed secundum quod est divinum in ipso homine.

rather than the more common later word 'operatio'.[5] The use of various expressions from different translations is common in the thirteenth century, and many medieval writers did not seem to insist on a consistent use of terminology. Like Albert, the anonymous author does not understand practical happiness to be an immediate end, but rather a mediate one. He distinguishes the immediate end of ethics, which is the awareness of actions, from the mediate one which is the act (*opus*) itself. More specifically he defines the immediate end of morality as the knowledge of truths, but the actions proceeding from such truths are remote and mediate. Moral knowledge of virtues and actions, however, is not absolute in the manner of metaphysical wisdom, but must be considered relative to the act.[6] Like earlier commentators the author of this work has some difficulty in determining the exact nature of human happiness. He implies that it is a state that somehow exists apart from the activities that comprise it. When comparing truth to friendship he indicates that truth is closer (*propinquior*) to happiness than friendship. He supports his position by referring to the relationship between speculative and practical happiness. The cognition of truth participates in supreme goodness to a higher degree than do social and political actions.[7] The language of the commentary indicates the assumption that happiness is something separate from truth and the social activities that lead one to union with the supreme good.

The relation of the two types of happiness is clear from the order that is the characteristic of reason. Eustratius had clarified Aristotle's position concerning the many best things (*plura optima*) that produce speculative and civic happiness in rational activity. Human reason seems to possess an order and a desire for superior beings and inferior powers. The first type of order produces contemplative happiness by which "human reason itself is somehow joined with the separate substances themselves." This union, as Aristotle says, consists in the act of wisdom, which considers the highest causes, God and the separate substances. Here the commentary provides

---

[5] E, f. 86ra: . . . quia secundum quod vult philosophus in Metaphysicis practica et theoretica diffinitur fine quia finis theorice est veritas, practice vero opus.

[6] E, f. 86va: Tertium dicimus quod opus [quod] est finis practice non est intelligendum de fine immediate, sed de fine mediato; sed immediatus et propinquius finis est cognitio operationum. Finis vero remotus et mediatus est ipsum opus quod immediatus finis huius sciencie est cognitio virtutum et operationis procedentium ex virtute; tamen illa cognitio non est absoluta, sed relata ad opus.

[7] E, f. 87vb: . . . sunt bona in comparatione etiam ad quod omnia alia dicuntur per compositionem que est ex participante et participato. E, f. 88ra: Sed veritas propinquior est huic bono quam homo amicus. Et ideo . . . veritas propinquior sit felicitati quam homo amicus. Hoc apparet de felicitate speculativa quam de felicitate civili.

an accurate reading of the theoretical life that Aristotle described in book X of the NE.[8] The other aspect of human reason that directs the lower powers performs best when it directs virtuous actions. The commentator locates the ability to produce virtue in the use of prudence, which perfects practical reason by moral virtues. Prudence and practical reason function with respect to the irascible and desiderative appetite. The guidance of the lower powers by prudence produces a second type of happiness.[9]

The author of this commentary never permits prudence to regulate the activities of the speculative intellect, since he, like all medieval commentators on the NE, considers its function to be the regulation of the appetitive powers that produce only moral virtues. In relation to happiness the practical life of virtue prepares the way for the true happiness that results from contemplation of truth. In this understanding of Aristotle the commentator is in complete agreement with the interpretation of Albert the Great.[10] Only contemplative happiness, as the perfection of the supreme human potentiality, can terminate desire, and, as such, it has the nature of perfect goodness. When considering the meaning of perfection the author distinguishes simple perfection from that perfection which pertains to human goods. Simple perfection lacks nothing, as Averroes noted in his commentary on the *Physics*. Only God, or the first cause, can be thought of as perfect in this way.[11] Perfection in the genus of human goods lacks nothing necessary to human life. Only happiness qualifies as this type of perfection since it includes both the essential goods of the soul and the incidental external goods.[12]

In a short passage the commentator offers an interpretation of happiness that contradicts his earlier conclusions of this topic. Whereas previously he had asserted that one is joined to happiness and that virtues prepare one for its attainment, he now claims that "happiness itself consists essentially in the goods of the soul, as in the virtues, but it consists incidentally in the

---

[8] E, ff. 88va–b.

[9] E, f. 88vb: Alius vero est respectus humane rationis ad vires inferiores, et secundum hoc etiam debetur [esse] aliud optimum. Illud autem optimum est debito modo regnere virtutes inferiores obedibiles et dirigere operationes in actu virtutis; sed hoc communiter inest homini per usum prudentie et per virtutes morales: per prudentiam inest quia illa perficit rationem practicam per virtutes morales quia ille perficiunt appetitum ut irascibilem et concupiscibilem. Et per ista debetur homini felicitas practica sive civilis. Sic igitur patet quod est duplex optimum quod duplex felicitas [est]. See above, p. 147, n. 79.

[10] E, f. 88vb.

[11] E, f. 88vb: Perfectum simpliciter est cui nulla perfectio deest omnino quo[d] dicit Commentator in quinto physicorum quod quoddam perfectum est cui nihil deest ... quod est deus sive causa prima. See above, p. 173, n. 13.

[12] E, f. 89ra.

external goods necessary to life."[13] This more accurate explanation of Aristotle's notion of happiness may not be entirely contradictory, if 'as in virtues' is understood broadly to include wisdom with the moral virtues. In this way the commentator may be referring to the intellectual union by which the virtuous activity of wisdom is the *finis quo*, or individual human activity that unites a person to the *finis cuius*, or the supreme object of contemplation.[14]

The commentator considers the question whether happiness consists in the act of the intellect or of the will very carefully. He notes correctly that there are contradictory opinions among his contemporaries, some of whom, such as Albert the Great and Thomas Aquinas, agree with Aristotle that happiness consists in an intellectual act. Others, however, most notably Henry of Ghent, consider happiness to be a voluntary act of love by which one is joined to the ultimate end.[15] He responds carefully by appealing to Aristotle's intention, which places happiness in an intellectual activity, even though desire moves the will toward the apprehended good. Like many of his contemporaries, the commentator of the Erfurt manuscript avoids the controversy by limiting his response to the intention of Aristotle, who clearly considers contemplative happiness to consist in the actualization of intellectual potentiality. His reference to the argument of Henry of Ghent may actually be closer to his own opinion, since he has indicated earlier how one is joined (*coniungitur*) to happiness.[16] The language here and in the earlier questions is remarkably similar.

b The virtue of prudence

The initial question on the topic of prudence considers the possibility that all virtues must be moral and that none can be intellectual. The author gives a number of arguments that restrict all virtues to moral ones. In his resolution the moral virtues are said to be so designated because they

---

[13] E, f. 89vb: Unde intelligendum quod ipsa felicitas essentialiter consistit in bonis anime ut in virtutibus, sed in bonis exterioribus necessariis ad vitam consistit insubstantialiter.

[14] See above, pp. 196–197.

[15] Henry of Ghent, *Quodlibet* I, 14, ed. R. Macken (Leuven: Leuven University Press, 1979), esp. pp. 86–88.

[16] E, f. 89vb: Quod de ista questione opiniones sunt contrarie. Aliqui enim dicunt cum philosopho quod felicitas consistit in operatione intellectus; alii vero sunt qui dicunt . . . in actu voluntatis qui est diligere quia per talem actum coniungitur aliquid fini ultimo. Quid autem de hoc sentiendum sit amplius forte in decimo huius. Dicendum tamen modo sine preiudicio quod . . . de intentione philosophi felicitas consistit in actu intellectus et non in actu voluntatis.

perfect the appetitive potency that obeys reason. The word, 'moral', not only implies habit, but also an inclination to act. Aristotle, however, distinguished between rational essentially, and rational according to obedience and participation. Moral virtues belong to the second type of rational acts. The commentator does not state explicitly that he classifies intellectual virtues as essentially rational, but he seems to assume that the reader will do so.[17] Choice is involved in every virtue including those which are classified as intellectual, but moral virtues are restricted to those which are the proper habits of the appetitive potency only. Any virtue derives its character from the object of choice, so that when the object of an action is truth, then the resulting actuality results in an intellectual virtue.[18]

A common question in the medieval commentaries on the NE is whether prudence is an intellectual or a moral virtue. It certainly seems to be moral in nature, since it is the form of moral virtues and its function as a guide to the appetite also seems to be characteristic of a moral virtue. The commentator repeats another common argument that favors prudence as a moral virtue when he says that any intellectual virtue may be forgotten, but, as Aristotle determined, prudence is never forgotten. The contrary position is based on the text of the NE, which the author interprets as follows: a virtue by which the soul expresses truth is an intellectual one; prudence allows the soul to express truth; it, therefore, must be an intellectual virtue.[19] The common definition of virtue as that which perfects the agent and renders his action good contributes to the designation of prudence as an intellectual achievement. Prudence's primary function, which renders the action good, depends upon the agent's ability to use reason and to deliberate about practical decisions. Prudence may operate in specific areas of endeavor, or simply be the ability to deliberate correctly about all things. To deliberate correctly is the proper act of reason and of the intellect.[20]

---

[17] E, ff. 107vb–108ra: Modo virtus moralis non solum dicitur a more secundum quod importat consuetudinem, sed etiam ut importat inclinationem ad operandum ... Unde philosophus distinxit rationale in rationale per essentiam et in rationale secundum obedienciam et participationem. Ostendit quod virtus moralis est in rationale per participationem quod est appetitus sensitivus qui dividitur in irrascibilem et concupiscibilem.

[18] E, f. 108ra.

[19] E, f. 108va: Oppositum patet per philosophum et arguitur ratione quia virtus qua verum dicit anima est virtus intellectualis; sed ipsa prudentia anime dicit verum circa agibilia; ergo etc.

[20] E, f. 108va: Intelligendum est ad hoc quod prudentia est virtus intellectualis. Virtus est quia ad virtutem pertinet perficere habentem opus cuius bonum reddit ut sepe dictum est. Sed prudentia opera hec in prudente perficit; enim proprium et opus eius bonum facit circa agibilia quia prudentia rationamur et consiliamur de agibilibus. Et hoc est opus bonum. Et ex isto apparet quod prudentia est virtus; est autem virtus intellectualis quia

The composer of the questions of Erfurt correctly recognizes the essential characteristic of proper deliberation to consist in syllogistic reasoning. He also realizes that all such reasoning, including moral syllogistic deduction, requires a principle from which the process begins.[21] Like Albert and Thomas, this commentator compares moral reasoning to theoretical deduction. He is vague about the specific dictates of the major proposition and claims only that it is the end of practical reason to which the means are directed. This end, unspecified here, is the principle of action that directs the process of practical reasoning. Prudence then is correct deliberation and reasoning about the good. The commentator concludes that the process of both intellectual and moral reasoning presupposes a principle that guides the syllogistic process.[22] The process of prudential reasoning may be identical to that of the theoretical syllogism, but no good principle may be attained without the virtue of the appetite. An evil appetite impedes reason and prevents the moral agent from recognizing an end as good. As a result, the process of prudence may be that of an intellectual virtue, but its subject remains primarily moral in nature. Like Albertus Magnus and Thomas Aquinas, the commentator sees aspects of both intellectual and moral virtues in the process of prudential reasoning.[23]

The commentator acknowledges the moral aspects of prudence and determines that the rectitude of the appetite depends upon moral virtue with respect to both the end and the means. Since prudence requires moral virtue it must have a number of moral virtues connected to it.[24] As a result of this connection, some list prudence among the moral virtues, but the anonymous author of Erfurt emphasizes the process of reason that

cuius est actus eius est habitus; sed actus prudentie est ratione consiliabilis quod determinat philosophus quia dicit quod prudentis in genere est recte consiliari in illo genere et prudentis simpliciter est recte consiliari de omnibus.

[21] E, f. 108va: Sed intelligendum est ulterius quod cum actus prudentie sit recta consiliatio que est quedam sillogizatio sive ratiocinatio, et cum quelibet syllogizatio habeat principium aliquod per quod ratiocinetur oportet ... hanc ratiocinationem que est recta consiliatio habere aliquod pro principio.

[22] E, f. 108va: Unde sicut ratiocinatio intellectualis speculativa (*s. l.*) presupponit aliquod principium unde demonstrat vel syllogizat sic; ratiocinatio practica que consilium dicitur habet principium ex quo procedit quod principium est finis operabilium humanorum, quia ex hoc ratio eorum que sunt ad finem accipitur. Et ideo finis est principium; et si principium ratiocinationis practice est finis, tunc recte ratiocinationis practice erit rectus finis; et cum prudencia sit recta consiliatio et ratiocinatio, ipsa erit de bono.

[23] E, f. 108va–vb.

[24] E, f. 108vb: Si igitur prudentia est recta consiliatio, et recta consiliatio non potest esse sine recto fine, et finis non potest esse rectus nisi appetitus sit rectus (rectitudo autem appetitus non potest esse sine virtute morali), tunc patet quod prudentia non est sine virtute morali[s], sed habet ipsas virtutes morales sibi annexas.

determines the proper means to an end. The essential nature of prudence
lies in the habit of reason, which clearly indicates that it must be numbered
among the intellectual virtues. The determining component to prudence is
the process of reasoning that is comparable to the method of thought in
theoretical sciences. Both practical and theoretical reasoning proceeds
from universals to particulars, as Aristotle and his medieval commentators
describe. Our commentator realizes that Aristotle thought the human
awareness of the first practical principles originated in experience of
particulars, and that the NE does not include natural or divine law in the
analysis of the prudential process.[25] The commentator, however, does
imply that human beings have a natural inclination by which they deliberate correctly about actions. Just as they have a natural ability to perceive
principles in speculative science, they also have a natural inclination to
recognize moral principles and to reach appropriate conclusions.[26] The
commentator does not say whether he is referring here to the concept of
synderesis, and he is reluctant to introduce into his analysis a notion that
does not appear in the work of Aristotle. These practical principles are the
ends of moral actions and produce in the appetite a desire for their
realization, which is the innate inclination of prudence. But prudence itself
is not innate since the practically wise person must develop a virtuous
habit. For the commentator Aristotle himself understood that there is such
a natural inclination within rational beings.[27]

The order that exists among moral virtue, correct appetite and prudence
is essential to proper action. In this order there is a beginning to virtue
(*inchoatio ad virtutem*). A proper moral procedure begins with an intellectual recognition of the end as good, followed by the satisfaction of the
appetite's desire for the end. Finally the practical intellect assumes a moral

---

[25] E, f. 109va: Dicendum quod prudentia non est a natura propter quod intelligendum quod
prudentia est habitus quo recte ratiocinamur de operabilibus. Ratiocinatio autem talis ex
universalibus et particularibus est quia oportet quod conclusio conformis sit premissis,
sicut etiam oportet in speculativis; eodem modo in practicis (in practicis *s.l.*) ex quo
conclusio est particularis. In ipsis operabilibus apparet alteram premissarum etiam esse
particularem. Hoc intellecto dicendum quod prudentia non est a natura quia illud quod
inest a principio extrinseco non inest a natura; sed prudentia etc., quia acquirat per
doctrinam ut iam tactum est per assuefactionem; ergo etc.

[26] E, f. 109va: Est tamen intelligendum quod inclinatio ad talem habitum inest a natura quia
sicut videmus in speculativis. Habemus naturalem inclinationem ad cognoscendum
prima principia et consequenter ad ipsas conclusiones. Sic etiam [in] operabilibus
habemus inclinationem naturalem.

[27] E, f. 109vb: Patet ... quod inclinatio ad prudentia[m] naturaliter inest nobis, licet
prudentia non insit nobis naturaliter ... quia tales habitus non insunt a natura sed
inclinationes ad ipsos, et sic intellexit philosophus.

principle, such as all proper means must be performed for the end. The virtue of prudence does not determine the end, but rather the intellect itself must do so. The commentator accepts Aristotle's idea that deliberation never considers the end, but merely accepts it as good.[28] For Aristotle, however, the prudential judgment does recognize and formulate proper first principles, as he explained in the sixth book of the NE. Individual experiences must at some point generate a practical rule, such as all light meats are healthy. These principles are an important part of the prudential process, but many of the medieval commentators ignored this element in Aristotle's explanation of the prudential process. Such an interpretation emphasizes the importance of the particular in the syllogistic prudential process and even excellent scholars can come to the same conclusion. T. Hoffmann in a recent article on prudential reasoning in the work of Thomas Aquinas argues that the role of the understanding (*nous*) is restricted in the practical syllogism to the particular contingent fact, and excludes the formulation of general principles from its function.[29] Aristotle, however, clearly indicates that *nous* does formulate general rules when one moves from individual perceptions to universal principles (*NE* 1143a32).

The composer of the commentary of Erfurt reformulates the question on prudence and other virtues when he asks whether one who has moral virtue must also have prudence, rather than considering Aristotle's assertion that with prudence come all other virtues. In recasting the question he ignores the more interesting claim of Aristotle concerning the primacy of practical wisdom. He also considers the problem primarily in terms of individual virtues, rather than responding to the more general question on the nature of prudence. He claims merely that one who has moral virtue must have prudence simply, as well as correct appetite. To have prudence 'simply' includes a cognition of the end and the means to it. The response does not address the question whether prudence denotes the possession of both theoretical and practical virtues. The commentator posits a reciprocal relation between moral virtue and prudence: one who has the prudence of all virtues also has moral virtue, and one who has moral virtue necessarily possesses prudence. The source for this answer is likely the commentary of Albertus Magnus, but our author moves even further away from the position of Aristotle.[30] Later in the commentary the author does indicate

---

[28] E, f. 109vb: Ita quod prudentia non determinitiva finis, sed intellectus speculativus.

[29] T. Hoffmann, "Prudence and Practical Principles," *Aquinas and the Nicomachean Ethics*, ed. T. Hoffmann, J. Müller and M. Perkams (Cambridge: Cambridge University Press, 2013), pp. 165–183.

[30] E, f. 110ra.

that the virtue of prudence does bring with it all other virtues when he asserts that "he who has prudence has all [virtues]." The reason that the *prudens* necessarily has all virtues is that such a person has right reason concerning the end and the means to the end. But this prudence one cannot have without all the virtues.[31] One might ask here whether this anonymous commentator captured the force and meaning of Aristotle's notion of practical wisdom, and makes prudence the guiding force in a complete human life. He does not seem to have done so, since he implies that prudence is merely the result of the exercise of different virtues and does not function as the directive force for decisions leading to the highest good. In the tenth book of his commentary he maintains a position common in the thirteenth century when he identifies practical happiness with the activity according to prudence. Prudence leads one to civic happiness because of its ability to rule the other virtues. Despite the claim of prudence's ruling function, the division of virtue into practical and speculative limits the reign of prudence to the moral virtues only. Wisdom, he argues, is superior to other virtues and its nobility renders speculative happiness more choice-worthy than practical goodness.[32]

The influence of Albert the Great on the doctrine of two happinesses and on the discussion of the nobility of the human intellect is evident in the commentary of Erfurt. The intellect is superior to the will when the former is considered simply and absolutely. The intellect's perfection arises from the species of what it knows. The dignity of the will consists in the soul's ability to be compared to what it possesses. The intellect's possession of the object of knowledge makes it superior to the will whose nobility is derived externally from the intellect's ability. The commentator argues in simpler terms when he argues that to know a stone is nobler than to desire it. The ability to understand an object is always superior to the will's reaction to it.[33] The will may be viewed as nobler than the intellect with respect to

[31] E, f. 110ra: Sed qui habet prudentiam (*corr. ex* primam) ille habet omnes [virtutes]. Cuius ratio est quia ille qui habet prudentiam necessario habet omnes virtutes quia talis habet rectam rationem ultimi finis et eorum que sunt ad finem; sed hanc prudentiam non potest habere sine omnibus virtutibus.

[32] E, f. 118ra: Sed duplex est virtus: quedam est practica, quedam speculativa. Et inter practicas virtutes perfectior et excellentior est ipsa prudentia, quia est aliorum regitiva. Felicitas ergo practica que est operatio secundum virtutem practicam consistit in operatione secundum prudentiam. Sed inter virtutes speculativas sapientia est virtus excellentior ... Felicitas ergo speculativa que est optima secundum virtutem speculativam in operacione huius virtutis que est sapientia ... felicitas speculativa eligibilior est.

[33] E, f. 117va: Intellectus nobilior voluntate quia nobilius est intelligere lapidem quam velle lapidem.

divine beings. The will has more intimate and produces a superior delight in the soul's relation to divine beings than does the intellect, since human beings can love what is divine more than they can understand it. The will, however, cannot in most cases attain a higher level of delight than that which the intellect presents to it.[34]

Contemplative happiness is superior to the practical life because its object is the most stable and delightful. The specific object of human happiness is the first cause. Any other object conveys to the agent a sense of regret because of the realization that something is lacking.[35] The commentator's discussion of happiness in book X of the NE does not stray far from the intention of Aristotle, and his assertion that in the act of contemplation one is assimilated to God in the highest degree (*maxime*) has its origins in the text of Aristotle and in book lambda of the *Metaphysics*. Perfect happiness consists in the best activity of reason whose excellence arises from the goodness of the potency and the realization of its object. The author cites Aristotle's description of the human intellect as something divine whose supreme intelligible object and its truth are ultimately found in the first cause and the separate substances. Here the commentator accepts Aristotle's doctrine on the supreme achievement of human beings. He makes no mention of the Christian doctrine of perfect beatitude in his commentary despite the obvious similarities in doctrine.[36]

c The commentary of Radulphus Brito

A second witness to the tradition of commentaries on the NE in the thirteenth century is the collection of questions attributed with good

[34] E, f. 117vb.
[35] E, f. 117va: Speculatio est circa obiectum stabilissimum, quia est circa primam causam que est delectabilissimum obiectum ... ipsa tamen speculatio non semper potest continuari cuius ratio est quia speculatio indiget operatione sensuum qui fatigantur et laborant in operando ... Propter quod etiam non ponitur felicitas in speculatione alterius obiecti quam prime cause ... quia non est respectu optimi obiecti, ex hoc tamen quod aliquis scit se intelligere aliquid scit hoc non esse optimum, [et] tristatur.
[36] E, f. 117vb: Quod perfecta felicitas hominis (*s.l.*) in speculatione intellectus consistet. Cuius ratio est quia secundum quod manifestum est ... felicitas perfecta consistit in operatione. Cum ergo felicitas sit optimum rationabile est ut in optima operatione consistat; sed optima operatio est speculatio quia operatio bona reddit ex bonitate potentie et obiecti; sed potentia ad speculationem est quid optimum quia per talem potentiam maxime assimilamur deo. Est enim ipse divinissimum eorum qu in nobis sunt, scilicet intellectus. Obiectum enim speculationis est optimum quia inter omnia cognoscibilia maxime cognoscibile est intelligibile; et hoc maxime verum est de divinis ut de causa prima et substantiis separatis.

reason to Radulphus Brito.[37] This work of the late thirteenth century has a number of positions in common with the anonymous commentary of Erfurt and other literary products of this era. All these works owe a great debt to the efforts of Albertus Magnus and Thomas Aquinas, who flourished in the most creative period in the exposition and assimilation of Aristotle's moral philosophy. After their contributions the later medieval commentators seem content to explain more fully Aristotle's positions in the directions provided by his two greatest interpreters. The common positions that appear in the commentary of Radulphus and in the manuscript in Erfurt do not necessarily indicate a common source, as R.-A. Gauthier argued,[38] since the late thirteenth-century commentaries display a tendency to accept established positions on Aristotle's doctrines. They valued originality less highly than a thorough exposition of Aristotle's text and of earlier interpretations. Still Radulphus's commentary provides a way to elucidate further the understanding of important moral doctrines in the late thirteenth and early fourteenth century.

Radulphus lists several opinions concerning the subject of Aristotle's work on ethics. He says that Eustratius considered it to be the betterment of the individual human being so that one may become good. Others say that happiness is its subject, and still others maintain the topic of the NE to be virtue or individual practices. Radulphus accepts for the present the subject of ethics to be the good that is ordered to the end (*bonum agibile ad finem ordinatum*). In other words the NE considers the action of a human being in itself (*operatio hominis secundum se*).[39] Radulphus admits that the NE examines the nature of virtue, but only as it is generated by actions, or insofar as it is the principle of actions. No one, he says, considers virtue except as it is performed in itself. The point of departure in ethics is the existence and nature of *bonum agibile*, which is ordered to a proper end.[40]

d The goal of human existence

The proper end of human actions is happiness, as Aristotle determined in the NE. Since happiness consists in the operation of the speculative

---

[37] See I. Costa, *Questiones*, pp. 99–137. On the life and works of Radulphus Brito, see W. Courtenay, "Radulphus Brito: Master of Arts and Theology," *Cahiers de l'Institut du Moyen-âge grec et latin*, 76 (2005), pp. 131–158.

[38] R.-A. Gauthier, "Trois commentaires 'averroistes' sur l'Ethique à Nicomaque," *Archives d'histoire doctrinale et littéraire du moyen âge*, 16 (1947–1948), pp. 334–336 and O. Lottin, *Psychologie et morale* ... III, pp. 621–650.

[39] *Questiones*, p. 184.   [40] *Questiones*, p. 184.

intellect, especially with respect to the first intelligibles, and practical
happiness results from the activities to be performed, Aristotle determined
that the *bonum agibile* of one person ordered to the end is more properly
the subject of ethics than the end itself.[41] In emphasizing the activity more
than the end of action as the subject of ethics, Radulphus differs from his
anonymous contemporary of the manuscript in Erfurt, who claimed the
end to be the proper subject of the science of ethics. Radulphus treats the
topics of book I of the NE more extensively than those of any other book,
and the number of questions demonstrate his interest in the nature of
goodness, the subject and proper student of ethics, and the meaning and
cause of human happiness. There are forty-two questions on book I of the
NE, while no other book has more than twenty-seven. Book VII has only
five questions and there is none in books VIII and IX. Whether these
questions were lost or reflect the teaching activity of the Arts masters at
Paris is a topic for further research.

Since Radulphus's positions in his questions are similar to those of the
commentator of Erfurt, Albertus Magnus and Thomas Aquinas, only a few
of his more interesting discussions require examination here. In the question whether there is one ultimate end for all human beings he makes a
distinction common in this age. The ultimate end may be viewed in two
ways, either according to its nature (*ratio*), or with regard to that in which
this end exists. In his response Radulphus makes three assertions: (1) there
should be one extrinsic end that is unique in number; (2) for all persons
there should be one intrinsic end according to their species and its relation
to the ultimate end; (3) that in which this nature of the ultimate end
consists differs in individuals. For Radulphus the extrinsic end can only
be one for all, but the intrinsic end may also be thought of as one
specifically with regard to its nature. Finally the activity in which this
nature consists is diverse in individuals.[42] With these distinctions in
place Radulphus may claim that the extrinsic end for all is the first cause
that is numerically one. The specific commonality in the intrinsic end
comes from the desire for the ultimate end, which fulfills and satisfies the

---

[41] Questiones, p. 184.
[42] Questiones, p. 197: Dicendum quod ultimus finis potest considerari dupliciter: vel
quantum ad rationem eius, vel quantum ad illud in quo existit ultimus finis. Etiam
ultimus finis potest esse vel intrinsecus vel extrinsecus. Hoc viso dico tria ad questionem.
Primo: quod omnium hominum debet esse unus finis extrinsecus, unus etiam numero.
Secundo dico quod omnium hominum debet esse unus finis ultimus intrinsecus secundum speciem quantum ad rationem ultimi finis. Tertio dico quod illud in quo consistit
hec ratio ultimi finis secundum diversos est diversificatum.

human appetite. His explanation for the differences within the intrinsic
end lies in the individuals' beliefs that constitute the final end. Some may
think it to be honor, riches, or pleasure, but Aristotle and others thought it to
be the contemplation of truth.[43] Radulphus departs here from the opinion of
Thomas Aquinas, who addressed similar ideas in the *Summa theologiae*
where he distinguishes the intrinsic ends by noting the diverse manner
and profundity of attaining knowledge of the first cause. Radulphus does
not really answer the question that would explain how the attainment of
contemplative happiness would differ in individuals. Thomas had dismissed
the idea that the identification of happiness with lesser goods produces
different ends among those who are termed happy. For Thomas each
contemplative achieves an intellectual union with the first cause differently
through the individual act of actualizing the soul's supreme potential, even if
the object of thought is identical for all. Thomas answers the more difficult
philosophical problem of how happiness may be considered both the same
activity of contemplation for all human beings and how it may be uniquely
individuated by their different acts.[44] Radulphus merely notes that different
people believe different objects to be diverse ultimate ends.

In determining the relative merits of contemplative and active lives
Radulphus distinguishes between two senses of better (*melius*): better
may indicate what is more honorable or more useful. Which of these is
of greater value to God Radulphus dismisses as irrelevant to philosophy,
since it is a theological issue. The NE considers which life is better, and
undoubtedly the life of contemplation is more honorable and simply
better. Like Albert, Radulphus claims the contemplative life exists for its
own sake, while the active life exists for the sake of something else. Because
the active life is sought for something other than itself, it may be praiseworthy, but not honorable. Again following Albert, he considers the active
life to lead to contemplation, which derives its superiority in the contemplative assimilation to divine substances. The ability to lead a human being
to an intellectual union with God conveys great dignity to the life of
philosophy.[45] The active life, however, is more useful because it remedies
the defects in the body and soul. In the civic arena one is considered not
only as an individual, but also as part of a domestic and political group. The
active life, however, derives more worth through its contribution toward
the life of contemplation.

Radulphus ascribes correctly this interpretation to Albert the Great, who
distinguished between two types of happiness. Albert said that one can

---

[43] Questiones, p. 198.   [44] See above pp. 196–197.   [45] Questiones, p. 224.

consider each kind of happiness in two ways: according to its worth and dignity; or according to utility with regard to life's necessities.[46] In the first way contemplative happiness is greater than civic happiness since it is in a human being according to the best part of human nature, and makes one similar to God. Practical happiness, which arises from the practice of moral virtues is more closely related to the corporeal nature of a person, but is more important in the second manner, since it allows one to procure and to order the elements for a human life.[47] Radulphus's admiration for the contemplative life is so great he boldly asserts that according to human perfection philosophers, who contemplate the truth, are nobler than kings or princes. In matters of business and politics, however, the civic authorities are more important than the contemplatives.[48]

When discussing the state of human happiness, Radulphus again finds his inspiration in the writings of Albert the Great. Radulphus declares succinctly that happiness is indeed the simply perfect good among human acts and activities.[49] The term 'simply perfect', without further designation refers only to the first cause, which has in itself the perfection of all beings, as Averroes made clear in his commentary on the *Metaphysics*. Since human achievements can never contain every possible perfection, happiness cannot be described as simply perfect without the further restriction of 'in the genus of human actions'. Its perfection originates in its ability to terminate simply the motion of the human appetite. Anyone, who is not corrupted, seeks nothing beyond the state of human perfection, which is happiness itself.[50] To explain further the meaning of human perfection Radulphus employs a distinction found in the earlier works of Albert and Thomas. The argument that what requires external goods cannot in itself be perfect leads Radulphus to the discussion of happiness according to its essence and happiness with a certain luster (*decor*). He cites Thomas in his resolution to the question when he argues that what lacks an intrinsic good pertaining to its essence cannot be simply perfect. But what lacks an extrinsic good as an ornament (*decor*) is not necessarily imperfect:

---

[46] Questiones, p. 557: ... dico, secundum quod dicit Albertus, per distinctionem: quia nos possumus considerare felicitatem practicam et speculativam secundum principalitatem dupliciter: aut secundum honestatem et dignitatem aut secundum utilitatem necessitatis vite.

[47] Questiones, p. 557.   [48] Questiones, p. 558.

[49] Questiones, p. 226: Secundo dico quod inter actus et operationes humanas felicitas est bonum simpliciter perfectum.

[50] Questiones, p. 226.

It can be said, just as brother Thomas says, that these exterior goods do not pertain to the essence of happiness, but only to a certain embellishment of it, and therefore even if something lacks these goods in this way it does not mean that it is not perfect.[51]

Any addition to the essence of an object would render the object imperfect, but any good that does not pertain to the essence may be considered extrinsic to its nature. The necessities and luxuries that make life more desirable add luster and beauty to human existence, but are not essential components of happiness.

The resolution to the question whether happiness is a self-sufficient good leads Radulphus to discussions concerning the nature and meaning of human happiness. He distinguishes among what is necessary for happiness, what is useful and instrumental to it, what results from it, and what is concomitant to it. What is essential to happiness is the activity according to the intellect. Since the intellect may be either speculative or practical, its actualizations are also so divided. Following Albert, Radulphus divides happiness into practical, which he identifies with prudence, and speculative, which consists in the contemplation of the supreme objects of thought. The activity of the practical intellect is the highest good in action, or right reason of action, which he calls again the act of prudence. The supreme good among speculative actions is the contemplation of the first beings. At this point in the commentary Radulphus seems to accept Thomas Aquinas's notion of human happiness as a combination of contemplative and practical activity: "Therefore, in this speculation according to the intellect, either speculative or practical, human happiness consists."[52] The assertion here that human happiness consists in both speculative and practical activity does not mean that Radulphus does, in fact, prefer Thomas's interpretation of the question to that of Albert, since he may merely mean that both types of actions may qualify for the designation of happiness. His previous and subsequent discussions on the topic clearly indicate his preference for Albert's position, which sees in the NE two distinct types of human happiness.

---

[51] Questiones, p. 227: Vel potest dici, sicut dicit frater Thomas, quod ista bona exteriora non pertinent ad essentiam felicitatis, sed solum ad quemdam decorem ipsius, et ideo quamvis indigeat istis isto modo, non oportet propter hoc quin sit bonum perfectum. See also Thomas Aquinas, SLE, pp. 58–59, ll. 115–125; A. Celano, "The Concept of Worldly Beatitude in the Writings of Thomas Aquinas," *Journal of the History of Philosophy*, 25 (1987), esp. pp. 218–222.

[52] Questiones, p. 228: Ergo in ista speculatione secundum intellectum sive speculativum sive practicum consistit humana felicitas.

Self-sufficient as a description of happiness means that Aristotle determined it to make a life worthwhile and lacking nothing. Radulphus, however, claims that happiness that exists essentially does not meet the requirements of a self-sufficient good because it needs other benefits, such as riches, for both active and contemplative virtues.[53] He seems to have misunderstood Aristotle's statement that if happiness were numbered as merely one among good things, it would become more desirable by the addition of other desirable objects. Aristotle does not measure happiness quantitatively as a sum of goods, but rather qualitatively, since it encompasses all that is necessary to a worthwhile life. Radulphus argues that happiness in all its aspects, which are essential activities, instruments and results, comprise a *per se* sufficient good. In Albert's terms only *felicitas secundum posse*, which lacks no external goods, such as friends or wealth, can be considered truly self-sufficient.[54] Here Radulphus completely reverses Aristotle's position, which was succinctly explained by Thomas Aquinas: "And so happiness of which we speak now has sufficiency in itself, namely because it contains in itself everything which is necessary to a human being; not however, everything which can come to a human being."[55] Radulphus believes that Aristotle's description of self-sufficiency means that nothing may be added to the state of happiness, whereas Thomas and Aristotle maintain that it is essentially complete even, if it may be enhanced by an abundance of material goods. Aristotle himself implies this distinction when he refers to a state of happiness with the benefits of fortune as a type of beatitude.[56]

The concept of self-sufficiency helps to clarify the differences in the two types of human happiness. Contemplative happiness requires fewer exterior goods than does practical happiness. Contemplation, which consists

---

[53] Questiones, p. 229.

[54] Questiones, p. 229: Si autem accipiamus felicitatem quantum ad omne illud requisitum ad felicitatem, et quantum ad pertinentia essentialiter ad eius rationem et quantum ad omnia alia ibi requisita sicut coadiuvantia vel organa vel consequentia et sic de aliis, sic felicitas est bonum per se sufficiens: quia illud quod solitarium facit aliquam vitam per se sufficientem et per se eligibilem nullo extrinseco indigentem, tale est bonum per se suficiens; modo felicitas accepta isto modo, ut dictum est, facit talem vitam, quia tunc felix non indiget bona exterioribus nec amicis nec aliis requisitis ad felicitatem; ideo felicitas isto modo est bonum per se sufficiens, et sic intellgit Philosophus quod est bonum per sufficiens. See above, p. 133.

[55] SLE, p. 33, ll. 198–201: Et sic felicitas de qua nunc loquitur habet per se sufficientiam, quia scilicet in se continet omne illud quod est homini necessarium, non autem omne illud quod potest homini advenire …

[56] A. Celano, "Aristotle on Beatitude," *Ancient Philosophy*, V, 2 (1985), pp. 205–214.

only in the activity of the speculative intellect, needs only life's few necessities, as Seneca and Cicero recognized. Practical happiness, however, which consists in the act of prudence and is the activity of moral virtues, requires far more external goods. This latter type of happiness involves interaction with family friends and neighbors. The demands of the practical life produce a greater need for extrinsic goods than does the solitary life of the contemplative.[57]

The difficult question of the relation of virtue to happiness leads Radulphus to distinguish sharply between the activity of virtue and the virtue itself. He contends that it is possible for someone to possess a virtue and never act according to it. As an example, he considers a person who possesses the habit of generosity, but who lacks money; he cannot, therefore, act with respect to this virtue.[58] As a result of the dichotomy between habit and activity, Radulphus concludes that human happiness consists not in virtues, but rather in activity according to virtue, and most of all according to the supreme virtue.[59] He continues by stating that since happiness is the ultimate good, it cannot consist in something ordered to another. Virtues then cannot comprise the supreme good because of their order to actions. Habits, which are the virtues, are always directed to actions, just as a primary act exists for the sake of a secondary act.[60] In further discussions on the differences between primary and secondary acts, Radulphus distinguishes further the virtuous habits from the resulting actions. He declares the secondary acts to be more perfect than the primary ones because the former cannot exist without the latter, whereas the primary act (habit) can exist without its corresponding result (virtue).[61]

Radulphus is certainly surprising in his assertion of the superiority of the action over the habit, since the latter requires the former. One might logically assume the reverse position that such dependence renders the operation less perfect than its preceding habit. Radulphus does not consider the temporal priority of the operations that are needed to create the habit.

[57] Questiones, p. 232. The clearest expression of Radulphus' acceptance of Albert's division of happiness into two distinct types is as follows (Questiones, p. 248): Dico per distinctionem quod duplex est felicitas: quedam enim est contemplativa et quedam est practica.

[58] Questiones, p. 210.

[59] Questiones, p. 211: Dicendum quod felicitas non consistit in virtutibus. Secundo dico quod consistit in operationem secundum virtutem, et maxime secundum supremam virtutem. Cf. the position of Albertus Magnus, above, p. 137.

[60] Questiones, p. 211.   [61] Questiones, p. 236.

He asserts merely that "... actions are more perfect than the habit or the virtues themselves, because the posterior is always more perfect; now actions are posterior to virtues, for virtues are ordered to actions."[62] Using arguments from the early thirteenth-century commentaries on the NE, Radulphus makes the obvious claim that someone acting in a good activity cannot possibly not act well. On the other hand, someone with the habit of virtue may not exercise it, if one is sleeping or otherwise impeded. It does not occur to Radulphus that the actions are the very virtues themselves.[63] He considers the assertion that the virtues are nobler than the activities to be false, since the former are ordered to the latter. The argument for the superiority of that which endures longer is irrelevant here, since Radulphus judges virtues and actions to have different genera. Virtues belong to the genus of quality, and activities (*operationes*) belong to the genus of action (*actus*). Activities are the final causes with respect to virtues and like all final causes or ends they are nobler than their efficient causes.[64] Radulphus ignores the reciprocal relation between habit and activity, and his view of virtue as a habit that may, or may not, be exercised leads him to differentiate happiness from virtue, and virtue from its act to a far greater degree than appears in the NE.

Radulphus understands well the dynamic element in Aristotle's concept of happiness. The operation of virtue actualizes the soul's potentialities, which eliminates the soul's substance, potency, nature and habits as possible definitions of happiness. What remains then can only be the activity of the soul, since lower human potencies cannot qualify for the ultimate human good. All activities including those of the practical intellect contribute to the final human perfection that comes from contemplation of the first intelligible beings.[65] The work of Albert the Great on moral and intellectual virtues again inspires Radulphus's understanding of the meaning of happiness. Since happiness arises from the activity of the speculative intellect, knowledge and virtues must perfect the intellect. Because the

---

[62] Questiones, p. 211: ... operationes sunt perfectiores habitu sive ipsis virtutibus, quia posterius semper est perfectius; modo operationes sunt posteriores virtutibus: virtutes enim ordinantur ad operationes.
[63] Questiones, p. 211.   [64] Questiones, pp. 211–212.
[65] Questiones, p. 238: ... si felicitas esset operatio humana, ergo cum multe sint operationes humane multe essent felicitates, dico quod non oportet, quia omnes operationes humane sunt ordinate ad ultimam eius perfectionem ... et omnes operationes intellectus sunt ordinate ad ultimam operationem que consistit in contemplatione primorum intelligibilium ... sed operationes que sunt secundum intellectum practicum ordinantur ad operationem que est secundum intellectum speculativum.

virtues are temporally prior to knowledge they assist the wise man in the quest for contemplation by calming the passions and preparing the way for the solitary pursuit of truth.[66]

The insistence that Aristotle's intention clearly places happiness in the act of the intellect differs little from the responses of Albert and Thomas,[67] but Radulphus admits that some theologians may think differently. Although the Philosopher is clear on this question, Radulphus concedes there may be some doubt about this position. Radulphus summarizes the counter-argument of Henry of Ghent and other late thirteenth-century theologians as follows. The will is brought to God essentially and according to the mode that He has in Himself, but the intellect cannot be conveyed to God in this manner.[68] The intellect comes to God according to His way of being (*secundum modum essendi*) and according to the manner of comprehending Him. The mode of God's being in itself is nobler than the manner of existence in human beings; the will's activity, therefore, brought to God according to manner of divine being is nobler than the operation of the speculative intellect. For this reason some theologians assert that happiness must consist in the act of the will. Radulphus is careful to cite this position only and prefers to remain silent concerning its validity: "Whether this is so or not according to faith I do not even consider, nevertheless according to the Philosopher it should be said that happiness consists in the activity of the speculative intellect."[69] Radulphus ventures to explain how Aristotle would have resolved the question, if faced with the theological position. When someone claims the will is brought to God according to His mode of being, one should understand that the will follows cognition, since the will is a type of appetite and all desire follows cognition. When one says the will is conveyed to God according to the mode of being, one speaks falsely because the will is so moved only insofar as there is understanding. The will cannot desire or possess anything without a prior apprehension. No one can understand God as He is or in His being, nor can one desire Him in this manner.[70] This argument demonstrates Radulphus's caution and skill,

---

[66] Questiones, p. 240.
[67] Questiones, p. 241: ... dico secundum intentionem Philosophi quod felicitas consistit in actu intellectus et non in actu voluntatis.
[68] Questiones, p. 242.
[69] Questiones, p. 242: Utrum tamen ita sit vel non secundum fidem, de hoc non intromitto me, tamen secundum Philosophum diceretur quod felicitats consistit in operatione speculativi intellectus ...
[70] Questiones, p. 242.

since he refrains from explicit criticism of such a powerful and influential figure as Henry of Ghent. He is, however, able to provide a thorough refutation of the voluntaristic position in his hypothetical Aristotelian response to the problem.[71]

Radulphus asserts unequivocally that Aristotle accepted the doctrine of natural law[72] and that its principles function similarly to those in theoretical sciences. Just as in science when one comprehends the meaning of terms and immediately accepts them as true, so too in action does one assent immediately to certain practical principles. Examples of these first principles are to avoid evil and practice good, and to refrain from harming another arbitrarily. These commands to which the practical intellect immediately assents are the components of natural law.[73] Although Aristotle discussed only natural law, jurists differentiate between natural law and the law of nations (*ius gentium*). Jurists think that natural law reflects the 'animal' nature of human beings and is therefore limited to principles concerning innate animal traits, such as the procreation, nourishment and education of the young. What the legal experts call the law of nations addresses the rational nature of humanity. Examples of its principles are to favor friends and benefactors, harm evildoers and enemies, and to protect legates and ambassadors. Radulphus claims that all human beings observe such laws. Although Aristotle was not aware of the legalistic distinctions, Radulphus assumes that he included the principles of the *ius gentium* under his concept of natural law.[74] Radulphus considers the commands to sacrifice to the gods and to join males and females as additional moral imperatives, but his discussion adds little to the medieval understanding of natural law. The recognition of the force of the commands of natural law furnishes the basis for the idea that the prudent person recognizes universal principles. Radulphus argues that the first principles of action should be known naturally. When comprehended they lead immediately to assent. The practical intellect immediately accepts the command to pursue good and avoid evil. The principles serve as the ends to which all subsequent acts are directed. The cognition

---

[71] For a discussion of the position of Henry of Ghent, see R. Macken, "La volonté humaine, faculté plus élevée que l'intelligence selon Henri de Gand," *Recherches de Théologie ancienne et médiévale*, 42 (1975), pp. 5–51 and R. Macken, "Heinrich von Gent im Gespräch mit seinen Zeitgenossen über die menschliche Freiheit," *Franziskanische Studien*, 59 (1977), pp. 125–182.

[72] Questiones, p. 460: Sed est intelligendum quod ius naturale, quod dicitur a Philosopho ius naturale ...

[73] Questiones, p. 460.   [74] Questiones, p. 460.

of the imperatives of natural law become extremely important in the prudential process, and the immediate recognition of the principles of action is a natural element in the virtue of prudence.[75]

e Practical wisdom and virtue

Radulphus does not directly raise the question concerning Aristotle's assertion that with practical wisdom come all other virtues, but he does discuss the relation of prudence to other virtues in a few questions. He asserts the need for prudence in living or acting well. He identifies living well (*bene vivere*) with acting well (*bene operari*) and to do so absolutely requires the exercise of prudence.[76] The choice of the phrases, *bene vivere* and *bene operari*, clearly indicates Radulphus's intention to limit prudence only to the moral virtues. As we have seen, the complete description of Aristotle's concept of happiness contains both *cognitio Dei* and *bene vivere* (or *operari*).[77] The former term designates the theoretical component to the Aristotelian ideal of happiness, while the latter term specifies the practical life of moral virtue. The exclusion of *cognito Dei* here displays the author's intention to restrict prudence to the practice of moral activities.

   Although prudence regulates the moral virtues, Aristotle clearly demonstrated it to be an intellectual virtue, which Radulphus freely admits. He finds its intellectual nature in the ability to think rationally and syllogistically (*ratiocinari et sillogizare*). These rational abilities are clear in the intellect's ability to deliberate about the means to acquiring the immediately perceived ends of action.[78] Radulphus describes the rational process as a combination of intellectual reasoning and right desire:

> ... although prudence is an intellectual virtue, nevertheless it always presupposes correct appetite and consequently the other moral virtues, because prudence is the correct ratiocination of the means to an end; now correct ratiocination begins from a correct principle determined to a correct conclusion. The correct principle in action is the end, because the end is the principle of all actions; therefore, in prudence one must have a correct assessment of the end which is the principle of actions. Now one cannot have a correct assessment of the end, unless one has an ordered and correct appetite, because the appetite is that which is brought to the end; prudence, therefore, presupposes an ordered and correct appetite. Because the

---

[75] Questiones, pp. 507–508.

[76] Questiones, p. 495: Dicendum quod prudentia est necessaria ad hoc quod homo bene vivat. Quia bene vivere est bene operari; modo ad bene operari necessario requiritur prudentia; ergo ad bene vivere necessario requiritur prudentia.

[77] See above, pp. 137 and 189–192.   [78] Questiones, p. 494.

appetite is ordered and made correct by the moral virtues, prudence presupposes other moral virtues.[79]

Not only does prudence presuppose the other moral virtues, the reverse is also true, since moral virtues require prudence. Prudence is necessary because moral virtues only incline the appetite to correct action. An inclination is insufficient for acting well since correct judgment and reasoning about the means to the end are also required. Prudence furnishes the ability to deliberate correctly and to determine the proper means with respect to any moral virtue.[80] The intellectual nature of prudence comes from its function in directing the appetite, which the moral virtues cannot do, since they provide only the inclination to act well. What directs the appetite is the intellectual process of correct reasoning. In the precise analysis of prudence the proper determination of the end is a function of correct appetite, while the judgment about the proper means depends upon the function of prudence. Like other medieval commentators Radulphus, at times, limits prudence to the means and, at other times, acknowledges its need to recognize the end.[81]

The treatment of Aristotle's concept of practical wisdom has by the late thirteenth century developed in some decidedly un-Aristotelian ways. The concepts of perfect prudence, perfect moral virtue, natural law and the restriction of prudence to moral decisions alone are not part of Aristotle's moral philosophy and may be contradictory to his thought. The medieval commentators attempt to understand Aristotle in a way that does not oppose their own moral principles, but the practice of exposition of the text and the reverence for tradition inhibited innovation and creativity in their commentaries on the NE. The more profound contributions to moral philosophy in the later medieval period do not appear in commentaries on Aristotle's text, but rather in theological works, such as *Summae*, Commentaries on the *Sentences* and Quodlibetal Questions, of Henry of Ghent, John Duns Scotus and William of Ockham, among others. At the end of the thirteenth century a number of commentaries on the text of the NE appeared, but despite small refinements in the interpretation of Aristotle's work, the authors were content for the most part to follow doctrines that were well established. The more controversial questions and original solutions concerning the primacy of the will over the intellect, of human volitional freedom and of the relation of worldly happiness to perfect beatitude appear far more often in works other than

---

[79] *Questiones*, p. 494.   [80] *Questiones*, p. 494.   [81] *Questiones*, p. 496.

expositions of Aristotle's thought.[82] Without the earlier carefully constructed explanations of Aristotle's philosophy of the commentators on
the text of the NE, however, it seems doubtful that these innovations in
moral philosophy and theology would have occurred.

---

[82] See, among many other studies, the work of R. Macken already cited; M. Stone, "Henry of
Ghent on Freedom and Human Action," *Henry of Ghent and the Transformation of
Scholastic Thought, Studies in Memory of Jos Decorte*, ed. G. Guldentops and C. Steel
(Leuven: Leuven University Press, 2003), pp. 201–225; A. Wolter, *Duns Scotus on the Will
and Morality*, ed. W. Frank (Washington: The Catholic University of America Press,
1997); M. M. Adams, "The Structure of Ockham's Moral Theory," *Franciscan Studies*, 29
(1986), pp. 1–35 and "Ockham on Will, Nature and Morality," *The Cambridge
Companion to Ockham*, ed. P. Spade (New York: Cambridge University Press, 1999),
pp. 245–272.

9

Conclusion

The origin of philosophical moral theory lies in Socrates's statement that the unexamined life is not worth living.[1] Before the Socratic-Platonic examination of the good life, ethics consisted largely in obedience to the law and in a military code of conduct.[2] Although Socrates served as a soldier, he offered a new vision of human responsibility, one in which an individual must decide for oneself which actions contribute to a moral life. His admonition to examine a life is taken now as an obvious element in moral self-development, but what is often overlooked is Socrates's implication that a standard is needed by which human existence may be measured. The mere examination of a life does not render it good, since a person like Hitler, who examined his life in *Mein Kampf*, can be said to have met Socrates's demand to consider a life. While self-investigation may be an element within the good life, it alone provides nothing more than individual reflection. Socrates would require that the life be measured in a way that produces a judgment about its moral worth, which lies in the beneficial effects of actions upon the soul.

Plato provided such a measure by which every object and act may be judged when he sought a standard that would be universal and eternal. Since nothing in the material world could qualify, the Platonic measure is divine and transcendent. All objects in their being and intelligibility are related to the immaterial divine forms. A universal concept, such as beauty itself, which few modern thinkers would consider real, is a true being in its eternal form, and the standard by which all inferior beautiful objects may

---

[1] *Apologia* 38a.
[2] See the monumental studies of W. Jaeger, *Paideia: The Ideals of Greek Culture*, tr. G. Highet (Oxford: Oxford University Press, 1986), esp. v. I, and W. Guthrie, *A History of Greek Philosophy* (Cambridge: Cambridge University Press, 1979–1981), esp. vv. I and II.

be measured. In the *Symposium* Socrates relates the story of his philosophical education directed by Diotima, a wise woman of Mantinea, who
teaches him the connection between true beauty and the derived manifes-
tations of it in the material world. Anyone who has regarded beautiful
things properly will become aware of something wondrous that provides
meaning to all former efforts at understanding the nature of beauty. If one
contemplates beauty's common element, one gains a unified understanding of beauty itself.[3] The intuition that such perfect beauty exists recognizes
its true nature as everlasting, immutable and universal. It is beauty absolute, separate, simple, everlasting and entirely unchanged by objects that
gain their beauty by participation in it.[4] Rather than merely considering the
form an objective metaphysical and epistemological unifying element,
Diotima extends it to the moral realm:

This, my dear Socrates ... is that life above all others which man should live in the
contemplation of beauty absolute ... But what if man had eyes to see the true
beauty–the divine beauty, I mean, pure and clear and unalloyed, not clogged with
the pollutions of mortality and all the colors and vanities of human life ...
Remember how in that communion only beholding beauty with the eye of the
mind, he will be enabled to bring forth, not images of beauty but realities ... and
bringing forth and nourishing true virtue to become the friend of God and be
immortal, if mortal man may.[5]

Whatever Plato's final doctrine concerning the separate existence of forms
turned out to be,[6] he retained always the Socratic ideal of a divine model
and the quest for the soul's immortality as the basis for moral decisions. For
Socrates and Plato the truly good person is one,

born to arrive towards reality, who cannot linger among that multiplicity of things
which man believes to be real, but holds on his way ... until he has laid hold upon
the essential nature of each thing with that part of his soul which can apprehend
reality because of its affinity therewith; and when he has by that means approached
real being and entered into union with it ... so that at least having found knowledge and true life and nourishment, he is at rest from his travail.[7]

The entire thrust of Socratic ethics is to direct human beings away from the
imperfections of the world and toward a perfect existence that culminates

---

[3] *Symposium*, 210d6–e1: κατίδῃ τινὰ ἐπιστήμην μίαν τοιαύτην, ἥ ἐστι καλοῦ τοιοῦδε. See
also *Phaedo* 100d7.
[4] *Symposium*, 211a–b5.
[5] *Symposium*, 211d1–212a7. For the works of Plato, I have used the translations of B. Jowett
with some minor changes, unless otherwise noted.
[6] D. Ross, *Plato's Theory of Ideas* (Oxford: Clarendon Press, 1951).
[7] *Republic*, 490a–b; also Phaedo 79d.

in a union of the intellective soul with the perfect objects of knowledge, the forms. When responding to a question concerning "the fair measure of truth" Socrates responds: "No measure that falls in the least degree short of the whole truth can be quite fair in so important a matter. *What is imperfect can never serve as a measure;* though people sometimes think enough has been done and there is no need to look further."[8] The perfect measure is applied to moral action when Socrates argues in the *Theaetetus*:

> God is supremely just and what is most like him is the man who has become just as it lies in human nature to be ... There are two patterns set up in the world. One is divine and supremely happy; the other has nothing of God in it, and is the pattern of the deepest unhappiness. This truth the evildoer does not see.[9]

The measure of human goodness is divine and those who are to become happy recognize the basis for moral actions and those who do not accept the divine foundation cannot become truly good. Plato's divine pattern in the world serves as the moral paradigm for everyone. Plato's ethical theory may seem too demanding for modern readers who may judge his moral goals so lofty that "no one can in fact achieve them."[10] Plato, himself, seems untroubled by the loftiness of his standards as he indicates in the *Republic*. When Glaucon doubts that the republic described by Socrates could exist anywhere on earth, Socrates agrees, but reminds Glaucon of the pattern in heaven for anyone who wishes to see it and model actions upon it. Whether it actually exists, or will ever exist on earth, does not trouble Socrates at all.[11]

The enduring message of Platonic moral theory lies in its acceptance of eternal standards that serve as universal models of right action. While they are ultimately unattainable during a human lifetime they direct all toward a universally applicable rule of conduct.[12] Plato does not think that the importance of the form is lost by the human need to adapt customs and laws to political needs.[13] His "solution to the problem of objectivity is given ... by the theory of forms. The form of justice is common to all that we describe as

---

[8] *Republic*, 504c: ἀλλ', ὦ φίλε, ἦν δ' ἐγώ, μέτρον τῶν τοιούτων ἀπολεῖπον καὶ ὁτιοῦν τοῦ ὄντος οὐ πάνυ μετρίως γίγνεται· ἀτελὲς γὰρ οὐδὲν οὐδενὸς μέτρον. δοκεῖ δ' ἐνίοτέ τισιν ἱκανῶς ἤδη ἔχειν καὶ οὐδὲν δεῖν περαιτέρω ζητεῖν.
[9] *Theaet.* 176 c–e, tr. Levett, rev. M. F. Burnyeat (Indianapolis: Hackett, 1990). See also J. Annas, *Platonic Ethics, Old and New* (Ithaca, London: Cornell University Press, 1999), p. 8, where she argues convincingly that "becoming like God" is a unifying theme in Plato's philosophy.
[10] J. Annas, *op. cit.*, p. 52.   [11] *Republic*, 592b.   [12] *Republic*, 472b–d.
[13] *Laws*, 875d–e.

just ... and it also provides the standard to which we must refer in judging the rightness of conduct as well as legislation."[14]

Like many of Plato's doctrines the notion of immutable universal moral standards provoked a critical reaction from Aristotle. As we have seen in Chapter 2, Aristotle makes the final arbiter of moral rectitude not divinely inspired models, but the reasoned choices of the practically wise person. While those seeking precise moral formulations will become disappointed in their search through Aristotle's works, he would himself remind them not to seek more precision than their investigation allows. Aristotle recognizes the importance of circumstances, customs and individual talents that enter into all moral actions. His ethics tends toward a reasoned conservatism, since he places great faith in the ability to construct a rational and effective moral tradition. He recognizes that even if Plato's proposed social innovations may in theory improve society, they constitute little more than philosophical musings, since they have no possibility of implementation. He describes a moral skill that resembles athletic excellence in that the best players with a mastery of accepted practices provide innovative methods for their profession. An example would be the swinging volley in tennis, or the one-handed catch in baseball. New equipment and the players' skill allow for novel methods of play that had been universally condemned in the past, but now such techniques have become routine parts of the sport. What these athletes accomplish arises from their recognition that changing circumstances permit innovations that lead to the desired goal of athletic success. Those with practical wisdom can likewise improve moral practices within a society. Recognizing the impact of technology upon manufacturing productivity, opponents to child labor could more easily pass laws prohibiting the economic exploitation of children. They recognized that a more just society could evolve into a community in which the misuse of children is prohibited. The theoretical foundation for their opposition required the appropriate circumstances for their legislation. Those with practical wisdom used the existing moral tradition to improve their communities' practices. Such legislation in less developed countries, whose families relied upon children to provide income and economic help, required more time to implement.

For Aristotle the human measure of moral conduct is far more effective than a complete reformulation of political practice and moral ideas based

---

[14] G. Striker, "Origins of the Concept of Natural Law," *Proceedings of the Boston Area Colloquium in Ancient Philosophy*, 2 (1987), p. 84. Also p. 85: "... he [Plato] recognized that no human being could acquire and keep the kind of insight and motivation he expected from his ideal rulers."

upon a theoretical model. The failure of the Marxist regimes in Eastern Europe, whose governments were instituted and maintained by force, demonstrates how difficult it is to build a society based on a revolutionary theory with no basis in past practices. One might argue that countries with strict gun control laws have far fewer violent deaths and murders than the United States, and that for the safety of its citizens America should do likewise. But the proponents of gun control laws have met with little success because the tradition of the private possession of weapons is a long established practice. Even obvious immoral practices, such as slavery and legal discrimination, were slow to change because of the traditional practices that supported them. Persons of practical wisdom, such as Martin Luther King, had to demonstrate how these traditions could be replaced by better practices that would benefit everyone in a more just society.

Both Plato and Aristotle recognized the flexibility and mutability of human moral goodness, but they did so in different ways. Plato posited eternal standards by which all beings may be known and judged, but recognized the limitations of human beings to reach these standards. Aristotle, however, described certain universal laws as applicable to all political states (EN 1134b17–30), but, as G. Striker observes: "Aristotle also held that the practically wise or decent person's decisions would be objectively right though they do not result from the application of fixed rules."[15] The *phronimos* has far more freedom in Aristotle's ethical theory than the just person in Plato's theory, since practical wisdom extends to the entire range of human decisions. While murder and fraud may be universally proscribed, the *phronimos* determines when killing and deception may be considered good, especially in service to a nobler end. The wise person may arrange an individual life in the way that best leads to goodness for himself and others.

The origins of the theory of natural law lie in the writings of the Stoics[16] and the question whether they prescribed universal mandates without exceptions need not concern us here. They did base their concept of law on the harmony between correct human actions and the natural order governed by a providential deity. The primary sources for the doctrine of

---

[15] G. Striker, *op. cit.*, p. 84.
[16] See B. Inwood, "Natural Law in Seneca," *Studia Philonica*, 15 (2003), pp. 81–99 and *Ethics and Human Action in Early Stoicism* (Oxford: Oxford University Press, 1985). Also G. Striker, "Ethics and Human Action in Early Stoicism," *Canadian Journal of Philosophy*, 19 (1989), pp. 91–100.

natural law in the Middle Ages were the works of Cicero and Seneca, but Aristotle, himself, provided an opportunity for his readers to assume the existence of universal divinely mandated laws. In his commentary on the NE Thomas ascribes to Aristotle a theory of natural law. Natural law judged according to its effect has a universal ability to lead all to good and away from evil. As a cause, Thomas argues, it does not originate in human opinion, but rather from nature itself. Thomas compares natural legal precepts to the indemonstrable principles of theoretical sciences. In law these commands can be specified, such as evil is to be avoided, to harm no one unjustly and to refrain from thievery.[17] These principles do not depend upon human perception, but arise from nature itself, and nature directs all human being to them.[18]

Although the innate principles of natural law represent a universal aspect of human nature, they do not always lead to correct actions. The close connection between natural law and the habit of virtue depends upon the relation between the knower and the known. As the dictates of natural law become incorporated into human laws they have an experiential force attained by custom. In customary laws practice may lead to a greater acceptance of false and immature statement (*fabulariter et pueriliter dicta*) than to a recognition of truth. Aristotle speaks of such human laws as directed to the maintenance of the city as the ultimate goal even if some of them may become frivolous when foolish customs are accepted. Thomas is suspicious of the efficacy of human institutions to lead human beings to true happiness (*ad veram felicitatem*). He prefers the "law divinely given," which directs human beings to happiness. Human institutions may in their development include falsehoods and errors, but "in the law of God no falsehood is contained."[19] Despite his admiration for Aristotle, Thomas accepts the absolute infallibility of scriptural law over the human reasoning process that produces a legal system that is rooted partially, at least, in customary practices. Moral reasoning, which does not err in recognizing universal commands, may be impeded by a number of causes when a particular act is chosen. At the moment of decision Thomas again prefers the guidance of a determined course of action prescribed by divine law to the more flexible determinations of human beings.

---

[17] SLE, pp. 304–305, ll. 34–57.   [18] SLE, p. 305, ll. 58–65.

[19] *In XII libros Metaphysicorum expositio*, ed. M.-R. Cathala and R. Spiazzi (Taurin, Rome: Marietti, 1964) II, lec. 5, n. 3. See also, A. Maurer, "Siger of Brabant on the Fables and Falsehoods of Religion," *Mediaeval Studies* 43 (1981), pp. 515–530.

Thomas's interpretation of the role of tradition in the development of civic institutions in Aristotle's moral and political philosophy is essentially correct. Aristotle, as noted in Chapter 2, relies heavily on traditional practices in the education of a good person and the development of the state. Like Mill, Aristotle has an optimistic view of the development of human practices, since he applies his general theory of knowledge to moral and political science. Like the one who develops an understanding of laws, such as light meat is healthy, through repeated experience, so too will a wise politician come to accept beneficial rules and reject harmful ones.

The debate on the nature of the foundation of just and moral conduct did not end in the Middle Ages. Hume's definition of virtue as that quality that provokes admiration from the observer and his basis for action on sentiment have some elements in common with Aristotelian moral theory. Hume, however, did not remain long without challenge, since Kant, most likely wary of an ethical foundation based on changing sentiments, provided a universal ground for ethics within human reason itself. Today when people respond to the question how they wish to be treated, the common response is 'fairly'. But what constitutes fair treatment? Should one, like Draco, offer the same response to every human predicament, or should one adjust responses to changing circumstances? The appeal of universal rules of conduct is patently obvious, but constraints, such as mandatory judicial sentencing, hamper a jurist's ability to account for mitigating circumstances. The opponents to universal principles, however, may find themselves forced to accept repugnant practices, such as the economic and sexual exploitation of children, if they are to maintain a position of accepting varying cultural practices. Cicero perhaps formulated the proper answer to the problem, when he stated succinctly that we certainly accept divine eternal principles of law, but we need to recognize how the wise person interprets them.[20] Cicero joins the strengths of both the Platonic and Aristotelian moral theories, but as is his custom, he quickly abandons his solution, and turns to a different topic.

The dictates of natural law have a direct bearing on the attainment of human fulfillment in medieval moral theory. Despite an overly optimistic view of how Aristotelian happiness leads to eternal beatitude, R. McInerny recognizes the connection between natural law and the goal of human life: "Of course natural law cannot be discussed without presupposing what was said earlier about the ultimate end. The precepts of natural law have to do precisely with the end . . . In its proper sense, a precept is a command to do

---

[20] Cicero, *De legibus*, I, vi, 19.

what will lead to an end."[21] McInerny argues further that Thomas reads a passage in the NE (1101a14–20) as Aristotle's admission that the ideal of happiness can only be imperfectly realized by human beings in this life. This admission allowed Thomas to subsume what Aristotle had to say into a richer vision of the ultimate good that overcomes the transitory accomplishments of human life.[22] This interpretation is common among those who wish to see a natural progression from the life of virtue described by Aristotle to the enjoyment of perfect beatitude that is the Christian moral goal. But Thomas's position is more complex, since he comments on this passage rightly about Aristotle's distinction between happiness in its essential activity and a type of philosophical beatitude that encompasses the added benefits of good fortune.[23] On Aristotle's own position concerning the soul's absolute perfection Thomas claims that the Philosopher left the question unanswered, since it was not entirely a question within the parameters of philosophical reasoning.

The commands of natural law harmonize with the first principles of practical science, as Thomas indicates in his commentary on the NE. When discussing justice and law, Thomas notes that both Aristotle and the medieval jurists discussed what is politically and legally right. Thomas understands Aristotle's concept of natural justice (*iustum naturale*) in two ways: the first pertains to its effect and power, since natural justice has a universal force that leads to good actions and prevents evil ones; a second way of considering natural justice discovers its roots in human nature itself. The description of natural law in the second sense closely resembles that of *synderesis*, whose principles, such as avoid evil and harm no one unjustly, are naturally known. Other legal imperatives may be derived from the ones that are naturally known.[24] A human being by its very nature is inclined to natural justice in two ways: (1) insofar as there is an element common to all living beings; (2) that proper human nature permits one to discern naturally good and evil. The jurists associate the first meaning of natural justice with acts, such as union of male and female and the education of the young. The law that follows the specific inclinations of human nature are rational, and the jurists call it *ius gentium* because all

---

[21] R. McInerny, "Thomistic Natural Law and Aristotelian Philosophy," *St. Thomas Aquinas and the Natural Law Tradition Contemporary Perspectives*, ed. J. Goyette *et al.* (Washington: The Catholic University of America Press, 2004), p. 34.

[22] Ibid., p. 33.

[23] A. Celano, "The Concept of Worldly Beatitude in the Writings of Thomas Aquinas," *Journal of the History of Philosophy*, 25 (1987), pp. 215–226 and *De virtutibus*, q. 1, a. 5, ad 8.

[24] SLE, pp. 304–305, ll. 34–57.

peoples accept practices, such as observing treaties and assuring the safety of ambassadors. The ignorance that hampers prudential decisions is involved in a wrong choice by which every evil person displays error. Ignorance results when the judgment of reason is swayed by the inclination of appetite. Ignorance of the particular does not excuse wrongdoing, but is the reason why human beings err. Ignorance of a universal judgment in practical science does, however, diminish culpability.[25]

The prudent person would not make an error with respect to either the universal command or the particular choice. Today the term 'prudent', often conveys a meaning of negative characteristics as outmoded, overly cautious and prudish. The profound understanding of moral wisdom of Aristotle's concept of *phronesis* has largely been lost in the evolution from practical wisdom to prudence. Although the *phronimoi* have an awareness of the importance of traditional practice, they are not bound by it. They may respect what is generally done, but may also alter their own moral choices in order to bring about what is good for themselves and their society. The internalized general principles may provide guidelines for action, but no specific imperatives. C. Trottmann claims that the medieval notion of *synderesis* constitutes a subversion of Aristotle's 'elitism'.[26] But the medieval adaptation of Aristotle's theory permitted less flexibility in decision-making, since the hierarchical order of the dictates of natural law provided more specific direction when courses of action conflicted. In a situation of contrary demands the order of natural law directs the prudent person to follow specific courses of conduct. The divine law would always overcome the civic, and the theoretical life would always overcome bio-logical duties. Albert's understanding of happiness as divided into two specific types, with the active life as a preparatory stage to contemplative virtue, reflects the reinterpretation of Aristotle's doctrine of wisdom.

Aristotle's virtue of practical wisdom is no less important today than it was in his time. The idea of fairness that is so important in contemporary society is not always easy to practice. Many daily decisions may require the judgments of wisdom and cannot be made in accordance with general rules with no regard for circumstances. A teacher may have certain attendance requirements in order for students to pass a course, but would be consid-ered 'unfair', if a student were to fail despite legitimate reasons for missing

---

[25] *De virtutibus*, q. 1, a. 6, ad 3.
[26] C. Trottmann, "La syndérèse selon Albert le Grand," *Albertus Magnus zum Gedenken nach 800 Jahren: Neue Zugänge, Aspekte und Perspektiven*, ed. W. Senner *et al.* (Berlin: Akademie Verlag, 2001), pp. 253–273, p. 265.

classes. If one student's failure to attend classes is caused by a medical emergency, while another's is due to a desire to spend a week surfing in Hawaii, then two different responses are warranted. The instructor should not merely apply a rule without consideration of the circumstances. Both students would fail to meet the requirements, but one is owed a different response than the other.

The desire for fairness has produced many rules, laws and regulations, but almost all of them remain subject to interpretation. Even the most absolute imperatives may in extraordinary circumstances be contravened. Few would reject a universal prescription against murder, but in an exceptional cases it could be justified. Von Stauffenberg executed his planned assassination of Hitler despite his own life being in no jeopardy, since he was a trusted member of the Army's general staff. Still he found reasons other than self-defense to take a human life. If he had succeeded, then millions of lives might have been spared in the final months of World War II.[27] Von Stauffenberg's motivation to save Germany from the insanity of 'total war' led him to plan and execute an assassination attempt.

Today he is honored as a heroic figure who died in service to his country. One might argue that Von Stauffenberg's act was not attempted murder, but rather a justifiable act of war. Whether his deed is redefined or remains a justified act of murder, a person with true wisdom must determine when such a step is needed. John Wilkes Booth's exclamation after his assassination of Abraham Lincoln (*sic semper tyrannis*) demonstrates his belief that he had pursued a noble course. To Booth, Lincoln was a tyrant who merited execution so that the South might be avenged. But the differences between Lincoln and Hitler are apparent to anyone who uses a reasonable standard by which to judge political leaders.

When such provisions, as 'reasonable standard', 'community standards' 'beyond reasonable doubt' or 'according to right reason', are used, they often provoke skepticism and mistrust. These terms are too general to apply to individual cases and rely too much on the judgment of individuals. As both Aristotle and Thomas Aquinas knew, the general ideals never come into question, but their application in particular cases and circumstances may be questioned. Again Cicero's understanding is most important. We need universal principles and the wisdom to apply them properly. No moral and ethical system can function without them.

---

[27] See I. Kershaw, *The End: The Defiance and Destruction of Hitler's Germany, 1944–1945* (London: The Penguin Press, 2011).

Bibliography

I Manuscripts

Cambridge, MS Peterhouse 206 (=C), ff. 285ra–307vb. Contains the commentary on the *Ethica vetus* and *nova* attributed to Robert Kilwardby.

Erfurt, Bibliotheca Amploniana, MS F 13 (=E), ff. 84r–119r. Contains the anonymous *Quaestiones in Ethicam*.

Florence, Naz. MS *conv. soppr.* G 4.853 (=F). Contains the commentary on the *Ethica vetus* and *nova* wrongly attributed to John Pecham.

Prague, Czech State Library (*olim* University) MS. III. F. 10 (=Pr). Contains the commentary on the *Ethica nova* attributed to Robert Kilwardby.

II Primary sources

Albertus Magnus. *De homine* (=DH), ed. H. Anzulewicz and J. Söder. *Alberti magni Opera omnia* 27, 2. Münster: Aschendorff, 2008.

Albertus Magnus. *De bono*, ed. H. Kühle *et al. Alberti magni Opera omnia* 28. Münster: Aschendorff, 1951.

Albertus Magnus. *De natura boni*, ed. E. Filthaut. *Albert magni Opera omnia* 25, 1. Münster: Ashcendorff, 1974.

Albertus Magnus. *In X Ethicorum*, ed. A. Borgnet. *Opera omnia* 7. Paris: Vives, 1891.

Albertus Magnus. *Quaestiones*, ed. W. Kübel and H. Anzulewicz. *Alberti magni Opera omnia* 25, 2. Münster: Aschendorff, 1993.

Albertus Magnus. *Super Ethica commentum et quaestiones libri quinque priores* (=SE), ed. W. Kübel. *Alberti magni Opera omnia* 14, 1. Münster: Aschendorff, 1968.

Aristotle. *Ethica Nicomachea* (=NE). ed. I. Bywater. Oxford: Clarendon Press, 1894. Nicomachean Ethics, tr. D. Ross. Oxford: Oxford University Press, 1908.

Aristotle. *Ethica Nicomachea*, Ethica Nova, ed. R.-A. Gauthier. *Aristoteles Latinus*. Leiden-Brussels and Brill, 1974, XXVI, fasc. 1–3.

Aristotle. *Eudemian Ethics*, ed. F. Susemihl. Leipzig: Teubner, 1884.

Aristotle. *Politica*, ed. W. Ross. Oxford: Clarendon Press, 1957.

Aristotle. *Ars Poetica*, ed. R. Kassel. Oxford: Clarendon Press, 1966.

Aristotle. *Ars Rhetorica*, ed. W. Ross. Oxford: Clarendon Press, 1959.

Aristotle. *Metaphysica*, ed. W. Ross. Oxford: Clarendon Press, 1924.

Augustine. *De civitate Dei*, XII, 9, ed. B. Dombart and A. Kalb. *Corpus christianorum series latina*, 47–48. Turnhout: Brepols, 1955.

Averroes. *Commentarium magnum in Aristotelis de anima libros*, ed. F. S. Crawford. *Corpus commentariorum Averrois in Aristotelem*, VI, I. Cambridge, MA: The Medieval Academy of America, 1953.

Bonaventure. *Commentaria in quatuor libros Sententiarum Magistri Petri Lombardi*. Doctoris Seraphici S. Bonaventurae Opera omnia, vv. 1–4. Quaracchi: Ad claras aquas, 1882–1889.

Bonaventure. *Iter mentis ad Deum. Doctoris Seraphici S. Bonaventurae Opera omnia*, v. 5. Quaracchi: Ad claras aquas, 1891.

Chartularium Universitatis Parisiensis (CUP), ed. H. Denifle and E. Châtelain. Paris, 1889.

Cicero. *De legibus*, ed. J. Powell. *M. Tulli Ciceronis De Re Publica, De Legibus* . . . Oxford: Oxford University Press, 2006.

Cicero. *De officiis*, ed. M. Winterbottom. *M. Tulli Ciceronis De Officiis*. Oxford: Oxford University Press, 1994.

Henry of Ghent. *Quodlibet* I, 14, ed. R. Macken. Leuven: Leuven University Press, 1979.

Hugh of St. Victor. *Didascalion*, ed. C. Buttimer. *Hugonis de Sancto Didascalion. De studio legendi*. Washington: The Catholic University of America Press, 1939.

Kant, I. *Grundlegung zur Metaphysik der Sitten*, Akademie Textausgabe. Berlin: Walter de Gruyter, 1903/1911.

Philip the Chancellor. *Philippi Cancellarii Parisiensis Summa de Bono* (=SDB), ed. N. Wicki. Corpus Philosophorum Medii Aevi: Opera philosophica mediae aetatis selecta, II. Bern: Francke, 1985.

Plato. *Platonis Opera*, ed. J. Burnet. Oxford: Oxford University Press, 1903.

Radulpus Brito. *Le questiones di Radulfo Brito sull' 'Etica Nicomachea' Introduzione e testo critico* (=Questiones), ed. I. Costa. Studia Artistarum, 17. Turnhout: Brepols, 2008.

Robert Kilwardby. *De ortu scientiarum*, ed. A. Judy. *Auctores Britannici Medii Aevi*, 4. Toronto, Oxford: The British Academy and The Pontifical Institute of Mediaeval Studies, 1976.

Statuta Antiqua Universitatis Oxoniensis (=St. Ox.), ed. S. Gibson. Oxford: Clarendon Press, 1931.

Thomas Aquinas, all works cited are from the Leonine edition, *Sancti Thomae de Aquino Opera omnia iussu Leonis XIII P.M. edita, cura et studia Fratrum Praedicatorum*. Romae: ad Sanctae Sabinae, 1882-ss., unless otherwise noted.

Thomas Aquinas. *Sententia libri Ethicorum* (=SLE), ed. Leon. 47, 1–2, 1969.

Thomas Aquinas. *Summa theologiae* (=S. th.), ed. Leon. 4–12, 1888–1906.

Thomas Aquinas. *Summa contra gentiles* (=SCG), ed. Leon. 13–15, 1918–1930.

Thomas Aquinas. *Quaestiones disputatae de veritate*, ed. Leon. 22, 1–3, 1972–1976.

Thomas Aquinas. *De divinis nominibus*, ed. C. Pera. Turin, Rome: Marietti, 1950.

Thomas Aquinas. *De virtutibus, Quaestiones disputatae de virtutibus in communi*, ed. E. Odetto. Taurin, Rome: Marietti, 1965.

Thomas Aquinas. *Scriptum super libros Sententiarum magistri Petri Lombardi epsicopi Parisiensis*, ed. P. Mandonnet and M. Moos. Paris: Lethielleux, 1929–1947.

Thomas Aquinas. *In XII libros Metaphysicorum expositio*, ed. M.-R. Cathala and R. Spiazzi. Taurin, Rome: Marietti, 1964.

William of Auxerre. *Summa aurea magistri Guillelmi Altissioderensi* (=SA), ed. J. Ribaillier. Paris: Spicelegium Bonaveturianum, 18, 1980–1987.

III Studies

Ackrill, J. "Aristotle on Eudaimonia," *Aristotle's Ethics: Critical Essays* (see Sherman, N.), 57–77.

Adams, M. M. "Ockham on Will, Nature and Morality," *The Cambridge Companion to Ockham*, ed. P. Spade. New York: Cambridge University Press, 1999, 245–272.

Adams, M. M. "The Structure of Ockham's Moral Theory," *Franciscan Studies*, 29 (1986), 1–35.

Annas, J. "Aristotle on Virtue and Happiness," *Aristotle's Ethics: Critical Essays*, ed. N. Sherman. Lanham: Rowman and Littlefield, 1999, 35–55.

Annas, J. *The Morality of Happiness*. New York and Oxford: Oxford University Press, 1993.

Annas, J. *Platonic Ethics, Old and New*. Ithaca and London: Cornell University Press, 1999.

Anzulewicz, H. "'Bonum' als Schlüsselbegriff bei Albertus Magnus," *Albertus Magnus zum Gedenken nach 800 Jahren: Neue Zugänge, Aspekte und Perspektiven*, ed. W. Senner *et al*. Berlin: Akademie Verlag, 2001, 113–140.

Anzulewicz, H. and Söder J., ed. and tr. *Albertus Magnus, Über den Menschen, De homine*. Hamburg: Felix Meiner Verlag, 2004.

Bejczy, I. *The Cardinal Virtues in the Middle Ages: A Study in Moral Thought from the Fourth to the Fourteenth Century*. Leiden: Brill, 2011.

Bossier, F. "L'élaboration du vocabulaire philosophique chez Burgundio de Pise," *Aux origines du lexique philosophique européen. L'influence de la latinitas. Actes du Colloque international organisé à Rome. Academia Belgica, 23-25 mai 1996*, ed. J. Hamesse. Louvain-la-Neuve: Fédération Internationale des Instituts d'Etudes Médiévales, 1997, 81–116.

Bossier, F. "Les ennuis d'un traducteur. Quatre annotations sur la première traduction latine de l'Ethique à Nicomaque par Burgundio de Pise," *Bijdragen. Tijdschrift voor filosofie en theologie*, 59 (1998), 406–427.

Bradley, D. *Aquinas on the Twofold Human Good*. Washington: The Catholic University of America Press, 1997.

Buffon, V. "Happiness and Knowledge in Some Masters of Arts before 1250: An Analysis of Some Commentaries on Book I of *Nicomachean Ethics*," *Patristica et Mediaevalia*, 25 (2004), 111–115.

Buffon, V. "Philosophers and Theologians on Happiness: An Analysis of Early Latin Commentaries on the *Nicomachean Ethics*," *Laval théologique et philosophique*, 60 (2004), 449–476.

Buffon, V. "The Structure of the Soul, Intellectual Virtues, and the Ethical Ideal of Masters of Arts in Early Commentaries on the *Nicomachean Ethics*," *Virtue Ethics in the Middle Ages: Commentaries on Aristotle's Nicomachean Ethics, 1200-1250*, ed. I. Bejczy. Brill's Studies in Intellectual History, 160. Leiden, Boston: Brill, 2008, 13–30.

Burnet, J. *The Ethics of Aristotle.* London: Methuen, 1900.

Burnyeat, M. F. "Aristotle on Learning to Be Good," *Aristotle's Ethics*, ed. A. O. Rorty. Berkeley: University of California Press, 1980, 69–92.

Callus, D. A. "The 'Tabulae Super Originalia Patrum' of Robert Kilwardby O.P.," *Studia Mediaevalia in honorem R.J. Martin.* Bruges: De Tempel, 1948, 243–270.

Celano, A., "Act of the Intellect or Act of the Will: The Critical Reception of Aristotle's Ideal of Human Perfection in the 13th and Early 14th Centuries," Archives d'histoire doctrinale et littéraire du moyen âge, 57 (1990), 93–119.

Celano, A. "Aristotle on Beatitude," *Ancient Philosophy*, V, 2 (1985), 205–214.

Celano, A. "Boethius of Dacia on the Highest Good," *Traditio*, 43 (1987), 199–214.

Celano, A. "The Concept of Worldly Beatitude in the Writings of Thomas Aquinas," *Journal of the History of Philosophy*, 25 (1987), 215–226.

Celano, A. "The End of Practical Wisdom: Ethics as Science in the Thirteenth Century," *Journal of the History of Philosophy*, 33 (1995), 225–243.

Celano, A. "The 'Finis Hominis' in the Thirteenth-Century Commentaries on the *Nicomachean Ethics*," *Archives d'histoire doctrinale et littéraire du moyen âge*, 53 (1986), 23–53.

Celano, A. "Peter of Auvergne's Questions on Books I and II of the *Nicomachean Ethics*: A Study and Critical Edition," *Mediaeval Studies*, 48 (1986), 1–110.

Celano, A. "Phronesis, Prudence and Moral Goodness in the Thirteenth Century Commentaries on the *Nicomachean Ethics*," *Mediaevalia Philosophica Polonorum*, 36 (2007), 5–27.

Celano, A. "Play and the Theory of Basic Human Goods," *American Philosophical Quarterly*, 28 (1991), 137–146.

Celano, A. "A Question of Justice: The Good Thief, Cain and the Pursuit of Moral Perfection," *Medieval Philosophy and Theology in the Long Middle Ages: A Tribute to Stephen F. Brown*, ed. R. Friedman, K. Emery and A. Speer, Studien und Texte zur Geistesgeschichte des Mittelalters, 105. Leiden, Boston: Brill, 2011, 321–350.

Celano, A. "The Understanding of Beatitude, the Perfection of the Soul, in the Early Latin Commentaries on Aristotle's *Nicomachean Ethics*," *Documenti e Studi sulla Tradizione Filosofica Medievale*, 17 (2006), 1–22.

Clark, M. *Augustine.* London, New York: Continuum Press, 1994.

Clark, S. *Aristotle's Man.* Oxford: Clarendon Press, 1975.

Cooper, J. "Contemplation and Happiness: A Reconstruction," *Synthese*, 72 (1987), 187–216.

Courtenay, W. "Radulphus Brito: Master of Arts and Theology," *Cahièrs de l'Institut du Moyen-âge grec et latin*, 76 (2005), 131–158.

Curzer, H. *Aristotle and the Virtues.* Oxford: Oxford University Press, 2012.

Dahan, G. "Une introduction à l'étude de la philosphie: *Ut ait Tullius*," *L'enseignement de la philosophie au XIIIᵉ siècle: Autour du 'Guide de l'etudiant du ms. Ripoll 109*, ed. C. Lafleur with J. Carrier. Studia artistarum, 5. Brepols: Turnhout, 1997, 3–58.

Deman, T.-H. *Saint Thomas d'Aquin, Somme théologique. La prudence: 2a-2ae, questions 47–56, traduction françaises, notes et appendices.* Paris, Tournai & Rome: Desclée & Cie, 1949.

DeMoss, D. "Acquiring Ethical Ends," *Ancient Philosophy*, 10 (1999), 63–79.

Dirlmeier, F. *Eudemische Ethik Übersetzt und kommentiert von Franz Dirlmeier.* Berlin: Akademie Verlag, 1984.

Farrell, D. *The Ends of Moral Virtues and the First Principles of Practical Reason in Thomas Aquinas*. Rome: Gregorian and Biblical Press, 2012.

Finnis, J. *Fundamentals of Ethics*. Washington, DC: Georgetown University Press, 1983.

Finnis, J. *Moral Absolutes: Tradition, Revision and Truth*. Washington, DC: Catholic University of America Press, 1991.

Finnis, J. *Natural Law and Natural Rights*, 2nd ed. Oxford: Oxford University Press, 2011.

Finnis, J. "Natural Law: The Classical Tradition," *The Oxford Handbook of Jurisprudence and Philosophy of Law*, ed. J. Coleman and S. Shapiro, S. Oxford & New York: Oxford University Press, 2002, 1–60.

Finnis, J. "Practical Reasoning, Human Goods and the End of Man," *Proceedings of the American Catholic Philosophical Association*, 58 (1984), 23–36.

Gadamer, H. G. *Nikomachische Ethik VI/Aristoteles*. Frankfurt am Main: Klostermann, 1998.

Gauthier, R.-A. "Arnoul de Provence et la doctrine de la 'fronesis', vertu mystique suprême," *Revue du Moyen Âge Latin*, 19 (1963), 135–170.

Gauthier, R.-A. "Comptes Rendus," *Bulletin Thomiste*, 8 (1947–1953), 75–86.

Gauthier, R.-A. "Le Cours sur l'Ethica nova d'un maitre ès Arts de Paris (1235–1240),") [=Le cours]. *Archives d'histoire doctrinale et littéraire du moyen âge*, 42 (1975), 71–141.

Gauthier, R.-A. "Trois commentaires 'averroistes' sur l'Ethique à Nicomaque," *Archives d'histoire doctrinale et littéraire du moyen âge*, 16 (1947–1948), 187–336.

Gauthier, R.-A. and Jolif, Y. *L'Éthique à Nicomaque, trans. et comm.* Louvain: Publications universitaires, 1970.

Gigon, O. *Die Nikomachische Ethik, eingeleitet und übertragen von Olof Gigon*. Zurich: Akademie Verlag, 1951.

Gilson, E. *The Christian Philosophy of St. Bonaventure*, tr. I. Trethowan and F. Sheed. Patterson: St. Anthony Guild, 1965.

Grisez, G. *Way of the Lord Jesus, v. 1: Christian Moral Principles*. Chicago: Franciscan Herald Press, 1983.

Grisez, G., Boyle J. and Finnis, J. "Practical Principles, Moral Truth and Ultimate Ends," *American Journal of Jurisprudence*, 58 (1987), 99–151.

Guthrie, W. *A History of Greek Philosophy*. Cambridge: Cambridge University Press, 1979–1981.

Hardie, W. F. R. "Aristotle on the Best Life for a Man," *Philosophy*, 54 (1979), 35–50.

Hardie, W. F. R. *Aristotle's Ethical Theory*. Oxford: Clarendon Press, 1968.

Hardie, W. F. R. "The Final Good in Aristotle's Ethics," *Philosophy*, 40 (1965), 277–295; repr. in *Aristotle: A Collection of Critical Essays*, 297–322 (see Moravcsik, J.).

Hissette, R. "La date de quelques commentaires à l'Éthique," *Bulletin de Philosophie Mèdièvale*, 18 (1976), 79–83.

Hittinger, R. *A Critique of the New Natural Law Theory*. Notre Dame: Notre Dame University Press, 1987.

Hoffmann, T. "Conscience and Synderesis," *The Oxford Handbook of Aquinas*, ed. B. Davies and E. Stump. Oxford and New York: Oxford University Press, 2012, 255–264.

Hoffmann, T. "Prudence and Practical Principles," *Aquinas and the Nicomachean Ethics*. T. Hoffmann, J. Müller and M. Perkams, ed. (1). Cambridge: Cambridge University Press, 2013, 165–183.

Hoffmann, T., Müller, J. and Perkhams, M., ed. (2). *Das Problem der Willenschwäche in der Mittelalterlichen Philosophie (The Problem of Weakness of Will in Medieval*

Philosophy), Rechérches de Théologie et Philosophie médiévales: Bibliotheca, 8. Louvain: Peeters, 2006.

Homiak, M. "Moral Character," *The Stanford Encyclopedia of Philosophy* (Spring 2011 Edition), Edward N. Zalta (ed.), URL = http://plato.stanford.edu/archives/spr2011/entries/moral-character/.

Inwood, B. *Ethics and Human Action in Early Stoicism.* Oxford: Oxford University Press, 1985.

Inwood, B. "Natural Law in Seneca," *Studia Philonica,* 15 (2003), 81–99.

Irwin, T. "Prudence and Morality in Greek Ethics," *Ethics,* 105 (1995), 284–295.

Jaeger, W. *Paideia: The Ideals of Greek Culture,* tr. G. Highet. Oxford: Oxford University Press, 1986.

James, M. R. *A Descriptive Catalogue of the Manuscripts in the Library of Peterhouse.* Cambridge: Cambridge University Press, 1899.

Joachim, H. H. *Aristotle the Nicomachea Ethics,* ed. D. A. Rees. Oxford: Clarendon Press, 1955.

Kenny, A. "Happiness," *Proceedings of the Aristotelian Society,* New Series 66 (1965–1966), 93–102.

Kershaw, I. *The End: The Defiance and Destruction of Hitler's Germany, 1944–1945.* London: The Penguin Press, 2011.

Kraut, R. *Aristotle on the Human Good.* Princeton: Princeton University Press, 1989.

Lafleur, C. *Quatre introductions à la philosophie au XIIIe siècle. Textes critiques et étude historique.* Publications de l'Institut d'études médiévales, XXIII. Montreal, Louvain: Vrin, 1988.

Lafleur, C. with Carrier, J. ed., *Le 'Guide de l'étudiant' d'un maitre anonyme de la faculté des arts de Paris au XIIIe siècle. Édition critique provisoire du ms. Barcelona, Arxiu de la Corona d'Aragó, Ripoll 109, fol 134ra-158va.* Québec: Faculté de Philosophie, Université Laval, 1992.

Langston, D. *Conscience and Other Virtues: From Bonaventure to Macintyre.* University Park, PA: Pennsylvania University Press, 2001.

Le Boulluec, A. "Recherches sur les origenes du thème de la syndérèse dans la tradition patristique," *Vers la contemplation. Études sur la syndérèse et le modalités de la contemplation de l'antiquité a la renaissance,* ed. C. Trottmann. Paris: Champion, 2007, 61–77.

Lehmann, P. *Mittelalterliche Bibliothekskataloge Deutschlands und der Schweiz.* Munich: Beck, 1969.

Lottin, O. *Psychologie et morale aux XIIe et XIIIe siècles.* Louvain, Gembloux: Abbaye du Mont César, Duclot, 1942–1949.

Luscombe, D. "Ethics in the Early Thirteenth Century," *Albertus Magnus und die Anfänge der Aristoteles-Rezeption im lateinischen Mittelalter: Von Richardus Rufus bis zu Franciscus de Mayronis,* ed. L. Honnefelder *et al.* Aschendorff: Münster, 2005, 657–684.

MacIntyre, A. *Whose Justice? Which Rationality?* Notre Dame: University of Notre Dame Press, 1988.

Macken, R. "Heinrich von Gent im Gespräch mit seinen Zeitgenossen über die menschliche Freiheit," *Franziskanische Studien,* 59 (1977), 125–182.

Macken, R. "La volonté humaine, faculté plus élevée que l'intelligence selon Henri de Gand," *Recherches de Théologie ancienne et médiévale,* 42 (1975), 5–51.

Marrou, H. I. *A History of Education in Antiquity,* tr. G. Lamb. New York: Sheed and Ward, 1956.

Maurer, A. "Siger of Brabant on the Fables and Falsehoods of Religion," *Mediaeval Studies*, 43 (1981), 515–530.

McCluskey, C. "Albertus Magnus and Thomas Aquinas on the Freedom of Human Action," *Albertus Magnus zum Gedenken nach 800 Jahren: Neue Zugänge, Aspekte und Perspektiven*, ed. W. Senner *et al*. Berlin: Akademie Verlag, 2001, 243–254.

McInerny, R. "Action Theory in St. Thomas Aquinas," *Miscellanea Mediaevalia 19, Thomas von Aquin Werk und Wirkung im Licht neuerer Forschung*, ed. A. Zimmermann. Berlin, New York: de Gruyter, 1988, 13–22.

McInerny, R. "Thomistic Natural Law and Aristotelian Philosophy," *St. Thomas Aquinas and the Natural Law Tradition Contemporary Perspectives*, ed. J. Goyette *et al*. Washington: The Catholic University of America Press, 2004.

Meersseman, G. ed. *Laurentii Pignon Catalogi et Chronica, accedunt Catalogi Stamensis et Upsalensis Scriptorum O.P.* Rome: Monumenta Ordinis Fratrum Praedicatorum Historica, XVIII, 1936.

Miller, J. ed. *The Reception of Aristotle's Ethics*, Cambridge: Cambridge University Press, 2013.

Minio-Paluello, L. "Note sull'Aristotele latino medievale, VII," *Rivista di Filosofia Neo-Scolastica*, 44 (1952), 485–495.

Moravcsik, J. *Aristotle: A Collection of Critical Essays*, Garden City: Anchor Books, 1967.

Mulchahey, M. *First the Bow Is Bent in Study: Dominican Education*. Toronto: Pontifical Institute of Mediaeval Studies, 1998.

Müller, J. "Duplex Beatitudo: Aristotle's Legacy and Aquinas's Conception of Human Happiness," *Aquinas and the Nicomachean Ethics* see Hoffmann, T., Müller, J. and Perkhams M., (2) 2013. 52–71.

Müller, J. "Ethics as a Practical Science in Albert the Great's Commentaries on the *Nicomachean Ethics*," *Albertus Magnus zum Gedenken nach 800 Jahren: Neue Zugänge, Aspekte und Perspektiven*, ed. W. Senner *et al*. Berlin: Akademie Verlag, 2001, 275–285.

Müller, J. *Natürliche Moral und philosophische Ethik bei Albertus Magnus*. Beiträge zur Geschichte der Philosophie und Theologie des Mittelalters: Texte und Untersuchungen, Neue Folge, 59. Münster: Aschendorff, 2001.

Müller, J. *Willenschwäche in Antike und Mittelalter. Eine Problemgeschichte von Sokrates bis zum Johannes Duns Scotus*. Leuven: Leuven University Press, 2009.

Nussbaum, M. "The Discernment of Perception: An Aristotelian Conception of Private and Public Rationality," *Proceedings of the Boston Area Colloquium of Ancient Philosophy*, 1 (1985), 151–201.

Nussbaum, M. *The Fragility of Goodness: Luck and Ethics in Greek Tragedy and Philosophy*. Cambridge: Cambridge University Press, 1986.

Owens, J. "The KALON in Aristotelian Ethics," *Studies in Aristotle*, ed. D. J. O'Meara. Washington: The Catholic University of America Press, 1981, 261–278.

Owens, J. "Value and Practical Knowledge in Aristotle," *Essays in Ancient Greek Philosophy IV: Aristotle's Ethics*, ed. J. Anton and A. Preuss. Albany: SUNY Press, 1991, 153–157.

Parry, R. "Episteme and Techne," *Stanford Encyclopedia of Philosophy*, ed. E. Zalta (Fall, 2007), URL= http://plato.stanford.edu/entries/episteme-techne/.

Payer, P. "Prudence and the Principles of Natural Law: A Medieval Development," *Speculum*, 54 (1979), 55–70.

Pelzer, A. "Le cours inédit d'Albert le Grand sur la morale à Nicomaque recuilli et rédigé par S. Thomas d'Aquin," *Revue néoscolatique de philosophie*, 24 (1922), 331–361, 479–520.

Perkams, M. "Aquinas on Choice, Will and Voluntary Action," *Aquinas and the Nicomachean Ethics*, ed. T. Hoffmann, J. Müller and M. Perkams. Cambridge: Cambridge University Press, 2013), 72–90.

Porter, J. "Contested Categories: Reason, Nature and Natural Order in Medieval Accounts of the Natural Law," *The Journal of Religious Ethics*, 24 (1996), 207–232.

Queneau, G. "Origine de la sentence 'Intellectus speculativus extensione fit practicus' et date du Commentaire du De Anima de S. Albert le Grand," *Recherches de théologie ancienne et medievale*, 21 (1954), 307–312.

Rackham, H. *Athenian Constitution, Eudemian Ethics and Virtues and Vices*. Cambridge: Harvard University Press, 1981.

Rhonheimer, M. *Natural Law and Practical Reason: A Thomist View of Moral Autonomy*, tr. G. Malsbary. New York: Fordham University Press, 2000.

Roberts, J. "Aristotle on Responsibility for Action and Character," *Ancient Philosophy*, 9 (1989), 23–36.

Rorty, A. O. "Virtues and Their Vicissitudes," *Midwest Studies in Philosophy*, 13 (*Ethical Theory: Character and Virtue*), ed. P. French *et al*. Notre Dame: University of Notre Dame Press, 1988, 136–148.

Ross, D. *Plato's Theory of Ideas*. Oxford: Clarendon Press, 1951.

Rowe, C. J. "The Meaning of *Phronesis* in the Eudemian Ethics," *Untersuchungen zur Eudemischen Ethik*, ed. P. Moraux *et al*. Berlin: de Gruyter, 1971, 73–92.

Schneyer, J. *Die Sittenkritik in den Predigten Philipps des Kanzlers*. Münster: Aschendorff, 1962.

Schollmeier, P. "Aristotle on Practical Wisdom," *Zeitschrift für philosophische Forschung*," 43 (1989), 124–132.

Sherman, N. ed. *Aristotle's Ethics: Critical Essays*. Lanham: Rowman and Littlefield, 1999.

Söder, J. "Die Erprobung der Vernunft. Vom Umgang mit Traditionen in *De homine*," *Albertus Magnus zum Gedenken nach 800 Jahren: Neue Zugänge, Aspekte und Perspektiven*, ed. W. Senner *et al*. Berlin, Akademie Verlag, 2001, 1–13.

Sokolowski, R. *Moral Action: A Phenomenological Study*. Bloomington: Indiana University Press, 1985.

Somme, L. T. "The Infallibility, Impeccability and Indestructibility of Synderesis," *Studies in Christian Ethics*, 19 (2006), 403–416.

Sorabji, R. "Aristotle on the Role of Intellect in Virtue," *Aristotle's Ethics*, ed. A. O. Rorty. Berkeley: University of California Press, 1980, 201–220.

Souchard, B. "La singulière primauté aristotélicienne de la raison théorique sur la raison pratique," *Vers la contemplation: Études sur la syndérèse et les modalités de la contemplation de l'antiquité à la renaissance*, ed. C. Trottmann. Paris: Honoré Champion, 2007, 27–45.

Sparshot, F. *Taking Life Seriously – A Study of the Argument for the Nicomachean Ethics*. Toronto: University of Toronto Press, 1996.

Stammkötter, F.-B. "Die Entwicklung der Bestimmung der Prudentia in der Ethik des Albertus Magnus," *Albertus Magnus zum Gedenken nach 800 Jahren: Neue*

Zugänge, Aspekte und Perspektiven, ed. W. Senner *et al.* Berlin: Akademie Verlag, 2001, 303–310.

Stegmüller, F. "Neugefundene Questiones des Siger von Brabant," *Recherches de Théologie et Philosophie Médiévale,* 3 (1931), 158–182.

Stewart, J. *Notes on the Nicomachean Ethics.* Oxford: Clarendon Press, 1892.

Stone, M. "Henry of Ghent on Freedom and Human Action," *Henry of Ghent and the Transformation of Scholastic Thought, Studies in Memory of Jos Decorte,* ed. G. Guldentops and C. Steel. Leuven: Leuven University Press, 2003, 201–225.

Striker, G. "Ethics and Human Action in Early Stoicism," *Canadian Journal of Philosophy,* 19 (1989), 91–100.

Striker, G. "Origins of the Concept of Natural Law," *Proceedings of the Boston Area Colloquium in Ancient Philosophy,* 2 (1987), 79–94.

Sturlese, L. *Die deutsche Philosophie im Mittelalter. Von Bonifatius bis zu Albert dem Großen (748–1280).* Munich: Beck, 1993.

Tracey, M. "Albert on Incontinence, Continence and Divine Virtue," ed. T. Hoffmann, J. Müller and M. Perkhams. (2). Louvain: Peeters, 2006, 197–220.

Tracey, M. "An Early 13th-Century Commentary on Aristotle's *Nicomachean Ethics* I, 4–10: The Lectio cum Questionibus of an Arts-Master at Paris in MS Napoli Biblioteca Nazionale, VIII G 8, ff. 4r-9v," *Documenti e Studi sulla Tradizione Filosofica Medievale,* 17, 2006, 23–70.

Tracey, M. "Prudentia in the Parisian summae of William of Auxerre, Philip the Chancellor, and Albert the Great," *Subsidia Albertina II: Via Alberti Texte-Quellen-Interpretationen,* ed. L. Honnefelder, H. Möhle and S. Bullido del Barrio. Münster: Aschendorff, 2009, 267–293.

Tracey, M. "Virtus in the Naples Commentary on the Ethica nova (MS Napoli Biblioteca Nazionale, VIII G 8, ff. 4r-9vb)," *Virtue Ethics in the Middle Ages: Commentaries on Aristotle's Nicomachean Ethics, 1200–1250,* ed. I. Bejczy. Brill's Studies in Intellectual History, 160. Leiden, Boston: Brill, 2008, 55–76.

Trottmann, C. "La syndérèse selon Albert le Grand," *Albertus Magnus zum Gedenken nach 800 Jahren: Neue Zugänge, Aspekte und Perspektiven,* ed. W. Senner *et al.* Berlin: Akademie Verlag, 2001, 253–273.

Trottmann, C. "La syndérèse, sommet de la nature humaine dans l'Itinerarium mentis in Deum," *Dionysius,* 18 (2000), 129–150.

Trottmann, C. *La vision béatifique, des disputes scolastiques à sa définition par Benoît XII.* Bibliothèque des ecoles françaises d'Athènes et de Rome, 289. Rome: Ecole française de Rome, 1995.

Trottmann, C. "*Scintilla synderesis.* Pour une auto-critique mediévale de la raison la plus pure en son usage pratique," *Miscellanea Mediaevalia, 27, Geistesleben in 13. Jahrhundert,* ed. J. Aertsen and A. Speer. Berlin, New York: de Gruyter, 2000, 116–130.

Vega, J. "Aristotle's Concept of Law: Beyond Positivism and Natural Law," *Journal of Ancient Philosophy,* 4 (2010), 1–31.

Verbeke, G. "L'éducation morale et les arts chez Aristote et Thomas d'Aquin," *Miscellanea Mediaevalia 22, Scientia und ars in Hoch-und Spätmittelalter,* ed. I. Craemer-Ruegenberg and A. Speer. Berlin: de Gruyter, 1994, 449–467.

Wallace, J. "Ethics and the Craft Analogy," *Midwest Studies in Philosophy,* 13 (*Ethical Theory: Character and Virtue*), ed. P. French *et al.* Notre Dame: University of Notre Dame Press, 1988, 222–232.

White, N. "Conflicting Parts of Happiness in Aristotle's Ethics," *Ethics*, 105 (1995), 258–283.

Wicki, N. *Die Philosophie Philipps des Kanzlers: ein philosophierender Theologe des frühen 13. Jahrhunderts.* Dokimion, 29. Fribourg: Academic Press, 2005.

Wieland, G. "Albertus Magnus und die Frage nach menschlichen Glück – zur ersten Kölner Ethikvorlesung," Kölner Universitätsreden, H. 80, *Albert der Große in Köln. Gehalten auf der Feierstunde zur 750sten Wiederkehr der Einrichtung des Kölner Generalstudiums der Dominikaner am 6. November 1998*, ed. J. Aertsen. Köln, 1999.

Wieland, G. "Ethica docens – ethica utens," *Miscellanea medievalia, 13, Sprache und Erkenntnis im Mittelalter*, ed. J. P. Beckmann *et al.* Berlin, New York: W. de Gruyter, 1981, II, 593–601.

Wieland, G. *Ethica – scientia practica. Die Anfänge der philosophischen Ethik im 13. Jahrhundert.* Beiträge zur Geschichte der Philosophie des Mittelalters, Neue Folge, 21. Münster: Aschendorff, 1981.

Wiggins, D. "Deliberation and Practical Wisdom," *Aristotle's Ethics*, ed. A. O. Rorty. Berkeley: University of California Press, 1980, 221–240.

Wolter, A. *Duns Scotus on the Will and Morality*, ed. W. Frank. Washington: The Catholic University of America Press, 1997.

Zavattero, I. "Le Prologue de Lectura in Ethicam Veterem du 'Commentaire de Paris' (1235–1240)," *Recherches de Théologie et Philosophie médiévales*, 77 (2010), 1–33.

Zavattero, I. "Moral and Intellectual Virtues in the Earliest Latin Commentaries on the Nicomachean Ethics," *Virtue Ethics in the Middle Ages: Commentaries on Aristotle's Nicomachean Ethics, 1200–1250*, ed. I. Bejczy. Brill's Studies in Intellectual History, 160. Leiden, Boston: Brill, 2008, 31–54.

Index

Printed in the United States
By Bookmasters